Predictive Methods in Next-Generation Computing

Scrivener Publishing
100 Cummings Center, Suite 541J
Beverly, MA 01915-6106

Next-Generation Computing and Communication Engineering

Series Editor(s): Dr. G. R. Kanagachidambaresan and Dr. Kolla Bhanu Prakash

Scope: The rapid growth of technology and new smart city development initiatives has made computing and communication an inevitable platform for all engineering domains. The need for a sophisticated ambient environment has resulted in the exponential growth of automation, robustness and artificial intelligence. Therefore, it is very important to address computing and communication issues in such environments in order to achieve better performance.

Edge computing has become an active research field supporting low processing power, real-time response time, and more resource capacity than IoT and mobile devices. It has also been considered to effectively mitigate loads on data centers, to assist artificial intelligence (AI) services, and to increase 5G services. Edge computing applications along with the IoT field are essential technical directions in order to open the door to new opportunities enabling smart homes, smart hospitals, smart cities, smart vehicles, smart wearables, smart supply chain, e-health, automation, and a variety of other smart environments.

However, any developments are made more challenging because the involvement of multi-domain technology creates new problems for researchers. Therefore, in order to help meet the challenge, this book series concentrates on next generation computing and communication methodologies involving smart and ambient environment design. It is an effective publishing platform for monographs, handbooks, and edited volumes on Industry 4.0, agriculture, smart city development, new computing and communication paradigms. Although the series mainly focuses on design, it also addresses analytics and investigation of industry-related real-time problems.

The main focus of the series includes but is not limited to the following research areas: Industry 4.0, Artificial Intelligence, Machine and Deep learning, Data science, Cognitive Engineering, Cognitive Analytics, CUDA system design, Cyber-physical systems, Quantum Machine Learning, Smart cities, Smart factory, Smart machining, Smart cutting tools, Sensors and Actuators, 5G and wireless technologies for industrial applications, prognostics and alert system. Additional areas of interest include Intelligent manufacturing, Smart healthcare and Transportation systems, Digital Twins, Rapid Prototyping and Manufacturing system, Low Energy Embedded system, Edge and Fog computing, Algorithm design, the Internet of Things and Cyber forensics, Cryptocurrency, Bitcoin and Blockchain Technology, Communication Protocol Design, Intelligent System design and Crowd Sensing, Smart Grid, Soft computing solutions, Microwave Antennas, Atmospheric & Ionospheric research, UAV and ROV monitoring, Signal Processing, System-on-chip and Embedded Design concepts.

Publishers at Scrivener
Martin Scrivener (martin@scrivenerpublishing.com)
Phillip Carmical (pcarmical@scrivenerpublishing.com)

Predictive Methods in Next-Generation Computing

An Approach Toward Sustainability

Edited by

R. Sathiyaraj

Rajesh Kumar Dhanaraj

K. Arun Kumar

Rutvij H. Jhaveri

and

A. Mohamed Abbas

Scrivener
Publishing

WILEY

This edition first published 2025 by John Wiley & Sons, Inc., 111 River Street, Hoboken, NJ 07030, USA and Scrivener Publishing LLC, 100 Cummings Center, Suite 541J, Beverly, MA 01915, USA

For more information about Scrivener publications please visit www.scrivenerpublishing.com.

Wiley Global Headquarters
111 River Street, Hoboken, NJ 07030, USA

For details of our global editorial offices, customer services, and more information about Wiley products visit us at www.wiley.com.

The manufacturer's authorized representative according to the EU General Product Safety Regulation is Wiley-VCH GmbH, Boschstr. 12, 69469 Weinheim, Germany, e-mail: Product_Safety@wiley.com.

Library of Congress Cataloging-in-Publication Data

ISBN 9781394248797

Cover image: Generated with AI using Adobe Firefly
Cover design by Russell Richardson

Set in size of 11pt and Minion Pro by Manila Typesetting Company, Makati, Philippines

Printed in the USA

10 9 8 7 6 5 4 3 2 1

Contents

Preface

The ever-evolving landscape of computing has witnessed a paradigm shift toward the adoption of predictive methods, intelligent algorithms, and sustainable technologies. As we step further into the era of next-generation computing, the confluence of Artificial Intelligence (AI), Machine Learning (ML), the Internet of Things (IoT), Blockchain, and sustainable system design is transforming how societies function and innovate. The edited volume titled *Predictive Methods in Next-Generation Computing* is a timely and comprehensive compilation of research that brings together diverse perspectives on the application of intelligent computational techniques for shaping a smarter and more sustainable future.

This book aims to explore how predictive analytics, driven by AI and allied technologies, can address real-world challenges across various domains such as healthcare, transportation, energy systems, smart cities, and secure digital ecosystems. Each chapter contributes a unique insight into how predictive methodologies are being used to build efficient, intelligent, and future-ready applications.

Beginning with an overview of intelligent computational techniques and their relevance in smart applications, the book transitions into sustainable design strategies and global development paradigms powered by predictive models. The role of intelligent systems in managing urban transport, traffic, and infrastructure is examined through dedicated chapters, highlighting the importance of data-driven planning for urban sustainability. Further, the application of IoT in secure and smart development, especially in the context of smart cities and traffic systems, is discussed with practical frameworks and models.

Healthcare and biomedical informatics are addressed through predictive diagnostics, exemplified by the use of Autoencoders and Principal Components in heart disease classification. The integration of Blockchain in managing medical data and decentralized financial systems illustrates the emergence of secure and transparent computing ecosystems.

Moreover, this volume also delves into the energy domain, focusing on renewable energy integration, data center optimization, and analytics for resource sustainability — critical aspects for the green transformation of digital infrastructure. This also addresses the security and privacy issues with the importance of safeguarding data in predictive environments, a growing concern in the age of ubiquitous computing.

This book is intended for researchers, academicians, industry professionals, and students who are eager to understand the cutting-edge advancements and applications of predictive methods in next-generation computing. It serves both as a reference for ongoing research and as a source of inspiration for developing innovative solutions to contemporary challenges. Additionally, the book provides the consideration and impact of technologies on lives of all stakeholders including industrialists and academicians, customers, government and policy makers. May this book serve as a catalyst for thought, innovation, and forward-looking collaboration in the next era of computational discovery.

1

Introduction to Intelligent Computational Technologies

C. Geetha[1], Sajithra S.[1], S. Srijayanthi[1], B. Reena[2*], I. Subha[3] and Sreelakshmi N.[4]

[1]R.M.K. Engineering College, Kavaraipettai, India
[2]Department of Computer Science and Engineering, Hindustan College of Engineering and Technology, Coimbatore, Tamil Nadu, India
[3]Zoho Labs, Chennai, India
[4]LBS Institute Technology for Women, Poojappura, Thiruvananthapuram, India

Abstract

Indeed, the convergence of smart technologies and sustainability imperatives is one of vital spectrum and focus in application development within the contemporary technological context. This chapter investigates the overlap in these domains by putting forward a framework for designing smart and sustainable applications *via* computational techniques. Building on cutting-edge Artificial Intelligence, Machine Learning, and Data Analytics technologies, it tackles challenging problems as efficiently as possible by maximizing resource utilization without compromising the environmental impact. The paper highlights some key concerns associated with the design, such as data acquisition, modeling, optimization, and deployment policy. Moreover, it discusses case studies and applications in different domains to clarify the effectiveness of intelligent computational techniques and their potential for enabling smart, sustainable development. By doing so, developers and stakeholders can work towards building novel pathways that lead to a more efficient, resilient, and environmentally conscious future. This chapter is all about gathering the right sets of elements/attributes or factors to utilize for different E-Governance services. As per this research, weak adoption factors of E-Governance have been identified and ranked using the fuzzy conjoint technique. These factors are ranked based on satisfaction levels, from highest to lowest: very satisfied, satisfied, neither/nor (ambiguous), dissatisfied, and very dissatisfied.

**Corresponding author*: reena.cse@hicet.ac.in

R. Sathiyaraj, Rajesh Kumar Dhanaraj, K. Arun Kumar, Rutvij H. Jhaveri and A. Mohamed Abbas (eds.) Predictive Methods in Next-Generation Computing: An Approach Toward Sustainability, (1–22)

The ranking of the above factors with satisfaction levels also defines whether the government needs to focus on or not to increase adoption.

Keywords: Smart technologies, sustainability, application development, intelligent computational techniques, artificial intelligence, machine learning

1.1 Introduction

Implementing e-services, or electronic services, will have a deeply rooted impact on every citizen of the nation. If the citizens are unwilling to consume these services, it virtually defeats the purpose of provisioning and consuming e-services as they are the primary consumers. This pressure therefore blasts the call to sieve out what factors can ascertain the suitability of such services. So, the suitable factors have already been identified by the researchers. These factors are addressed as infrastructure, cost, trust, time, accessibility literacy, language, willingness, age, gender, and people awareness [1]. The success of e-services depends on how satisfied people are with their usage. There aren't many private players in the community to meet this expectation, so we need support from the government as well. Internet connectivity, including its speed and bandwidth, is a crucial factor when implementing e-services across the country. Another thing to consider is that there are new technologies out. In the case of a multilingual country, these e-services should also be multilingual. Given the variations in demand preferences for end-users across the country, it is essential to understand what specific factors play a critical role in ensuring that consumers adopt e-services. Hence, this chapter will rank acceptance factors through fuzzy joint model statistics to address the sluggish access to e-governance services. The Fuzzy Conjoint Model was proposed by Turksen and Wilson [2] in 1994. This order of factors was also validated with other ranking approaches such as those proposed by Biswas [3] and Wang [4].

1.2 Literature Survey

Most theories are based on the Davis Technology Acceptance Model (1989) [5], the Unified Theory of Acceptance and Use of Technology, the Theory of Reasoned Action (TRA) [6], the Diffusion of Innovation, etc. Tashfeen Miral Screwvala extended the work of Carter and Belanger (2005) [7] by identifying the 'purpose of use' factor. When deploying technology-based electronic services, the security of existing information is a highly important factor. E-services [8] introduced by the government offer numerous benefits, including increased reusability of information and citizens' satisfaction by sharing it with general public. The author tested an e-governance service introduced by the city council of New Delhi, India [9]. The central idea is that, based on literature research, it can be assumed that the adoption of these services depends on how citizens perceive government electronic services. Table 1.1 lists some of the theories discussed by

Table 1.1 Some empirical theories about adoption models.

Model/theory	Factors/items	Definitions	Authors
A Unified Model of E-Governance Adoption (UMEGA)	Perceived service quality and recommendation	Recognizing the quality and trust of service to the government, as well as the intent to use and recommend e-government services.	Mensah *et al.*, 2020 [11]
TAM2 (Extended Technology Acceptance Model)	Thought/Image	An image of a person after using an innovative service.	Venkatesh, 2000 [15]
	Voluntariness	Personal evaluation of the voluntary use of innovative services.	Moore and Benbasat, 1991 [16]
	Job relevance	Identify the system that applies to his or her work.	
	Quality of output	Comparison with the previous version.	

(*Continued*)

Table 1.1 Some empirical theories about adoption models. (*Continued*)

Model/theory	Factors/items	Definitions	Authors
DOI (Diffusion of Innovation)	Benefits	How is the E-Governance service advantageous over its predecessor?	Rogers and Shoemaker, 1971 [17]
	Complexity	The system is relatively difficult to use and understand.	
	Observability	Determine the output of innovation.	

Table 1.2 Factors/attributes affecting the adoption of E-Governance services.

Factors	Description	Authors
Perceived service quality and intention to use	Service quality, intention to use, and recommendations to others.	Mensah *et al.*, 2020 [11]
Transaction security	Transaction security when using e-government applications.	Rehman M. *et al.*, 2012 [19]
Transparency/fairness	Determine the transparency of electronic services.	Bertot *et al.*, 2010 [20]
Corruption avoidance	How much corruption will be reduced after the introduction of e-government services?	Bertot *et al.*, 2010 [20]
Perceived risk	Risks associated with the use of e-government applications.	Be'langer, Carter, 2008 [22]

(*Continued*)

Table 1.2 Factors/attributes affecting the adoption of E-Governance services. (*Continued*)

Factors	Description	Authors
Trust in the government	Evaluate the level of government confidence in using e-services introduced by the government.	Saxena, 2005 [23]
Trust in the internet	Describe public confidence in the use of the Internet and applications.	Leitner, 2003 [25]
Customer support	Determine the level of customer support while using e-government services in case of stuck.	De Ruyteer *et al.* 2024 [26]

researchers [10] that the study or research found. Table 1.2 presents the key attributes affecting e-governance adoption.

Researchers have also examined the assessment of government websites, applications, and mobile apps. Jain *et al.* (2004) [27] proposed an evolutionary fuzzy system for evaluating supplier performance using the linguistic nature of supplier and manufacturer attributes.

Besides the various factors discussed above, some matters also need consideration, including but not limited to interoperability with other systems, resource management, and policy standardization [28]. In this context, the purpose of this chapter is to measure e-government service evaluation factors. The fuzzy conjoint model is also utilized in ranking and selecting of the suitable factors from them [2].

Conduct collaborative statistical analysis on survey data to understand the overall picture of each product and its attributes, characteristics, advantages, etc., based on columns in Likert scales like 'satisfied' and 'very satisfied'. With the survey data responses handy, you—or anyone else, for that matter—could evaluate our product as a service. Every individual has unique requirements, and according to their preferences, they tend to respond to a variety of products and services. There's no accounting for taste. Fuzzy set theory can be used for ambiguous, uncertain, and undefined tastes. As far as civic satisfaction goes, we're pretty much talking about some form of Likert-scale linguistics to begin with: HS - Highly Satisfied, S - Satisfied, N - Neutral, DS - Dissatisfied, HDS - Highly Dissatisfied. Several literature reviews identify factors such as trust in the Internet and avoidance of corruption. However, the lack of interoperability, inability to process resources within its system, and policy standardization are some of the challenges.

Based on the above, this chapter will deal with evaluating factors that are implementable to enable the launch of e-government services. The government has launched e-governance services across various sectors and aims to analyze whether they are reaching all citizens effectively. Choose one of the following needs, describe the consequences if access rates do not meet expectations, and classify them accordingly.

In this way, we are thus able to present the fuzzy conjoint model in a chapter as an effective method of statistically analyzing survey response data and ranking factors from highest significance to lowest influential factor.

1.3 Methodology

The present subchapter finally introduces how the methodology is applied to finding key influencers on factors for eGovCA-launched services. We can represent the architecture to assess the factors of influence, as shown in Figure 1.1 below. Based on this architecture, which appears in a pictorial form in Figure 1.2, we use prior literature mainly to discern all the different components that affect e-services adoption. Around those parameters, a prepared questionnaire is available. The questionnaire was distributed to various people in Saudi Arabia to assess their satisfaction with e-services.

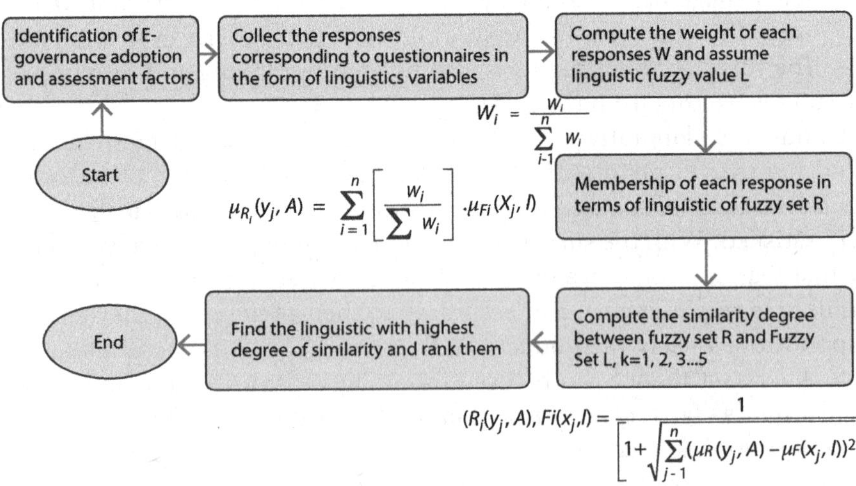

Figure 1.1 Architecture of assessing the adoption factors.

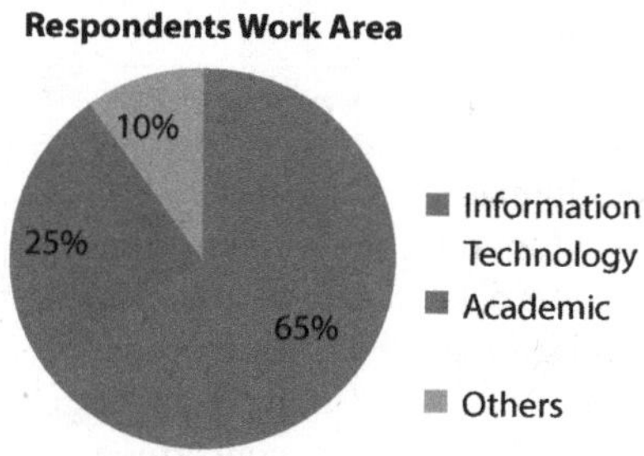

Figure 1.2 Respondents' work area.

These responses are then summed for a Likert scale by the fuzzy conjoint model. The details of all but one of these operations are covered in this section of the chapter.

1.4 Simulation Metrics

In this subchapter, the simulation metrics setup is provided in Table 1.1. The goal column represents the purpose of the research. The object/entity column represents the objects based on which decisions need to be made. The questions column represents the research questions, and the output parameters represent the variable based on which the goal is achieved.

1.4.1 Identification of E-Governance Adoption and Assessment Factors

Table 1.3 shows the various acceptance and evaluation factors described in influential theories on the deployment of E-Governance services.

According to literature searches, researchers' focus is primarily on factors such as trust in the internet. However, it is seen that some elements are missing, such as interoperability with other systems, resource handling, capacity building, intelligence, and policy standardization.

1.4.2 Sample Data Collection Using Questionnaire

To understand the importance of these factors, we run a survey using a questionnaire that is similar to what has been identified above. The HELP LINK is https://imgur.com/aH5SF8R. Referring to the same uploaded image in Figure 1.3 of the sample questionnaire (since my surveys are

Table 1.3 Simulation metrics.

Goal	Object/entity	Questions	Output parameters
Identification of E-Governance adoption attributes and ranking of these factors.	Questionnaire of adoption factors data and survey data.	What are E-Governance adoption factors and their ranking concerning satisfaction levels?	Using the fuzzy conjoint model, factors are ranked from highest to lowest concerning satisfaction levels.
101 responses are collected after the survey.	Demographic distinguishing	Survey data collected based on objects provided.	Demographic distinguishing/1, overall satisfaction/2, intelligence/3, trust in government/4, compatibility/5, instructiveness/6, facilitation at rank/7, and intention/8.
The methodology is verified with two other approaches.	Demographic distinguishing, compatibility	Survey data collected based on objects provided.	Ranks are determined for Wang and Biswas's approaches.
A Spearman's rank correlation and hypothesis is assumed to validate the methodology.	Ranks of all approaches	How can the methodology be validated?	The null hypothesis is rejected and the alternative hypothesis is accepted concerning the methodology.

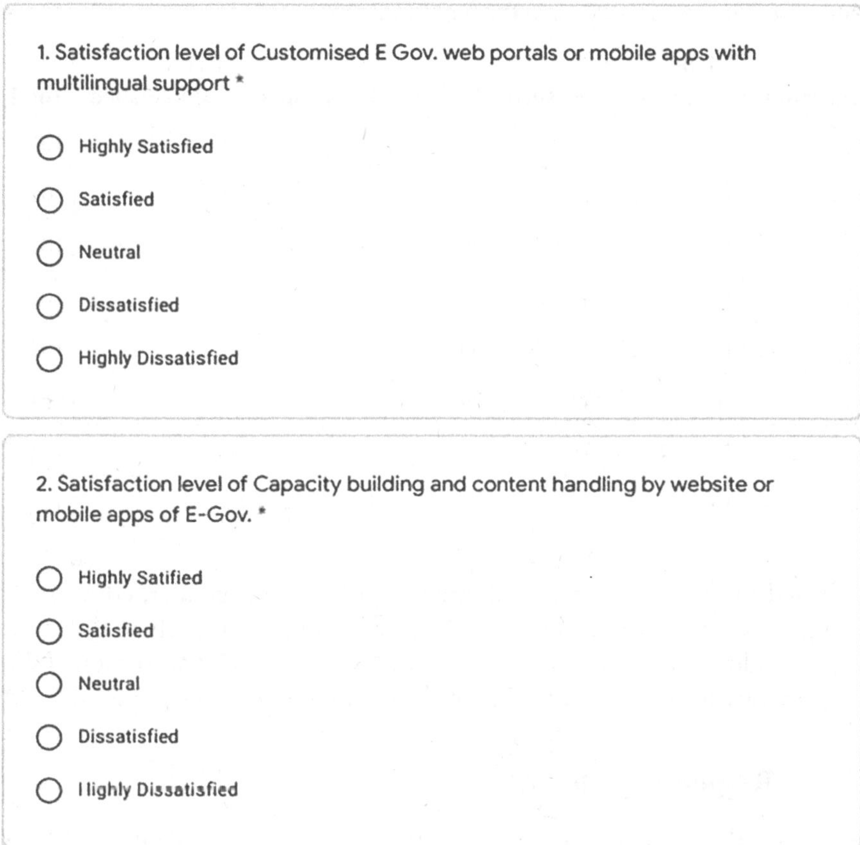

Figure 1.3 Sample questionnaire.

published/shared *via* Google Forms by social sites, WhatsApp group, and email). Data in metadata file has been thoroughly processed, as shown in Figure 1.3.

Identify the respondents and specify the organizations they are affiliated with.

The responses are as follows: Highly Satisfied (L1), Satisfied (L2), Neutral (L3), Dissatisfied (D4), and Highly Dissatisfied (H1). So we measured the responses of people on a Likert scale (1–5). Unified Table 1.4: Citizen's Responses • Stratified sampling. The whole population is stratified based on some characteristic in this process, which is called Strata. The strata are

Table 1.4 Citizens' responses to the questionnaire.

Questions	Highly satisfied	Satisfied	Neutral	Dissatisfied	Highly dissatisfied	Total
Q1	21	66	11	3	0	101
Q2	18	60	19	4	0	101
Q3	16	3	26	56	0	101
Q4	10	10	17	62	2	101
Q5	17	44	33	7	0	101
Q6	16	58	24	3	0	101
Q7	11	53	27	10	0	101
Q8	13	70	16	1	1	101

stratified by two demographical strains. In this case, gender, educational background, and age group. We can extract samples in each of the layers using random sampling: 101 replies, 77.9% men vs. 22.1% women. Table 1.5 provides an overview of influential factors in e-governance services.

1.4.3 Respondent Details

Figure 1.4 describes that the age group of most respondents is from 16 to 30 (31%), followed by those aged between 31 and 45 (43). A total of 24% were between 39 and 60, while only 0.4 % were over 60 years old. The figure also demonstrates that 65% of respondents are from the IT area, 25% are from academia, and only the last 10% are allocated to others. This finding is converted to multiple-choice questions with more than one correct option (checkbox).

1.4.4 Fuzzy Conjoint Model

A fuzzy conjoint model, proposed by Turksen and Wilson, is used to determine the attributes' rank as shown in Figure 1.1. The linguistic representation was based on the Likert scale as Highly Satisfied (HS), Satisfied

Table 1.5 E-Governance services influential factors.

S. no.	Influential factors	Attributes
1	Satisfaction level of customized E-Governance web portals or mobile apps with multilingual support.	Demographic distinguishing
2	Satisfaction level of capacity building and content handling by the website or mobile apps of E-Governance.	Compatibility
3	Satisfaction level of standardization of policies and IT laws.	Trust in the government
4	Satisfaction level in detection frauds after implementing E-Governance services.	Intelligence
5	Satisfaction level for artificial intelligence-enabled E-Governance websites and mobile apps.	Instructive
6	Satisfaction level for common service center (CSCs) establishment for accessing E-Governance services.	Facilitation
7	Experience with previous E-Governance services/ apps.	Intention to use
8	Overall satisfaction.	Satisfaction

(S), Neutral (N), Dissatisfied (DS), and Highly Dissatisfied (HDS). Figure 1.5 presents the correlation between e-governance adoption and user satisfaction.

The linguistic variables of the Likert scale for surveys are defined as Lk= {Highly Satisfied (L1), Satisfied (L2), Neutral (L3), Dissatisfied (L4), and Highly Dissatisfied (L5)}. The assumed membership values for the Likert scale are shown in Table 1.6.

1.4.4.1 *Calculation of Weight for Each Respondent*

The weight for each respondent corresponding to the attribute is calculated.

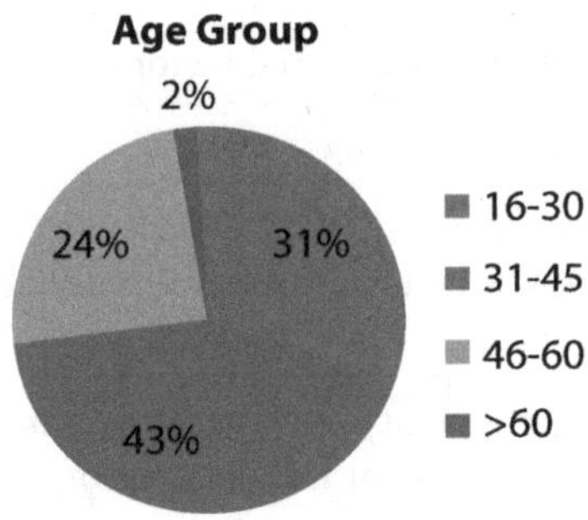

Figure 1.4 Respondents' age group.

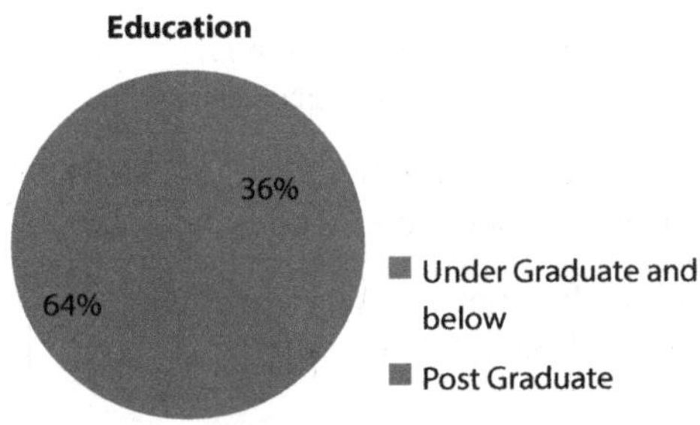

Figure 1.5 Respondents' educational background.

1.4.4.2 Calculating the Similarity Degree

Equation has been used to calculate the similarity degree between fuzzy responses [R] and fuzzy set [L]. The highest degree of similarity linguistic value is obtained.

The steps of the fuzzy conjoint model (Turksen and Wilson's) are as follows:

Table 1.6 Assumed membership value of the fuzzy set of Likert's scale.

Fuzzy set/ linguistic variables	Highly satisfied	Satisfied	Neutral	Dissatisfied	Highly dissatisfied
L1	1.0	0.7	0.5	0.0	0.0
L2	0.7	1.0	0.6	0.0	0.0
L3	0.0	0.3	1.0	0.7	0.3
L4	0.0	0.0	0.4	1.0	0.6
L5	0.0	0.0	0.0	0.4	1.0

Step 1: Data Collection
Step 2: Preprocessing
Step 3: Model Training
Step 4: Performance Evaluation

1.5 Computation

This subchapter discusses computation steps as per the algorithm.

1.5.1 Computation of Fuzzy Vector of Responses

Table 1.7 shows the membership value of each response to linguistics variables for the questionnaire calculated as follows:

$$(0.207921\times1.0+0.653465\times0.7+0.108911\times0.0+0.029703\times0.0+0\times0)= 0.665347.$$

1.5.2 Computation of Similarity Degree

Table 1.9 shows the degree of similarity between respondents' data fuzzy values in Table 1.8 and the Likert scale fuzzy set in Table 1.6. The highest value in each row represents the level of satisfaction in terms of the Likert scale, and ranks are determined based on the highest value in each

Table 1.7 Fuzzy vector of respondents to the linguistic variables of the questionnaire.

Questions	Highly satisfied	Satisfied	Neutral	Dissatisfied	Highly dissatisfied
Q1	0.207921	0.653465	0.108911	0.029703	0
Q2	0.178218	0.594059	0.188119	0.039604	0
Q3	0.158416	0.029703	0.554455	0.554455	0
Q4	0.09901	0.09901	0.168317	0.613861	0.019802
Q5	0.168317	0.435644	0.326733	0.069307	0
Q6	0.158416	0.574257	0.237624	0.029703	0
Q7	0.108911	0.524752	0.267327	0.09901	0
Q8	0.128713	0.693069	0.158416	0.009901	0.009901

Table 1.8 Membership value of each response in linguistics variables for the questionnaire.

Questions	Highly satisfied	Satisfied	Neutral	Dissatisfied	Highly dissatisfied
R1	0.665347	0.831683	0.616832	0.105941	0.050495
R2	0.594059	0.775248	0.649505	0.171287	0.330693
R3	0.179208	0.306931	0.873267	0.942574	0.499010
R4	0.168317	0.218812	0.522772	0.739604	0.438614
R5	0.473267	0.651485	0.700000	0.298020	0.139604
R6	0.560396	0.354455	0.673267	0.196040	0.089109
R7	0.476238	0.681188	0.676238	0.069307	0.574257
R8	0.613861	0.830693	0.642574	0.124752	0.063366

row. Further, ranking between attributes is assigned from highest to lowest. For example, for question 1, the second column represents the highest value which falls under the "satisfied" column. As observed, row 1 has achieved the highest rank, i.e., 0.827282, under the linguistic variable "satisfied." Thus, row 1 is assigned as rank 1. Likewise, the other ranks have been calculated. The cell (1,1) value of Table 1.9 is calculated as:

1/(1+(sqrt((0.665347-1.0)^2+(0.831683-.7)^2+(0.616832-.50)^2+(0.105941-0.0)^2+(0.050495-0.0)^2)))=0.716371.

The results shown in Figure 1.6 indicate that 15% of citizens are highly satisfied with the services, 45% are satisfied with the services, 22% are neutral, 18% of citizens are dissatisfied with the E-Governance services, and no citizens are highly dissatisfied. After applying the discussed model for ranking the factors, it was found that citizens are dissatisfied with fraud detection, which falls under the intelligence category, and neutral about the formation of IT laws, which falls under trust in the government, after implementing the E-Governance services.

Table 1.9 Calculation of similarity degree as well as rank among attributes.

Attribute	Highly satisfied	Satisfied	Neutral	Dissatisfied	Highly dissatisfied	Rank
Demographic distinction	0.716371	**0.827282**	0.483831	0.398270	0.387289	1
Compatibility	0.634615	**0.689452**	0.502259	0.428731	0.421996	5
Trust in the government	0.409137	0.416437	**0.723077**	0.623769	0.455038	4
Intelligence	0.436751	0.438604	0.702525	**0.754649**	0.520841	3
Interactiveness	0.604486	**0.649517**	0.533583	0.371410	0.318636	6
facilitation	**0.615864**	0.588741	0.540590	0.429504	0.429504	7
Intention to use	0.555495	**0.587718**	0.506422	0.438929	0.454655	8
Satisfaction	0.687772	**0.806620**	0.480052	0.403812	0.390663	2

Bold values indicate the most significant parameter contributing to e-governance adoption.

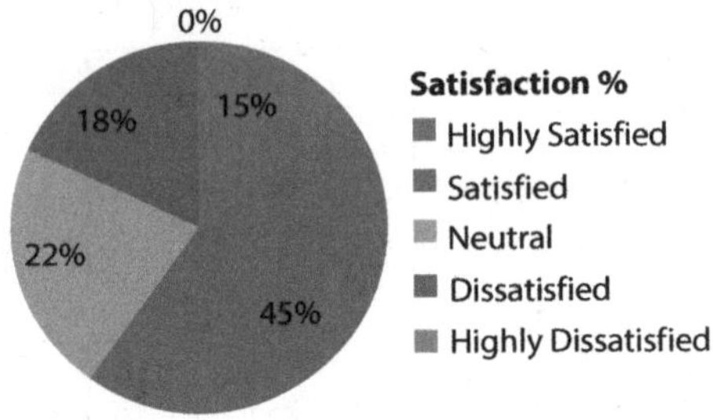

Figure 1.6 Respondents' satisfaction %.

1.5.3 Result Analysis

The E-Governance adoption factors that influence citizens are shown in Table 1.10. The bold rows show dissatisfaction and neutrality among citizens.

The results in Table 1.10 show that citizens are dissatisfied with the intelligence capability of E-Governance applications as a weak factor and neutral concerning IT policies and laws.

The factors ranking from highest to lowest as per Table 1.11 are: demographic distinguishing ranked at rank 1, overall satisfaction at rank 2, intelligence at rank 3, trust in the government at rank 4, compatibility at rank 5, instructiveness at rank 6, facilitation at rank 7, and intention to use at rank 8.

Table 1.10 Identified influential factors.

Questions	Satisfied/ dissatisfied/ neutral	Factors
Satisfaction level in detection of frauds after implementing E-Governance services.	Dissatisfied	Intelligence
Satisfaction level of Standardization of policies and IT laws.	Neutral	Trust in the government

Table 1.11 Similarity degree and ranking of attributes—Biswas's approach.

Questions	Highly satisfied	Satisfied	Neutral	Dissatisfied	Highly dissatisfied	Rank
Q1	0.894218	**0.901364**	0.572241	0.250530	0.060754	1
Q2	0.767042	**0.854482**	0.659394	0.414147	0.263595	4
Q3	0.409940	0.471944	**0.875875**	0.785287	0.432318	2
Q4	0.334983	0.351511	0.741151	**0.797290**	0.633151	5
Q5	0.735233	**0.758255**	0.686191	0.435383	0.207594	7
Q6	**0.65813**	0.621996	0.565008	0.341323	0.14441	8
Q7	0.742062	**0.767728**	0.659512	0.450234	0.406004	6
Q8	**0.871628**	0.075543	0.608703	0.276185	0.075543	3

Bold values indicate the most significant parameter contributing to e-governance adoption.

1.5.4 Validation

Further, this subchapter describes how to use different approaches to validate the rankings. The approach used for comparison is Biswas and Wang's approaches for the same dataset.

The cell (1,1) value of Table 1.11 is calculated as follows: (0.665347×1.0+0.831683×0.7+0.616832×0.5+0.105941×0.0+0.050495×0.0)/max((0.665347×0.665347+0.831683×0.831683+0.616832×0.616832+0.105941×0.105941+0.050495×0.050495),(1.0×1.0+0.7×0.7+0.5×0.5+0.0×0.0+0.0×0.0))=0.894218. Table 1.12 summarizes the ranking of e-governance adoption factors.

A. Wang's Approach Wang has given a formula for similarity degree values between two fuzzy sets $\tilde{A}$ & $\tilde{B}$ as follows:

Hypothesis

H_0 : No rank difference in various approaches (Null Hypothesis).

H_1 : Rank differences in various approaches.

A Spearman's rank correlation test has been applied for validating the rank between attributes. In this validation process, the rank difference between the two approaches was calculated. The Z-score is calculated using the formula

Table 1.12 Similarity degree and rank among attributes—Wang's approach.

Questions	Highly satisfied	Satisfied	Neutral	Dissatisfied	Highly dissatisfied	Rank
Q1	**0.852079**	0.924752	0.515446	0.455446	0.531881	1
Q2	**0.741058**	0.744158	0.551089	0.491089	0.535842	4
Q3	0.575842	0.577624	**0.78604**	0.722376	0.620594	3
Q4	0.506535	0.486535	0.700396	**0.780792**	0.573267	5
Q5	**0.732277**	0.712277	0.618416	0.558416	0.547723	6
Q6	0.748119	**0.780792**	0.566931	0.506931	0.531881	7
Q7	**0.720396**	0.700396	0.606535	0.546535	0.559604	8
Q8	**0.712079**	0.602079	0.471287	0.471287	0.527921	2

Bold values indicate the most significant parameter contributing to e-governance adoption.

Table 1.13 shows a statistical analysis of the fuzzy conjoint model associated with Biswas and Wang's models. Column 1 in Table 1.13 defines the attributes, and columns 2, 3, and 4 show the ranking of the different approaches.

Table 1.13 Comparison table of T&W, Biswas, and Wang's approaches.

Attribute – (A)/ States	T&W (1994)- (B)	Biswas (1995)- (C)	Wang (1997)- (D)	$Diff_1$= B-C	$Diff_2$= B-D	$(Diff_1)^2$	$(Diff_2)^2$
Q1	1	1	1	0	0	0	0
Q2	5	4	4	1	1	1	1
Q3	4	2	3	1	2	1	4
Q4	3	5	5	2	-2	4	4
Q5	6	7	6	0	-1	0	1
Q6	7	8	7	0	-1	0	1
Q7	8	6	8	0	2	0	4
Q8	2	3	2	0	1	0	1

1.5.5 Limitations and Future Study

An individual survey is not suitable for real-time or short-term problems because surveys collect data at a specific point in time. Thus, it is problematic to measure population change without conducting more than one survey at different times. There are always chances that people may provide dishonest answers. Additionally, people may misunderstand the survey questions and can give wrong answers, which may lead to wrong predictions.

1.6 Summary

The chapter consists of fuzzy conjoint methodologies for evaluating E-Governance services and determining both weak and strong adoption factors. Several adoption/causative factors have been posited for E-Governance. The results indicate that 60% are highly satisfied or satisfied with the service, and 18% are dissatisfied with the provision of E-Governance services. Whereas, 22% of respondents have a neutral opinion of these services. It is also learned that even though people are neutral to policy/IT law-related satisfaction, they are dissatisfied with the intelligence factor determining satisfaction in automatically detecting fraud or corruption. Moreover, this ranking is also confirmed by other two approaches, namely Biswas and Wang's approaches, which are verified on a similar dataset. This result indicates that the method by Turksen and Wilson for ranking government electronic services is valid. It is also observed that in order to implement smart governance requires intelligent techniques. Citizens are also not fully satisfied with intelligent technology just if E-Governance applications. Therefore, smart E-governance instructiveness, intelligence, and public trust will be successfully implemented, making them a high-priority factor. Another prominent fraud detection model found in e-Government applications is based on the dissatisfaction of citizens about its efficiency in detecting fraud. This model is used in India's customs export incentive/refund system, which will be explained in the next chapter.

Bibliography

1. Smith, J. and Jones, A., Smart Cities: *Designing Sustainable Urban Systems*, Springer, Berlin, Germany, 2020.

2. Turksen, I.B. and Wilson, I.A., A fuzzy set model for multi-criteria decision making. *Fuzzy Sets Syst.*, 64, 1, 21–32, 1994, https://doi.org/10.1016/0165-0114(94)90240-2.
3. Biswas, R., Fuzzy preference ordering in group decision making. *Fuzzy Sets Syst.*, 86, 3, 277–283, 1997, https://doi.org/10.1016/S0165-0114(96)00131-6.
4. Wang, X., Integrating fuzzy multi-criteria decision analysis with real options to evaluate power generation technologies. *Fuzzy Sets Syst.*, 119, 1, 47–60, 2001, https://doi.org/10.1016/S0165-0114(99)00098-1.
5. Sharma, S. and Gupta, R., *Advancements in Data Analytics for Environmental Monitoring*, IGI Global, ACM, New York, USA, 2019.
6. Gao, L. and Zhang, H., *Machine Learning and Data Analytics for Smart Cities*, CRC Press, Taylor & Francis, London, UK, 2017.
7. Carter, L. and Bélanger, F., The utilization of e-government services: Citizen trust, innovation and acceptance factors. *Inf. Syst. J.*, 15, 1, 5–25, 2005, https://doi.org/10.1111/j.1365-2575.2005.00183.x.
8. Anupama Namburu, D., Sumathi, R.R., Rutvij, H., Jhaveri, R.K.D., Subbulakshmi, N., Balusamy, B., FPGA-Based Deep Learning Models for Analysing Corona Using Chest X-Ray Images. *Mobile Inf. Syst.*, 2022, Article ID 2110785, 14, 2022.
9. Akhtar, N. and Khan, S., *Smart City Technologies for Sustainable Urban Development*, CRC Press, IEEE, New York, USA, 2020.
10. IEEE, *IEEE International Smart Cities Conference Proceedings*, IEEE, 2019.
11. Mensah, I.K., Mi, J., Domfeh, K.A., E-government service adoption: The moderating role of gender on citizens' trust and risk perception. *Int. J. Public Admin.*, 43, 4, 303–314, 2020, https://doi.org/10.1080/01900692.2019.1628055.
12. Chen, H. and Chau, M., *Data Mining for the Social Sciences: An Introduction*, University of California Press, Springer, Berlin, Germany, 2016.
13. Kuo, M. and Sarkis, J., *Smart Technologies for Sustainable Supply Chain Management*, Springer, 2020.
14. United Nations, *World Urbanization Prospects: The 2018 Revision*, 2019.
15. Venkatesh, V. and Davis, F.D., A theoretical extension of the Technology Acceptance Model: Four longitudinal field studies. *Manag. Sci.*, 46, 2, 186–204, 2000, https://doi.org/10.1287/mnsc.46.2.186.11926.
16. Moore, G.C. and Benbasat, I., Development of an instrument to measure the perceptions of adopting an information technology innovation. *Inf. Syst. Res.*, 2, 3, 192–222, 1991, https://doi.org/10.1287/isre.2.3.192.
17. Rogers, E.M. and Shoemaker, F.F., *Communication of Innovations: A Cross-Cultural Approach (2nd ed.)*. Free Press, 1971.
18. Bhattacharya, A. and Das, S., *Digital Governance: Models and Technologies*, Springer, MIT Press, Cambridge, Massachusetts, USA, 2018.
19. Rehman, M., Esichaikul, V., Kamal, M., Factors influencing e-government adoption in Pakistan. *Transform. Gov.: People, Process and Policy*, 6, 3, 258–282, 2012, https://doi.org/10.1108/17506161211251263.

20. Bertot, J.C., Jaeger, P.T., Grimes, J.M., Using ICTs to create a culture of transparency: E-government and social media as openness and anti-corruption tools for societies. *Gov. Inf. Q.*, 27, 3, 264–271, 2010, https://doi.org/10.1016/j.giq.2010.03.001.
21. Marullo, A. and Zappia, G., *Big Data and the Smart City*, Springer, IOS Press, Amsterdam, Netherlands, 2017.
22. Bélanger, F. and Carter, L., Trust and risk in e-government adoption. *J. Strateg. Inf. Syst.*, 17, 2, 165–176, 2008, https://doi.org/10.1016/j.jsis.2007.12.002.
23. Schaffers, H. and Komninos, N., *Smart Cities and the Future Internet*, Springer, CRC Press, Boca Raton, Florida, USA, 2018.
24. Heeks, R., *ICT4D 1.0: The Next Generation of ICT for Development*, Oxford University Press, IEEE, New York, USA, 2017.
25. EEA, *Resource Efficiency in Europe: Policies and Approaches in 31 Countries*, European Environment Agency, Elsevier, Amsterdam, Netherlands, 2019.
26. Agyemang, F. and Adedoja, G., *Green Computing Strategies for Energy-Efficient Design*, IGI Global, Taylor & Francis, London, UK, 2018.
27. Jain, V., Wadhwa, S., Deshmukh, S.G., Supplier selection using fuzzy association rules and neural network. *Int. J. Technol., Policy Manag.*, 4, 2, 141–157, 2004, https://doi.org/10.1504/IJTPM.2004.004765.
28. Saravanakumar, P., Sundararajan, T.V.P., Dhanaraj, R.K., Nisar, K., Memon, F.H., *et al.*, Lamport certificateless signcryption deep neural networks for data aggregation security in wsn. *Intell. Autom. Soft Comput.*, 33, 3, 1835–1847, 2022.

2

Design of Smart and Sustainable Applications Using Intelligent Computational Techniques

R. Rajitha Jasmine[1]*, Jhansi Ida[2], P. Rajesh[3], K.V. Sreelekha[4], N. BanuPriya[2] and Dilli Babu M.[5]

[1]*Department of Information Technology, R.M.K. Engineering College, Kavaraipettai, India*
[2]*Department of Computer Science and Engineering, R.M.K. Engineering College, Kavaraipettai, India*
[3]*Department of Data Science, SASTRA Deemed University Chennai Campus, Chennai, India*
[4]*Department of Computer Science and Engineering, LBS Institute Technology for Women, Thiruvananthapuram, India*
[5]*Department of IT, Panimalar Engineering College, Poonamallee, India*

Abstract

In all areas of government, several technological services have already been introduced. The use of electronic governance has many benefits, such as streamlining the administration of government services, increasing communication between government and non-government institutions, reducing corruption, identifying fraud, and making government services accessible 24/7. The four main pillars upon which electronic governance rests are the following: exchanges between the government and its citizens, businesses, employees, and other governments. The widespread use of these services is crucial to their success. As a result, a plethora of opportunities to evaluate and implement these services' analyses become available. In this research, we look at the variables that could influence these services' adoption rates. To do this, a questionnaire is developed using the elements that influence the adoption of E-Governance. To identify the weak components, survey data is processed using the fuzzy conjoint model. Additionally, the degree of

**Corresponding author*: rrj.it@rmkec.ac.in

R. Sathiyaraj, Rajesh Kumar Dhanaraj, K. Arun Kumar, Rutvij H. Jhaveri and A. Mohamed Abbas (eds.) Predictive Methods in Next-Generation Computing: An Approach Toward Sustainability, (23–46)

satisfaction or dissatisfaction is used to score these aspects. This research shows that people aren't happy with how well E-Government services can identify fraud. As a result, E-Governance services must be enhanced to identify fraud by the government better. Electronic filing and clearance of exports and imports is one of the major E-Government applications of India's customs. In this era of automated customs clearance, the Indian customs agency has fallen victim to a number of scams, including those involving shipping bills, exporters, licensing, smuggling, falsified documents, and duty drawback fraud. A unique set of procedures exists for identifying various forms of fraud. Export drawback fraud is a big financial scam. Currently, there is no smart way to identify fraudulent export drawbacks. To achieve this, a model has been developed to detect potential export incentive/drawback fraud. Intuitionistic fuzzy sets and game theory are the basis of a two-tier fraud detection model that determines the sensitivity of export bills. To identify potential drawback frauds, a customs officer is given instructions for manually inspecting products based on their sensitivity.

Keywords: Smart electronic governance, blockchain technology, intelligent techniques, e-governance adoption factors, fraud detection capability, export drawback fraud

2.1 Introduction

It is possible to provide all of a government's functions digitally, according to the notion of electronic governance. Derived from the Greek "kebernon," the English term "governance" denotes leading, controlling, managing, or cooperating with an established authority. Development and the end of poverty both depend on good administration. Digital governance, smart governance, the electronic society, electronic administration, etc., are all novel applications of this idea. The government has had to reevaluate its strategies for providing services to its citizens in light of the fast development of new technologies. However, there are several obstacles to quickly adjusting to the changes. Governments worldwide are actively working to increase the number of public-private partnerships that contribute to the planning and execution of public projects. The success of electronic governance relies heavily on the information technology (IT) infrastructure, which encompasses things like the internet, connection, speed, and public knowledge of the benefits of utilizing electronic services. More expansions of smart city governance emerge from E-Governance theory, which in turn leads to smart governance theory [1]. Transparency, accountability, responsibility, as well as cost reduction are the overarching goals of all forms of governance. In a democratic society, they are the bedrock principles. Predicting trends and making informed choices in advance may be possible using the data from E-Governance applications. Several E-Governance projects, including e-health, e-ports, e-districts, e-results, e-transport, e-customs, and e-passports, have already been launched by the Indian government [2]. With 27 Mission Mode Projects (MMPs) covering domains such as lands, customs, transportation, treasury, police, village panchayat, employee exchange, health, and more, the Indian government's National Electronic Governance Plan (NeGP) was established under the Department of Information Technology. All MMPs are created, tested, and run by the National Informatics Centre (NIC), which is part of the Government of India's Department of Electronics and Information Technology (DEITY) 1 [2].

Words like "SMART" stand for straightforward, ethical, responsible, quick to respond, and open about their inner workings. Governance changes the tight-knit imperative relationships between people, companies, governments, NGOs, and workers [3]. One may say that knowledge, data content, connectivity, and capital are the four mainstays of E-Governance [4]. Additionally, an electronic society is promoted *via* e-governance, which places an emphasis on people's electronic involvement. Indian residents may now more easily engage with their government *via* three new portals: dial.gov.in, mygov.gov.in, and india.gov.in. From these exchanges emerges the notion of adaptive governance, which holds that public opinion should inform policymaking. The effective execution of all societal electronic services is hindered by several factors, including but not limited to citizens' literacy, awareness, involvement, poverty, trust in services, customization, citizen engagement, connection, linguistic domination, infrastructure, and many more. Overspending, service delivery delays, and an inability to adapt to new technologies are some of the reasons why E-Government services fail, as highlighted by the author [5]. Now more than ever, with the advent of new data analytics tools, it is necessary to examine data and make predictions. Traditional databases, which were used by earlier apps, are not very efficient. Predictions are made using statistical approaches and structured data is the mainstay of application development. However, the idea of "Big Data" emerged with technological progress. The data in Big Data is not structured. Unstructured data may be analyzed and patterns can be predicted with the help of Big Data analytics. False or incomplete information may be present in Big Data. Data selection, dissemination, and analysis are the three main steps in developing a complete system. The leadership of any nation can no longer afford to ignore the viewpoints expressed on social media, which have quickly become the most popular platforms for such expressions. In his discussion of the pioneer of unstructured datasets, Morabito [6] mentions concepts like crowdsourcing, the IoT, and the participation of public objects.

By using the internet and a decentralized network of remote servers, operating systems, databases, and bandwidth, cloud computing makes it possible to outsource computer tasks to third parties. Pattern recognition, data integration, data sharing, modeling, transmission, prediction, and real-time data analytics are some of the particular needs handled by Munne [7]. Technologies that allow for pattern detection and cross-checking are useful for creating pattern blueprints. You may use analytics approaches based on machine learning to in-memory databases to get real-time insights. Acquiring data aids in the transmission of data in real time. Storming and codifying are the two methods of data gathering used by Optimex. The analytical database can be used with predictive analysis approaches. Applying natural language processing techniques allows for the detection of human speech. Modeling and simulation can be accomplished with the help of a temporal database. Agarwal [8] used data analytics and machine learning (ML) approaches to predict societal unrest, improbable events, conflicts, or demonstrations. A variety of analytical frameworks, including those for sentiment, prediction, comparison, behavioral, fraud, and more, have been laid forth [9]. An important problem in E-Governance is the widespread use of e-services by the general public. Trust in the Internet, the government, and other stakeholders were among the many adoption criteria highlighted by the research. Other considerations were related hazards, data security, complexity, corruption, fraud detection capabilities, and comparable advantages. The researchers have been unable to determine the relative strength of these variables. After E-Governance systems are put into place, there is a dearth of studies examining the capacity to identify fraud. Duty drawback fraud and fabricated documents in customs clearance are additional problems for the Indian customs agency. Fuzzy logic theory may be used to anticipate the likelihood of fraud in Indian customs, which can be used to avoid duty drawback fraud. The Indian customs service may use cutting-edge blockchain technology to stop forgeries of papers. Blockchain is a cutting-edge technology that eliminates the need for a central authority by facilitating the creation of an immutable, distributed record of all system transactions. People can make direct or indirect use of objects over the internet thanks to the Internet of Things (IoT). E-Governance applications might therefore benefit from methods of artificial intelligence, agile technology, blockchain, and the internet of Things [31, 32].

As part of its public service delivery system, every nation's government addresses both known and unknown atmospheric influences. It would be impossible to ensure the effective execution of services using broad ideas and theories in this context. This can only be accomplished by attending to the specifics of the service delivery process. The government needs strong communication skills to engage with its people. What we call "e-society" is really just a term for the open and accessible society made possible *via* the widespread use of information and communication technology (ICT). On several levels—federal, state, district, block, and village—the Indian government has already launched programs to bring electronic services to people's homes and bring them together. The government of India has set up Common Service Centers (CSCs) to provide electronic services to all citizens, whether they live in an urban or rural location, in this digital age [9]. Factors that may affect people's ability to use electronic services include their level of education, income, awareness, language proficiency, knowledge of available resources, and proficiency with information technology. These are significant obstacles to the effective adoption of e-services in underdeveloped nations. As a result, these digital services need to facilitate two-way communication between public entities and their constituents, among other interested parties; yet, there are a number of obstacles and voids that can hinder their widespread adoption and use. To keep the public's interest in these services high, it is necessary to examine the problems and how to fix them. The elements that may affect the ranking and acceptance of electronic services are the subject of research investigations. To encourage adoption, the government should prioritize the characteristics that are least satisfied after ranking them according to their degree of satisfaction. Additionally, several instances of fraud have been uncovered across various government agencies. The traditions of India are one example. A literature review uncovered several forms of fraud inside the Indian customs service, including but not limited to smuggling, false document presentation, filing of shipping invoices, exporters, licensing, and different forms of fraud. In addition to this, the study employs AI approaches to prevent 17 instances of government fraud. Additional applications of blockchain technology in this study include the safe mining of blockchain transaction blocks and blockchain-based customs clearance in India.

While conducting this research, we saw several gaps in our understanding of how to best use E-Governance services to improve the delivery of public services. a) Every single person in the nation is profoundly affected by the introduction and use of electronic services. The point of permitting e-services is rendered moot if a significant portion of the population does not use them, even if citizens constitute the primary users of these services. Finding out what elements influence service usability and appropriateness is thus important. b) Improvements in E-Governance include the ability to electronically file import and export paperwork as well as invoices. As a result, the submission of import and export bills of entry and related paperwork will no longer need human verification. The item tariff schedule determines the import duty. To encourage export activities, the government pays incentives to exporters. A percentage of the invoice value of the exported products is used to determine the incentive/discount. To gain greater incentives, dishonest exporters inflate the worth of the exported goods. Therefore, customs inspectors have a very difficult duty in determining the true worth of exported commodities to identify and prevent drawback fraud. c) Over 40 distinct kinds of LPCO (Licenses, Permissions, Certificates, and Other authorization) are granted by various government agencies for use in customs processing of import and export paperwork. For several reasons, the Directorate General of Foreign Trade (DGFT) in India provides licenses both digitally and manually. Importers and exporters are also responsible for producing compliance reports for the DGFT. Nevertheless, these certifications are often provided by hand. Unfortunately, not every division understands the significance of these credentials. For usage on a global scale, a certificate of origin or origin guarantee is produced. Both exporters and importers are capable of producing fake documentation. It is necessary to digitally alter the application, issue, and use of these certificates to prevent such fraudulent practices. d) After that, the customs official's nodes check the details of the provenance certificate, and the next step is to put those facts into the blockchain ledger. To prevent dishonest nodes controlled by the government from inserting fake papers into the blockchain ledger, an effective solution is necessary. To remedy the problems with conventional forms of government, this study introduces the idea of smart electronic governance, which uses blockchain technology in conjunction with intelligent tactics. A new way to improve the efficiency, openness, and responsibility of government operations is smart electronic governance, which uses intelligent systems like machine learning and natural language processing in conjunction with blockchain's intrinsic qualities of decentralization, transparency, and immutability. The feasibility and efficacy of smart electronic governance will be investigated *via* case studies and empirical research, demonstrating how it may change the face of government in the information age.

2.2 Background

Gathering the right components, features, or criteria to utilize different E-Government services is the main topic of this chapter. Weak adoption aspects of E-Government are identified in this study paper. The fuzzy conjoint approach is used to rate the adoption criteria and identify the weak ones. According to the degree of satisfaction, the elements are graded from highest to lowest: very pleased, satisfied, neutral, dissatisfied, and very unhappy. Whether or not the government should prioritize certain elements to boost adoption depends on how they rank with satisfaction levels. The introduction of electronic services, sometimes known as E-services, affects every person in the country. Citizens are the main target audience for these services; therefore, any dissatisfaction among a sizable portion of the population would render them useless. Because of this, it is crucial to identify key criteria that establish the appropriateness of these services. The following elements have been previously recognized by the researchers as being relevant: infrastructure, cost, trust, time, accessibility, literacy, languages, willingness, age, gender, and people's awareness [10]. Ensuring user satisfaction with these e-services is crucial for a successful deployment. The government also needs this since many private entities in the community provide the same degree of expectation. Major considerations for the nationwide rollout of e-services are the availability, velocity, and capacity of the internet connection. Another aspect to think about is emerging technologies. These e-services need to be multilingual if the nation in question has more than one official language. It is important to discover the key elements that influence customers' acceptance of e-services since user needs vary throughout the country. Consequently, this section ranks acceptance criteria that could impact the rate of E-Government service access using fuzzy conjoint model data.

2.2.1 Adoption Models and Theories

The majority of theories draw on earlier work by Davis, such as the Technology Acceptance Model (TAM), UTAUT, TRA, DOI, (Diffusion of Innovation), etc. The utility intent aspect was brought forward [11]. The four key areas of e-management, e-commerce, e-services, and e-democracy that make up e-governance were identified [12]. The anticipated performance was suggested by Venkatesh *et al.*, 2003 as an important component in addressing citizens' trust in using services to enhance their jobs. Expectations of efforts have also been addressed [13]. Considerations related to the intended application are discussed [14]. Deploying technology-based electronic services also raises serious concerns about the security of current information. The government's e-services have several positive effects, including making information more reusable and making residents happier *via* more public access to formerly private data. [15] indicated that the intention to use e-government websites is significantly affected by both intrinsic and cognitivist elements. For the purpose of public trust and contentment with technology, [16] put out a unified theory. Using an E-Governance service that the New Delhi Municipal Council in India had implemented, the author put the suggested concept to the test. This assumption is dependent on the public's opinion of government electronic services, according to the reviewed literature. Performance expectation, effort expectancy, social influence, enabling circumstances, faith in technology, government, and citizen satisfaction, and a few more criteria not included in Table 2.1 were also the focus of several writers. [17] looked at how socio-demographic characteristics affected the study. In the Philippines, these characteristics may be categorized as internet and information technology accessibility, public perception of e-government, knowledge of e-services, and the use of

Table 2.1 Some empirical theories about adoption models.

Model/theory	Factors/items	Definitions	Authors
A Unified Model of E-Governance Adoption (UMEGA)	Perceived service quality and recommendation	Recognizing the quality and trust of service to the government, the intent of using and recommending e-government services.	[18]
Trust Literature	Faith	Trust in actor providing the service.	[19]
UTAUT (User Theory of Acceptance and Use of Technology)	Performance	Determining the performance after using innovation service.	[20]
	Social influence	Assessment of social impact after using innovative services.	
	Facilitating condition	An organizational and technical architectural framework for using innovative systems.	

(*Continued*)

Table 2.1 Some empirical theories about adoption models. (*Continued*)

Model/theory	Factors/items	Definitions	Authors
TAM2 (Extended Technology Acceptance Model)	Thought/Image	An image of a person after using an innovative service.	[21]
	Voluntariness	Personal evaluation for the voluntary use of innovative services.	[22]
	Job relevance	Identify the system that applies to his or her work.	
	Quality of output	Comparison with the previous version.	
Theory of Reasoned Action (TRA)	Attitudes	How do citizens feel about using e-governance services?	[23]
	Subjective norms		
Technology Acceptance Model (TAM)	Usefulness	Identifying the use of a system.	
	Ease of useful	Ease of use of service.	
DOI (Diffusion of Innovation)	Benefits	How is the E-Governance service advantageous over its predecessor?	[24]
	Complexity	The system is relatively difficult to use and understand.	
	Observability	Determine the output of innovation.	

digital e-government. You may find a comprehensive overview of the elements influencing the adoption of digital government services in Table 2.2.

Consequently, the fuzzy conjoint model is ranked from most influential to least in this chapter as a viable option for statistically assessing survey data.

Table 2.2 Factors/attributes affecting the adoption of E-Governance services.

Factors	Description	Authors
Perceived service quality and intention to use	Service quality, intention to use, and recommend to others.	[25]
Information security	Evaluate the security of information.	[26]
Transaction security	Transaction security when using e-government applications.	[27]
Transparency/fairness	Determine the transparency of electronic services.	[28]
Corruption avoidance	How much corruption will be reduced after the introduction of e-government services?	[29]
Availability of resources	Identify the availability of resources in e-government applications.	[30]

2.3 Methodology

The approach to identifying the important factors of government-launched electronic services is covered in this section. To discover the many elements that affect the adoption of e-services, the architecture largely depicts literature research. The next step is to use these criteria to inform the development of a questionnaire. Many individuals fill out this survey so we can gauge how happy they are with the e-services. A fuzzy conjoint model is used to examine the gathered answers based on a Likert scale. In this section of the textbook, we go over each of these processes in depth.

2.3.1 Simulation Metrics

Table 2.3 provides the configuration for the simulation metrics in this section. The objective of the research is represented in the goal column. The items requiring a decision are shown in the object/entity column. The research question is represented in the questions column, and the variable depending on the aim is represented by the output parameters.

Table 2.3 Simulation metrics.

Goal	Object/entity	Questions	Output parameters
Identification of E-Governance adoption attributes and ranking of these factors.	Questionnaire of adoption factors data and survey data.	What are E-Governance adoption factors and ranking of them concerning their satisfaction level.	Using fuzzy conjoint model, factors are ranked from highest to lowest concerning their satisfaction level.
101 responses are collected after the survey.	Demographic distinguishing, Compatibility, Trust in government, Intelligence, Interactive, Facilitation, Intention to use, and Satisfaction.	Survey data collected based on objects provided.	Demographic distinguishing/1, overall satisfaction/2, intelligence/3, trust in the government/4, compatibility/5, interactiveness/6, facilitation at rank/7, and intention/8.
The methodology is verified with two other approaches.	Demographic distinguishing, Compatibility, Trust in the government, Intelligence, Interactive, Facilitation, Intention to use, Satisfaction	Survey data collected based on objects provided.	Ranks are determined for Wang and Biswas's approaches.
A Spearman's rank correlation and hypothesis is assumed to validate the methodology.	Ranks of all approaches	How can the methodology be validated?	The null hypothesis is rejected and an alternate hypothesis is accepted concerning methodology.

2.3.2 Identification of E-Governance Adoption and Assessment Factors

Table 2.1 displays the many assessment and acceptance criteria outlined in prominent theories about the implementation of E-Government services.

According to literature searches, researchers are mostly concerned with issues like online trust. Things like intelligence, policy standardization, capacity creation, resource management, and interoperability with other systems are noticeably absent.

2.3.3 Sample Data Collection Using Questionnaire

The identified variables are surveyed using the same questionnaire to understand their significance. Figure 2.1 displays the questions that make up the sample questionnaire. We use Google Forms to publish and share surveys on social media, WhatsApp groups, and *via* email. Colleagues in the academic and information technology fields are among the respondents. A scale from "Highly Satisfied" (L1) to "Highly Dissatisfied" (L4) is used to gather the answers (L5). People are asked to rate their answers on a Likert scale that ranges from 1 to 5. Table 2.4 displays the results obtained

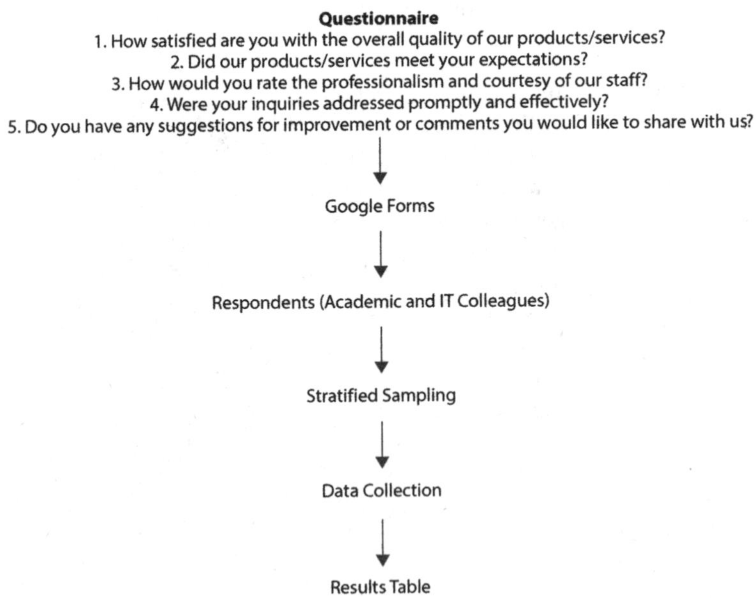

Figure 2.1 Sample questionnaire.

Table 2.4 Citizens' responses to the questionnaire.

Questions	Highly satisfied	Satisfied	Neutral	Dissatisfied	Highly dissatisfied	Total
Q1	21	66	11	3	0	101
Q2	18	60	19	4	0	101
Q3	16	3	26	56	0	101
Q4	10	10	17	62	2	101
Q5	17	44	33	7	0	101
Q6	16	58	24	3	0	101
Q7	11	53	27	10	0	101
Q8	13	70	16	1	1	101

from respondents. A stratified sampling technique is used, which involves dividing the whole population into strata based on gender, level of education, and age. Each of these levels has a sample taken from it using a random sampling technique. A grand total of 101 responses were received, with 77.9% male respondents and 22.1% female respondents. Among the respondents, 64% have postgraduate education and above, while 36% are graduate or below. The citizen's responses are shown in Table 2.4.

2.3.4 Respondent Details

Figure 2.2 shows that 31% of respondents are aged 16–30, 43% are aged 31–45, 24% are aged 46–60, and 2% are over 60. Figure 2.3 shows the

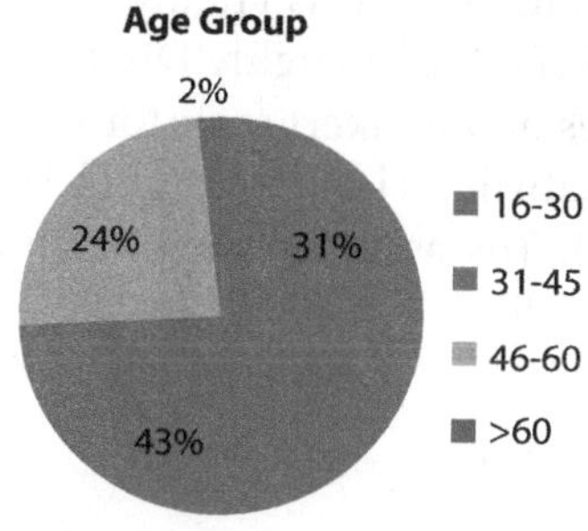

Figure 2.2 Respondents' age group.

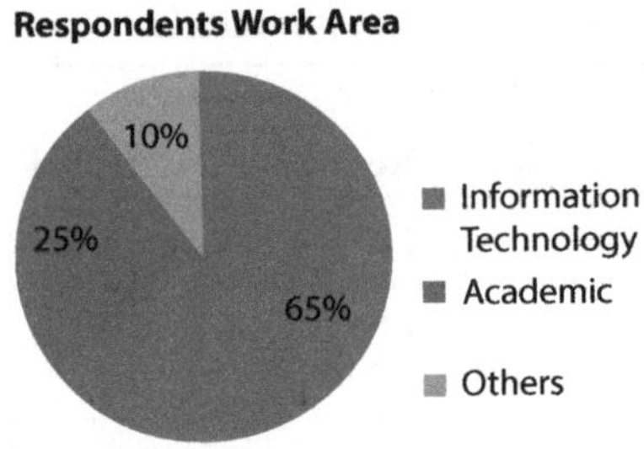

Figure 2.3 Respondents' work area.

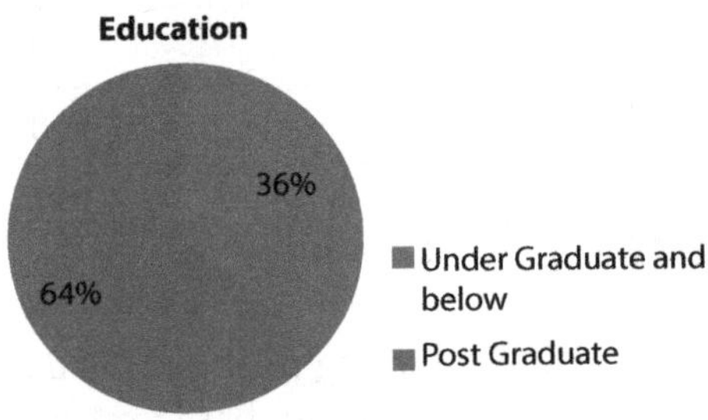

Figure 2.4 Respondents' education.

respondents' work areas, indicating that 65% of the respondents are from IT, 25% are from academics, and 10% are from other areas. Figure 2.4 shows the education levels of respondents, with 64% of respondents being postgraduates and 36% being graduates and below.

2.3.5 Fuzzy Conjoint Model

A fuzzy conjoint model, proposed by Turksen and Wilson, is used to determine the attributes' rank as shown in Figure 2.5. The linguistics representation was based on the Likert scale as Highly Satisfied (HS), Satisfied (S), Neutral (N), Dissatisfied (DS), and Highly Dissatisfied (HDS).

The linguistic variables of the Likert scale for surveys are defined as Lk= {Highly Satisfied (L1), Satisfied (L2), Neutral (L3), Dissatisfied (L4), and Highly Dissatisfied (L5)}. The assumed membership values for the Likert scale are shown in Table 2.5.

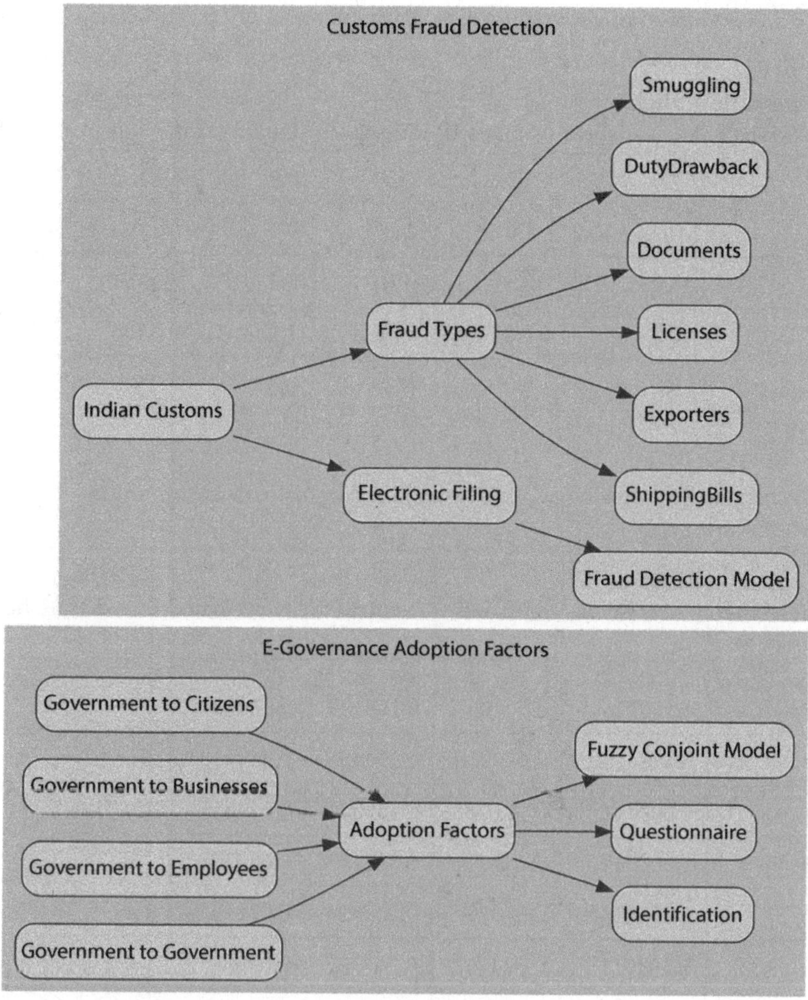

Figure 2.5 Architecture of assessing the adoption factors.

2.3.5.1 *Calculating the Similarity Degree*

i. Computation of the Weight Vector of All Respondents

Table 2.6 shows the weight vector of the respondent in linguistics variables for the questionnaire, calculated using equation 2.1. According to Table 2.5, responses are collected in the form of linguistic variables. The weight

Table 2.5 Assumed membership value of the fuzzy set of Likert's scale.

Fuzzy set/ linguistic variables	Highly satisfied	Satisfied	Neutral	Dissatisfied	Highly dissatisfied
L1	1.0	0.7	0.5	0.0	0.0
L2	0.7	1.0	0.6	0.0	0.0
L3	0.0	0.3	1.0	0.7	0.3
L4	0.0	0.0	0.4	1.0	0.6
L5	0.0	0.0	0.0	0.4	1.0

Table 2.6 Fuzzy vector of respondents to the linguistic variables of the questionnaire.

Questions	Highly satisfied	Satisfied	Neutral	Dissatisfied	Highly dissatisfied
Q1	0.207921	0.653465	0.108911	0.029703	0
Q2	0.178218	0.594059	0.188119	0.039604	0
Q3	0.158416	0.029703	0.554455	0.554455	0
Q4	0.09901	0.09901	0.168317	0.613861	0.019802
Q5	0.168317	0.435644	0.326733	0.069307	0
Q6	0.158416	0.574257	0.237624	0.029703	0
Q7	0.108911	0.524752	0.267327	0.09901	0
Q8	0.128713	0.693069	0.158416	0.009901	0.009901

vector for the respondents of the linguistic variable (Table 2.6) is determined as cell (1,1) after using equation 2.1, where cell (1,1) = 21/101 = 0.207921.

ii. Computation of Fuzzy Vector of Responses

Table 2.7 shows the membership value of each response to linguistics variables for the questionnaire, calculated using equation 2.2. As per Table 2.5, responses are collected in the form of linguistic variables. After that, the fuzzy membership value for respondents to linguistic variables

Table 2.7 Membership value of each response in linguistics variables for the questionnaire.

Questions	Highly satisfied	Satisfied	Neutral	Dissatisfied	Highly dissatisfied
R1	0.665347	0.831683	0.616832	0.105941	0.050495
R2	0.594059	0.775248	0.649505	0.171287	0.330693
R3	0.179208	0.306931	0.873267	0.942574	0.499010
R4	0.168317	0.218812	0.522772	0.739604	0.438614
R5	0.473267	0.651485	0.700000	0.298020	0.139604
R6	0.560396	0.354455	0.673267	0.196040	0.089109
R7	0.476238	0.681188	0.676238	0.069307	0.574257
R8	0.613861	0.830693	0.642574	0.124752	0.063366

in Table 2.7 is calculated after applying equation 2.1 as follows: cell (1,1) = (0.207921×1.0+0.653465×0.7+0.108911×0.0+0.029703×0.0+0×0) = 0.665347.

iii. Computation of Similarity Degree

Table 2.8 shows the degree of similarity between respondents' data fuzzy values in Table 2.7 and Likert's scale fuzzy set in Table 2.6. The highest value in each row represents the level of satisfaction in the form of the Likert scale, and ranks are found based on the highest value in each row. Further, ranking between attributes is assigned from highest to lowest. For example, for question 1, the second column represents the highest value, which falls under the satisfied column. As observed, row 1 has achieved the highest rank, i.e., 0.827282, under the linguistic variable "satisfied", thus row 1 has been assigned as rank 1. Likewise, the other ranks have been calculated.

The cell (1,1) value of Table 2.8 is calculated as follows:

1/(1+(sqrt((0.665347-1.0)^2+(0.831683-.7)^2+(0.616832-.50)^2+(0.105941-0.0)^2+(0.050495- 0.0)^2)))=0.716371.

The result shown in Figure 2.6 is that 15% of citizens are highly satisfied with the services, 45% are satisfied, 22% are neutral, 18% of citizens are

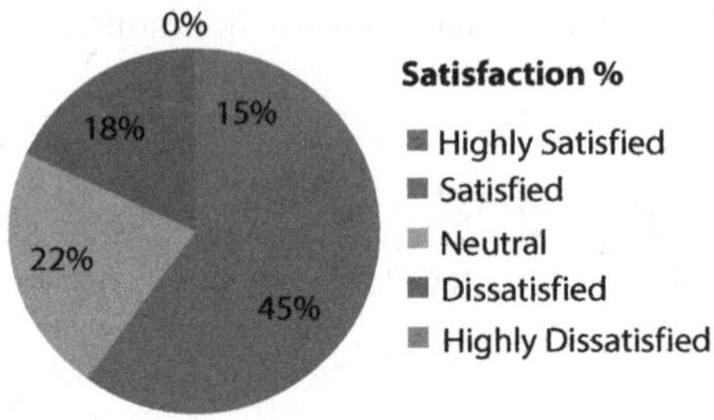

Figure 2.6 Respondents' satisfaction %.

Table 2.8 Calculation of similarity degree as well as rank among attributes.

Attribute	Highly satisfied	Satisfied	Neutral	Dissatisfied	Highly sissatisfied	Rank
Demographic distinguishing	0.716371	**0.827282**	0.483831	0.398270	0.387289	1
Compatibility	0.634615	**0.689452**	0.502259	0.428731	0.421996	5
Trust in government	0.409137	0.416437	**0.723077**	0.623769	0.455038	4
Intelligence	0.436751	0.438604	0.702525	**0.754649**	0.520841	3
Interactiveness	0.604486	**0.649517**	0.533583	0.371410	0.318636	6
facilitation	**0.615864**	0.588741	0.540590	0.429504	0.429504	7
Intention to use	0.555495	**0.587718**	0.506422	0.438929	0.454655	8
Satisfaction	0.687772	**0.806620**	0.480052	0.403812	0.390663	2

Bold values indicate the highest or most significant result in each category.

dissatisfied, and no citizens are not highly dissatisfied. After that, the discussed model was applied for the ranking of the factors, it was found that citizens are dissatisfied with fraud detection which falls under the intelligence category, and neutral with the formation of IT laws, which falls under trust in the government after implementing the E-Governance services.

2.4 Result Analysis

The E-Governance adoption factors that influenced citizens are shown in Table 2.9. The bold rows show dissatisfaction and neutrality among

Table 2.9 Identified influential factors.

Questions	Satisfied/ dissatisfied/ neutral	Factors
Satisfaction level in detection of frauds after implementing E-Governance services.	Dissatisfied	Intelligence
Satisfaction level of Standardization of policies and IT laws.	Neutral	Trust in government
Satisfaction level of customized E-Governance web portals or mobile apps with multilingual support.	Satisfied	Demographic distinguishing
Satisfaction level for CSCs establishment for accessing E-Governance Services.	Satisfied	Facilitation
Satisfaction level of capacity building and content handling by the website or mobile apps of E-Governance.	Satisfied	Compatibility
Overall satisfaction.	Satisfied	Satisfaction
Satisfaction level for AI-enabled E-Governance websites and mobile apps.	Satisfied	Interactive
Experience with previous E-Governance services/Apps.	Satisfied	Intention to use

citizens. The result in Table 2.9 shows that citizens are dissatisfied with the intelligence capability of E-Governance applications, which is identified as a weak factor, and neutral concerning IT policies and laws.

The factors ranking from highest to lowest as per Table 2.8 are as follows: demographic distinguishing at rank 1, overall satisfaction at rank 2, intelligence at rank 3, trust in the government at rank 4, compatibility at rank 5, interactiveness at rank 6, facilitation at rank 7, and intention to use at rank 8.

Conducting multiple surveys at different times allows for trend analysis and improved accuracy. There are always chances that people may provide dishonest answers. People may misunderstand the survey questions and can give wrong answers that may lead to wrong predictions. Table 2.10 shows the Similarity degree and ranking of attributes—Biswas's approach.

Table 2.10 Similarity degree and ranking of attributes—Biswas's approach.

Questions	Highly satisfied	Satisfied	Neutral	Dissatisfied	Highly dissatisfied	Rank
Q1	0.894218	**0.901364**	0.572241	0.250530	0.060754	1
Q2	0.767042	**0.854482**	0.659394	0.414147	0.263595	4
Q3	0.409940	0.471944	**0.875875**	0.785287	0.432318	2
Q4	0.334983	0.351511	0.741151	**0.797290**	0.633151	5
Q5	0.735233	**0.758255**	0.686191	0.435383	0.207594	7
Q6	**0.65813**	0.621996	0.565008	0.341323	0.14441	8
Q7	0.742062	**0.767728**	0.659512	0.450234	0.406004	6
Q8	**0.871628**	0.075543	0.608703	0.276185	0.075543	3

Bold values indicate the highest or most significant result in each category.

2.5 Conclusion

This chapter explores fuzzy conjoint methodologies for assessing E-Governance services and identifies weak and strong adoption factors. Multiple adoption/influential factors have been proposed for E-Governance. The results show that 60% are very satisfied or satisfied with the service, 18% are dissatisfied, and 22% are neutral concerning E-Governance services. It is also found that while people are neutral about policy/IT law-related satisfaction, they are dissatisfied with the intelligence factor, which determines satisfaction in automatically detecting fraud or corruption. Additionally, this ranking is validated using Biswas and Wang's approaches using the same dataset. The result shows that Turksen and Wilson's method for ranking government electronic services is reliable. It is also found that implementing smart governance requires intelligent techniques. Citizens are now dissatisfied with embracing intelligent technology in E-Governance applications. Therefore, successful implementation of smart E-Governance requires interactiveness, intelligence, and public to be high-priority factors. Citizens are dissatisfied with the efficiency of fraud detection in e-government applications, so the next chapter describes the fraud detection model in India's customs export incentive/refund system.

References

1. Abbasi, A. and Chen, H., *Cyber intelligence: Concepts, methodologies, tools, and applications*, Information Science Reference, Springer, Berlin, Germany, 2012.
2. Al-Fuqaha, A., Guizani, M., Mohammadi, M., Aledhari, M., Ayyash, M., Internet of Things: A survey on enabling technologies, protocols, and applications. *IEEE Commun. Surv. Tutorials*, 17, 4, 2347–2376, 2015.
3. Athanasiadis, I.N. and Mitkas, P.A., *Computational intelligence methods for bioinformatics and biostatistics*, Springer, IEEE, New York, USA, 2018.
4. Bojanova, I. (Ed.), *Fog computing: Concepts, frameworks and technologies*, Springer, California Law Review, Berkeley, USA, 2018.
5. Chen, M., Mao, S., Liu, Y., Big Data: A survey. *Mobile Networks Appl.*, 19, 2, 171–209, 2014.
6. Dehuri, S., Cho, S.B., Ghosh, A., *Nature-inspired computing: Concepts, methodologies, tools, and applications*, Information Science Reference, IEEE, New York, USA, 2011.
7. Durresi, A. and Barolli, L. (Eds.), *Advances in mobile cloud computing and Big Data in the 5G era*, Springer, IEEE, New York, USA, 2017.
8. Elgendy, N. and Attiya, G., *Intelligent renewable energy systems: Modelling and control*, CRC Press, Tow Center for Digital Journalism, New York, USA, 2018.
9. Sathish, R. and Kumar, D.R., Proficient algorithms for replication attack detection in Wireless Sensor Networks—A survey, in: *2013 IEEE International Conference ON Emerging Trends in Computing, Communication and Nanotechnology (ICECCN)*, IEEE, pp. 1–7, 2013, March.
10. Garroppo, R.G. and Giordano, S. (Eds.), *Energy-aware system design: Algorithms and architectures*, CRC Press, Privacy Enhancing Technologies, Cambridge, UK, 2015.
11. Han, J. and Kamber, M., *Data mining: Concepts and techniques*, Morgan Kaufmann, Macmillan, New York, USA, 2011.
12. Saravanakumar, P., Sundararajan, T.V.P., Dhanaraj, R.K., Nam, Y., Kadry, S., Ruzicka Indexed Regressive Homomorphic Ephemeral Key Benaloh Cryptography for Secure Data Aggregation in WSN. *J. Internet Technol.*, 22, 6, 1287–1297, Nov. 2021.
13. Malathy, S., Vanitha, C.N., Narayan, N., Kumar, R., Gokul, R., An Enhanced Handwritten Digit Recognition Using Convolutional Neural Network, in: *2021 Third International Conference on Inventive Research in Computing Applications (ICIRCA)*, IEEE, 2021.
14. Jie, L. and Masud, M.A.H., *Sustainable computing: Informatics and systems*, CRC Press, ACM SIGSAC, New York, USA, 2018.

15. Kumar, V. and Zhang, Q., *Social media mining: An introduction*, Cambridge University Press, Auerbach Publications, Boca Raton, Florida, USA, 2015.
16. Lee, K., Din, I.U., Khan, Z.A., *Big Data analytics: A management perspective*, Springer, Springer, Berlin, Germany, 2019.
17. Lefebvre, H., Doyon, M., Venne, S. (Eds.), *Urban environmental governance in India: Bureaucracy, democracy and the socio-environmental context*, Springer, San Diego Law Review, San Diego, USA, 2018.
18. Li, Z., Zhu, S., Chen, L., *Big Data application architecture Q&A: A problem-solution approach*, Apress, IEEE, New York, USA, 2016.
19. Liu, Y. and Wang, Z. (Eds.), *Resource allocation for wireless networks: Basics, techniques, and applications*, Springer, IEEE, New York, USA, 2018.
20. Maimó, R. and Vallés, M.S. (Eds.), *Data science and Big Data computing: Frameworks and methodologies*, Springer, Duke Law Technology Review, Durham, USA, 2017.
21. McAfee, A. and Brynjolfsson, E., Big Data: The management revolution. *Harv. Bus. Rev.*, 90, 10, 60–68, 2012.
22. Ntalampiras, S. (Ed.), *Multimedia Big Data computing for IoT applications: Concepts, paradigms and solutions*, Springer, Harvard University Press, Cambridge, Massachusetts, USA, 2019.
23. Ozsu, M.T. and Valduriez, P., *Principles of distributed database systems*, Springer, ACM, New York, USA, 2011.
24. Pahikkala, T. and Airola, A. (Eds.), *Feature selection for data and pattern recognition*, Springer, Elsevier BV, Amsterdam, Netherlands, 2018.
25. Patnaik, S. and Lee, C.H., *Intelligent computing for sustainable energy and environment*, CRC Press, Neural Information Processing Systems, New York, USA, 2019.
26. Rahmani, A.M., Rehmani, M.H., Rachedi, A., Touati, F. (Eds.), *Smart cities and homes: Key enabling technologies*, Springer, University of Pennsylvania Law Review, Philadelphia, USA, 2017.
27. Shi, Y., Zhang, Z., Zomaya, A.Y. (Eds.), *Fog computing: Concepts, frameworks and applications*, Springer, ACM Fairness, Accountability, and Transparency Conference, New York, USA, 2016.
28. Singh, R. and Tripathi, M., *Renewable energy integration: Challenges and solutions*, CRC Press, Nature Machine Intelligence, London, UK, 2018.
29. Tama, B.A. and Ndunguru, G.T. (Eds.), *Proceedings of the Second International Conference on SCI 2018*, Springer, arXiv.org, Cornell University, USA, 2018.
30. Tianfield, H. and Rammig, F.J. (Eds.), Advances in computational intelligence systems. *Contributions presented at the 19th UK Workshop on Computational Intelligence*, Lancaster, UK, Springer, IEEE, New York, USA, September 4-6 2019.

31. Ramana, T.V., Ghantasala, G.S., Sathiyaraj, R., Khan, M. (Eds.), *Artificial Intelligence and Machine Learning for Smart Community: Concepts and Applications*, Springer, Berlin, Germany, 2024.
32. Mohanty, A., Rahamathunnisa, U., Sudhakar, K., Sathiyaraj, R., Age of Computational AI for Autonomous Vehicles. *Artif. Intell. Auton. Veh.*, 25–54, 2024.

3

Intelligent Predictive Analysis for Sustainable Global Development

Rajalakshmi S.[1]*, Swetha R.[1], Vaishali N.[1], P. Umaeswari[2], S. Senthil Kumar[3] and S. D. Uma Mageswari[4]

[1]*Department of Electronics and Communication Engineering, R.M.K. College of Engineering and Technology, Puduvoyal, Tamil Nadu, India*
[2]*Department of Computer Science and Business Systems, R.M.K. Engineering College, Kavaraipettai, Tamil Nadu, India*
[3]*Department of Mechanical Engineering, R.M.K. College of Engineering and Technology, Puduvoyal, Tamil Nadu, India*
[4]*Department of Science and Humanities, R.M.K. Engineering College, Kavaraipettai, Tamil Nadu, India*

Abstract
Intelligent predictive analysis plays a crucial role in steering global development toward sustainability by harnessing the power of data-driven insights and advanced technologies. This paper explores the significance of predictive analytics in addressing complex global challenges such as climate change, poverty, healthcare, and resource management. By leveraging machine learning algorithms, big data analytics, and artificial intelligence techniques, predictive models can forecast future trends, identify potential risks, and inform proactive strategies for sustainable development. Moreover, integrating intelligent predictive analysis with decision-making processes enables policymakers, businesses, and organizations to make informed choices that optimize resource allocation, mitigate environmental impacts, and promote inclusive growth. This paper highlights key applications, challenges, and opportunities associated with intelligent predictive analysis for achieving sustainable global development objectives.

Keywords: Predictive analytics, sustainable development, machine learning, big data, artificial intelligence, decision-making

**Corresponding author*: srajalakshmi312@gmail.com

R. Sathiyaraj, Rajesh Kumar Dhanaraj, K. Arun Kumar, Rutvij H. Jhaveri and A. Mohamed Abbas (eds.) Predictive Methods in Next-Generation Computing: An Approach Toward Sustainability, (47–64)

3.1 Introduction

Nowadays, the multilayered fictional neural networks [1] that utilize the back-propagation rule composition are widely used due to their effective coaching contents. Back-propagation is a technique used within neural network schemes where input impression is propagated through the network, and the output is adjusted based on the weights. It is used in several applications, such as face apprehension, economic and weather foretelling, and character acceptance. Project implementation is done by examining the knowledge and constructing appropriate exercise tests. Additionally, the quantity of invisible neurons is discovered in particular layers for accurate behavior.

3.2 Literature Survey

It is one of the exhausting and necessary operational significance. It is dispensed with the help of the environmental condition services available on the planet. It represents a classical practice that gathers various explicit areas of understanding. The task seems to be complex inside the meteorological area. The entire determination area unit is condemned inside the suspicious side. Various scientists have utilized the assumptive weather portrait [2]. The area unit is produced on the accidental generator variations. The output represents the competent knowledge related to the weather. These kinds of portraits are elaborated terribly for the estimation. It is not adapted to the changing knowledge patterns and is not under the prognosis. It is not documented in several formula performances. These real-life bearings [3] are clearly described by 'artificial neurons' that are being understood from the participation.

3.2.1 Concepts of ANN

It is related to the nursing economical ADP system. The central concept of ANN is based on the concept of the biological NN [4]. It is also known as "connectionist systems", "parallel distributed process systems", or "artificial neural systems". It needs an extra unit assortment. The area unit is joined in some format or pattern to allow communication among the units. These units are also known as the neurons or nodes. The processors are straight forwarded by the area unit, and they function in a parallel manner [5]. The general ANN model is given in Figure 3.1.

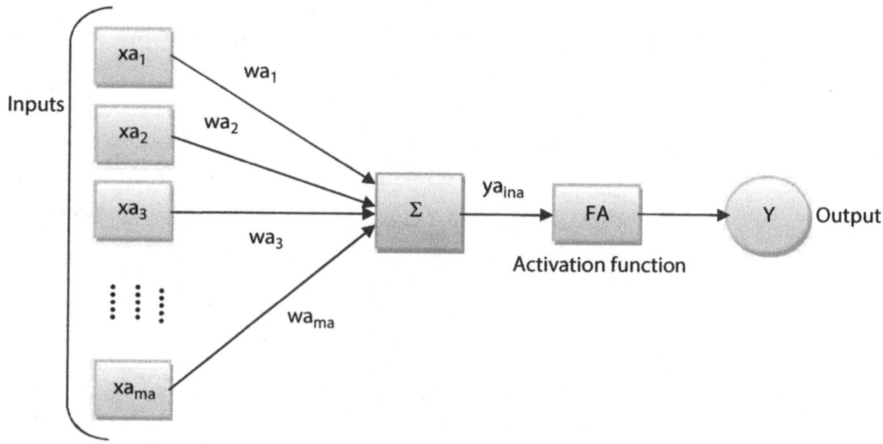

Figure 3.1 General ANN model.

Each somatic cell is joined with a distinct somatic cell *via* an affiliation link. Each affiliation link is associated with a weight that contains the data with consideration of the sign. These are the supportive data for the neurons in handling a chosen downside. Next, the load inhibits or excites the signal during the process of communication [6]. Each somatic cell is composed of an inside state that is called the nursing activation signal. The output signals are attained by joining the activation rule and input signals, and they can then be transmitted to distinct units.

3.3 Proposed Work

Generally, the short-generation precipitation describes the conditions during a specific period. The storm precipitation was confirmed by activating immediate neighboring access, ANN [7], and distinct auto-regressive moving moderate construction methods. The analysis of the ANN seems to be reliable. However, in the case of low precipitation replication, the results seem to be repetitive.

3.3.1 Layout of a Neural Network

The input and output knowledge must be established because they are measured in different units. There is no correlation between the output and input values. Once the normalized knowledge is attained, the next

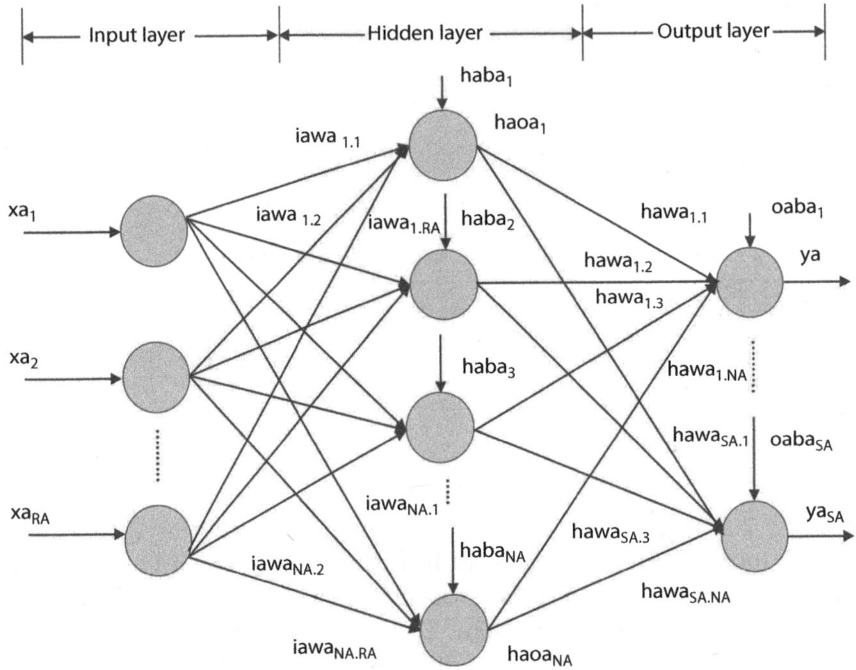

Figure 3.2 Neural network layout.

step is to train the computer file exploitation with the help of the MATLAB back-propagation rule [8]. The neural network layout is depicted in Figure 3.2.

The general ANN model usually comprises three superimposed layers [9] utilizing back-propagation learning. The coaching is guided by a rule that captures the positive percentage related to the computer file. The performance of a network is clearly shown in Figure 3.3.

3.3.2 Neural Network Structure

This somatic cell is composed of a single output and multiple inputs. Each input is varied using a weight. This weight is multiplied by the input. The somatic cell combines these weighted inputs, and with the help of activation and threshold, the output can be obtained. This characteristic reveals the functionality of the real neurons [10]. The ANN is based on the three consequent building blocks, namely, activation function learning, weight adjustment, and network topology [11].

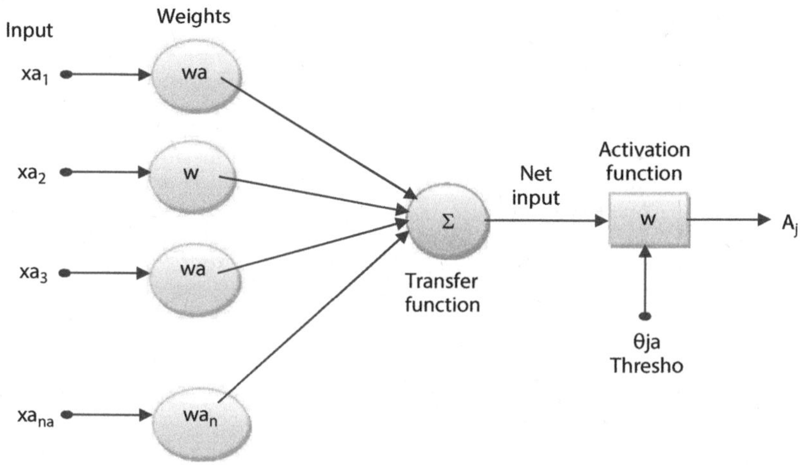

Figure 3.3 Performance of a network.

3.3.3 Back-Propagation Neural Network

In general, the input layer considers [12] the signal distribution from the external world. These signals are analyzed by the hidden layers, which act as feature detectors or categorizers. The output layer combines the detected options and generates the final output. It is also employed in the conceptualization of the operations of the layers. This method cannot be considered in a more virtual manner. The delineated functions are not localized or specified.

3.3.4 SVM

SVM represents a "supervised machine learning rule" [13]. It is employed for regression or classification challenges. It is mostly utilized in classification conflicts. Every data point is plotted in terms of an *na*-dimensional space, where *na* represents several options. Each feature corresponds to a specific coordinate. Classification is accomplished by using a hyperplane that separates the two categories. A graphical representation is depicted in Figure 3.4.

3.3.5 Learning Sequence of NN

The process of learning in an NN is referred to as training. Similar to sports coaching, NN training requires a tutor who defines the NN [14] regarding

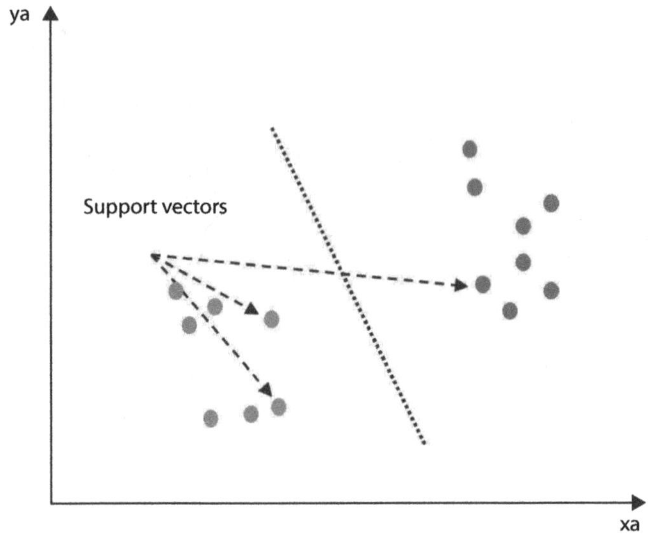

Figure 3.4 Graphical read.

the responses it has to perform. The error is calculated as the difference between the required and the actual response, and some of this error is propagated backward through the network. For every somatic cell inside the network, the error is utilized to regulate the threshold and weight values. Hence, to ensure the error and time inside the network response are minimum for the identical inputs.

3.3.6 Forage Progressive Network

An improved lined fodder leading medicine is composed of several layers in its preparation. A converting components layer performs the accurate computations that gorge and settle the outcomes across several layers. The nearby thickness constructed its own pathway and highlighted the significance of an extra layer. A considerable amount of waste generates the core media at the network assembly. The exclusive side is composed of the estimation that is not dependent in terms of the absorption [15]. The external layer inside the absorption layer and the determinative layer forms the productivity layer. The covering area of these two layers forms the invisible layers.

3.3.7 Neural Network Learning

There exists a great challenge in organizing the neurons [16] themselves and the mechanisms employed by the array of neurons in adapting their characteristics to the external stimuli. Nowadays, a huge count of experimental neural network structures is in use, reflecting the ongoing research in the field.

In the above equation, the output of the pre-synaptic neuron at time *ta* is defined by $ya_{ja}(ta)$, the input value from the pre-synaptic neuron at time *ta* is defined by $xa_{ia}(ta)$, and the constant and positive learning rate is defined by α.

3.3.8 Model Somatic Cell

Here, the characteristics, arithmetic, and structure of the back-propagation network [17] are described. This is considered the generalized neural network that is widely used nowadays. A back-propagation network is constructed using the below fashion. Initially, several arrays and neurons are taken to create a layer. Each layer contains all the inputs that are joined to the external inputs or the preceding layer. However, these two similar layers are not considered at the same interval [18]. Each layer contains all the outputs that are joined to the external outputs or the succeeding layer. These also do not occur at the interval of the same layer. These are mostly a fully connected one. Each somatic cell [19] is joined to a single external input or every preceding layer output if the somatic cell is inside the initial layer. Each somatic cell contains an output that is joined to every somatic cell inside the succeeding layer.

3.3.9 Fabricated Visual Structure

A visual structure represents the framework of computations that are activated through a study of a biological sensory conversion. The area unit is composed of various visual organizations ranging from simple to highly complex. The biological visual conversion occurs in the area unit.

3.3.10 Neuron Weight Adjustment

This corrective process is known as the back-propagation [20]. This name represents the form of the NN. It is given in a repetitive and endless manner for every group of inputs. On the basis of the inputs, the corresponding outputs are generated. This technique continues since the total or individual errors inside the responses execute until there are no measurable errors or it crosses a nominative level. The coaching material is learned by the NN. It is possible to stop the coaching technique and utilize the NN for offering the responses to the novel computer file.

3.4 Results and Discussion

The two tools used for implementation are MATLAB's Nntool and Nftool. Nntool serves as the data manager or open network manager. The single and multi-layer algorithms are enforced inside the knowledge or the open network manager. Nftool, on the other hand, is the NN fitting tool that defines the back-propagation rule. A minimum MSE was achieved and a graph was constructed among the target and the anticipated values. The value of the rainfall prediction is given in Table 3.1.

The performance related to the back-propagation rule of a single layer is shown in Figure 3.5.

Table 3.1 Value of rainfall prediction.

Rainfall data for the Ahmad Yani station (mm/h)			
No	**1**	**2**	**3**
Year	2015	2016	2017
"January"	2590	2176	2375
"February"	2260	2053	2140
"March"	870	1080	1140
"April"	1170	810	1110
"May"	548	326	360
"June"	307	210	846
"July"	314	523	364
"August"	0	235	236
"September"	304	124	0
"October"	243	1026	0
"November"	182	546	504
"December"	245	1524	639

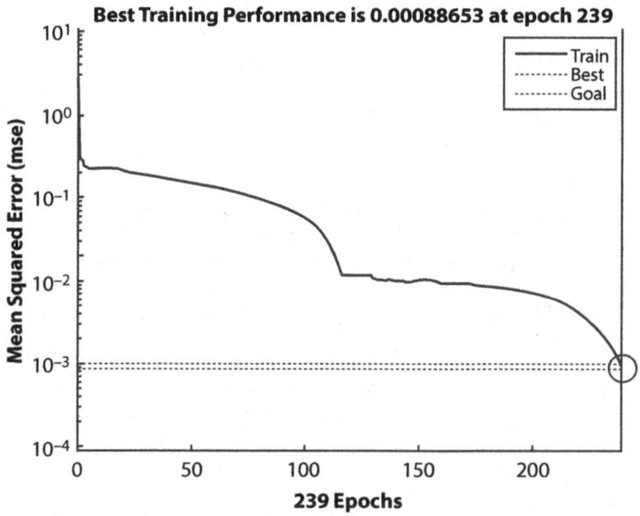

Figure 3.5 Performance related to the back-propagation rule (single layer).

3.4.1 Normalization of Knowledge

The attained input and output knowledge must be normalized since they are of various units. In the other case, there exists no correlation between the output and input values. Initially, the mean of the entire information was considered for the precipitation, wind speed, and humidity.

Next, *SD* and quality deviation of the entire parameters on the basis of the individual were computed.

The normalized data are given in Table 3.2.

Once the normalized knowledge is attained, the computer file undergoes training and coaching for the implementation of MATLAB BPA. The projected ANN method resembles a three-layer superimposed back-propagation learning approach. For this process, 70% of the computer file is considered for the coaching process. Hence, out of the 400 samples, 280 are considered for the coaching process, and these area units are chosen randomly from the set of knowledge. Thus, for every trial of information coaching, the rule chooses the coaching sample in a random format from the entire group. It does not resemble a quick and hard set of knowledge such that, for any training information, there exists a tendency to attain the completely distinct values of MSE that, in turn, relies upon 70% of the computer file selected for the coaching. The remaining 60 samples are not considered for validation and testing. The graph for the precipitation prediction having target values is given in Figure 3.6.

Table 3.2 Normalized data.

Rainfall data result normalization			
No	**1**	**2**	**3**
Year	2015	2016	2017
"January"	0.9000	0.7721	0.8336
"February"	0.7981	0.7341	0.7610
"March"	0.3687	0.4336	0.4521
"April"	0.4614	0.3502	0.4429
"May"	0.2693	0.2007	0.2112
"June"	0.1948	0.1649	0.3613
"July"	0.1970	0.2615	0.2124
"August"	0.1000	0.1726	0.1729
"September"	0.1939	0.1383	0.1000
"October"	0.1751	0.4169	0.1000
"November"	0.1562	0.2686	0.2557
"December"	0.1757	0.5707	0.2974

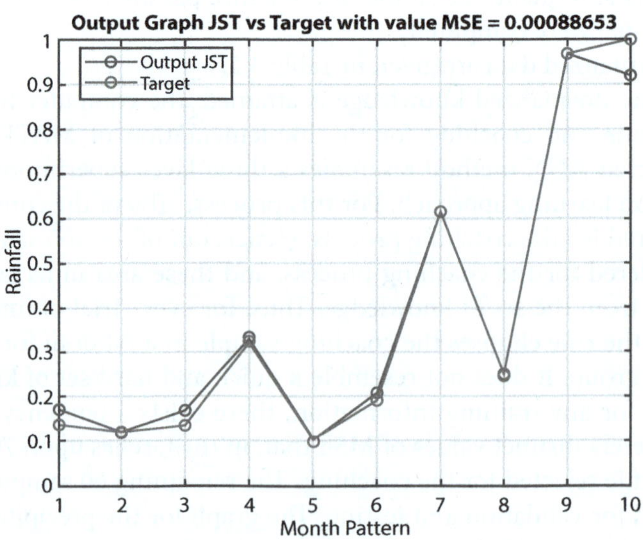

Figure 3.6 Precipitation prediction having target values.

3.4.2 Testing and Validation

The testing process ends when the information coaching is finished, and the error is displayed below the level of tolerance. The BPA maintains the computer file for half an hour for the validation as well as the testing process. Hence, among the 400 samples, 60 samples are used for the testing process, and another 60 samples are used for the validation process. The comparison of foreseen and actual knowledge after the process of testing is finished; the outcomes are saved inside the space, and a graph is considered among the foreseen and the specific output. The associate graph of three regression plots of the back-propagation rule or the single layer is given in Figure 3.7.

The nursing economical technique examined the two forms of knowledge that is available in the North American nation. It also computes the accuracy of the method. A graph was constructed among the foreseen and the particular values that revealed a better degree of similarity among them. It proved that the ANN method is appropriate in the process of prediction.

3.4.3 Error Measures

The various error measures used here are described below.

(a) SMAPE: "SMAPE is an accuracy measure based on percentage errors".

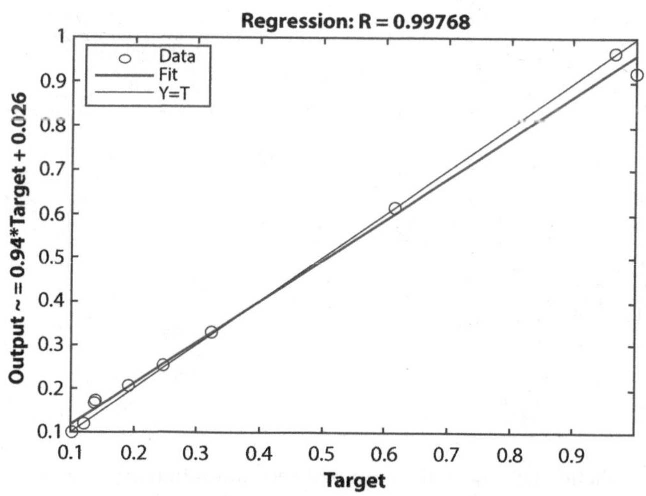

Figure 3.7 Associate graph of three regression plot of back-propagation rule.

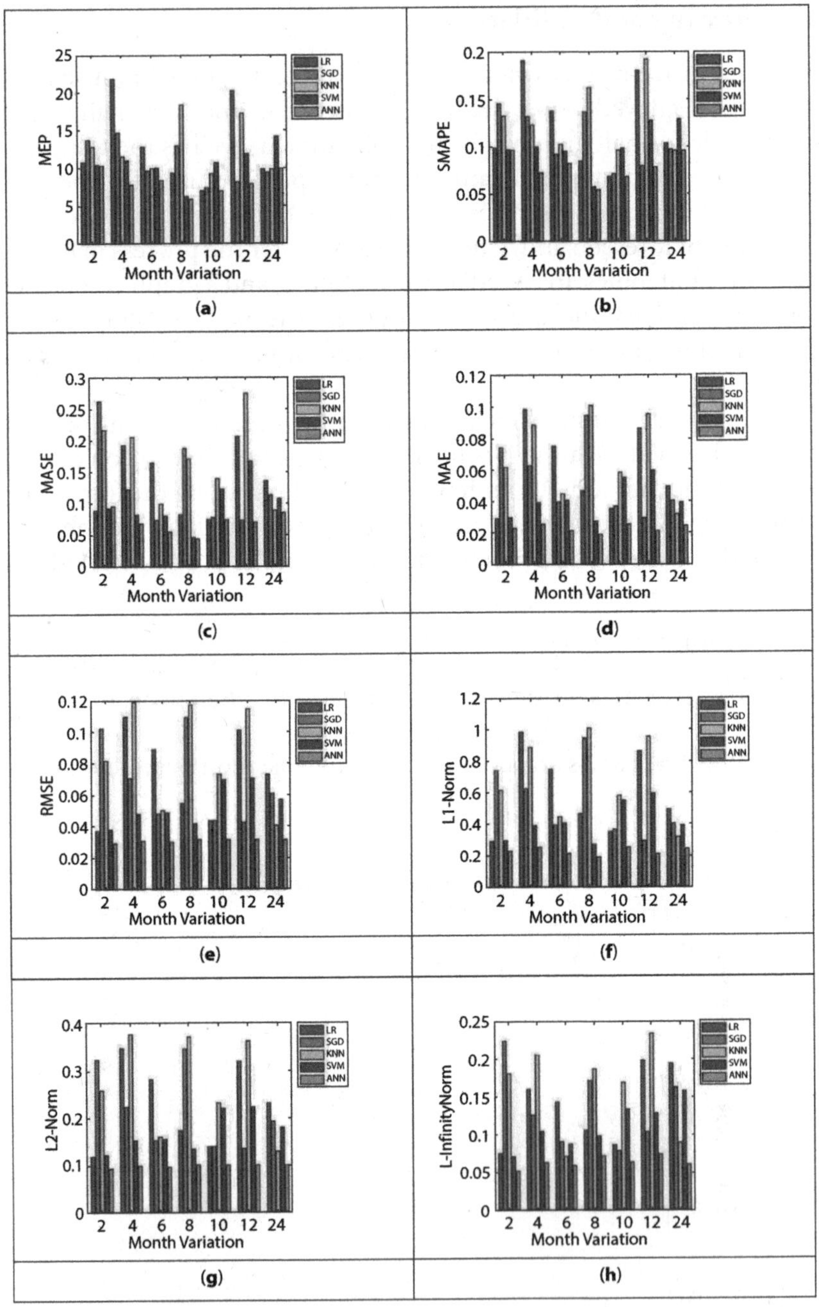

Figure 3.8 Prediction analysis of the proposed and conventional models in terms of (a) MEP, (b) SMAPE, (c) MASE, (d) MAE, (e) RMSE, (f) L1 norm, (g) L2 norm, and (h) L-infinity norm.

3.4.4 Prediction Analysis

The predictive analysis of the suggested and existing machine learning models is given in Figure 3.8. From Figure 3.8(a), it is evident that the MEP of ANN at the 12-month variation is 33.33%, 52.94%, 11.11%, and 61.90% higher than SVM, KNN, SGD, and LR, respectively. Hence, it is obvious that the recommended ANN-based prediction method attains better outcomes than the remaining techniques.

3.4.5 Overall Prediction Analysis

The SMAPE of ANN at the 24-month variation is 0.62%, 32.59%, 16.46%, 76.19%, 40.79%, and 22.68% better than 2-, 4-, 6-, 8-, 10-, and 12-month variations.

3.4.6 Actual and Predicted Value Analysis

The actual and predicted value analysis for the years 2016 to 2019 is given in Figure 3.9. From Table 3.3, in the year 2016, regarding the actual value, for the 1st month, the range is 40; for the 2nd month, the range is 1; for the 3rd month, the range is 38; for the 4th month, the range is 18; for the 5th month, the range is 78; for the 6th month, the range is 40; for the 7th month, the range is 40; for the 8th month, the range is 160; for the 9th month, the

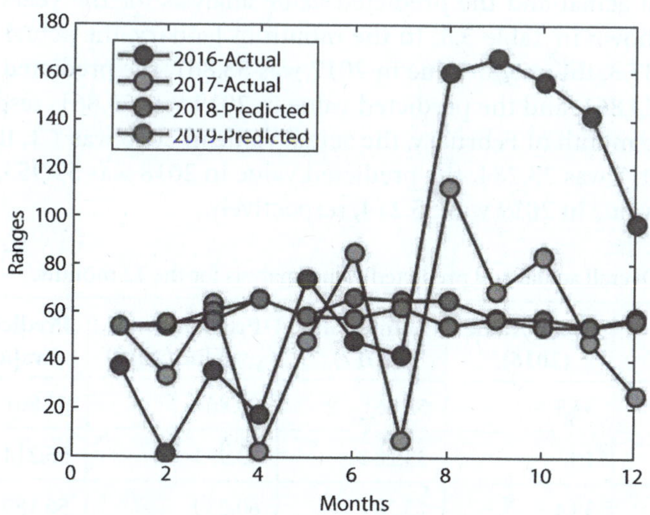

Figure 3.9 Actual and predicted value analysis in terms of months and ranges.

Table 3.3 Overall prediction analysis in terms of various error measures for different months.

Error measures	Month variation						
	2	4	6	8	10	12	24
"MEP"	10.423	7.8238	8.4616	5.9219	7.0391	7.9691	10.049
"SMAPE"	0.097319	0.072946	0.08305	0.054894	0.068697	0.078834	0.096716
"MASE"	0.095755	0.068117	0.055324	0.043803	0.074409	0.070613	0.085381
"MAE"	0.022759	0.025273	0.021349	0.019055	0.025289	0.02113	0.024428
"RMSE"	0.029133	0.030939	0.030169	0.031607	0.031496	0.031471	0.031502
"L1 Norm"	0.22759	0.25273	0.21349	0.19055	0.25289	0.2113	0.24428
"L2 norm"	0.092126	0.097837	0.095402	0.09995	0.099599	0.099521	0.099617
"L-infinity norm"	0.050905	0.062384	0.058192	0.071207	0.062958	0.073367	0.059843

range is 165; for the 10th month, the range is 158; for the 11th month, the range is 140; and for the 12th month, the range is 100, respectively.

3.4.7 Overall Actual and Predicted Value Analysis

The overall actual and the predicted value analysis for the years 2016 to 2019 are shown in Table 3.4. In the month of January, the actual value in 2016 was 37.3, the actual value in 2017 was 53.861, the predicted value in 2018 was 53.861, and the predicted value in 2019 was 53.861, respectively. During the month of February, the actual value in 2016 was 1.1, the actual value in 2017 was 33.284, the predicted value in 2018 was 53.953, and the predicted value in 2019 was 55.214, respectively.

Table 3.4 Overall actual and predicted value analysis for the 12 months.

Months	Actual value (2016)	Actual value (2017)	Predicted value (2018)	Predicted value (2019)
January	37.3	53.861	53.861	53.861
February	1.1	33.284	53.953	55.214
March	35.4	63.287	60.239	56.189

(Continued)

Table 3.4 Overall actual and predicted value analysis for the 12 months. (*Continued*)

Months	Actual value (2016)	Actual value (2017)	Predicted value (2018)	Predicted value (2019)
April	17.3	1.9445	65.147	65.145
May	73.5	47.63	58.086	58.087
June	47.9	84.531	65.793	57.198
July	42	6.696	64.765	61.814
August	159.4	111.83	64.725	54.15
September	165.3	68.536	57.349	56.939
October	155.5	83.17	57.15	53.796
November	141.5	47.585	53.992	53.765
December	96.8	25.516	57.664	56.43

3.5 Summary

The neuron's growth was linked to ANN training, which is considered to minimize MSE. Among the right dependable processes, the BPA was considered the most effective method. The traditional approach represented optimal data activities for knowledge transformation. The "lean" method is somewhat generation-exhausting but is still considered an optimal operational exercise. The multi-layer index is better than the single-layer rule condition that is associated with the administration process. Nntools was highlighted as the best algorithm because it excels in nursing preferences relative to all other algorithms, except for the BPA. Generally, the higher the amount of admission knowledge, the lesser the MSE for the coaching process. The effectiveness of either the output or input knowledge is established when they are of high quality. The network methods provided here can be efficiently employed for the missing values of rainfall prediction at various places of choice. The feed-forward distributed time delay network is important for this process because this network employs sequential data for the training process. Additionally, this idea could be further developed to forecast short-term rainfall in a given region, which could enhance rain crop forecasting and flood management systems. A comparison of several ANN techniques and optimization methods can be made to attain more appropriate prediction outcomes. From the analysis, the MASE was improved by 12.5%, 66.67%, 41.67%, and 63.16% compared to SVM, KNN, SGD, and LR, respectively. Therefore, the prediction outcomes using ANN are superior to those from the other methods.

References

1. Parry, M.L., *et al.*, *Climate Change 2007: Impacts, Adaptation and Vulnerability. Contribution of Working Group II to the Fourth Assessment Report of the Intergovernmental Panel on Climate Change*, Cambridge University Press, USA, 2007.
2. Li, Y. and Wu, X., Climate data analysis and modeling using support vector machines. *Int. J. Climatol.*, 28, 9, 1253–1264, 2008.
3. Mendoza, G.A. and Martins, H., Multi-criteria decision analysis in natural resource management: A critical review of methods and new modelling paradigms. *For. Ecol. Manage.*, 230, 1–3, 1–22, 2006.
4. Rosenzweig, C. and Hillel, D., *Climate Change and the Global Harvest: Potential Impacts of the Greenhouse Effect on Agriculture*, Oxford University Press, USA, 2008.
5. Huang, G.B., *et al.*, Extreme learning machine: Theory and applications. *Neurocomputing*, 70, 1–3, 489–501, 2006.
6. United Nations Development Programme, *Sustainable Development Goals: 17 Goals to Transform Our World*, United Nations Publications, USA, 2015.
7. IPCC, Climate Change 2014: Synthesis Report, in: *Contribution of Working Groups I, II and III to the Fifth Assessment Report of the Intergovernmental Panel on Climate Change*, IPCC, 2014.
8. Dietterich, T.G., Ensemble methods in machine learning, in: *Multiple Classifier Systems*, pp. 1–15, Springer, 2000.
9. Sachs, J.D., *et al.*, *The Age of Sustainable Development*, Columbia University Press, 2019.
10. Friedman, J., Hastie, T., Tibshirani, R., *The Elements of Statistical Learning (Vol. 1)*, Springer series in statistics, 2001.
11. World Bank, *World Development Report 2017: Governance and the Law*, World Bank Publications, 2017.
12. Toulmin, C. and Guèye, K., *Land Use, Soil Fertility Management and the Future of Agricultural Systems in Sub-Saharan Africa*, vol. 101, Gatekeeper Series, 2001.
13. Hastie, T., Tibshirani, R., Friedman, J., *The Elements of Statistical Learning: Data Mining, Inference, and Prediction*, Springer Science & Business Media, 2009.
14. World Health Organization, *Preventing Disease through Healthy Environments: A Global Assessment of the Burden of Disease from Environmental Risks*, World Health Organization, USA, 2015.

15. Sathyamoorthy, M., Kuppusamy, S., Nayyar, A., *et al.*, Optimal emplacement of sensors by orbit-electron theory in wireless sensor networks. *Wireless Netw.*, 28, 1605–1623, 2022.
16. Steffen, W., *et al.*, Planetary boundaries: Guiding human development on a changing planet. *Science*, 347, 6223, 1259855, 2015.
17. Ramasamy, M.D., Dhanaraj, R.K., Pani, S.K., Das, R.P., Movassagh, A.A., Gheisari, M., Liu, Y., Porkar, P., Banu, S., An improved deep convolutionary neural network for bone marrow cancer detection using image processing, in: *Informatics in Medicine Unlocked*, vol. 38, p. 101233, Elsevier BV, India, 2023.
18. United Nations, *Transforming Our World: The 2030 Agenda for Sustainable Development*, United Nations, 2015.
19. Stocker, T.F., *et al.*, Climate Change 2013: The Physical Science Basis, in: *Contribution of Working Group I to the Fifth Assessment Report of the Intergovernmental Panel on Climate Change*, Cambridge University Press, 2013.
20. Arvindhan, M. and Kumar, D.R., Adaptive Resource Allocation in Cloud Data Centers using Actor-Critical Deep Reinforcement Learning for Optimized Load Balancing, in: *International Journal on Recent and Innovation Trends in Computing and Communication*, vol. 11, pp. 310–318, Auricle Technologies, Pvt., Ltd, USA, 2023.

4

Intelligent Transport System and Traffic Management Frameworks

S. Srijayanthi[1]*, T. Sethukarasi[1], Sankar R.[2], T. Ramesh[1], Nayana B. M.[3] and S. Vijayakumar[1]

[1]*Department of Computer Science and Engineering, R.M.K. Engineering College, Kavaraipettai, India*

[2]*Department of Computer Science and Engineering, S. A. Engineering College, Chennai, India*

[3]*Department of Computer Science and Engineering, LBS Institute Technology for Women Poojappura, Thiruvananthapuram, India*

Abstract

The tremendous growth in transport systems and the increase in the number of vehicles over the past several decades have created a significant problem for urban areas, that is traffic congestion. An enormous traffic jam of cars built up earlier this week next to the Qianmen Gate of Beijing City. In recent years, traffic congestion analysis has come forward as a significant challenge; numerous scholars concentrate on the root causes of traffic congestion. Here, some recent research work points out the cause of traffic jams in one direction and suggests an alternate route for another direction. On the other hand, traffic forecasting needs to modernize traffic models that can analyze these actual traffic condition statistics. Intelligent Transport Systems (ITS) aims to improve the quality of mobility and its sustainability by gathering input technology with engineering solutions *via* communication methods. Besides that, other studies of ITS from the standpoint of artificial intelligence (AI) have been done. ITS exercises a capillary network of sensors strung over the roads and uses this information to transform traffic information such as flow, speed, and density. This allows the administration to judge traffic dynamics more accurately and conduct control operations more effectively. This research proposes a smart road transportation domain that takes fuel consumption models as its basic framework for making approximate traffic forecasts

**Corresponding author*: ssj.ad@rmkec.ac.in

R. Sathiyaraj, Rajesh Kumar Dhanaraj, K. Arun Kumar, Rutvij H. Jhaveri and A. Mohamed Abbas (eds.) Predictive Methods in Next-Generation Computing: An Approach Toward Sustainability, (65–82)

and analyzing traffic flow disturbances. Moreover, it suggests the application of a multi-agent system method for traffic light control with deviation, a tool for avoiding congestion that utilizes only sparse distributed message passing. Firstly, the framework introduced is smart road traffic prediction and alleviation based on the genetic model put forward by the author, as it can reduce fuel use. Its powerful optimization can rely on statistical models. Poisson Distribution, for example, is applied to forecast car arrival probability from historical data.

***Keywords*:** Intelligent transport systems (ITS), traffic light controller, multi-agent system, poisson distribution, artificial intelligence (AI), big data analytics

4.1 Introduction

For intelligent traffic management, accurate traffic prediction and regulation of traffic lights are basic steps. Otherwise, the efficiency of traffic systems cannot be improved. There is a pressing need for a traffic management system in urban areas to predict and control the flow of traffic. Forewarning about traffic helps to prevent a traffic jam before it's too late. As a rule, the city traffic forecast uses historical and real-time data on the flow of traffic, as well as data from previous road traffic reports. As information technology grows, mobile phones, sensors or other devices are widely used to analyze the traffic condition. This paper discusses the use of machine learning algorithms and techniques of big data analysis for forecasting and managing congested traffic flows.

Traffic congestion is a global menace. The population explosion, particularly the increase in number of vehicles, has been unprecedented. India's population growth and economic expansion are second only to China's. Many cities throughout India are plagued with traffic congestion problems. Intelligent Transportation Management Systems (ITMS) have been widely used in developed countries, but their application to major cities in India is hampered by practical limitations. These include slow growth in infrastructure and rapid increases in the number of vehicles carried (both land use and cost crowds). Digital flight monitors must provide traffic flow information to passengers who need to make changes in their journey plans due to overcrowding at airports. It would be most useful to predict short-term traffic flow to maintain freeway networks. This traffic flow forecast is based on using real-time data to predict traffic status in the subsequent 5 to 20 minutes. In the world of today, every nation is striving to make its traffic management system better or more efficient. Different methods have been used in studies to predict freeway traffic in urban areas.

The solution must be found. Some of the possible ways to solve this problem include parking restrictions, changing school schedules so that rush hour is reduced, installing traffic counters, good traffic planning, speed limits and lane splitting, setting up flyovers, building a subway (metro), and publicizing programs to enhance people's understanding of living in an overpopulated city. To reduce traffic congestion, we need a new model of traffic flow management. This thesis focuses on developing a model for traffic flow control that eliminates traffic congestion and enables fluid traffic to circulate uniformly. The most appropriate causes and solutions for traffic congestion vary according to the location.

4.2 Background Study

However, existing research is geared towards overseeing the flow of traffic and reducing congestion. Additional research focuses on traffic prediction and over 50% of the models are for short-term traffic prediction, Nonparametric approaches are those that do not require any statistical distribution assumption to be made of the data such as the kernel regression (Vlahogianni and Karlaftis, 2013). These approaches pay particular attention to the model's structure as well as real-time traffic scenarios. To enhance the accuracy of prediction, ARIMA (Williams and Hoel, 2003) and STARIMA (Pfeifer & Deutsch 1980) were suggested as the two methods of choice. Data mining machine learning models mostly use about six methods to predict traffic. These methods are: classification tree model (CTM) artificial neural network (ANN) (Liu, Y *et al.* 2007), support vector machine (SVM) (Ding *et al.* 2008), and support/relevance vector machine (SVM/RVM). Improved Transportation Infrastructure (ITI) is essential to solving these types of problems. Yet, the sudden increase in traffic volume alongside urban growth creates demand for big data analytics, which can handle and develop the traffic system in an orderly manner (Vlahogianni *et al.*, 2008). Regression techniques have been proposed to model vehicle arrivals using real-time data on the road (Lippi *et al.* 2013). An accurate travel forecasting method named traffic prediction (Liu, Z *et al.* 2016) uses road network correlation and sparse traffic sampling.

The fixed-type controller approach has been modified by (Chiu and Chand, 1993). They programmed these controllers to manage preset timings for each series. This solution was applied to various types of traffic scenarios, especially undisciplined traffic. Several research algorithms have aimed to avoid the fixed cyclic controller system, but an efficient approach is much needed by ITS to reduce traffic problems.

One thing doesn't work properly. To avoid a jam-like phenomenon, a certain number of considerations are needed at the same time. Vehicle speed and length were seen as two of the most important factors in the traffic management system.

4.3 Methodology

There has been a recent uptick in the number of cars on the road. All the while, the quantity of traffic signs and the number of ways has increased. The increased visibility of traffic signs has led to the expectation that drivers would get used to and be attentive to all traffic indicators (Taştimur *et al.*, 2016). When it comes to driver aid and traffic safety systems, traffic sign detection is crucial (Swathi & Suresh 2017). However, current detecting methods sometimes only work with a limited selection of traffic signals. Near roadways, you'll see traffic signs that warn drivers of impending danger and provide them with important information. Accidents may occur when drivers aren't paying attention, are caught off guard by bad weather or high traffic, or both. As a result, the system must be able to detect and identify these traffic signs autonomously and then notify the driver.

The ability to automatically classify and recognize panel information has the potential to be life-changing for driver assistance applications (Wu and Ranganathan, 2012). Since traffic sign identification relies on form, text, and color recognition, many computer vision algorithms still face certain challenges. These challenges include distinguishing between different text characters by removing outliers and correctly comprising words using text recognition to convert pixel-based text into readable code (Gonzalez *et al.*, 2011). There are several emerging approaches to automated visual recognition that show promise in addressing the aforementioned problems and identifying traffic signs (Gonzalez and Yebes, 2014). As a result, researchers use a wide range of techniques for traffic sign identification and detection.

To avoid accidents and provide safe driving, this study employs an image-executing approach for traffic signal identification. To begin, we take a picture. Then, we send it to a color space designer, who will convert it to greyscale. After that, we check the image for the feature extraction approach, which uses a Harris corner detector and a Laplace operator to choose the scale. For edge detectors, the Sobel operator is used. The next step is to use adaptive fuzzy clustering for segmentation, and finally, a massively trained artificial neural network is used to identify traffic signs. The importance of classification and segmentation in this study will be quickly shown in the section that follows.

4.3.1 Segmentation–Fuzzy Clustering

To divide a picture into useful sections with shared or relevant characteristics, one may use an image segmentation technique. Simplicity, or the representation of a picture in a meaningful and easily analyzable fashion, is the primary goal of segmentation. An important first step in analyzing images is picture segmentation. Segmenting a picture into smaller pieces that have common characteristics is the main objective of image segmentation. Here, picture segmentation is used for traffic sign recognition, which is one of several uses of image segmentation (Kaur and Kaur, 2014). A picture is divided into sections based on how similar they are. Included in this procedure are methods for increasing regions, methods for thresholding regions, and methods for dividing and merging regions. Regions with a common pixel set were identified in these photos. This strategy is also used by clustering algorithms. Based on a number of established criteria, these photos were classified into sets with shared characteristics (Gonzalez and Woods, 2002).

Furthermore, many new ideas and methods from other fields have led to the development of picture segmentation algorithms that combine elements of several approaches [31, 32]. The so-called class is a group of items with the same name. Clustering relies on approach-specific criteria and rules of classification. Clustering is a statistical technique that groups together things that have similar characteristics. An exceedingly wide-ranging perspective is presented in this explanation. Objects may be considered "similar" in many ways when discussing their similarities and differences; for example, they can have comparable dimensions, directions (vectors), magnitudes, shapes, colors, and so on. As previously stated, a "cluster" or group consists of related object sets that differ in relation to a certain property. Clustering algorithms are of utmost relevance in many cognitive and computational applications that need items to be divided into separate groupings for more efficient execution. This study uses an image segmentation process with the fuzzy clustering technique.

4.3.2 Fuzzy Clustering

Using a membership function that enables membership with a given degree, fuzzy logic provides a mathematically ordered way to cope with fundamentally inaccurate notions. It has proven useful in several crisis-related fields. Among its many applications, it has found use in pattern recognition and the interval [0, 1] (Malhotra *et al.*, 2014). Traditional superset (Boolean) logic has been expanded to include the concept of partial truth—truth values between "totally false" and "totally true"—in fuzzy logic. Fuzzy logic has an approximated form of underlying thinking. Every aspect of fuzzy logic is handled by the membership function. A unique way to determine fuzzy word membership is to measure the distance between each cluster center and each data point. By grouping similar characteristics into explicitly defined clusters, the fuzzy clustering approach may divide data into manageable chunks. There is only one cluster that each data point in the sample space is associated with. Instead of data points, cluster centers are traversed after data partitioning is finished (Han and Kamber, 2006; Ayech *et al.*, 2010). The next part of this research will show how to use an artificial neural network for traffic sign identification, which is done using a classification approach.

4.4 Artificial Neural Network (ANN)

The nodes are seen as "artificial neurons" in one kind of network, Artificial neural networks are the term given to this (ANNs). An artificial neuron is a computer model inspired by real neurons (Gershenson, 2003). A natural neuron's membrane or dendrites may form synapses, which allow the

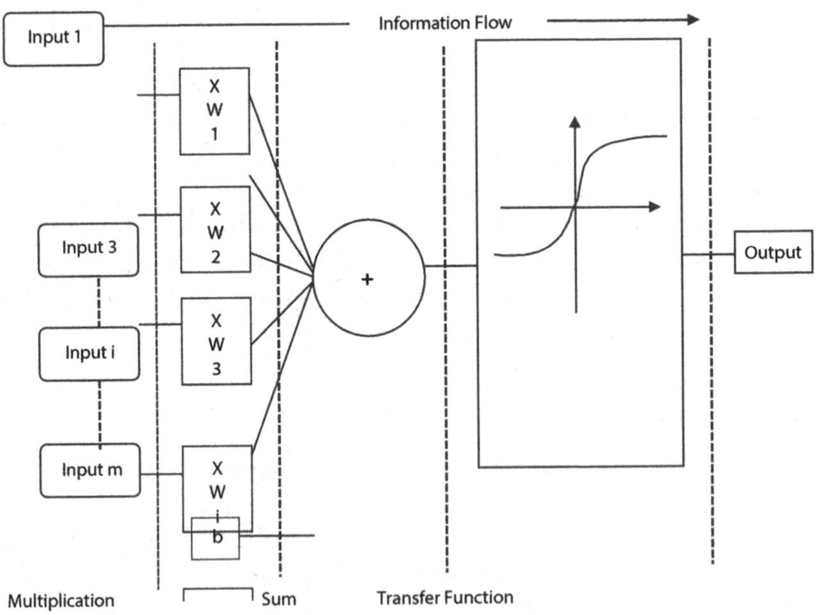

Figure 4.1 Working principle of an artificial neuron.

neuron to receive impulses. When the strength of the incoming impulses exceeds a certain threshold, the neuron is activated and sends out a signal along its axon. This signal has the potential to excite additional neurons by being passed to subsequent synapses. Artificial neural networks (ANNs) are mathematical representations that aim to mimic the structure and operation of real-life neural networks. An artificial neuron, a simple mathematical model (function), is the basic building element of any artificial neural network (Andrej *et al.*, 2011). The activation, summation, and multiplication set of rules are the simplest in this design. Each input value is multiplied by its unique weight at the entry of the artificial neuron.

The central component of an artificial neuron contains the sum function, which adds together all of the inputs and weighted biases. The total of the inputs and weighted biases is sent *via* the activation function, also known as the transfer function, at the exit of the artificial neuron (Figure 4.1). To reduce false positives in computerized traffic sign identification, a pattern-recognition approach called massive training artificial neural network (MTANN) is used as a filter on top of an artificial neural network (ANN). MTANN can directly process picture data since it is composed of modified multilayer ANN. To train MTANN, a large number of subregions are used, both from input photos and teacher images, with the latter providing a distribution for the "probability of being nodule." By feeding an input picture into MTANN, we can generate an output image. This section will demonstrate the predicted method of using MTANN for traffic sign detection.

4.5 Proposed Methodology

An introduction to image processing and key methods used for traffic sign detection is provided in the preceding section. Capturing the picture, converting the colors, segmenting it, and finally recognizing it are all components of the image processing process. This study employs the effective MTANNs method for traffic sign recognition in accordance with the aforementioned steps (Celikoglu, 2014). To deliver the RGB pictures, the acquired image is transformed into an RGB color scheme. Three distinct color channels—red, green, and blue—are extracted from the original picture. Because outdoor photographs' colors are sensitive to changes in lighting, it's challenging to get good results during detection. According to Dean and Jabir (2013), the collected picture is then transformed from RGB to YCbCr to lessen the impact of lighting variance.

4.5.1 Detection and Extraction of Traffic Sign

4.5.1.1 Image Extraction and Pre-Processing Using YCbCr

The specified dimensions for the taken picture are 320 × 420 pixels. The most common color space utilized by cameras is RGB (Kaplan *et al.*, 2012). Three separate pictures are extracted from the original: one each for the green, red, and blue color channels. Due to the difficulty of object recognition and the impact of lighting fluctuations on RGB, the RGB format is very sensitive to the chromatic variations of daylight.

Using the AAM, which is described below, the following object detection method takes the transformed YCbCr pictures and uses them to identify the traffic sign with less error.

4.5.1.2 Active Appearance Model (AAM)

In the second phase of the traffic light cycle focuses on adjusting signal timing based on real-time congestion levels, objects are detected from the picture by analyzing their form characteristics using an AAM algorithm. This method correctly locates the items by separating them from other objects of similar color (Martins and Batista, 2008). AAM can match a class of deformable objects to a certain sign (e.g., changes in the size or shape of the sign). An annotated picture collection is necessary for AAM to construct a traffic sign model. According to Nguwi and Kouzani (2008), AAM learns its model parameters, changes in grey levels, and shape control modes from a training set. With 60 points labeled around the key features and over 10,000 intensity values collected in the traffic sign area, the training set may include more than 30 traffic signs. This is where the 45 parameters that make up the appearance model are defined; these parameters account for 95% of the addressed variance in the training set.

4.5.1.3 Extracting the Region of Interest

Once the items and their relevant shapes have been detected, a specific area may be extracted from the object. Within this synthesized panel, the four-character description can be used to identify potential candidate regions. Points at intersections and corners may be located with a Harris detector.

4.5.1.3.1 Exploring Keypoint Extraction with the Harris Corner Detector

One fundamental idea underpins the Harris corner detector (Le *et al.*, 2011): the picture intensity will fluctuate substantially in several directions at a corner. Alternatively, it may be expressed by looking at the intensity variations caused by changes in a local window. When the window is moved in any direction, the visual intensity changes significantly at a corner point. The Harris detector bases its corner judgments on the second moment matrix, following this idea and a smart decomposition. Important information may be highlighted by extracting the corners.

4.5.1.4 Edge Detection Using Sobel Operator

Image processing, specifically edge detection methods, makes use of the Sobel operator (Zheng *et al.*, 2010). To be more precise, it calculates a near-gradient of the picture intensity function and is therefore a discrete differentiation operator. At every picture point, the Sobel operator yields one of two things: the matching gradient vector or its norm. Computationally, the Sobel operator is cheap since it convolves the picture with a tiny, separable, integer-valued filter in both the horizontal and vertical directions. However, when it comes to high-frequency picture fluctuations, the gradient approximation it generates is tiny.

4.5.1.4.1 Design of the Sobel Filter (Gupta and Mazumdar, 2013)

The majority of edge detection algorithms are based on the premise that a very steep intensity gradient or a discontinuity in the intensity function constitutes an edge. Under this assumption, the edge may potentially be discovered by taking the derivative of the intensity value throughout the picture and finding the spots where the derivative is highest. A vector representing the gradient has components that measure the x- and y-distance changes in pixel values.

One way to find whether there is a gradient discontinuity is to determine the gradient's change at (i, j).

4.5.1.5 Segmentation Using Adaptive Fuzzy Clustering

In addition, the adaptive fuzzy clustering technique efficiently analyzes each picture pixel and aids in the identification of groups associated with those pixels (Afrose and Bhuiyan, 2012). The traffic sign's N-shape is split into C groups *via* adaptive fuzzy clustering. We use weights ranging from 0 to 1 to show how important each shape is to each category. The dimensions of the matrix U are C × N. To normalize the matrix value, we sum together all the weighted values of a particular shape in matrix U. (e.g., single character, number, and symbol).

Where the convergent factor prevents the cluster from being oversplit and α is a constant (CF). Without excessive separation of characters, numbers, and symbols in the traffic panel, the clustered form identifies the potential candidate and the area of attention.

4.5.1.6 Tracking the Detected Sign

The size of a panel on the side of the road can vary. When a traffic panel is discovered in N consecutive frames—where N is a function of panel size and occlusion—the multi-frame detection method (Gómez *et al.*, 2010) is used to confirm the panel's detection.

4.5.2 Recognition of Traffic Sign

The area of interest is verified as a traffic sign by the recognition module, and the sign is identified (Chen *et al.*, 2013). The panel's traffic sign may be identified with the help of the MTANN. For MTANN training, a teaching picture with the nodule distribution is used in conjunction with a large number of subregions taken from the input photos (Suzuki, 2009). Massive training entails a high dimensionality of zones in each input subvolume and a large number of subregions. Utilizing MTANN, which is both time-consuming and effective, will expedite the identification of traffic signs. To sort traffic signs from non-traffic signs with the best possible false positive ratio. In the following section, we expand MTANN's capabilities.

4.5.2.1 MTANN Training Model for Classification

For the purpose of training, ten photographs that are not traffic signs and thirty images of varying sizes and types of environments were used. The training area is split into 30 identical zones, each measuring 6 × 6 pixels, and retrieved from each traffic sign. Each zone is 30 × 30 pixels in size. The relevant teaching area is used to obtain the teaching value for each zone. Every traffic sign includes 30 characteristics that are part of the trained model.

4.5.2.2 Multiple MTANN Training Models

To enhance the expanded capability of a single MTANN, a combination of numerous MTANNs is used, which are then organized in parallel. Differentiating the traffic sign from other signs is its primary function. Each MTANN follows the same training technique as the previous one, using the input photos and instructor images. To differentiate between traffic signs and non-traffic signs, the characteristics used are the scores of each MTANN. A mixing ANN that can distinguish between ten distinct types of signs (including traffic signs) is used to aggregate the scores from each MTANN. For mixed ANNs, the result is a linear output. The trained mixing ANN assigns a lower probability to non-traffic signs and a higher probability to traffic signs, distinguishing between true positives and false positives.

4.5.2.3 MTANN Classification

An output layer in MTANN identifies the traffic sign, while the hidden layer uses a log sigmoid function with 20 units. For testing purposes, the trained MTANN is fed the original picture (Tuia and Camps-Valls, 2009). Scanning the source picture with the trained MTANN yields the output image. The threshold for each trained MTANN is based on the score, which distinguishes between traffic signs and non-traffic signs. Using a trained set that removes as many non-traffic signs as feasible while leaving all traffic signs in place determines the threshold.

4.6 Results and Discussion

Several types of roadside traffic panels were used to evaluate the suggested system's efficacy in detecting and recognizing traffic signs.

4.6.1 LiU Traffic Sign Database

In Figure 4.2, you can see the recorded video pictures of the signs connected to traffic, which occur every five frames.

After collecting photos from the LiU traffic sign database, the suggested methods for detecting these signs are applied (Houben *et al.*, 2009). The obtained pictures are transformed into YCbCr images, after which the item is identified with the help of the AAM, and a specific area is removed. Using MTANN, many descriptors are collected from the extracted area

Figure 4.2 Sample LiU traffic sign video images.

and recognized. To measure the system's efficiency, we use the following measures.

In contrast to the SC's exclusive focus on form and color, the backtracking algorithm (BTG) & spanning tree (ST) approach gives more weight to letters than symbols. The suggested technique focuses on the traffic panel's symbols, shapes, and text regardless of lighting conditions. A two-dimensional graph called a Receiver Operating Characteristic (ROC) curve shows the true-positive rate on the Y-axis and the false-positive rate on the X-axis. As shown in Figure 4.3, ROC curves serve as valuable tools for depicting and comparing classifier performance. In comparison to the current approaches, the suggested approach accurately distinguishes between traffic signs and non-traffic signals.

Figure 4.4 is a graphical depiction of the identification rate for several categories of traffic signs. While 90% of people can identify the mandatory

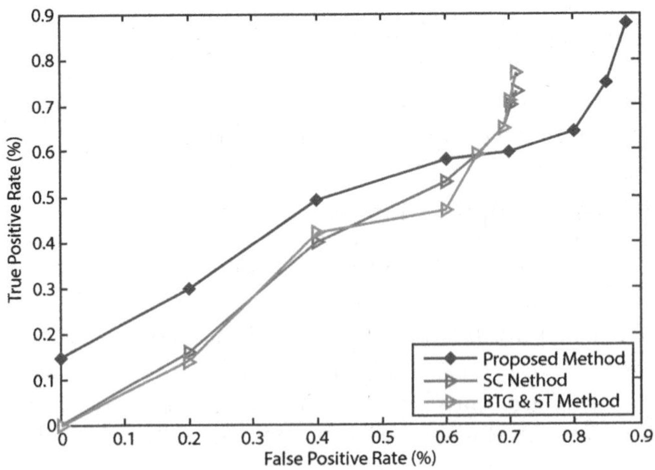

Figure 4.3 ROC curve for different methods.

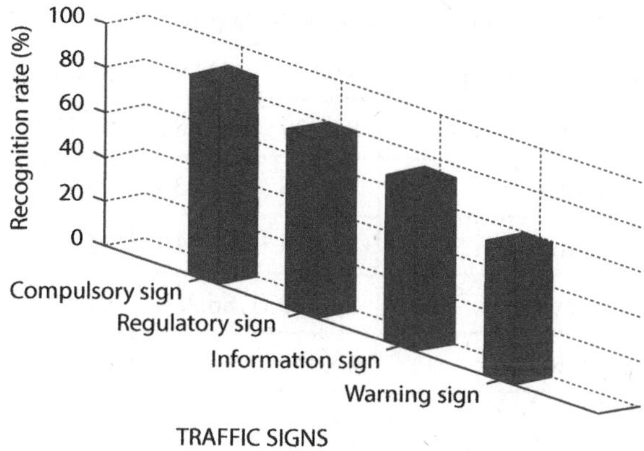

Figure 4.4 Recognition rate for different categories of traffic signs.

sign, only 80% can do the same for the regulatory sign, 72% for the information sign, and 60% for the warning sign.

A number of procedures are carried out by the suggested approach to identify the shapes, letters, and symbols, while the traditional approaches primarily focus on individual items inside the traffic panel.

4.6.2 Investigations of Various Classification Techniques

Classifiers in this domain are evaluated using a variety of measures, including precision, recall, accuracy, F-measure, and error rate. The classifiers that are compared are Support Vector Machine (SVM), Artificial Neural Network (ANN), and Massive Training Network for Artificial Neural Systems (MTANN). Using the following metrics, we can compare the classification strategy with dataset 2's 10,000 photographs and dataset 1's 20,000 photos:

Table 4.1 shows the results of comparing several classifiers for dataset 1. The results in Table 4.1 demonstrate that the suggested MTANN performs better than an alternative classifier, with an improved accuracy rate of 91.49%, recall of 93.13%, F-measure of 94.14%, and a decreased error rate of 8.51%.

Table 4.2 shows the results of comparing several classifiers for dataset 2. The table shows that compared to other existing classifiers, the suggested MTANN achieves better results in terms of accuracy (88.552%), recall (92.307%), F-measure (90.929%), and precision (88.552%). Additionally, it has a reduced error rate of 12%.

Table 4.1 Comparison of various classifiers for dataset 1.

Metrics/techniques	SVM	ANN	MTANN
Precision (%)	86.999	89.084	93.173
Recall (%)	90.786	91.335	95.108
F-measure (%)	88.893	90.210	94.140
Accuracy (%)	84.510	86.250	91.49
Error rate (%)	15.490	13.750	8.51

Table 4.2 Comparison of various classifiers for dataset 2.

Metrics/techniques	SVM	ANN	MTANN
Precision (%)	77.519	84.615	89.552
Recall (%)	83.334	85.937	92.307
F-measure (%)	80.426	85.276	90.929
Accuracy (%)	75.5	81	88
Error rate (%)	24.5	19	12

You can see the difference in accuracy between datasets 1 and 2 in Figure 4.5. The results demonstrate that the proposed MTANN outperforms the control and input datasets in terms of accuracy. With a precision value of 93.173% in dataset 1, MTANN outperforms the other classifiers. In contrast, the accuracy values of the other two current classifiers, SVM and ANN, are 86.094% and 86.099%, respectively.

The error rates of datasets 1 and 2 are shown in Figure 4.5. Both datasets demonstrate that the suggested MTANN has a greater error rate. Compared to other classifiers, MTANN's error rate of 8.51% in dataset 1 is greater. On the other hand, the error rates for the two other current classifiers, SVM and ANN, are 15.490% and 13.750%, respectively. Out of all the classifiers tested in dataset 2, MTANN had the highest error rate at 12%. On the other hand, the error rates for the two other current classifiers, SVM and ANN, are 24.5% and 19.9%, respectively.

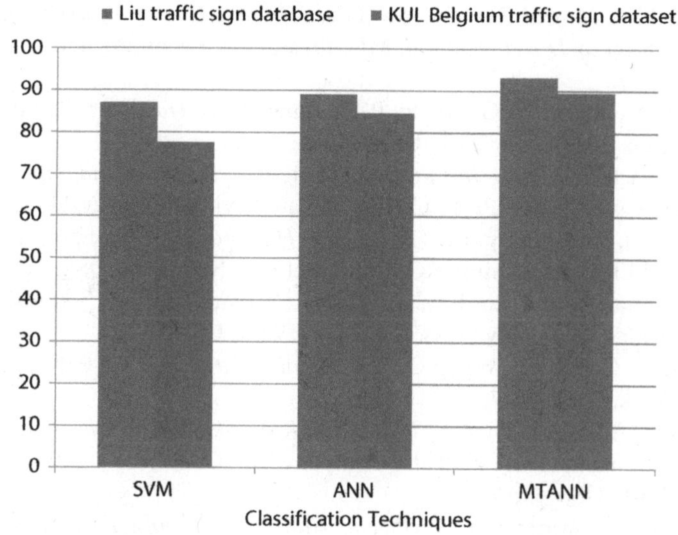

Figure 4.5 Precision comparison of datasets 1 and 2.

4.7 Summary

This study's methodology, which included a variety of approaches for detecting and recognizing traffic signals on road panels, proved to be a successful strategy. To get around RGB's light sensitivity, you may convert it to YCbCr color space, which will result in a greyscale picture. The use of AAM for shape model creation produces satisfactory results regardless of whether the traffic signs are partially or completely obscured. Using adaptive fuzzy clustering, we can extract the area of interest containing the potential text, numbers, and symbols from the synthesized picture. To improve the algorithm's performance, multi-frame analysis examines the traffic sign detection data to determine its sensitivity and selectivity. To enhance prediction accuracy and decrease the number of false positives, several MTANNs are trained for each class. The results demonstrate the rapid and reliable nature of this procedure's traffic sign detection and identification capabilities.

References

1. Ahuja, R.K. and Maheshwari, R.P. (Eds.), *Handbook of Research on Intelligent Transport Systems and Travel Behavior Analysis*, IGI Global, Springer, Berlin, Germany, 2018.

2. Ben-Akiva, M. and Bierlaire, M. (Eds.), *Discrete Choice Analysis: Theory and Application to Travel Demand*, MIT Press, UCLA Law Review, Los Angeles, USA 2019.
3. Cairns, S., Atkins, S., Goodwin, P., *Comprehensive Transport Planning*, Taylor & Francis, IEEE, New York, USA, 2019.
4. Coifman, B., *Modeling the Internet of Things: Development and Implementation of Frameworks*, CRC Press, California Law Review, Berkeley, USA, 2017.
5. Dargay, J. and Hanly, M. (Eds.), *The Handbook of Transport Economics*, Edward Elgar Publishing, ACM Transactions, New York, USA, 2020.
6. De Palma, A. and Lindsey, R., *Discrete Choice Methods with Simulation*, Cambridge University Press, IEEE, New York, USA, 2018.
7. Duan, L., Cheng, H., Wang, Q., *Data Mining with Big Data*, CRC Press, IEEE, New York, USA, 2017.
8. Elberse, A., *Blockbusters: Hit-making, Risk-taking, and the Big Business of Entertainment*, Henry Holt and Company, Tow Center for Digital Journalism, New York, USA, 2017.
9. European Commission, *Intelligent Transport Systems: From Research and Development to Deployment of Cooperative Systems*, Publications Office of the European Union, Big Data Society, London, UK, 2019.
10. Fagnant, D.J. and Kockelman, K., *Preparing a Nation for Autonomous Vehicles: Opportunities, Barriers and Policy Recommendations*, Transportation Research Part A: Policy and Practice, Privacy Enhancing Technologies, Cambridge, UK, 2018.
11. Federal Highway Administration, *Traffic Analysis Toolbox Volume XII: Traffic Analysis Tools Case Study Report*, FHWA Publications, Macmillan, New York, USA, 2018.
12. Golob, T.F. and Recker, W.W., *Travel Survey Methods: Quality and Future Directions*, Elsevier, ProPublica, New York, USA, 2019.
13. Hensher, D.A. and Button, K.J. (Eds.), *Handbook of Transport Strategy, Policy and Institutions*, Emerald Group Publishing, International Journal of Uncertainty and Fuzziness, Singapore, 2019.
14. Koenig, R., *Integrated Public Transport: Design, Operation and Management*, CRC Press, ACM SIGSAC, New York, USA, 2018.
15. Mahmassani, H.S., *Dynamic Network Traffic Control: Algorithmic and Optimization Aspects*, Springer, Auerbach Publications, Boca Raton, Florida, USA, 2018.
16. Nakamura, F. and Kuroda, K. (Eds.), *Advances in Mobility as a Service Systems*, Springer, Springer, Berlin, Germany, 2017.
17. OECD, *Transport Infrastructure Investment and Development for Tourism*, OECD Publishing, San Diego Law Review, San Diego, USA, 2019.
18. Pietrzykowski, M., *Urban Traffic Management System: A Case Study in Szczecin, Poland*, Procedia Computer Science, IEEE, New York, USA, 2018.
19. Quak, H.J. and de Gier, J. (Eds.), *Human Factors in Traffic Management*, CRC Press, IEEE, New York, USA, 2019.

20. Regan, M.A. and Lee, J.D., *Driver Distraction: Theory, Effects, and Mitigation*, CRC Press, Duke Law Technology Review, Durham, USA, 2018.
21. Rutherford, G.S. and Wiley, M.W. (Eds.), *Urban Transportation Planning: A Decision-Oriented Approach*, Springer, Science, Technology & Human Values, USA, 2018.
22. Scharf, K., *Analyzing Big Data with Spark and Python*, O'Reilly Media, Harvard University Press, Cambridge, Massachusetts, USA, 2019.
23. Schrank, D. and Eisele, B., *Urban Mobility ScorecardTexas A&M Transportation Institute*, 2017.
24. Short, J. and Koppelman, F. (Eds.), *Handbook of Transport Modeling*, Elsevier, Elsevier BV, Amsterdam, Netherlands, 2019.
25. Sperling, D. and Gordon, D., *Two Billion Cars: Driving Toward Sustainability*, Oxford University Press, Neural Information Processing Systems, New York, USA, 2019.
26. Transportation Research Board, *Traffic Signal Systems Operations and Design*, TRB, University of Pennsylvania Law Review, Philadelphia, USA, 2017.
27. Vuchic, V.R., *Urban Transit Systems and Technology*, John Wiley & Sons, ACM Fairness, Accountability, and Transparency Conference, New York, USA, 2018.
28. Waraich, A., *Next-Generation Wireless Technologies: 4G and Beyond*, Cambridge University Press, Nature Machine Intelligence, London, UK, 2017.
29. World Bank, *Urban Transport Strategy Review*, World Bank Publications, IEEE, New York, USA, 2019.
30. Wright, M., *Autonomous Vehicles: Opportunities, Strategies, and Disruptions*, CRC Press, Springer, Berlin, Germany, 2018.
31. Sathiyaraj, R., Bharathi, A., Khan, S., Kiren, T., Khan, I.U., Fayaz, M., A genetic predictive model approach for smart traffic prediction and congestion avoidance for urban transportation. *Wireless Commun. Mobile Comput.*, *2022*, 1, 5938411, 2022.
32. Rajendran, S., Sabharwal, M., Hu, Y.C., Balusamy, B. (Eds.), *Artificial Intelligence for Autonomous Vehicles: The Future of Driverless Technology*, John Wiley & Sons, 2024.

5

Internet of Things in Smart and Secure Applications Development-Based Sustainability

S. Vijayakumar[1*], A. Thilagavathy[1], Sankar R.[2], T. Ramesh[1], N. BanuPriya[1] and S. Srijayanthi[1]

[1]*Department of Computer Science and Engineering, R.M.K. Engineering College, Kavaraipettai, India*

[2]*Department of Computer Science and Engineering, S.A. Engineering College, Chennai, India*

Abstract

In a nutshell, the IoT operates on an entirely new regime in which smart objects interconnect and communicate data so that they can operate machinery or physical equipment. The connection is the reason smart and truly secure apps can be built across so many varied domains. These areas include urban infrastructure, transportation, smart grids, and energy management systems in commercial buildings that want to radically reduce power bills and are at the head of that list of water usage, as well as agriculture—food grown in large-scale greenhouses on city peripheries and fish farms—and healthcare. To do so, the majority turns to using oceans of IoT devices that increasingly control our natural sustainability problems like wasting assets around, protecting nature, or actively recycling energy reuse. This chapter discusses mainly the Internet of Things (IoT), smart applications, security, and sustainability. It also looks at smart and secure solutions aligned with IoT to meet sustainability targets. It discusses themes such as data privacy, the degree of interoperability, and whether implementing IoT technology in an ecologically conscious manner is energy efficient, exposing many advantages and disadvantages. The chapter also presents multiple illustrations and case studies where the issues of sustainability have been dealt with, comprehensively using an IoT solution. These technologies have many applications: intelligent transportation

**Corresponding author*: svk.cse@rmkec.ac.in

R. Sathiyaraj, Rajesh Kumar Dhanaraj, K. Arun Kumar, Rutvij H. Jhaveri and A. Mohamed Abbas (eds.) Predictive Methods in Next-Generation Computing: An Approach Toward Sustainability, (83–106)

systems, smart energy management systems, waste management, and precision agriculture being a few. It also examines different strategies and principles to secure sustainable IoT-based applications in detail developed throughout this chapter. Essentials for hardened security measures to mitigate threats include, but are not limited to, authentication, packet integrity verification mechanisms (PIV), encryption, and access policy control, as strong firmware upgrade mechanisms should be delivered.

Keywords: Internet of Things, IoT, smart applications, sustainability, security, smart cities, environmental protection, energy management

5.1 Introduction

The Internet of Things has been one major trend and revolution this decade, drastically changing how we interact and operate across many aspects of our daily lives or the way business processes are conducted. The advent of the Internet of Things (IoT) [1–10] makes it possible to connect devices, facilitating smooth data exchange and resulting in smart, secure apps that enhance efficiency enabling sustainability programs. Among just a handful of the wide range of innovative solutions created based on IoT technology are those in healthcare, agriculture transportation, and energy management. The use of IoT-enabled apps that track environmental factors and optimize resource usage can help achieve sustainability goals even more. This first section provides an overview of how ideas about sustainability, methods for smart application development, and technologies employed by such applications are converging [11–20]. It highlights the importance, as well as urgency of securing essential infrastructure and data in IoT networks with robust security. It also highlights the importance of collaboration between stakeholders to foster scalable and interconnected solutions that promote sustainability. This paper helps in surfacing some of the critical thoughts, challenges, and opportunities around making sustainable safe smart apps using IoT technology. This report aims to inspire further research and development on this hugely expanding horizontal field by examining state-of-the-art practices as well as future trends, to foster a better interconnected, efficient, sustainable world [21–30].

By the end of this decade, estimates suggest that there will be billions of networked devices exploding on an unprecedented scale from what has been a rapid growth in IoT device deployments over recent years [2]. As this proliferation of connection has matured, the astonishing opportunities for innovation and efficiency across sectors have paralleled concerns about security, privacy, and its impact on our environment. One of the main reasons for the proliferation of IoT is its capability to enable sustainability through connected devices. Businesses can digest and process huge amounts of sensor data to better understand energy usage, resource use, and environmental impact. By using data to inform decisions, they are able to uncover areas of waste and improve operations that create real benefits beyond carbon emissions in the form of lower consumption-reducing ecological footprints. At the same time, there are crucial security issues associated with IoT devices being employed on a large scale. Because these devices are connected to the network, more cyber assaults such as data breaches and even bodily injury caused by a hack have become increasingly large problems. Consequently, robust security must be implemented across the IoT ecosystem to authenticate and encrypt devices, segment networks, or implement Intrusion Detection Systems. Also, because industries like healthcare and banking are involved—which involves sensitive data any way you see it—user data needs to be protected at all costs in IoT applications. Developers should integrate privacy-by-design principles in their process, and comply with data protection standards as the best way to earn users' trust and reduce the spillover of private information. Privacy, security, and the wider impact on our environment are just some of the concerns related to IoT (The Internet of Things). We spend a lot of energy and resources in making them, then using them, and ultimately disposing of them (adding to garbage/waste). To address this concern, companies developing IoT devices should strive to create these products and design them in such a way that allows for the utmost energy efficiency and recyclability. On our part, we can maintain each one of those to reach its intended time when these devices last through individual as well as organizational recycling. IoT has a huge potential to channel and support our environmental challenges, guiding us into the next step of more holistic or less centrally driven global efforts in living together. Before that promise is achieved, however, data privacy and security concerns will have to be sorted out—not only in the home but also for us here on earth. The combined power of the Internet of Things (IoT) is perfectly poised to help us build a more prosperous sustainable future for generations to come, where systems are developed safely and responsibly, working with all stakeholders in open forums.

In many places, a move toward these smart approaches to devices and architecture, especially in combination with the Internet of Things (IoT) [3], has great potential to make significant sustainability gains in an effort to more fully appreciate this junction's potential contributions.

Firstly, the Internet of Things enables intelligent applications that save resources on a larger scale in areas such as agriculture, manufacturing, and energy management. Real-time data collected from sensors and devices can help organizations identify inefficiencies, enabling them to take specific actions that result in waste reduction and increased efficiency. This not only improves sustainability among companies but also saves a significant amount while preserving resources.

IoT devices help with environmental monitoring because this allows the storage of physical quantities such as temperature, water quality, and air quality [5]. Authorities, such as mayors and city planners, can use this data to locate sites of heavy pollution or possible environmental hazards nearby, allowing them to take action to reduce these risks. Over time, this aids in meeting sustainability goals through better environmental stewardship and reduced depletion of natural resources.

Also, IoT enables better integration of renewable energy sources with the power grid [6]. IoT sensors embedded in smart grids provide real-time monitoring and control of electricity generation and transmission from suppliers to consumers. This increased flexibility makes our energy infrastructure better suited for renewable energy adoption—enhancing wind and solar integration while improving resilience and sustainability.

5.2 Literature Survey

New developments in IoT [10] technology have opened the door to creative approaches to improving sustainability in several areas. An example of such an application is the sustainable agricultural smart water management system based on the Internet of Things. This system optimizes irrigation methods by using real-time data from soil moisture sensors and weather predictions, thereby saving water resources. However, as pointed out in "Securing IoT Devices: Challenges and Solutions," security issues arise with the broad use of IoT devices. Ensuring the integrity and confidentiality of IoT data is the focus of this article, which delves into authentication procedures, encryption protocols, and intrusion detection systems. Additionally, as discussed in "Sustainable Energy Management Utilizing IoT-enabled Smart Grids," [11] smart grids connected to the Internet of Things allow for the integration of renewable energy sources and the real-time monitoring and control of energy usage.

5.3 Methodology

There is a data accumulator in the database module that records network traffic to collect real-world data. Additional synthesized datasets may be obtained using this module from the generative adversarial network. Along with that, it protects the Industrial Internet of Things (IIoT) network's central station-to-node and node-to-node communications [17]. Without sufficient data samples, it is often challenging to train an IDS model with a greater classification accuracy. Additionally, there is a data imbalance issue during classification algorithm training due to the relatively high number of benign data samples compared to attack/abnormal data. Appropriate methods for dealing with issues of class imbalance are implemented in this module. To prepare the data for classification methods, the preprocessing module examines the packets, converts them, and creates class labels. The IDS models that were created make use of preprocessing methods including standardization, data cleansing, and one-hot encoding.

The feature selection [18] module applies a suitable feature selection (FS) method to minimize the feature space to manage data flows that are rich in features and have greater dimensions in massive systems like the IIoT system. Integrating the right optimizer for parameter adjustment greatly improves the efficacy of the suggested FS approach. To identify the most important dataset characteristics, this study uses enhanced salp swarm optimization (SSO). By combining the idea of the β-HC algorithm with the standard salp swarm optimizer, the FS algorithm's exploration skills are enhanced, leading to a more efficient feature selection process. This combination is used in a classifier to make the IDS model work better. To detect cyberattacks, this research makes use of a stacked sparse autoencoder. A bird swarm optimization approach considerably improves the stacked sparse autoencoder (SSAE) classifier's classification performance. Below, you will find a detailed explanation of the four components that make up the suggested structure.

5.3.1 Module for the Database

The data accumulator in the database module captures network traffic from IIoT devices in real-time, allowing for the collection of data. Using data preparation methods, the packets are treated before being included in the dataset. To gather packets and extract properties from them, a packet capture program (like Wireshark) operates within the data accumulator. A huge amount of data, usually regular data, is generated by the interactions of an IIoT network's sensors and actuators. However, a malicious actor might try to launch an assault by compromising the communication lines or the sensing devices. Thus, the data collector collaborates with a firewall to identify such data samples, making the system resilient against any cyber assault. The generative adversarial networks can also provide database modules with synthetic datasets. Higher classification accuracy while training the IDS model is often not possible without a sufficient dataset. Additionally, there is a data imbalance issue during classification algorithm training due to the relatively high number of benign data samples compared to attack/abnormal data. One effective deep learning (DL) method is generative adversarial network (GAN), which can learn the pattern of a given dataset and then generate new datasets that are linked to it. A combination of the dataset's actual and synthetic samples is used to train the IDS's classifier module. Only real-world datasets, such as Next-generation knowledge discovery dataset (NSL-KDD) and canadian institute for cybersecurity distributed denial-of-service dataset (CIC-DDoS), are utilized to train the proposed binary sparrow algorithm-intrusion detection system (BSA-IDS) model. In contrast to the two other models, Improved generative adversarial network-intrusion detection system (IGAN-IDS) and Fused IGAN-IDS,, which are trained on both generated and original datasets [19]. To distinguish between different data sources, all samples are gathered in real-time and stored in a database with the proper labels.

5.3.2 Information Preparation Section

Data packets in the real world [20] can come from a variety of sources and may be inaccurate, invasive, unnecessary, hasty, repeated, or even missing certain movements or events. This highlights the need to clean up the source data before using it for feature extraction and evaluation. As a result, gaining valuable insights from data streams necessitates the application of certain captivating strategies. To prepare packets for classification algorithms, the preprocessor converts them, examines them, and creates class labels for the data. The built IDS models make use of data cleaning, standardization, and one-hot encoding as preprocessing methods.

Cleaning Up Data [21]: Ensuring that the database used for analytics accurately represents the data samples under consideration is the primary objective of data cleaning. Unintentionally adding anomalies to a database, such as outliers or codes that include various forms of missing values (e.g., skip patterns, genuinely missing, renunciations, etc.), can severely impact the data analytics system's performance. Data processing approaches, on the other hand, allow for improved outcomes from dataset processing, with better judgments and results produced by more accurate and descriptive data samples. Data scrubbing, also known as cleaning, is an essential step in the study's suggested IDS models [22] that eliminates entries that are not relevant, incomplete, or redundant and locates missing values in the mentioned datasets. This procedure guarantees accurate, efficient, and trustworthy findings. By using the preprocessing methods provided by the simulator, the superfluous characteristics from the NSL-KDD and CIC-DDoS databases are removed. Also, to prevent the classifiers from being confused during training, this method gets rid of any white or blank gaps in the data samples.

Quick Encoding: This research employs a one-hot encoding method to deal with output characteristics and non-numerical attributes (such as service, protocol type, and label) by transforming the non-numerical qualities into numerical values. This method uses a single bit to express categorical qualities in bit vectors. Unfortunately, most DL algorithms struggle when faced with features that have absolute values. Hence, before feeding these characteristics into classifiers, they must be converted into integer values. Two well-known methods in data processing for converting strings of non-numerical characters into integers are ordinal and one-hot encoding. This research uses these methods to find integer values for items that are not numbers [23]. For example, to implement the NSL-KDD, the communication protocols user datagram protocol (UDP), transmission control protocol (TCP), and internet control message protocol (ICMP) are given the numbers 2, 1, and 0, respectively. For the other characteristics to be converted to integer values, a similar method is used. The data records' binary tags consist entirely of ones and zeros. Figure 5.1 illustrates the IDS model architecture.

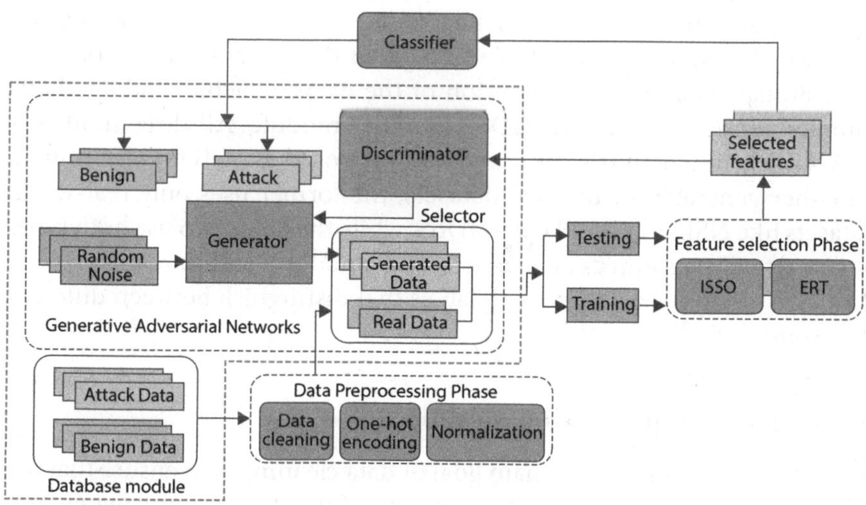

Figure 5.1 Overall architecture of the proposed IDS models.

To manage the data flow of massive systems like the IIoT system, which is rich in features and has larger dimensions, the feature selection module applies a suitable FS method to shrink the feature space. Adding the right optimizer for parameter adjustment makes the suggested FS approach [24] much more successful. To identify the most important dataset characteristic, this study uses enhanced salp swarm optimization (SSO).

5.3.3 Database Module

In order to collect data in real-time, the database module includes a data accumulator that captures network traffic from IIoT devices. Using data preparation methods, the packets are treated before being included to the dataset. To gather packets and extract properties from them, a packet capture program (like Wireshark) operates within the data accumulator. A huge amount of data, usually consisting of normal data, is generated by the interaction of sensors and actuators in an IIoT network [26]. However, a malicious actor might try to launch an assault by compromising the communication lines or the sensing devices. Thus, the data collector collaborates with a firewall to identify such data samples, making the system resilient against any cyber assault.

The generative adversarial networks may also provide database modules with synthetic datasets. Higher classification accuracy during training is often not possible with the IDS model [27] in the absence of a sufficient dataset. Additionally, there is a data imbalance issue during classification algorithm training due to the relatively high number of benign data samples compared to attack/abnormal data. One effective DL method is GAN [28], which can learn the pattern of a given dataset and then generate a new, similar dataset. A combination of the dataset's actual and synthetic samples are used to train the IDS's classifier module. All three models—IGAN-IDS, Fused IGAN-IDS, and the proposed BSA-IDS—are trained on either generated or original datasets; the former uses only real-world datasets like NSL-KDD and CIC-DDoS, while the latter two use both types of datasets. Data samples are collected continuously and in real-time, and they are stored in a database with labels that distinguish between different data sources.

5.3.4 Data Preprocessing Module

Achieving Data Purity: The main goal of data cleaning is to ensure that the analytics database is a good representation of the data samples being considered. The data analytics system's performance may be adversely affected if anomalies, including outliers or codes with different types of missing values (e.g., skip patterns, actually missing, renunciations, etc.), are accidentally added to the database. On the other side, data processing methodologies provide better judgments and results from dataset processing, thanks to more accurate and descriptive data samples. One crucial step in the proposed IDS models in this study is data cleansing or data scrubbing. It entails searching the designated datasets for missing values and eliminating entries that are irrelevant, incomplete, or duplicate. Results that are precise, quick, and reliable are assured by this method. The simulator's preparation procedures remove unnecessary features in the NSL-KDD and CIC-DDoS databases. This approach also removes blank or white spaces from the data samples to ensure the classifiers do not become confused when training.

Rapid Encoding: To handle output attributes and non-numerical qualities (including service, protocol type, and label), this study uses a one-hot encoding approach to convert the non-numerical qualities into numerical values. Bit vectors expressing category attributes are represented by this approach using a single bit. Features having absolute values are a real challenge for most DL algorithms. Therefore, it is necessary to transform these attributes into integer values before passing them into classifiers. Ordinal and one-hot encoding are two popular techniques in data processing for turning strings of non-numerical characters into numbers. For instance, the NSL-KDD requires the communication protocols UDP, TCP, and ICMP to be assigned the values 2, 1, and 0, respectively. A similar procedure is used for the conversion of the other attributes to integer values. However, one-and-zero binary tags are already present in all of the data records.

Standardization: The class imbalance problem has a detrimental effect on classifier performance, as previously shown. Therefore, it is crucial to standardize these disparities to a tolerable extent. Consider how the big "Src Bytes," "Dst Bytes," "Duration," and "Src Bytes" numbers in the CIC-DDoS dataset may impact the relatively small "Num Failed Logins" statistics.

In intrusion detection systems (IDS) models, this technique enhances classifier performance and dependability by eliminating bias issues, allowing rapid convergence, and significantly decreasing testing and training times.

5.3.5 Optimal Feature Selection Module

These days, deep learning algorithms are crucial in the digital world. Using deep learning in real-time applications causes problems with databases with more dimensions. Databases often include information that is not really relevant or required, according to many studies. Current IDS models rely on classification techniques that are rendered ineffective by these superfluous, redundant attributes and noisy data. To construct an effective decision-making system, it is crucial to choose appropriate attributes for training and testing. The capacity of intrusion detection systems to reliably and efficiently identify attacks has also been significantly impacted by the real-time apps' huge irrelevance and superfluous features. Furthermore, IDSs constructed using these challenges are infamously difficult to understand, resource-intensive, and time-consuming during validation and training. So, picking features is a crucial part of our research.

Reducing the number of features or parameters associated with classifiers is the objective of feature engineering. It prioritizes characteristics to set off an alarm when an abnormality is found. Eliminating features that do not add much to threat detection is also a part of it. Eliminating superfluous and irrelevant data not only improves the classifier's generalizability and performance but also reduces the total time cost. An essential quality of a good classifier is its capacity to generalize, which helps to avoid overfitting on specific datasets. In this work, feature selection and other optimization issues are better tackled by metaheuristic algorithms. The feature selection difficulty is successfully addressed by developing two methods: an upgraded salp swarm optimizer and a highly randomized tree-based attribute selection. Salp swarm optimizer is one of the metaheuristic algorithms that is thought to be relevant. Unfortunately, the diversity problem impacts all optimizers, including the salp swarm optimizer, making it impossible to avoid a less-than-ideal result. This research creates an improved salp swarm optimizer, a variation of the salp swarm optimization method, to fix these problems.

The conventional SSO approach is enhanced with two crucial enhancements to rectify its deficiencies. One change is a new formula for adjusting the salp locations. Expanding the variety of SSO choices is the primary enhancement. The second update integrates the hybrid hierarchical clustering (H-HC) algorithm with the regular SSO to improve the ability to explore the world. The ISSO method considers the evaluation function when deciding which characteristic is most essential. The rule engine will choose the feature with the lowest occurrence count when two subsections are equal in value. Inputting the selected qualities into the classification algorithm is the next stage in constructing the intrusion detection model and detecting cyberattacks. Extremely random trees are used in decision tree (DT) techniques that employ information gain (IG) to rank and classify attributes. The tree's nodes represent classes or labels at the top, features' potential value at the bottom, and the links between features that lead to excellent judgments shown by branches. By determining the IG and entropy for each node in the DT, this study identifies which qualities to search for. The disparity between the entropy levels before and after splitting defines the IG. Many DTs with k attributes are used to calculate the IG value. Consequently, the sum of IG for every attribute is calculated by comparing the gain values of various DT levels. The classification approach incorporates the outputs of all the de-correlated randomized tree sets. Parameter values are accepted in this work after extensive testing of various amalgamations and selection of the optimal subset. If we want to prevent underfitting, we may sort the attributes by relevance and remove the ones with the lowest values. The next step is to choose the remaining characteristics.

5.3.6 Classification Module

The proposed intrusion detection systems utilize an IDS model grounded in bird swarm optimization to spot questionable behavior in IIoT networks. A stacked sparse autoencoder is combined with BSA to improve cyberattack detection and security breach categorization. The Autoencoder (AE) network is a kind of neural network that can find data even when tags are not there. Modules for encoding and decoding or reconstruction form the backbone of this network, which is trained *via* unsupervised backpropagation. The encoding module first flattens the original data, which the decoding module subsequently reconstructs. The objective of the training phase of the AE is to learn the internal attribute pattern of the dataset and to decrease the restoration error between the input and rebuilt data.

A sparse AE is an autoencoder that uses sparsity penalties as part of its training criteria. To train the network to process a single record efficiently, it is usual practice to construct the loss function by penalizing activations of hidden layers. Conversely, deep attributes that are not very complimentary to the real ones are produced by most sparse autoencoders since they train without considering the actual properties of the network architecture. Using layered sparse AE and efficient feature engineering, the authors of this paper tackle these difficulties. Stacking sparse AEs includes connecting the output of one hidden layer to the input of the next hidden layer in a multi-layer sparse AE architecture. In this configuration, the outputs of each AE are linked directly to the inputs of the AE that follows it. This study recommends sorting samples of data from IIoT networks using an SSAE. It is possible to combine the fundamental characteristics even further to create even more essential classification criteria using deep attributes in SSAE. To enhance its classification performance, SSAE employs the BSA approach.

5.4 Generative Adversarial Network

One of the most important and well-known DL approaches is the ability to produce features in malicious attack data that may avoid and mislead defensive systems. This allows one to witness the actual network assault. Two separate neural networks, a generator (G) and a differentiator (D), work together to improve the system *via* mutual reinforcement and competition. The generator creates malicious samples that seem like real data traffic but include a twist that renders them inauthentic. An entry's likelihood of having come from the real database is what a differentiator is supposed to ascertain. Used as a detractor, it can now tell the difference between real and fake products. The attackers do not know the basic parameters of the intrusion detection model, thus it is up to the differentiator to understand and teach the generator.

Figure 5.2 shows the concept of an intrusion detection system (IDS) that creates adversarial attacks using GANs. While the generator is used for adversary development, the differentiator excels in classifying data samples in the context of attack detection and classification. Throughout the learning phase, these two modules are in a constant state of competition: one module, the generator, is trying to lure the other, the differentiator, into falling for its tricks. This interesting zero-sum game allows both modules to enhance their performance.

The training phase of a GAN begins with sorting the learning dataset into benign and malicious samples. After adding some noise, the malicious samples are sent to the generator to be transformed into adversarial samples. The black-box intrusion detection system (BB-IDS) can distinguish between benign and malicious attack samples. To train the black-box IDS, the differentiator uses the recognized labels. The differentiator's outputs and the BB-IDS model's outputs are used to calculate the losses for both the generator and the differentiator.

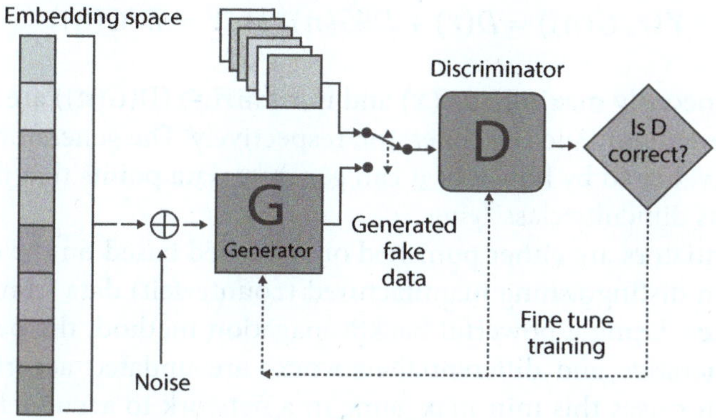

Figure 5.2 General architecture of GAN.

Given that the latent space noise input is n and the generator transfer function is G, the generated output function is (n). Similarly, r represents the actual sample, which is a set of one-dimensional vectors similar to different specified qualities. The differentiator unit's transfer function is represented by D. The differentiator takes two sets of inputs, denoted as a and (n). In its autonomous module version, the differentiator trains to compute the goal function by acting as a binary classification algorithm. As seen in Equation 5.1, the differentiator's output may be sensibly represented.

$$0, Y = D(r) \tag{5.1}$$

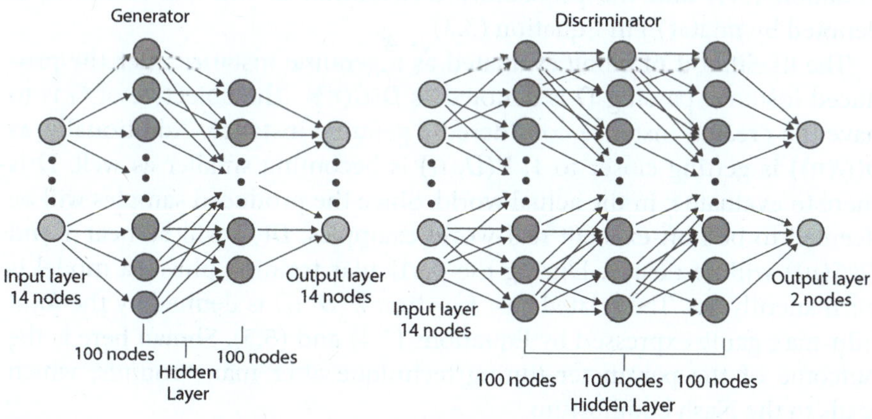

Figure 5.3 Structure of generator and differentiator in GAN.

$$Y(r, G(n)) = D(r) + D(G(n)) \{1, Y = D(G(n)) \tag{5.2}$$

Simultaneously maximizing (x) and minimizing (D($G(n)$)) are the goals of the differentiator and the generator, respectively. The generator's performance is evaluated by how well it can generate data points that the differentiator has difficulty classifying.

Differentiators are either punished or rewarded based on the degree of difficulty in distinguishing manufactured (counterfeit) data from authentic instances. Using a powerful backpropagation method, the parameters of the generative and differential networks are updated accordingly. A differentiator uses this min-max game in a network to accurately classify authentic and fake inputs. The model takes into account the combined impact of the differentiator and generator. So, the goal of a differentiator is to increase (D). Equation 5.3 has two parts: one has to do with better detection of real data samples and the other with better detection of created or false samples. To minimize (G), which is the differentiator cost function, it is necessary to fine-tune the generator settings. An appropriate representation of the same is given by Equations 5.3 and 5.4.

$$Max\mathrm{D}\ V(D) = E\mathrm{rpdata(r)}[\log D(r)] + E\mathrm{n{\approx}pn(n)}[\log(1 - D(G(n))] \tag{5.3}$$

$$Min\mathrm{G}\ V(G) = E\mathrm{n{\approx}pn(n)}[\log(1 - D(G(n))] \tag{5.4}$$

The prior distribution of the actual instances is denoted by $pn(n)$ in Equation (5.4) and the probability distribution of the real instances is denoted by $p\mathrm{data}(f)$ in Equation (5.3).

The likelihood of being evaluated as a genuine instance after the produced instance passing D is denoted as $D(G(n))$. The objective of G is to have the created instance considered a genuine instance. Additionally, as $b(G(n))$ is getting closer to 1, $V(D, G)$ is becoming smaller as well. D is there to evaluate r in the actual world. Since the produced samples will be deemed to be non-existent real-world examples, $D(f)$ will be near 1 and $D(G(n))$ will be near 0. During the particular training phase, a model is permanently set. The related cost function $X(D, G)$ is defined by the joint min-max game expressed by Equations (5.4) and (5.5). Shown here is the outcome of the parameter tuning technique after many rounds, which leads to the Nash equilibrium.

$$MinGMaxD\ V(G, D) = E\text{rpdata(r)}[\log D(r)] + E\text{n}{\approx}\text{pn(n)}[\log(1 - D(G(n))] \tag{5.5}$$

Since the generator is unaware of the database, it produces predictions at random. To start, the differentiator can easily tell the weak generator forecast apart from real data samples. It is possible for the differentiator to mistake the generator's fake samples for genuine ones when the generator's estimate grows and begins to seem more and more like actual data points from the database. Due to the increased losses it endures, the differentiator eventually learns to distinguish between generator-generated data and actual samples. In response to the differentiator's improved performance, the generator produces higher-quality data. If both networks are unable to improve once the differentiator reaches 50% classification accuracy, training should end. This process, called a min-max game, is an example of tactical pressure between competing decision-makers. Players in a min-max game avoid making hasty decisions to keep their maximum discrimination loss to a minimum. While two difficult multi-layer perceptron classification networks are part of the basic GAN model, any neural network model may be used by an efficient GAN model.

5.5 Datasets Used in This Work

Choosing the right databases to test IIoT network IDS models is turning out to be a real challenge. According to Aldwairi *et al.* (2018) [31], several studies have consistently investigated the importance of obtaining data samples that mimic real-world behavior without alteration or anonymization. If data is to be shared or made publicly available in response to certain requests, it will be severely modified or impossible to identify. A lot of private data will end up being thrown out or rendered unreliable because of this.

5.5.1 NSL-KDD Dataset

To tackle these problems, Tavallaee *et al.* (2009) [32] created a new database named NSL-KDD. It contains chosen records from the whole KDD database and complies with all the given limitations. This new database is an open-source database called NSL-KDD. Based on their probability distributions, the threat samples in this database are classified into four kinds as follows:

Looking Into: The collection of data about a system's computer equipment with the intent to change the security state of that system is a cyber threat.
Dos Attacks: These occur when the attacker discards approved user access to a network or makes processor or memory components very occupied or busy to accept permitted user requests.
User to Root (U2R) Attacks: In these attacks, the hacker impersonates a valid user and gains access to the network *via* that account. This account might have been obtained through social engineering, password sniffing, a dictionary attack, or some other means. The intruder may exploit the system's weakness to get root access.
Remote-to-Local (R2L) Cyberattacks: In these attacks, an attacker gains access to a system locally by exploiting its vulnerabilities and gaining unauthorized access using approved user information.

Table 5.1 lists a few of the attacks that have been carried out on the NSL-KDD dataset. According to Tavallaee *et al.* [32], this database consists of characteristics that according to Stirrat and Perrett (2009) [33], can be placed into three primary categories:

Intrinsic Properties: Property All features of Trojan detection are delayed, unwanted, and give even the most likelihood to collect from a Transmission Control Protocol/Internet Protocol (TCP/IP) friendship, and this variety estimates all of them.
Data Stream Attribute: According to Lee *et al.* (1999) [34], there are two sub-categories of features in this type that are looked at with respect to a window interval. In one sub-category, "Same Node Features" diversifies your entities according to service connections that share the same endpoint as the current connection and studies the service statistics and protocol enactment. In another sub-category, "Same Service Features" differentiates your entities according to service connections that share the

Table 5.1 Attack instances in NSL-KDD.

Class	Example attacks
Probing	ipsweep, nmap, portsweep, satan
DoS	back, land, neptune, pod, smurf, teardrop
U2R	buffer_overflow, loadmodule, perl, rootkit
R2L	ftp_write, guess_passwd, imap, multihop, spy, phf, warezclient, warezmaster

same analogous service as the current connection. These traits are called temporally linked aspects. On the other hand, many of the slow probing attacks check the ports (port or node) more frequently, every 1, 2, or 10 seconds, but with a longer cadence (> 2 seconds). Lowering the 2-second interval to what the assault will result in will still not generate these invasion patterns. This is solved by computing the same Port and Service feature but using a window of 100 connections instead of two seconds. These are connection-concerned traits.
U2R and R2L Attacks: U2R and R2L belong to DoS and probing threats and have no unique characteristics of attack instances that show consistent indicators. This is because DoS and probing attacks tend to have many service connections to some ports for continuous time, while R2L and U2R attacks often need only one connection and only within the data part of the packet. To identify these kinds of attacks, content elements are essential to track unusual behaviors in the payload, e.g., the number of failed logins.

Table 5.2 lists the 41 features of the NSL-KDD database used for differentiating data types, where 38 properties are numerical, and the remaining three are symbolic.

According to Tavallaee *et al.* [32], the dataset contains significantly fewer samples for outliers compared to normal ones. Indeed, according to Kim *et al.* [35], incursions occur frequently in standard data sets for the same reason as stated by Chawla *et al.* [36]. As you learn and test hypotheses while experimenting, it is important to take into account the ratio between Attack-to-Normal samples. Research captures samples that are used to fulfill data to get exactly 50% normal and 50% attack samples; this may be the balanced dataset. To ensure balanced training, the dataset should contain a similar number of attack and normal samples. Concurrently, this approach restricts samples across both groups from being reused, ensuring finer-grained testing of greater precision and thus a more accurate learning phase.

5.5.2 CIC-DDoS Dataset

In the CIC-DDoS database, there are 50,063,112 data samples. Out of this, 56,863 are non-traffic and 50,006,249 are traffic cases (Sharafaldin *et al.*, 2018) [37]. The database contains the data of 12 DDoS attacks with 84 associated characteristics. These attack samples are built around TFTP, DNS, SNMP, MSSQL, UDP-Lag, LDAP, SSDP, SYN attack, NTP, PortScan, and Web-DDoS. According to their probability distributions, the threats in this database are categorized into four types of attacks.

Table 5.2 Statistics of NSL-KDD.

Class	Number of instances	Distribution (%)
Normal	67343	53.45
DoS	11656	9.25
PRB	45927	36.45
R2L	995	0.79
U2R	52	0.041
Total	125973	100

1. TFTP Vulnerability: This is a kind of cyberattack that uses trivial file transfer protocol (TFTP) servers accessible from the internet. By default, it generates a file request where the TFTP server sends data to the requesting node, regardless of file name differences.
2. Cyberattack with a Connection to SNMP: This is a volumetric attack that uses the SNMP protocol to spam a large scale of data (in other words, hundreds of gigabits per second) into the network connection of the victim, rendering the victim unable to connect to the network.
3. Domain Name System (DNS)-Only Attack: This is an attack that relies on a DNS reflection being exploited by an attacker to flood a particular IP address with random queries using a botnet.
4. Microsoft SQL Server (MSSQL) Cyberattack: This is a reflection attack where an attacker impersonates the target MSSQLServer by faking an IP and performing the scripted request using the same fake IP address.
5. NetBIOS-Based Attack Vulnerability: This is more reflection-based—all an attacker has to do is send a target node a spoofed "Name Release" or "Name Conflict" message, and all NetBIOS data will be rejected.
6. User Datagram Protocol (UDP)-Lag: A cyberattack based on the recipient node with IP packets consisting of UDP data packets, which disrupts/slows down its function.
7. Attack Related to Lightweight Directory Access Protocol (LDAP): In this attack, an attacker tries to create large responses reflecting a target server by issuing queries to a vulnerable LDAP server available.
8. Simple Service Discovery Protocol (SSDP) Cyberattack: This cyberattack happens when an attacker sends a flood of packets to a target node *via* UPnP networking protocols.

9. SYN-Flooding Attack: This is a basic form of cyberattack using the normal three-way handshake (i.e., sending SYN, sending SYN-ACK, and replying with an ACK), exploiting the victim network server resources causing the server to stop responding.
10. Network Time Protocol (NTP) Amplification Cyberattack: In this attack, an attacker uses the NTP server feature to inundate (flood) a target client-server or other network with high-volume UDP datagrams. This threat can render the receiver and its communication links unusable to legitimate data streams.
11. PortScan: This is a cyberattack that performs a network security audit by scanning many ports of a particular node or the whole network. It scans with the help of requests to know what services are running on a remote host.
12. Web-DDoS-Related Cyberattack: In this attack, the hacker uses an original HTTP request (i.e., POST/GET: HTTP Methods (POST - Submit Data, GET - Retrieve Data)) to hack a web server or an application.

Table 5.3 illustrates 84 attributes of attempts to distinguish normal and malicious flows in the CIC-DDoS database.

The statistics for the CIC-DDoS dataset are summarized in Table 5.4.

5.6 Performance Measures Used for Evaluation

To examine the proposed IDS models' effectiveness, this study applies some important evaluation metrics, such as accuracy (ACC), sensitivity (SEN), specificity (SPE), precision (PRE), false negative rate (FNR), false positive rate (FPR), Jaccard similarity score [30], ρ-values, attack detection rate (ADR), and the consumed time for training and testing. The greater the value of these performance measures (except FNR, FPR, ρ-values, and time consumption), the better the performance of the IDS models.

Another measurement for the efficiency of the proposed IDS model is the false positive and the false negative ratios.

JavaScript stylesheets (JSS) measures how well a data classifier is working. The JSS, when evaluated on a dataset, quantifies the similarity of the contended class to the actual class of a sample in the filesystem.

Wilcoxon rank-sum test is a non-parametric statistical test. In this work, this evaluation is done to determine if the considered IDS model provides a significant augmentation with respect to another model. The rank-sum test and its effect on the intended model and each of the other models are evaluated at a 5% significance level. P-values above 5% mean that there is no significant difference between the two related values. Similarly, p-values < 5% indicate that there is a significant difference at this level. The results can be used as proof that the improvement obtained by the proposed IDS

Table 5.3 Attributes of CIC-DDoS dataset (Sharafaldin *et al.*, 2018) [37].

S. no.	Feature name	S. no.	Feature name	S. no.	Feature name	S. no.	Feature name
1	Flow ID	2	Source IP	3	Source Port	4	Destination IP
5	Destination Port	6	Protocol	7	Timestamp	8	Flow Duration
9	Total Fwd Packets	10	Total Backward Packets	11	Total Length of Fwd Packets	12	Total Length of Bwd Packets
13	Fwd Packet Length Max	14	Fwd Packet Length Min	15	Fwd Packet Length Mean	16	Fwd Packet Length Std
17	Bwd Packet Length Max	18	Bwd Packet Length Min	19	Bwd Packet Length Mean	20	Bwd Packet Length Std
21	Flow Bytes/s	22	Flow Packets/s	23	Flow IAT Mean	24	Flow IAT Std
25	Flow IAT Max	26	Flow IAT Min	27	Fwd IAT Total	28	Fwd IAT Mean
29	Fwd IAT Std	30	Fwd IAT Max	31	Fwd IAT Min	32	Bwd IAT Total
33	Bwd IAT Mean	34	Bwd IAT Std	35	Bwd IAT Max	36	Bwd IAT Min
37	Fwd PSH Flags	38	Bwd PSH Flags	39	Fwd URG Flags	40	Bwd URG Flags
41	Fwd Header Length	42	Bwd Header Length	43	Fwd Packets/s	44	Bwd Packets/s

(*Continued*)

Table 5.3 Attributes of CIC-DDoS dataset (Sharafaldin *et al.*, 2018) [37]. (*Continued*)

S. no.	Feature name	S. no.	Feature name	S. no.	Feature name	S. no.	Feature name
45	Min Packet Length	46	Max Packet Length	47	Packet Length Mean	48	Packet Length Std
49	Packet Length Variance	50	FIN Flag Count	51	SYN Flag Count	52	RST Flag Count
53	PSH Flag Count	54	ACK Flag Count	55	URG Flag Count	56	CWE Flag Count
57	ECE Flag Count	58	Down/Up Ratio	59	Average Packet Size	60	Avg Fwd Segment Size
61	Avg Bwd Segment Size	62	Fwd Header Length	63	Fwd Avg Bytes/ Bulk	64	Fwd Avg Packets/ Bulk
65	Fwd Avg Bulk Rate	66	Bwd Avg Bytes/ Bulk	67	Bwd Avg Packets/ Bulk	68	Bwd Avg Bulk Rate
69	Subflow Fwd Packets	70	Subflow Fwd Bytes	71	Subflow Bwd Packets	72	Subflow Bwd Bytes
73	Init Win bytes forward	74	Init Win bytes backward	75	act data pkt fwd	76	min seg size forward
77	Active Mean	78	Active Std	79	Active Max	80	Active Min
81	Idle Mean	82	Idle Std	83	Idle Max	84	Idle Min

models is statistically relevant, as most of the p-values in the comparisons are < 5%, illustrating this behavior.

The cost of model building and testing refers to the time required to train and evaluate the proposed IDS for detecting new attack samples. This research adopts such timing costs to assess the performance detection process.

Table 5.4 Statistics of the CIC-DDoS dataset.

Class	Number of instances	Distribution (%)
Normal	56863	0.11
DDoS_TFTP	20082580	40.11
DdoS_SNMP	5159870	10.31
DdoS_DNS	5071011	10.13
DdoS_MSSQL	4522492	9.03
DdoS_NetBIOS	4093279	8.18
DdoS_UDP	3134645	6.26
DdoS_SSDP	2610611	5.21
DdoS_LDAP	2179930	4.35
DdoS_SYN	1582289	3.16
DdoS_NTP	1202642	2.40
DdoS_UDP-Lag	366461	0.73
DdoS_WebDDoS	439	0.00
Total	50063112	100

5.7 Conclusion

This chapter summarizes some of the advanced IDS models and their capabilities to aid in building a strong defense mechanism for seamless interaction among all the elements in the IIoT network environment without any fear of potential threats. Efficient DL algorithms for feature selection, classification, and optimization steps are proposed in the framework. Developed attack detection models distinguish the normal activities of the attackers in the network traffic. If the detection is perfect, an alarm will be used to alert the administrator about potentially dangerous situations. This chapter further elaborates on how the synthetic dataset is created using GAN to train the classifier that is used in the IDS model.

References

1. Atzori, L., Iera, A., Morabito, G., The Internet of Things: A survey. *Comput. Netw.*, 54, 15, 2787–2805, 2010.
2. Perera, C., Zaslavsky, A., Christen, P., Context aware computing for the Internet of Things: A survey. *IEEE Commun. Surv. Tutor.*, 16, 1, 414–454, 2014.
3. Gubbi, J., Buyya, R., Marusic, S., Palaniswami, M., Internet of Things (IoT): A vision, architectural elements, and future directions. *Future Gener. Comput. Syst.*, 29, 7, 1645–1660, 2013.

4. Al-Fuqaha, A., Guizani, M., Mohammadi, M., Aledhari, M., Ayyash, M., Internet of Things: A survey on enabling technologies, protocols, and applications. *IEEE Commun. Surv. Tutor.*, 17, 4, 2347–2376, 2015.
5. Ray, P.P., A survey on Internet of Things architectures. *J. King Saud Univ. Comput. Inf. Sci.*, 28, 3, 257–273, 2016.
6. Roman, R., Lopez, J., Mambo, M., Mobile edge computing, fog : A survey and analysis of security threats and challenges. *Future Gener. Comput. Syst.*, 78, 680–698, 2013.
7. Kouicem, D.E., Lagraa, N., Moussaoui, S., A survey of security and privacy in Internet of Things: From the perception layer to the network layer. *J. Netw. Comput. Appl.*, 116, 1–16, 2018.
8. Dinh, T.T.A., *et al.*, A survey of mobile cloud computing: Architecture, applications, and approaches. *Wireless Commun. Mobile Comput.*, 13, 18, 1587–1611, 2013.
9. Zheng, Y., *et al.*, A comprehensive survey on wireless body area networks: PHY, MAC, and network layers solutions. *J. Med. Syst.*, 37, 1, 1–14, 2013.
10. Borgia, E., The Internet of Things vision: Key features, applications, and open issues. *Comput. Commun.*, 54, 1–31, 2014.
11. Miorandi, D., Sicari, S., De Pellegrini, F., Chlamtac, I., Internet of things: Vision, applications and research challenges. *Ad Hoc Netw.*, 10, 7, 1497–1516, 2012.
12. Choudhary, V., Guha, P., Pau, G., Dhanaraj, R.K., Mishra, S., Automatic Classification of Cowpea Leaves Using Deep Convolutional Neural Network, in: *Smart Agricultural Technology*, p. 100209, Elsevier BV, Springer, Berlin, Germany, 2023.
13. Fernandez-Carames, T.M. and Fraga-Lamas, P., A review on the use of blockchain for the Internet of Things. *IEEE Access*, 6, 32979–33001, 2018.
14. Shi, W., *et al.*, Edge computing: Vision and challenges. *IEEE Internet Things J.*, 3, 5, 637–646, 2016.
15. Atzori, L., *et al.*, The social Internet of Things (SIoT)–When social networks meet the Internet of Things: Concept, architecture and network characterization. *Comput. Netw.*, 56, 16, 3594–3608, 2017.
16. Chen, M., *et al.*, Smart factory of industry 4.0: Key technologies, application case, and challenges. *IEEE Access*, 6, 6505–6519, 2018.
17. Afshar, S., *et al.*, Internet of Things (IoT) applications: A systematic review. *Technol. Soc.*, 55, 137–154, 2018.
18. Goyal, D., *et al.*, Recent advances in Internet of Things (IoT): A review. *J. Comput. Electron. Agric.*, 139, 1–13, 2016.
19. Aloi, G., *et al.*, A survey of machine learning techniques for IoT devices and sensors. *Comput. Electr. Eng.*, 75, 297–317, 2019.
20. Bassi, A., *et al.*, A survey of architectures and scenarios in IoT-enabled smart cities. *IEEE Access*, 6, 7606–7625, 2018.
21. Prakash, V., Williams, A., Garg, L., *et al.*, Cloud-Based Framework for Performing Digital Forensic Investigations. *Int. J. Wireless Inf. Netw.*, 29, 419–441, 2022.

22. Li, S., *et al.*, Industrial big data analytics for prediction of remaining useful life of machine tools. *IEEE Access*, 6, 65961–65970, 2018.
23. Sundmaeker, H., *et al.*, *Vision and challenges for realising the Internet of Things*, Cluster of European Research Projects on the Internet of Things (CERP-IoT), IEEE, New York, USA, 2010.
24. Zeng, D., *et al.*, Cloud computing-based manufacturing: IT framework, architecture, and platform. *IEEE Trans. Ind. Inf.*, 9, 3, 1212–1222, 2013.
25. Zhou, K., *et al.*, Machine learning on big data: Opportunities and challenges. *Neurocomputing*, 237, 350–361, 2016.
26. Lee, E.A., Cyber physical systems: Design challenges, in: *2008 11th IEEE international symposium on object and component-oriented real-time distributed computing*, IEEE, pp. 363–369, 2008.
27. Kambatla, K., *et al.*, Trends in big data analytics. *J. Parallel Distrib. Comput.*, 74, 7, 2561–2573, 2014.
28. Ali, A., Dhanaraj, R.K., Nayyar, A., A high performance-oriented AI-enabled IoT-based pest detection system using sound analytics in large agricultural field, in: *Microprocessors and Microsystems*, vol. 103, p. 104946, Elsevier BV, Elsevier, Amsterdam, Netherlands, 2023.
29. Estrin, D., *et al.*, Open data: Opportunities and challenges. *IEEE Internet Comput.*, 19, 4, 68–71, 2015.
30. Guinard, D. and Trifa, V., Interacting with the Internet of Things: An open end-to-end architecture for IoT. *IEEE Commun. Mag.*, 54, 7, 32–39, 2016.
31. Aldwairi, T., Al-Hussaini, M., Al-Khamaiseh, S., Evaluating the performance of machine learning techniques in the classification of NSL-KDD intrusion detection dataset. *Int. J. Comput. Sci. Inf. Secur.*, 16, 9, 97–104, 2018.
32. Tavallaee, M., Bagheri, E., Lu, W., Ghorbani, A.A., A detailed analysis of the KDD CUP 99 data set, in: *Proceedings of the 2009 IEEE Symposium on Computational Intelligence for Security and Defense Applications (CISDA)*, pp. 1–6, IEEE, 2009, https://doi.org/10.1109/CISDA.2009.5356528.
33. Stirrat, M. and Perrett, D.I., Valid facial cues to cooperation and trust: Male facial width and trustworthiness. *Psychol. Sci.*, 21, 3, 349–354, 2009, https://doi.org/10.1177/0956797610362647.
34. Lee, W., Stolfo, S.J., Mok, K.W., A data mining framework for building intrusion detection models, in: *Proceedings of the 1999 IEEE Symposium on Security and Privacy*, pp. 120–132, IEEE, 1999, https://doi.org/10.1109/SECPRI.1999.766909.
35. Kim, G., Lee, S., Kim, S., A novel hybrid intrusion detection method integrating anomaly detection with misuse detection. *Expert Syst. Appl.*, 41, 4, 1690–1700, 2014, https://doi.org/10.1016/j.eswa.2013.08.066.
36. Chawla, N.V., Bowyer, K.W., Hall, L.O., Kegelmeyer, W.P., SMOTE: Synthetic Minority Over-sampling Technique. *J. Artif. Intell. Res.*, 16, 321–357, 2002, https://doi.org/10.1613/jair.953.
37. Sharafaldin, I., Lashkari, A.H., Ghorbani, A.A., Toward generating a new intrusion detection dataset and intrusion traffic characterization, in: *Proceedings of the 4th International Conference on Information Systems Security and Privacy (ICISSP)*, pp. 108–116, 2018, https://doi.org/10.5220/0006639801080116.

6

Modern Application for Smart Applications in Traffic Management

S. Selvi[1]*, A. Jasmine Gilda[1], K.V. Sreelekha[2], N. Banu Priya[1], Sajithra S.[1] and Lekshmi S. R.[3]

[1]R.M.K. Engineering College, Kavaraipettai, Tamil Nadu, India
[2]Department of Computer Science and Engineering, Hindusthan College of Engineering and Technology, Coimbatore, India
[3]LBS Institute Technology for Women Poojappura, Thiruvananthapuram, India

Abstract

As defenses against privacy invasion, Masquerade Technologies has contracted the third-party company Titian Media to lease its consumer database, which contains two hundred and thirty-six million names. This database consists of information about 90% of China's population. Because credit card is tied to a person's income and other information instead of the operating institution, thus rebuilding this model can immediately expose users' private information to the public, and those affected may take prompt legal action. Like it or not, traffic congestion is something the public cannot tolerate. This paper proposes an IoT-based traffic management solution to address traffic-related issues and guide ambulance drivers to find the signal status and choose the path where traffic flow can be manipulated. Traffic violations can be identified by onsite traffic officers controlled over the Internet. The system involves a framework where a couple of sensors, like infra red (IR) sensor and radio frequency identification (RFID), interface with node Microcontroller Unit (MCU) to operate in line with the principles of IoT. Normal cities can be changed to clever ones by taking advantage of this technique. IoT can play a major role in advancing this type of process. Along with the proposed new method of testing out the number of automobiles that pass by, traffic flow at its source will also smoothen up. The proposed method is general and can be easily implemented in any metropolitan city. This proposed work provides transportation authorities, urban planners, and lawmakers with information they can use

**Corresponding author*: ssi.cse@rmkec.ac.in

R. Sathiyaraj, Rajesh Kumar Dhanaraj, K. Arun Kumar, Rutvij H. Jhaveri and A. Mohamed Abbas (eds.) Predictive Methods in Next-Generation Computing: An Approach Toward Sustainability, (107–124)

to improve mobility, build more sustainable cities, and keep up with the newest innovations in smart traffic management.

Keywords: Safety, efficiency, sustainability, urbanization, IoT, artificial intelligence

6.1 Introduction

Finding an empty parking spot in a city may be a tiresome ordeal for drivers. In addition to the energy and time wasted, the emissions from vehicles contribute to pollution in the environment throughout this procedure [1]. If the motorist is unable to find a parking spot, they may get irate and park illegally, increasing the risk of an accident. Unless we find a way to reduce the ever-increasing traffic on our roads, this situation will only worsen in the years to come. Numerous automated unoccupied parking spot identification systems have been developed as a result of this problem's recognition by both industry and academia [2]. To illustrate the point, gate arm counters placed at parking spaces' entrances and exits may provide the overall inventory of available unoccupied lots, but they cannot direct the car to a specific vacant spot. Alternatively, you might install magnetic or ultrasonic sensors for every batch. Commercial alternatives exist. This subset of automated parking spot identification systems has recently attracted a lot of attention due to falling camera prices and developments in computer vision and machine learning [3].

One of the most desired amenities by city inhabitants is a smart parking management system that updates vehicles in real-time on the number and location of available parking spots. Using established parking lot borders, this study suggests a machine learning method for autonomously detecting empty lots in delimited parking spots.

Using publicly available datasets that include pictures of actual parking spots, the suggested technique stands up to big intra-class variability of automobiles as well as substantial differences in size and position within each lot.

Smart parking systems that use convolutional neural networks achieve very accurate classifications, but they are incompatible with the new paradigm of disconnected feature extraction and analysis and need very expensive hardware. Systems that handle images in the network's periphery need efficient processing, small features, and the ability to extract and classify features independently.

6.2 Related Work

To identify available parking spots, histogram of oriented gradients (HOG) characteristics are merged into a comprehensive 3D model of the parking lot in [10]. To identify parking and unparking occurrences, [11] employs gaussian mixture model (GMM) background subtraction in conjunction with transience map analysis. In addition to using a comparable method, Kalman filter tracking is also used in [12–16].

It is a diminutive variant of the well-known AlexNet. Another parking dataset, CNRPark-Ext, is introduced in [17]. [18] detects parking status using a 3D cuboid model of each lot using multilayer characteristics. However, it takes a lot of effort to manually define the 3D structure of the parking lots. To simplify matters and eliminate, or at least mitigate, the impacts of inter-object occlusion, it is possible to define the lot borders directly in the pictures while considering the camera viewpoint [19]. Because of this, it satisfies the energy and bandwidth requirements of a wireless application while producing less multimedia data. However, due to the limited processing capacity at the nodes, the system relies on basic visual data (the hue histogram of each parking lot), which leads to slightly poor accuracy. Vehicle detection in prohibited lanes is a related topic. To determine how long a car has been parked, the authors of [20] encode spatial-temporal data pertaining to halted cars in a heat map. [21] detects cars parked illegally by using spatio-temporal maps of intersection sites.

Using sensors placed on vehicles (such as surround-view cameras) to identify available parking spots is an alternative area of study that has recently gained traction [22–25]. Techniques based on free space and methods based on parking slot marking are two broad categories into which the various approaches fall [23]. Finding vacant spaces between cars is the goal of free space techniques, while approaches based on slot markings search for painted parking slot markings [24].

6.3 Delimited Spaces: Proposed Method

To solve this issue using machine learning, we can first collect data from the parking lots and then feed it into a trained classifier that can tell us which lots are empty and which ones are full. Only visual attributes, not motion ones, are usable since the automobiles never move. There are two types of vehicle cosmetic features: global and local. Occlusion and variations in lighting may significantly impact global characteristics. Most current methods for detecting vehicles rely on local characteristics and some kind of geometric restriction, either implicit or explicit, in their interrelationship. To make use of the feature vectors for vehicle and non-vehicle classification, it is common practice to model the backdrop in the same way. The majority of its use, however, has been in static environments, such as car rearview cameras for on-road driver assistance, where the perspective does not change. From one picture to the next, the geometric limitations between the features are preserved. The size and position of vehicles might vary greatly from one parking area to another. Depending on where you are, the camera could provide a front, back, side, or top perspective. Vehicles in nearby areas often partially block these views. Additionally, there are two possible methods to park a vehicle in the same space.

The provided local qualities will vary from one place to another over time. A potential approach in this case would be to create a set of feature templates and compare the local features in each location to these templates, without imposing geometrical constraints between the features. The bag of features (BoF) representation effectively achieves this.

Also included in the databases are the lot boundaries, or the four corners of a rectangle. Our approach for addressing problems consists of four steps:

1. Make a new image for each lot using the aforementioned tools.
2. For every lot, create a vector using the BoF format. Figure 6.1 shows the some example of delimited parking spaces.

Figure 6.1 Some examples of delimited parking spaces.

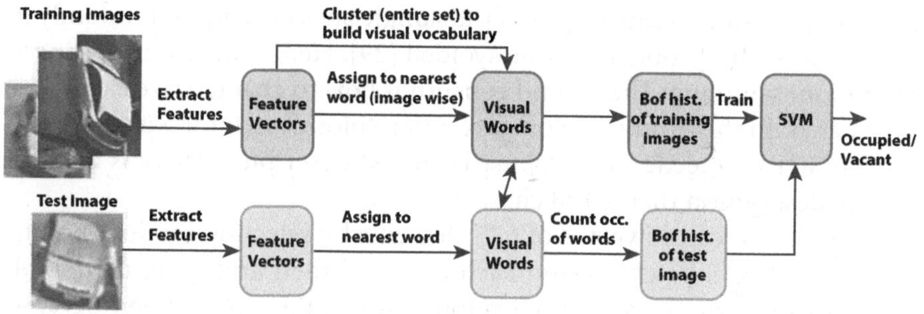

Figure 6.2 Block diagram of the proposed method for delimited spaces.

6.3.1 Bag of Features (BoF)

A number of computer vision applications, including picture classification and image retrieval [26], have benefited from the bag of features approach's [27] rise to the top in recent years. It is possible that CNN-based deep learning algorithms have recently outperformed the bag-of-features technique for picture categorization. However, smaller-scale applications, like surveillance, where there are fewer training pictures and less computer power, make the BoF technique a good competitor.

An improvement on the bag of words method, the bag of features method sorts text documents into groups according to their contents. Although it shows how often the words appear, the depiction does not convey their location in the text. The vocabulary words are selected in a way that allows them to discriminate between different types of documents. It is possible to categorize texts using the bag of words representation in conjunction with strong classification algorithms.

The use of BoF representation to depict cars, however, has been the subject of very few publications.

6.4 Implementation Details

There are a lot of choices at each stage in the BoF's multi-step process. It is necessary to decide on implementation details such as picture sampling, image description, descriptor quantization, and classification. Identifying relevant areas inside images is the primary concern.

On unoccupied lots with a simple concrete surface, the situation is worse than on inhabited lots. Even with the lowest corner threshold setting, sufficient points were detected. Conversely, these level areas serve as a helpful indicator that the property is unoccupied. Another popular option is to sample using a regular grid. If the sample sites are chosen randomly in each picture, this problem may be avoided [29]. Hence, we use an approach of random sampling. The second concern is how to characterize each sampled patch. In this study, we compare a raw color descriptor with the well-known SURF (Speeded Up Robust Features) descriptor. There is a SURF feature description that is 128 characters long.

We create a feature vector of 675 elements by selecting random points, defining a 15x15 patch around each one, and then arranging their RGB values as a vector. The size of the automobiles in the cropped photographs was taken into account while deciding on this patch size. You cannot get unique designs on a vehicle with a smaller patch size. The simplicity, ease of calculation, and visual nature of this raw color descriptor are its main features. The possibility of combining SURF with color descriptors is also investigated.

6.4.1 Datasets

There are three distinct parts to the PKLot dataset: UFPR04, UFPR05, and PUCPR. Each part contains 28, 40, and 100 monitored parking lots, respectively. The first two parts show the same parking spot from various vantage points. The third one provides a higher-altitude shot of a different parking lot than the previous two. The photographs are taken at five-minute intervals using an inexpensive camera in various weather conditions over several days. There are also individual parking lot cropped pictures available. Each subset contains 105, 485, 165, 785, 695, and 899 photos of segmented lots, respectively. In each frame, eXtensible markup language (XML) files are tagged with the occupancy status of all lots.

Despite its modest size, the CNRPark dataset comprises 12,584 photos of a parking lot shot from two distinct angles. With 144,965 photos taken by nine cameras with varying degrees of field of view on several days in varying weather conditions, the CNRPark-Ext dataset expands upon the original CNRPark dataset and adds occlusions caused by trees, lampposts, and other vehicles. Compared to PKLot, the picture quality at CNRPark and CNRPark-Ext appears to be higher. Unfortunately, you can only download segmented photos of certain parking lots. Hence, certain patches do not line up with the exact lot borders. In contrast, the segmented pictures in the PKLot dataset are either square or rectangular in shape and range in size to reflect the lot borders. Our BoF technique works well with photos of varying sizes and does not need any image scaling, unlike convolutional neural network (CNNs). The accuracy metric is used to measure the performance of classification systems.

An important aspect of BoF is the selection of the visual dictionary. The effect of a larger visual term lexicon on classification accuracy is the subject of the first study.

Figure 6.3 displays the sample frame. There are more than 100,000 individual photos of segmented lots, with 44% being inhabited and 56% being unoccupied. These images are taken under varying weather conditions and on various days. You may only utilize images captured on the same day for testing or training, not both. The PKLot authors propose this evaluation methodology to prevent duplicate cars from showing up in both the training and testing sets at the same time. The word counts that are examined are 500, 1,000, and 1,500 words, as shown in Figure 6.6. Both situations use

Figure 6.3 Output image from dataset 1.

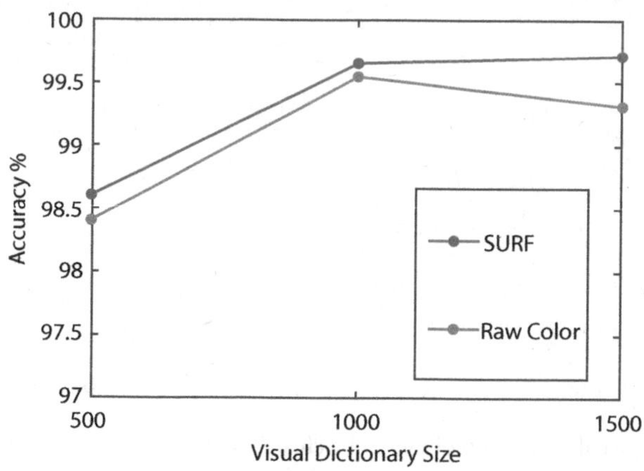

Figure 6.4 Accuracy graph of proposed work.

random sampling. The feature histogram of a picture is built by assigning the descriptors to the closest visual word. If more than one visual word is very close to a particular description, the closest one will be used to describe that aspect size keeps growing, the number of identical terms in the assignments keeps growing, and the discriminative capability keeps decreasing.

6.4.2 Experiment 2: Original and Split Dictionaries

A different approach to building the visual lexicon is investigated in this experiment. Compared to the vocabulary in Figure 6.5, this 1,000-word lexicon is somewhat more discriminative. In both instances, some visual

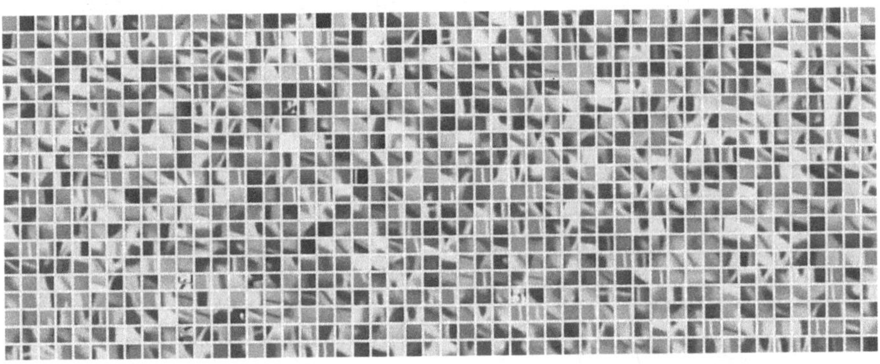

Figure 6.5 Output dataset of UFPR04.

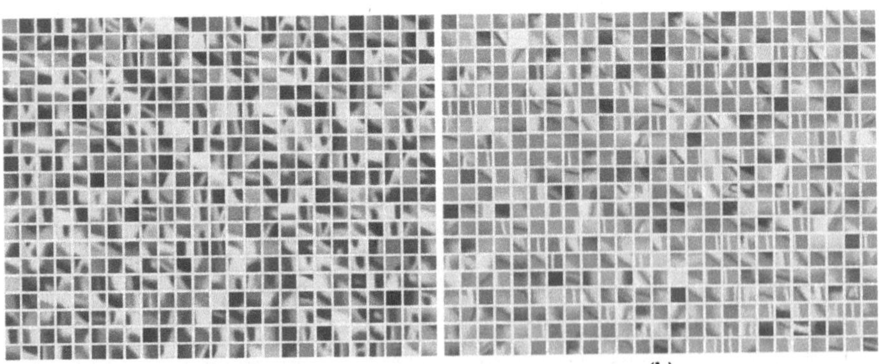

Figure 6.6 The visual dictionary obtained by clustering features from occupied and vacant training images separately: (a) 500 words from the occupied class, (b) 500 words from the vacant class.

terms, such as edges with different orientations, are seen as having low-level semantic meaning, while others, like car components, are perceived as having higher-level semantic meaning. Figure 6.4 displays the classification accuracy for the PKlot-UFPR04 and CNRPark databases using the original dictionary and the Split dictionary.

6.4.3 Experiment 3: Feature Fusion

The naïve color descriptor's high classification accuracy, which is close to SURF's (which uses just grayscale values) performance, suggests that color is useful for differentiating automobiles from backgrounds. Another experiment is carried out by merging the SURF and color descriptors in two distinct methods to see whether there would be a performance advantage from integrating the two. In the first scenario, visual dictionary learning precedes the combination of color and SURF descriptors (Desc. concat.). The second scenario involves learning two visual dictionaries and then merging the histograms that are produced (Hist. concat.).

The fact that classification accuracy is enhanced in both instances suggests that the color and SURF descriptors work well together. Table 6.1 displays the results of testing the concatenation techniques on the CNRPark dataset, which demonstrate an increase in accuracy.

We employ a portion of the training set for learning the visual dictionary and training the support vector machine (SVM) to show that our technique needs less training than CNNs. A randomly chosen 30% of the photos from CNRPark and CNRParkExt cameras C1–C8 make up the training set. The CNN trained by [20] takes full advantage of this collection, which

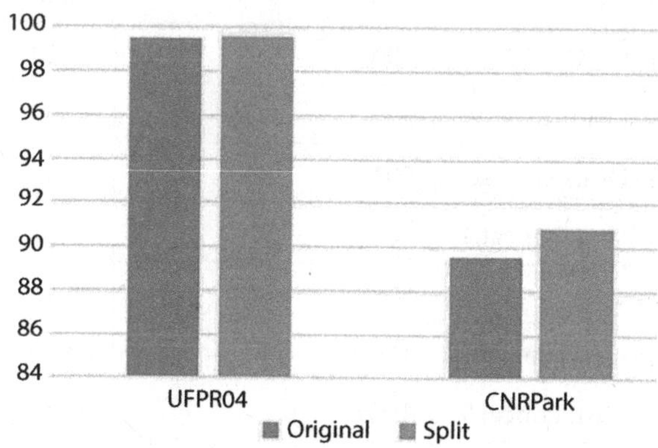

Figure 6.7 Classification accuracy with original and split dictionaries.

Table 6.1 Accuracy improvement with feature fusion-CNRPark.

Method	Accuracy
Prop(SURF desc.)	88.44
Prop(Color desc.)	90.89
Prop(Desc. concat.)	91.24
Prop(Hist. concat.)	91.10

includes photographs taken from a variety of perspectives. In [21], this set of training data is represented by CNRPark+ExtTrain C1–C8. When conducting tests, we adhere to the same test set as previously described in [22] (denoted by CNRParkExtTest). The suggested technique achieves classification accuracy similar to convolutional networks with this tiny percentage of training data. Utilizing half of the training set improves accuracy compared to mAlexNet [23], which trains on the whole set. When there

Table 6.2 Performance with reduced training.

Method	Training images used	Accuracy
Prop(SURF desc.)	30%	96.31
Prop(Color desc.)	30%	93.76
Prop(Desc. concat.)	30%	95.75
Prop(Hist. concat.)	30%	95.12
mAlexNet	30%	90.28
Prop(SURF desc.)	50%	95.18
Prop(Color desc.)	50%	96.50
Prop(Desc. concat.)	50%	96.48
Prop(Hist. concat.)	50%	96.57
mAlexNet	50%	96.42
Prop(Desc. concat.)	100%	96.48
Prop(Hist. concat.)	100%	96.59
mAlexNet	100%	95.88

Table 6.3 Generalization performance.

Method	Train on	Test on	Accuracy
Prop(SURF desc.)	PKLot2Days	CNRPark	78.27
Prop(Color desc.)	PKLot2Days	CNRPark	80.23
Prop(Desc. concat.)	PKLot2Days	CNRPark	81.15
Prop(Hist. concat.)	PKLot2Days	CNRPark	81.69
mAlexNet	PKLot2Days	CNRPark	82.88
LBP	PKLot2Days	CNRPark	65.31

are fewer training examples available, the suggested technique works much better, according to the test findings [4–9]. Table 6.2 displays the findings of this experiment's accuracy analysis.

This experiment examines how well the suggested strategy may be applied to different situations. When compared to the state-of-the-art methodologies, the accuracy values shown in Table 6.3 demonstrate competitive performance.

6.4.4 Results: Delimited Spaces

Using the three most current public parking datasets referenced in Section 6.3.3, we evaluate the suggested approach for delimited spots. The results are compared to state-of-the-art methodologies and given in terms of classification accuracy.

The histograms are quite sparse since computing performance was prioritized, and only 10 characteristics were extracted from each picture (at least 990 of the 1,000 bins are empty). Vectors with a high degree of sparsity boost performance [28].

There are two main benefits to the suggested strategy. The first is that the original rectangular photos may be used in a variety of sizes. Time is saved during training and testing by skipping the procedure of picture scaling. Using pictures of a certain size also makes it harder to adapt the algorithm to other situations, such as the one described in the non-delimited space proposal, where features need to be recovered from areas with irregular shapes caused by background removal. The second perk of the suggested approach is that it minimizes the number of photographs needed for training, which is a huge plus for any system like this that aims for real-world implementation.

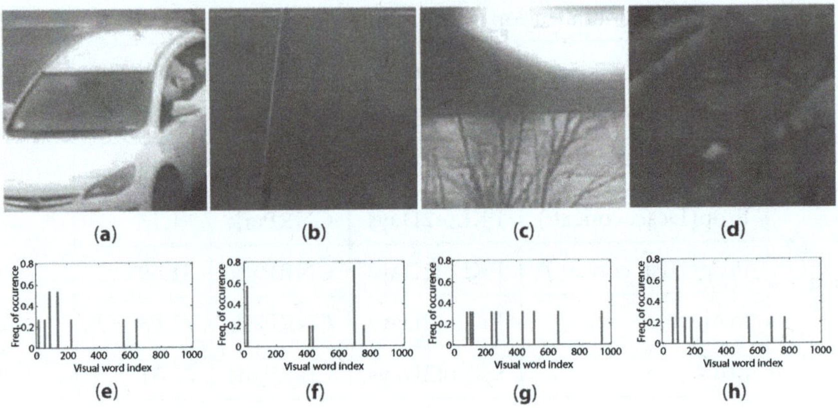

Figure 6.8 A collection of data using AlexNet.

Table 6.4 Summary of results.

Method	Dataset	Accuracy
Prop(Desc. concat.)	UFPR04	99.72
Prop(Hist. concat.)	UFPR04	99.66
mAlexNet	UFPR04	99.54
Mean	UFPR04	99.64
LPQu	UFPR04	99.55
Hue Hist.	UFPR04	96.00
Prop(Desc. concat.)	CNRPark	91.24
Prop(Hist. concat.)	CNRPark	91.10
mAlexNet	CNRPark	90.71
LBP	CNRPark	87.21
Prop(Hist. concat.)	CNRParkExt	96.59
Prop(Desc. concat.)	CNRParkExt	96.48
mAlexNet	CNRParkExt	95.88
AlexNet	CNRParkExt	96.85

Table 6.5 Confusion matrix for CNRPark-Color desc.

Known	Predicted occupied	Vacant
Occupied	3581	389
Vacant	173	2028

6.5 Non-Delimited Spaces: Proposed Method

There are parking spots that do not have their own distinct lots. Cars of all shapes, sizes, and orientations may be scattered over the parking lot. The two processes are known as hypothesis testing and hypothesis creation, respectively [30]. To generate hypotheses, we use background subtraction, and to verify them, we repeat our previous procedure using BoF+SVM.

6.5.1 Background Subtraction for Hypothesis Generation

The initial step in locating possible vehicle zones is to use a sample-based background removal technique, much like the ones described in Chapter 2. Because they all assume the backdrop is exposed often, background subtraction algorithms have a tough time detecting items like parked automobiles that stay still for extended periods. Backgrounds are obscured and the background model is not refreshed when automobiles are parked for long durations.

Incorrect initialization is another potential cause of ghost areas. For example, if an automobile is in the initialization frames but then goes out of the frame, the foreground will be the exposed backdrop. Background subtraction cannot be relied upon alone for detection purposes. Background subtraction is, therefore, reserved for detection suggestions only (hypothesis generation). If the background removal method produces an incorrect hypothesis—for example, a previously hidden background region—the trained SVM classifier will disprove it during the hypothesis verification phase. In contrast, detection will go unnoticed if background subtraction is unable to provide a hypothesis for a zone containing a vehicle. Camouflage, where the vehicle's color scheme closely matches that of the surrounding environment, could cause this to occur. Consequently, we sacrifice some accuracy in favor of a lower rate of false negatives by adjusting the parameters of our background removal method. For this application, the relevant parameters of the sample-based background subtraction are as follows:

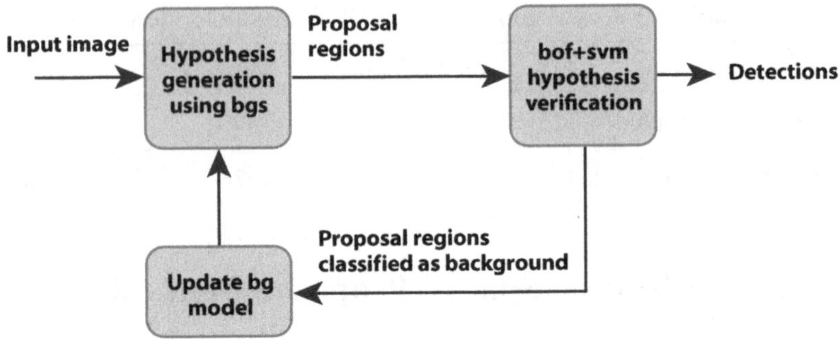

Figure 6.9 Block diagram of the proposed method for non-delimited spaces.

#min = 3, minimum number of matches needed = 3; distance threshold in each color channel = 10; and number of samples in the background model = 20. This implies a closer #min = 3 and a stricter R = 10 distance requirement when contrasted with the techniques given in Chapter 2. When contrasted with the general-purpose approaches discussed in Chapter 2, this leads to an increase in the number of false positives and false negatives. Prior to this, it was said that the act of verifying the hypothesis fixes false positives but not false negatives.

Similar to the first two chapters, this one explains how to initialize and segment the model, as well as post-process and identify shadows. However, instead of updating the background model immediately, it waits until the SVM classifier output is ready. The SVM updates all pixels in the hypothesized areas, including ghost regions, that are classified as background. The updated pixel value is substituted into the backdrop model to replace a random sample during the update.

For each frame, the potential object areas are identified using the pixel-level background removal and shadow detection technique. The SVM classifier processes the BoF characteristics obtained from the hypothesized areas and assigns a vehicle or non-vehicle classification to each region, as shown in Figure 6.9.

6.5.2 Results: Non-Delimited Spaces

Figure 6.10b is another test frame from the same folder; however, in this one, three automobiles are parked, while during the initialization phase, all of the cars were present, as seen in Figure 6.10c. The bottom right corner of Figure 6.10c has a ghost blob caused by the automobile parked beneath the tree during the initialization frame. Figure 6.10a

(a) (b) (c)

Figure 6.10 (a) Sample initialization frame, (b) test frame, and (c) result of background subtraction on the test frame.

shows that the automobile is heavily obscured by vegetation. Thus, the matching blob in Figure 6.10c is not completely clean; there are missing parts of the vehicle. However, since it is still linked, feature extraction treats the whole area as one. Before feeding them into the SVM classifier, BoF characteristics are retrieved from all six areas. All six areas—three for objects and three for backgrounds—were accurately identified by the classifier.

No more ghost regions in subsequent frames thanks to the revised backdrop model (see Figures 6.10c). No data pertaining to the lot borders were used in this experiment. In this non-delimited example, we manually counted the cars and calculated the Precision and Recall metrics as the ground realities are not accessible.

Multiple vehicles could be mistakenly identified as one due to blob merging since the BoF histogram is built region-wise. Convexity analysis of the blobs is one of the ways that have been suggested in the literature as a way to separate the blobs.

6.6 Conclusion

This study tackles the issue of parking space shortages, which is a significant concern for those who drive in metropolitan areas. Experimental analysis is used to examine and identify the optimal options for the sampling process, dictionary size, descriptors, and descriptor fusion. For this binary classification task, a small visual dictionary size of 1,000 is determined to be adequate, since it decreases processing time. It is possible to handle many video feeds at once since this application has a moderate real-time demand, which is readily accomplished (in fact, updating the parking status once per minute or so should be plenty).

References

1. Zhang, H. and Sun, Y., Smart Traffic Management System Based on Internet of Things Technology. *IEEE Access*, 8, 12567–12580, 2020.
2. Wei, L. and Cao, Y., Artificial Intelligence in Traffic Management: A Review. *Transp. Res. Part C Emerg. Technol.*, 103, 34–48, 2019.
3. Yang, Y. and Wang, F., Big Data Analytics in Traffic Management: A Survey. *IEEE Trans. Intell. Transp. Syst.*, 20, 5, 1800–1812, 2018.
4. Liu, X. and Yu, B., Real-Time Traffic Management System Based on IoT and Big Data Technologies. *J. Mod. Transp.*, 25, 3, 257–270, 2017.
5. Lee, K. and Ha, J., Intelligent Transportation Systems: New Trends and Challenges. *J. Adv. Transp.*, 2019, 7834523, 1–14, 2019.
6. Department of Transportation, DOT Publications, Washington, D.C., USA, 2020.
7. Abdul-Rahman, H. and El-Kharashi, M., Smart Traffic Management using Machine Learning Techniques. *Int. J. Comput. Sci. Inf. Secur.*, 16, 4, 115–128, 2018.
8. European Commission, *Intelligent Transportation Systems for Smart Cities*, EC Publications, European Commission, Brussels, Belgium, 2017.
9. Li, J. and Tang, L., Urban Traffic Management Based on Big Data Analytics. *J. Traffic Transp. Eng.*, 6, 2, 210–225, 2019.
10. Memon, S. and Shaikh, Z., IoT-based Traffic Management System: A Review. *J. Comput. Netw. Commun.*, 2018, 4369823, 1–11, 2018.
11. Li, Z. and Liu, L., Deep Learning Applications in Traffic Management: A Comprehensive Review. *IEEE Trans. Intell. Transp. Syst.*, 21, 4, 1501–1515, 2020.
12. World Bank, *Smart Mobility Solutions for Urban Traffic Management*, World Bank Publications, World Bank, Washington, D.C., USA, 2019.
13. United Nations, *Smart Cities for Sustainable Development: Traffic Management Strategies*, UN Publications, United Nations, New York, USA, 2018.
14. Chien, S. and Tsai, J., Smart Traffic Management Systems: Concepts and Applications. *J. East. Asia Soc. Transp. Stud.*, 2017.
15. Ghosh, S. and Saha, M., Smart Traffic Management using IoT and Cloud Computing. *Int. J. Eng. Res. Appl.*, 9, 7, 92–102, 2019.
16. Al Ogaili, R.R.N., Alomari, E.S., Alkorani, M.B.M., *et al.*, Malware cyberattacks detection using a novel feature selection method based on a modified whale optimization algorithm. *Wireless Netw.*, 29, 2, 213–226, 2023.
17. National Institute of Standards and Technology, NIST Publications, Gaithersburg, Maryland, USA, 2020.
18. Khan, M. and Asif, M., IoT-based Traffic Congestion Management: A Review. *J. Commun.*, 12, 5, 98–112, 2017.

19. Rajesh Kumar Dhanaraj, S.K., Seifedine Kadry, B.-G.K., Byeong-Gwon Kang, Y.N., Probit Cryptographic Blockchain for Secure Data Transmission in Intelligent Transportation Systems, in: 網際網路技術學刊, vol. 23, pp. 1303–1313, Angle Publishing Co., Ltd, Taipei, Taiwan, 2022, https://doi.org/10.53106/160792642022112306013.
20. Liang, X. and Zhang, H., Fuzzy Logic Control for Adaptive Traffic Signal Management. *J. Adv. Transp.*, 2019, 6845231, 1–10, 2019.
21. Khatua, D. and Mohapatra, S., Urban Traffic Management through IoT and Cloud Computing. *Procedia Comput. Sci.*, 140, 343–350, 2018.
22. International Organization for Standardization, *ISO Standards for Intelligent Transportation Systems*, ISO Publications, Geneva, Switzerland, 2017.
23. Yang, Z. and Wang, H., Smart Traffic Management using Wireless Sensor Networks. *J. Sens.*, 2020, 8523467, 1–13, 2020.
24. Liu, W. and Wu, L., Intelligent Traffic Management based on Edge Computing. *IEEE Trans. Ind. Inf.*, 2018.
25. Roobini, S., Kavitha, M., Sujaritha, M., Rajesh Kumar, D., Cyber-Security Threats to IoMT-Enabled Healthcare Systems, in: *Cognitive Computing for Internet of Medical Things*, pp. 105–130, Chapman and Hall/CRC, Boca Raton, Florida, USA, 2022.
26. Wang, Y. and Cheng, Z., Cloud Computing Applications in Traffic Management. *Future Gener. Comput. Syst.*, 95, 112–124, 2017.
27. European Union, *Smart Traffic Management Solutions for Sustainable Cities*, EU Publications, European Union, Brussels, Belgium, 2018.
28. Yu, C. and Lee, Y., Smart Traffic Management using Machine Learning and IoT. *J. Ambient Intell. Hum. Comput.*, 10, 5, 1102–1115, 2019.
29. Transportation Research Board, *Emerging Technologies in Traffic Management*, TRB Publications, Washington, D.C., USA, 2020.
30. Al-Qatab, A. and Harbi, A., Smart Traffic Management with Geographic Information Systems. *J. Geogr. Inf. Syst.*, 9, 3, 98–110, 2018.

7

Artificial Intelligence and Deep Learning in Healthcare: Evaluation, Opportunities, Challenges and Future Prospects Technologies in Healthcare Systems

Rakesh Ahuja[1]*, Gurpreet Kour Khalsa[2], Vijaita Kashyap[1], Himanshi Babbar[1], Ravi Kumar Sachdeva[1] and G. S. Pradeep Ghantasala[3]

[1]*Chitkara University of Institute of Engineering and Technology, Chitkara University, Punjab, India*

[2]*SRM Institute of Science & Technology Delhi NCR Campus Modinagar Ghaziabad, Uttar Pradesh, India*

[3]*Department of Computer Science and Engineering, Alliance University, Bengaluru, India*

Abstract

Advances in drug research are made possible by artificial intelligence techniques. Numerous obstacles and hurdles, including poor effectiveness, off-target delivery, lengthy development times, and high costs, affect drug research and development. Moreover, a huge amount of complicated data sets that are available from proteomics, genomes, clinical trials, and microarrays block the procedure of drug evolution. In this sense, Artificial intelligence (AI) and deep learning (DL) are critical components of the drug development process. There are several drug discovery methods, such as structure-based virtual screening and ligand-based virtual screening, pharmacophore modeling, polypharmacy prediction of toxicity, based on virtual screening, peptide synthesis, drug monitoring, drug release, drug repositioning, physicochemical activity, and activity quantitative-based structure have been developed. This chapter describes the function of AI and DL in drug discovery. It also covers how many applications, what tools are being used, and what obstacles AI and DL are facing. In short, the chapter discusses the rise of AI

**Corresponding author*: ahuja2305@gmail.com

R. Sathiyaraj, Rajesh Kumar Dhanaraj, K. Arun Kumar, Rutvij H. Jhaveri and A. Mohamed Abbas (eds.) Predictive Methods in Next-Generation Computing: An Approach Toward Sustainability, (125–148)

and DL in drug development and healthcare data analytics. Finally, it discusses the encounters of artificial intelligence and deep learning models with the aspect of future vision for developing rural health.

Keywords: Deep learning, artificial intelligence, machine learning, drug discovery, international health regulations

7.1 Introduction

In general, finding and manufacturing new remedies takes between the ages of ten and fifteen years, and the process is infamously costly, laborious, and wasteful. To put it frankly, failure is not rare, and when it does, it may have serious financial consequences [1]. Even though science has advanced and we now understand a great deal about how the human body functions, there has been a significant surge in data digitization in the pharmaceutical business in recent years [2]. Nonetheless, as digitalization advances, it becomes more difficult to gather, assess and use the information to cope with complex clinical circumstances. Artificial intelligence is being applied in many aspects of the healthcare sector, including the study and development of drugs, targeted therapies, pharmaceutical production optimization, and the discovery of novel medicines [3]. As a result, people need to exert less effort, and the industry can accomplish its goals more quickly. AI's Deep Learning (DL) field uses models that take into account topological changes over multiple layers. Speech recognition, picture processing, and natural language processing are just a few of the many uses for this method. Recently, DL has also been effectively employed in the production of novel pharmaceuticals [4]. According to predictions made by the McKinsey Global Institute, the quick proliferation of AI-guided computerization will significantly alter people's perceptions of their jobs [5]. This chapter has covered the development of the medication from its invention to the emergence of AI and DL.

7.1.1 Artificial Intelligence

In addition to the fundamental machine learning (ML) approach, artificial intelligence encompasses a range of technique fields such as cognition, information processing, and issue discovery. AI employs computers that are able to identify similarities in a set of data that has been processed and further categorized [6]. DL is a branch of machine learning that makes use of artificial neural networks (ANNs). The propagation of electronic signals

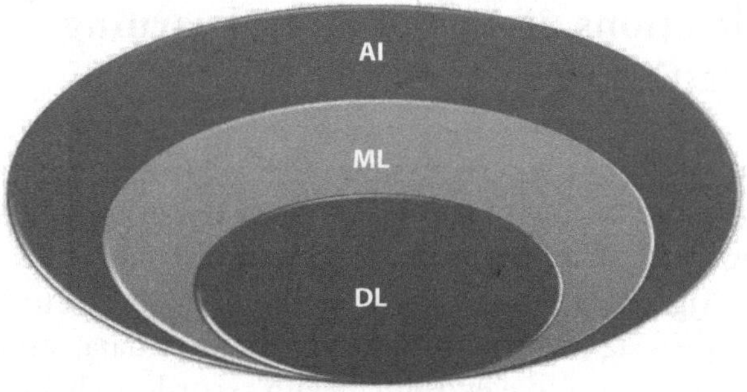

Figure 7.1 Relationship of AI, DL, and ML.

inside the neurological system is modeled. They consist of a network of interconnected, complicated computer units, including perceptrons, which resemble human biological neurons [7]. ANNs are made up of a succession of nodes. Each of these gets a different input and eventually transforms into an output, either individually or as a network, using methods for resolving problems. There are several forms of ANNs including recurrent neural networks (RNNs), convolutional neural networks (CNNs), and multilayer perceptron (MLP) networks which use any training processes, supervised or unsupervised. Figure 7.1 depicts the association among DL, AI, and ML [4, 8].

7.1.2 Deep Intelligence

In 1943, McCulloch and Pitts created the first artificial neuron model based on the description of nerve movement. This model was superseded by another, known as the perceptron, which is a two-layer neural network used for fundamental errands [9]. Back-propagation, a method for training effective multiplayer networks, was established in the late 1960s. DL is a subtype of ML that depicts high-level data abstractions by ANNs with numerous layers of asymmetric processing components. ANNs with logic like neural networks in human intelligence have now been established. Each neuron may be viewed as an algorithm, and its interconnectedness leads to a massive computer capability capable of completing complex computations [10]. Some AI applications and websites depend on DL to increase automation by handling cognitive and physiological tasks that previously required human intervention. Everyday items (such as chatbots, voice-command TV remotes, and banking fraud detection) and future innovations (like autonomous vehicles) rely on DL technology (such as self-driving cars) [11].

7.2 Applications of AI and Deep Learning in Healthcare

In the current age, with the progression of DL algorithms, the accessibility of huge datasets and the use of AI in healthcare has expanded to areas such as medical imaging, drug discovery, personalized medicine, and predictive analytics. Algorithms for DL have been demonstrated to be extremely successful at assessing massive volumes of medical data, such as medical images, genomics data, and electronic health records, to help with diagnosis and treatment decision-making [12]. AI and DL are fast transforming the healthcare business, making it simpler, more effective, and more customized. Here are some key ways AI and DL are evolving in healthcare:

7.2.1 Medical Imaging

Practitioners use AI to analyze images and diagnose more accurately. To diagnose the early signs of diseases like cancer, heart illness, brain diseases, etc., these algorithms are more helpful. Furthermore, DL is used for analyzing a vast collection of medical images like MRI scans, CT scans, and X-rays.

7.2.2 Personalized Medicine

AI can help personalize interventions based on a patient's individual characteristics and medical background. Instead of using a one-size-fits-all method, personalized medicine tries to change treatment plans based on the medical experiences and unique looks of each patient. With the help of AI and DL, medicine can be made according to a patient's need [13].

7.2.3 Precision Diagnostics

In hospitals, there is a vast amount of patient data such as medical pictures, genetic data, electronic health records (EHR), which can be accurately analyzed by AI and DL. This might lead to the development of more customized and efficient treatments.

7.2.4 Predictive Analytics

AI and DL algorithms can study large volumes of patient data to classify patterns and forecast outcomes. This can help physicians deliver more specialized and efficient care. AI and DL procedures can analyze the patient details, including medical history, genetics, and everyday problems, to forecast the likelihood of developing certain diseases. This can assist medical professionals in acting sooner to stop the progression of a disease [14]. Additionally, medical record analysis can be used by AI and DL algorithms to predict treatment response, or how a patient will react to therapy. This can help doctors decide which treatment plan is optimal for each patient, enhancing outcomes and minimizing side effects.

7.2.5 Drug Discovery

AI and DL techniques are being used to uncover new drug targets, accelerate drug discovery, and discover new applications for current medications. This might lead to more customized therapies with fewer adverse effects.

7.2.6 Drug Development

AI and DL are being increasingly used in drug development, with the aim of accelerating drug discovery process, reducing costs, and improving the efficiency of clinical trials. For example, in predictive modeling, AI and DL algorithms can analyze large datasets to predict the likelihood of drug candidate succeeding in clinical studies. This can help to prioritize drug candidates for further development and reduce the risk of drug failures. Large libraries of potential pharmaceutical compounds may be screened virtually using algorithms to identify those that have the best chance of being effective against a particular disease target. Thus AI and deep learning enhance drug development by accelerating discovery, reducing costs, and improving success rates through predictive modeling and virtual screening.

7.2.7 Remote Patient Monitoring

Wearable technology and sensors that can remotely monitor patients are being developed using AI. This can assist medical professionals in identifying early illness symptoms and in administering more prompt, focused care. In real-time monitoring, wearable technology and sensor data can be examined by DL and AI procedures to give clinicians the most recent information on a patient's health. This enables medical professionals to identify early illness symptoms and take action before the issue gets worse. On the other hand, AI and DL algorithms in predictive analysis can examine patient medical records to estimate the course of diseases and find individuals who may be at risk of developing certain conditions. AI-powered wearable technology enables real-time health monitoring, early disease detection, and predictive analysis for proactive medical care.

7.2.8 Electronic Health Records

AI is used to evaluate EHR and give real-time care insights to physicians. This saves both cost and time for healthcare providers and patients. Recurring trends and patterns in vast amounts of patient data in EHRs may be found with the help of data analysis techniques like AI and DL. This improves the outcomes of patients and the doctors get better choices for treating patients [15]. AI and DL are also used in the interaction of doctors and patients, and are useful for getting personalized health advice, appointments, and medications.

Additionally, the quality is improved by lowering hospitalization rates and raising patient satisfaction via the use of AI and DL algorithms.

All things considered, AI and DL are altering the drug discovery process, increasing personalized treatment, and speeding up and improving diagnosis. In the upcoming years, we should anticipate even greater advancements in healthcare as these technologies continue to develop.

7.3 Development of Deep Learning and Artificial Intelligence in Healthcare Sector

In the last decade, AI and DL have been evolving in the healthcare industry, and lately, there has been a lot of development. Although AI has been highly utilized in healthcare for an elongated period, significant breakthroughs in this area have been made with the development of DL, a subset of AI.

7.4 Analytics of Healthcare Data Through AI And DL

Healthcare data analytics is the process of investigating and rendering complicated medical data sets to detect recurring trends and patterns and extract insights that might influence healthcare decision-making. With the rapid advancements in AI and DL, healthcare organizations are increasingly turning to these technologies to improve their data analytics capabilities and enhance patient outcomes. Some of the popular models are describing below.

7.4.1 Machine Learning Models

A more specialized area of computer science that has progressed from the learning of recognizing patterns and estimating knowledge speculation in the field of AI is ML [16]. This technology traverses the entire build-up of the algorithm to make them learn and perform specific predictions on the given input data [17]. Such procedures for solving problems and performing computations are handled by designing a model from the input fed upon them and then interpreting the result in the form of predictions or conclusions instead of repeating those program instructions which are considered to be static in nature [18]. The most advent applications of ML include filtering spam, search engines, machine vision, and optical character recognition [19]. This technology is occasionally amalgamated with extracting hidden patterns [20] such as data mining, despite the fact that its main focus is on detailed analysis of data [21]. Based on the nature of learning and feedback received, ML algorithms are broadly categorized into three groups [22] and these are explained as follows:

7.4.1.1 Supervised Learning

It works with labeled inputs as well as output data. It deals with problems where available data consist of examples in labeled form. Its primary purpose is to teach you how to write a function that synchronizes input data items to corresponding output termed as labels. Supervised learning has the ability to enhance patient outcomes, optimize resource allocation, and minimize costs in the healthcare system. Overall, supervised learning has the potential to recover convalescent results, optimize resource allocation, and reduce costs in the healthcare system. It is crucial to remember that the accuracy and potency of the models depend heavily on the caliber of the labeled data that was used to train the algorithms. Additionally, healthcare providers must ensure that any models they use are transparent, explainable, and unbiased, in order to guarantee that they are producing the finest probable care to their patients.

7.4.1.2 Unsupervised Learning

No labeled data is available, and patterns need to be extracted from the given dataset on their own. It is considered a goal in itself. In the healthcare system, unsupervised learning can be used to inspect great quantities of facts and classify insights that may not be apparent through traditional analysis methods. Here are some examples of how unsupervised learning can be explained in the healthcare system. Overall, unsupervised learning has the potential to provide healthcare providers with valuable insights and improve patient outcomes. However, it is significant to communicate that unsupervised learning techniques can be difficult to interpret and may require domain expertise to interpret the results correctly. Additionally, healthcare providers must ensure that any insights gained through unsupervised learning are used in an ethical and responsible manner.

7.4.2 Reinforcement Learning

Here, agents who are intelligent work alongside the domain that keeps on changing and training itself to act along with them. In addition to this, another scenario that describes this type of learning is practicing for a game to be played against an opponent. Thus, it is considered as reaction-based learning methodology in which the particular agent is showing the behavior of learning and doing certain actions and analyzing the outcome.

7.4.3 Natural Language Processing (NLP)

The automatic or semiautomatic processing of human language is called NLP. Humans communicate with each other using natural language. Computers cannot interpret this data as they understand only 0s and 1s. There is a need for computers to be intelligent enough to know and respond to human speech. NLP provides machines the ability to read, understand, and drive meaning from human languages. The first step in NLP is segmentation where we require breaking the full document into constituent sentences. Then we need to explain these words individually to our algorithm. The process is called tokenization, and each word is called a token. After this, non-essential words called stop words are removed from the sentence. It leads to stemming where affixes are added to the stem and new words are provided. Lemmatization is done to obtain the root stem of the word, and then the concept of nouns, verbs, prepositions, and adjectives is explained to the machine by adding tags to the words. After performing pre-processing steps, the resultant data is given to the machine learning algorithm to create the NLP application.

7.4.4 Machine Vision

Machine vision provides methods for capturing visual information and is used in applications like robot guidance, process inspection, and analyzing parts being manufactured. This is used both in industrial and non-industrial applications providing guidance to the devices in their execution. Its center of attention is making copy of human perception to enhance machines to recognize and operate with the things in the same way as humans do, then training, and finally enabling computer to understand the visual world. Thus, it refers to automated system interpreting photographs or motion pictures just like humans. A huge amount of information is required for computer vision.

7.4.5 Data Mining

Data mining processes large data sets to identify patterns and relationships. It analyses the huge quantities of datasets and information to extract different intelligent patterns which aids establishments to crack hitches, forecast tendencies, and discover new occasions. It is also called knowledge discovery data (KDD). Relevant data for analysis are identified and assembled. Relevant steps are to be taken to get data ready to be mined. After mining, analysis and interpretation are done. Data mining algorithms create models for identifying meaningful patterns. Some of the data mining technique includes associations and correlations, classifications, clustering, and outlier detection. This analyzes the relationship between different items and helps organizations make favorable decisions in terms of sales, profits, strategies, and reducing costs.

7.4.6 Artificial Neural Networks

Artificial neural networks (ANNs) are also called neural networks. These are among the most advanced and widely used computing methods in machine learning, knowledge representation, and applying acquired expertise to optimize complex system outcomes [23]. These types of algorithms have gained their insights from the operations of the humanoid intelligence [24]. Similar to the working of the human brain, they have neurons that are distributed among different layers and are tied to each other. The terminology used for neurons is nodes. The network consists of base elements called nodes or processing elements or units and the connections that connect the input set to the output [25]. The layer which acts as input receives data and the output layer produces the final outcome. Each connection has a connection weight associated with it, and each neuron has its own limit value, also called threshold value and activation function. These systems have the capability of modifying their internal structure with respect to a functional objective. These are methods for computation and thus building different units based on the interrelated connections and approaches.

7.4.7 Fuzzy Logic

Fuzzy logic deals with information related to computational perception that is uncertain, partially true, or vague. It is a technique used for representing and processing such uncertain information. The truth ranges between completely true and completely false and it handles the concept of partial truth. A fuzzy model is the representation of relevant aspects of system behavior to obtain a better understanding of the system and makes forecasting and controlling behavior easy. This does not require fixed or noise-free inputs and can be altered easily to improve performance.

7.4.8 Expert System

One of the earliest research fields in artificial intelligence was Expert System. It was developed in 1970 and can be defined as a knowledge-based systems that can perform some tasks normally requiring human expertise. This is used to solve domain-specific problems and use inference procedures to solve them. It is basically a computer program constructed by utilizing the experience of the concerned professional. The user interface, interpretation engine, and information base are the three basic components of an expert system. The interface is used to take information as input in the readable format and pass it on to the inference engine which is the brain of an expert system. Here, inference rules are applied to derive conclusions, thus extracting knowledge from the knowledge base. The conclusions derived from the deterministic inference engines are assumed to be true and conclusions from the probabilistic inference engine contain uncertainty in their results. The inference engine uses either forward chaining, starting from facts and rules and then implementing the given rules, to sum up the final conclusions, or backward chaining, which begins from the final outcomes and works in the reverse direction to test and show the truthfulness of known facts. In addition to this, the knowledge base is similar to a database about a particular area, containing its information and rules.

7.5 Deep Learning Models

In the healthcare system, deep learning models have the potential to revolutionize how healthcare is delivered by improving diagnostic accuracy, predicting patient outcomes, and optimizing resource allocation. Here are some techniques of how deep learning models can be used in the healthcare system.

7.5.1 Convolutional Neural Networks (CNNs)

CNN has major applications in image processing and object detection. This model has multiple layers called the convolution layer, rectified linear unit (ReLU), and pooling layer. To carry out convolution operations, the filters in the convolution layer are used and then the next layer named ReLU performs operations on elements and the output turns out to be a rectified feature map. This map is fed as an input to the next layer called the pooling layer, where its dimensions are reduced, and a flattening procedure takes place in which two-dimensional arrays are mapped into a single linear array. Finally, a fully connected layer is formed where a flattened matrix is taken as an input and further classifies and identifies images.

7.5.2 Network Based on Long Short-Term Memory (LSTM)

LSTMs are used to memorize long-term dependencies. They are used to process entire sequences of data. They are an application of the Recurrent Neural Networks. Long-term dependencies are being remembered by these LSTMs and are used in types of work where memory and present condition about state are quite considerable. They process the entire available data while preserving long-term knowledge throughout the processing period, enabling categorization and time-bound predictions. Their key feature is the ability to retain information over time. LSTM has a chain-like structure containing four interacting layers and different memory blocks called cells. These cells are used for retaining information and different manipulations done by forget gates, input gates, and output gates. Their major area of applications are in language modeling, machine translation, and handwriting generation.

7.5.3 Recurrent Neural Networks (RNNs)

One more extensively utilized and approved algorithm in deep learning, natural language processing, and oration processing is Recurrent Neural Networks. They are very similar to artificial neural networks, which are more frequently used in language processing. Connections are established between nodes which in turn create a cycle. Due to its internal memory, it can memorize its previous inputs and exhibit dynamic temporal behavior. Data is accepted in the form of serial characteristics, and patterns are used to find the next state, as each pattern is assumed to be dependent on the previous state. The major issue with this approach is its speed. It becomes hectic to process long sequences and training can be difficult.

7.5.4 Generative Adversarial Network (GANs)

Generative deep learning algorithms are used for unsupervised learning. They create new instances resembling the training data. GANs are categorized into three major parts: the initial one is generative, which describes data generation in terms of probability; the second part is adversarial, which represents the training of a model; and finally, the third part is the network used for training purposes. GANs consist of three main components: generative for data generation, adversarial for model training, and a network for training implementation. In the training phase, both the generator and discriminator run in competition with each other and repeat several times, thereby improving themselves after each repetition. This approach is widely used in improving astronomical images, generating realistic images and cartoon characteristics, and rendering objects.

7.5.5 Radial Basis Function Networks (RBFNs)

The idea of RBFNs is derived from the theory of function approximation. This technique has a huge influence on keeping hold of as much as it can, which is one of the linear features of RBF. Contrary to this, it is considered that to achieve results that are quite general in nature, there should be some type of non-linear optimization [26]. The approach used here is a neural network based on feed-forward that makes use of an activation function called the radial basis function. This is composed of three major layers: the input layer, the hidden or invisible layer, and the output layer. The invisible layer is also referred to as a feature vector. This transforms the input signal into another form that acts as an input to the network to achieve linear separability. RBFN has an input vector fed to the input layer and the basis function finds the weighted sum of inputs. The Gaussian transfer function is contained in the hidden layer neuron, whose output is inversely proportional to the span from the midpoint of the neuron. The output achieved is a mix of radial basis function and neuron parameters that are in linear form.

7.5.6 Multilayer Perceptrons (MLPs)

It is a feed-forward neural network with multiple layers having activation functions. It consists of an input layer and an output layer, both of which are fully connected. Both layers are the same in number but may have multiple hidden layers. Data is fed to the input layer, and the layers are connected in the form of a graph, with the signal traveling in one direction.

Input along with weights is computed between the input layer and the hidden layer. The activation function is used further to identify the node to fire, and these functions mostly include sigmoid functions. Model training is done in such a way as to gain insight into the relationships between each other and gain an understanding of interdependencies between different variables.

7.5.7 Self-Organizing Maps (SOMs)

A Kohonen map, also known as an unsupervised learning technique, is trained using an algorithm that learns. It has been discovered to be useful in clustering and mapping approaches for mapping multidimensional data to lower dimensions, hence simplifying difficult situations for easier interpretation. At times, it becomes difficult for humans to gain insight and perceive high-dimensional data, so their SOMs are created to go through high-dimensional information. The very first step in this model is weight initialization and choosing any random vector from training data. To find the most likely input vector, every node is examined. The winning node is called the Best Matching Unit (BMU). After this step, neighbors of BMU are found, and this number decreases over time. The winning weight is awarded to the sample vector. The weight changes according to the closeness of a node. The weight adjustment in a neural network depends on a node's proximity to the Best Matching Unit (BMU). Nodes closer to the BMU undergo smaller updates, meaning they learn less, while those farther away experience greater adjustments.

7.6 Potential of AI and Deep Learning Models in Healthcare

The recent era is showing a huge transformation towards digitizing every kind of process in our lives. Advancements in technology have shown a greater impact on healthcare systems, completely changing the approach toward healthcare. The treatment and diagnostic processes of sickness have become simple and worthwhile because of artificial intelligence and recent technological advances [27]. Technical start-ups are using AI and deep learning models to detect diseases in advance and cure them easily before they become critical. The healthcare system has become a business platform based on technology where hospitals are acting like shoppers and are willing to pay huge amounts of sums for reputed machines such as scanners and accelerators [28]. Computer science has a major revolutionary technique named artificial intelligence, which is an impending domain that trains machines to do work on their own without any interference from humans [29]. There is a huge crunch of workers involved in healthcare due to the scarcity of doctors all over the world, factors covering tired and aging medical practitioners, and huge stipulations of persistent healthcare. It has been estimated on a large scale that there are over 17 million scarcities of healthcare workers, and contrary to this, the quantity of patients is increasing gradually. These medical problems can be solved by the use of artificial intelligence [30]. Medical technology is used from the most severe case to the simplest ones.

7.7 The Rise of AI and DL in Drug Discovery

The task of developing novel medicines is one that involves expertise from many fields. Each stage in the process of bringing a novel medicinal molecule to the market is well-defined and plagued with problems, delays, and additional costs. The process of finding a new pharmacological particle for healing reasons is still very time-consuming, expensive, and complex, despite significant advances in our knowledge of biological systems [31]. Given that AI may help with balanced pharmaceutical design, decision making, governing the proper therapy for a chronic condition, including tailored medicines, and managing clinical data created and utilizing it for future drug research, it is conceivable that AI will play a part in the growth of pharmacological goods from the laboratory to the patient's bedside. There are more than one thousand sixty molecules in the huge chemical era that makes it easy to make many pharmacological compounds. However, a lack of modern technology hinders the process of developing new drugs, creating a time-wastage and costly endeavor that may be aided by the help of artificial intelligence [32]. AI can detect hit and primary mixes, as well as speed up drug target confirmation and drug structure design optimization. AI has tremendous issues with data, including the size, growth, variety, and unpredictability of data. The datasets accessible to pharmaceutical firms for drug research may include millions of molecules, and typical ML systems may not be able to handle these sorts of data [33].

7.8 Application of AI in Drug Discovery

The greatest prevalent technique in medication growth is to create medicines such as chemicals, compounds, antigens, or innovative modalities such as short RNAs or cell treatments that modulate the activity of a biological target to change the disease state. Figure 7.2 depicts the many uses of drug discovery in AI. Repurposing, chemical synthesis, drug design, polypharmacology, and screening are just a few of the many areas where AI has proven useful in drug development. AI in designing drug molecules requires that medication molecules must be targeted correctly for effective therapy. The illness develops from the over-expression of several proteins. As a result, the target protein structure must be predicted while developing a therapeutic medication for a certain ailment. The target protein site is based on the plan of the chemical environment; therefore, AI can analyze compounds early in the fusion or manufacturing process to predict their effects on a target and assess safety, allowing for quicker decision-making and reducing potential risks [34]. Alpha Fold, a DNN-based AI tool, predicted 25 of 43 3D target protein structures by analyzing the nearby amino acids and the peptide bond angles. AI in medication design from scratch. The *de novo* drug technique has been extensively adopted in the development of medicinal molecules in recent years [35, 36]. The old technique of producing medications from scratch is giving way to developing DL approaches, with the former having the limitations of lengthy synthesis processes and problematic bioactivity prediction of the new molecule [37].

During drug screening, several predictions such as toxicity, bioactivity, and physicochemical qualities of medicines are produced. In toxicity, toxic effects may be avoided if the potential dangers of a medication molecule are known in advance [38]. Preliminary investigations often include costly cell-based *in vitro* tests followed by expensive animal experiments to

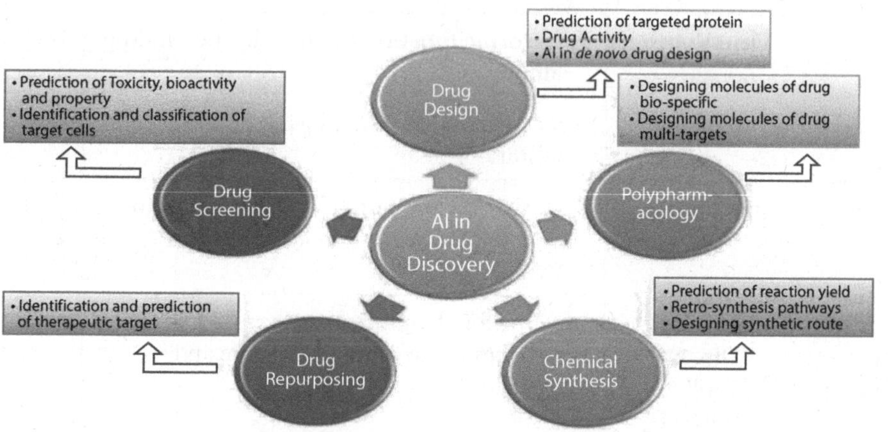

Figure 7.2 AI in drug discovery.

regulate a mixture's toxicity. LimTox, pkCSM, admetSAR, and Toxtree are only a few examples of low-cost digital systems. The efficiency of a drug is determined by the target protein or receptor affinity. Drug molecules that do not interact with the target molecule are ineffective. Drug molecules

Table 7.1 AI tool in drug discovery.

S. no.	Tools	Outline	Ref.
1	AlphaFold	The deep neural network used to forecast the tertiary structure of a protein has two versions AlphaFold1 and AlphaFold2	[43]
2	DeepChem	Chemical structure identification is performed via a DL technique implemented in a freely available Python package	[44]
3	DeepTox	Predict the toxicity of chemical Compounds using DL algorithm	[45]
4	Chemputer	Allows for more uniform reporting of chemical synthesis procedures	[46]
5	Deep Neural NETOSAR	Python-based system powered by computational methods for noticing compound chemical activity	[47]
6	ORGANIC	A tool for molecular generation that facilitates the creation of molecules with desired characteristics	[48]
7	DeltaVina	A rescoring function for drug-ligand binding affinity	[49]
8	PotentialNet	NNs are used to predict ligand binding affinity	[50]
9	JunctionTree	VAE Using a junction tree variational auto-encoder for *de novo* molecule design (VAE)	[51]
10	Open Drug Discovery Toolkit (ODDTs)	Pipeline for cheminformatics employing random forest score (RF)-Score and NNScore	[52]

may potentially interact with undesired proteins or receptors, causing harm [39]. Therefore, drug target binding affinity (DTBA) predicts drug–target interactions. As a result, while developing a novel drug, physicochemical factors such as volatility, diffusion coefficient, ionization degree, and intrinsic permeability must be considered. To make these predictions, scientists may employ a variety of artificial intelligence (AI)-based methods [40].

The capacity of AI to predict drug–target relationships was also employed to aid in the repurposing of traditional antibiotics and the avoidance of polypharmacy. Existing medications that have been repurposed are eligible for Phase II clinical trials right now [41]. Drug–protein interactions can also predict the possibility of polypharmacology, which is the ability of a pharmacological substance to bind to many receptors, resulting in unwanted side effects. AI can generate a new chemical based on polypharmacology principles and contribute to the creation of safer pharmaceutical molecules, as illustrated in Figure 7.2 [42]. Table 7.1 lists the AI tools utilized in drug discovery.

7.9 Challenges of AI And DL Models

In order for AI to be successful, vast amounts of data must be made available for the system to be trained on. Data access from several database providers may be costly for businesses, and it's important that the data be of good quality so that it can be used to anticipate outcomes with confidence [53]. Production, supply chains, sales, drug research, and clinical trials will all be computerized in the future thanks to "narrow AI," which requires a large amount of data to train. There are still several obstacles in the way of drug discovery: enhancing multi-target drug structure, improving virtual screening techniques, expanding the scope of computational chemogenomic research, improving the range and depth of computing resources on the web, and improving toxicity prediction techniques [54, 55]. Some pharmacological businesses have integrated AI, and it is expected that by 2025, AI-based solutions in the pharmaceutical sector will produce US$2.5 billion in income, through the medicinal industry spending over US$7.20 billion in 300+ deals between these years. Therapeutic businesses need clarity on the ability of AI technology to solve issues after it has been applied, as well as a grasp of the achievable objectives [56, 57].

7.10 Future Vision in Developing Rural Health

The use of ML and DL algorithms has the potential to change the healthcare business, particularly in rural health development. Massive amounts of health data can be analyzed by ML and DL algorithms, which can then be taught to identify patterns and make predictions that could inform clinical judgment and enhance patient outcomes. Here are some ideas for potential applications of ML and DL in the future to enhance rural health:

7.10.1 Telemedicine

In rural health, ML and DL could be used to help spread telemedicine. These techniques give doctors a better idea to look at patients' health. With the help of modern technology, people may not even need to travel great distances to see a doctor if they can be located and monitored remotely.

7.10.2 Disease Prediction and Prevention

Using ML and DL approaches, we may anticipate and avert the onset of diseases in rural areas [58, 59]. By analyzing population health data and identifying risk factors, healthcare providers may develop targeted preventive strategies and treatments to improve patient outcomes and halt the spread of illness.

7.10.3 Resource Allocation

Health data may be used to train ML and DL algorithms that can identify resource-intensive areas. Helping healthcare providers allocate resources more effectively and efficiently is crucial for ensuring that patients in remote areas can obtain the treatment they need [60].

7.10.4 Personalized Medicine

Personalized treatment can be given to patients who live far from hospitals with the help of ML and DL. To improve treatment results and decrease the likelihood of unpleasant consequences, medical practitioners may develop action plans that are specific to each patient by analyzing their health data and discovering trends [61, 62].

7.11 Conclusion

The development of novel medicines has been greatly impacted by recent advances in AI, such as the growth and improvement of more complex machine learning algorithms. Some of the most urgent issues facing the drug discovery industry can be resolved by artificial intelligence technology through the use of *in silico* methodologies for synthesis prediction, *de novo* drug design, and bio-activity forecasting. These include a reduction in early-stage costs, time, and labor demands. It is acceptable to assume that DL is a method that is based on ML. This chapter focuses on the theoretical foundations and current instances of good AI and DL applications in drug development.

References

1. Batool, M., Ahmad, B., Choi, S., A structure-based drug discovery paradigm. *Int. J. Mol. Sci.*, 20, 11, 2783, 2019 Jun 6.
2. Paul, D., Sanap, G., Shenoy, S., Kalyane, D., Kalia, K., Tekade, R.K., Artificial intelligence in drug discovery and development. *Drug Discov. Today*, 26, 1, 80, 2021 Jan.
3. Gupta, R., Srivastava, D., Sahu, M., Tiwari, S., Ambasta, R.K., Kumar, P., Artificial intelligence to deep learning: machine intelligence approach for drug discovery. *Mol. Diversity*, 25, 1315–60, 2021 Aug.
4. Jing, Y., Bian, Y., Hu, Z., Wang, L., Xie, X.Q., Deep learning for drug design: an artificial intelligence paradigm for drug discovery in the big data era. *AAPS J.*, 20, 1–0, 2018 May.
5. Vamathevan, J., Clark, D., Czodrowski, P., Dunham, I., Ferran, E., Lee, G., Li, B., Madabhushi, A., Shah, P., Spitzer, M., Zhao, S., Applications of machine learning in drug discovery and development. *Nat. Rev. Drug Discov.*, 18, 6, 463–77, 2019 Jun.
6. Cavasotto, C.N. and Di Filippo, J.I., Artificial intelligence in the early stages of drug discovery. *Arch. Biochem. Biophys.*, 698, 108730, 2021 Feb 15.
7. Rashid, M.B., Artificial intelligence effecting a paradigm shift in drug development. *SLAS Technol.*, 26, 1, 3–15, 2021 Feb.
8. Ju, Y., Zheng, L., Zhao, P., Xin, F., Wang, F., Gao, Y., Zhang, X., Wang, D., Lu, Y., Artificial intelligence recognition of pathological T stage and tumor invasion in rectal cancer based on large panoramic pathological sections. *Intell. Med.*, 2, 03, 141–51, 2022 Aug 28.
9. Gill, H.S., Murugesan, G., Mehbodniya, A., Sajja, G.S., Gupta, G., Bhatt, A., *Fruit Type Classification using Deep Learning and Feature Fusion*, 2022.

10. Sharma, B.B., Gupta, G., Vaidya, P., Basheer, S., Memon, F.H., Thakur, R.N., Internet of Things-Based Crop Classification Model Using Deep Learning for Indirect Solar Drying. Wirel. *Commun. Mob. Comput.*, 2022, 1, 1455216, 2022.
11. Rana, A., Vaidya, P., Kapoor, P., Gupta, G., Edge Preservation Gradient based Smoothing to Multiplicative the Image Noise, in: *2022 Second International Conference on Computer Science, Engineering and Applications (ICCSEA)*, IEEE, pp. 1–6, 2022, September.
12. Thakur, B., Kumar, N., Gupta, G., Machine learning techniques with ANOVA for the prediction of breast cancer. *Int. J. Adv. Technol. Eng. Explor.*, 9, 87, 232, 2022.
13. Thakur, B., Gupta, G., Kumar, N., Hybrid genetic model with ANOVA for predicting breast neoplasm using METABRIC gene data. *Mater. Today Proc.*, 56, 1847–1852, 2022.
14. Yousef, R., Gupta, G., Yousef, N., Khari, M., A holistic overview of deep learning approach in medical imaging. *Multimed. Syst.*, 28, 3, 881–914, 2022.
15. Rana, A., Vaidya, P., Gupta, G., A comparative study of quantum support vector machine algorithm for handwritten recognition with support vector machine algorithm. *Mater. Today Proc.*, 56, 2025–2030, 2022.
16. Tomar, A., Gupta, G., Salehi, W., Vanipriya, C.H., Kumar, N., Sharma, B., A review on leaf-based plant disease detection systems using machine learning. *Recent Innov. Comput.: Proc. ICRIC 2021*, 1, 297–303, 2022.
17. Gupta, G., Salehi, A.W., Sharma, B., Kumar, N., Vaidya, P., COVID-19: automated detection and monitoring of patients worldwide using machine learning, in: *Modeling, Control and Drug Development for COVID-19 Outbreak Prevention*, pp. 731–761, Springer, Cham, 2022.
18. Salehi, A.W. and Gupta, G., A prospective and comparative study of machine and deep learning techniques for smart healthcare applications. *Mob. Health Adv. Res. Appl.*, 163–189, 2021.
19. Baglat, P., Salehi, A.W., Gupta, A., Gupta, G., Multiple machine learning models for detection of Alzheimer's disease using OASIS dataset, in: *International Working Conference on Transfer and Diffusion of IT*, pp. 614–622, Springer, Cham, 2020, December.
20. Vanipriya, C.H., Malladi, S., Gupta, G., Artificial intelligence enabled plant emotion xpresser in the development hydroponics system. *Mater. Today Proc.*, 45, 5034–5040, 2021.
21. Upadhyay, S., Upadhya, A., Salehi, W., Gupta, G., The medical aspects of EMI effect on patients implanted with pacemakers. *Mater. Today Proc.*, 45, 5243–5248, 2021.
22. Saboori, R., Salehi, A.W., Vaidya, P., Gupta, G., Classification of Arrhythmia Using Machine Learning Techniques, in: *Innovations in Information and Communication Technologies (IICT-2020)*, pp. 445–452, Springer, Cham, 2021.

23. Gupta, G., Gupta, N., Gupta, A., Vaidya, P., Singh, G.K., Prediction of Alzheimer associated proteins (PAAP): a perspective to understand Alzheimer disease for therapeutic design. *Int. J. Bioinf. Res. Appl.*, 17, 4, 363–374, 2021.
24. Ahmadi, F., Gupta, G., Zahra, S.R., Baglat, P., Thakur, P., Multi-factor biometric authentication approach for fog computing to ensure security perspective, in: *2021 8th International Conference on Computing for Sustainable Global Development (INDIACom)*, pp. 172–176, IEEE, 2021, March.
25. Saboori, R., Sharma, B.B., Kumar, N., Gupta, G., IoT-based healthcare support services for arrhythmia: A review. *J. Xi'an Univ. Archit. Technol.*, 12, 1035–1039, 2020.
26. Gupta, G., Gupta, A., Barura, P., Jaiswal, V., Mobile health applications and android toolkit for alzheimer patients, caregivers and doctors, in: *Biological Forum–An International Journal*, vol. 11, pp. 199–205, 2019.
27. Salehi, A.W., Baglat, P., Gupta, G., Alzheimer's disease diagnosis using deep learning techniques. *Int. J. Eng. Adv. Technol.*, 9, 3, 874–880, 2020.
28. Salehi, A.W., Baglat, P., Gupta, G., Review on machine and deep learning models for the detection and prediction of Coronavirus. *Mater. Today Proc.*, 33, 3896–3901, 2020.
29. Gupta, G. and Thakur, P., *Image Compression Using Lossless Compression Techniques*, pp. 3896–3900, 2014.
30. Sharma, P. and Gupta, G., Proficient techniques and protocols for the identification of attacks in WSN: A review. *Indian J. Sci. Technol.*, 9, 42, 1–4, 2016.
31. Chandel, R. and Gupta, G., Image filtering algorithms and techniques: A review. *Int. J. Adv. Res. Comput. Sci. Software Eng.*, 3, 10, 198–202, 2013.
32. Lavecchia, A., Deep learning in drug discovery: opportunities, challenges and future prospects. *Drug Discov. Today*, 24, 10, 2017–32, 2019 Oct 1.
33. Tripathi, M.K., Nath, A., Singh, T.P., Ethayathulla, A.S., Kaur, P., Evolving scenario of big data and Artificial Intelligence (AI) in drug discovery. *Mol. Diversity*, 25, 1439–1460, 2021.
34. Zhou, S.F. and Zhong, W.Z., Drug design and discovery: principles and applications. *Molecules*, 22, 2, 279, 2017 Feb 13.
35. Scheeder, C., Heigwer, F., Boutros, M., Machine learning and image-based profiling in drug discovery. *Curr. Opin. Syst. Biol.*, 10, 43–52, 2018 Aug 1.
36. Réda, C., Kaufmann, E., Delahaye-Duriez, A., Machine learning applications in drug development. *Comput. Struct. Biotechnol. J.*, 18, 241–52, 2020 Jan 1.
37. Lo, Y.C., Rensi, S.E., Torng, W., Altman, R.B., Machine learning in chemoinformatics and drug discovery. *Drug Discov. Today*, 23, 8, 1538–46, 2018 Aug 1.
38. Patel, L., Shukla, T., Huang, X., Ussery, D.W., Wang, S., Machine learning methods in drug discovery. *Molecules*, 25, 22, 5277, 2020 Nov 12.
39. Singh, I., Rehni, A.K., Kalra, R., Joshi, G., Kumar, M., Aboul-Enein, H.Y., Ion exchange resins: Drug delivery and therapeutic applications. *Fabad J. Pharm. Sci.*, 32, 2, 91, 2007 Jun 1.

40. Dhiman, P., Kukreja, V., Manoharan, P., Kaur, A., Kamruzzaman, M.M., Dhaou, I.B., Iwendi, C., A novel deep learning model for detection of severity level of the disease in citrus fruits. *Electronics*, 11, 3, 495, 2022 Feb 8.
41. Vijayalakshmi, S., Balusamy, B., Dhanaraj, R.K. (Eds.), *AI-Powered IoT in the Energy Industry: Digital Technology and Sustainable Energy Systems*. Springer International Publishing, 2023.
42. Duch, W., Swaminathan, K., Meller, J., Artificial intelligence approaches for rational drug design and discovery. *Curr. Pharm. Des.*, 13, 14, 1497–508, 2007 May 1.
43. Dana, D., Gadhiya, S.V., St. Surin, L.G., Li, D., Naaz, F., Ali, Q., Paka, L., Yamin, M.A., Narayan, M., Goldberg, I.D., Narayan, P., Deep learning in drug discovery and medicine; scratching the surface. *Molecules*, 23, 9, 2384, 2018 Sep 18.
44. Sennan, S., Ramasubbareddy, S., Dhanaraj, R.K., Nayyar, A., Balusamy, B., Energy-efficient cluster head selection in wireless sensor networks-based internet of things (IoT) using fuzzy-based Harris hawks optimization. *Telecommun. Syst.*, 87, 1, 119–135, 2024.
45. Watson, O., Cortes-Ciriano, I., Taylor, A., Watson, J.A., A decision theoretic approach to model evaluation in computational drug discovery, 2018 Jul 24, arXiv preprint arXiv:1807.08926.
46. Zhavoronkov, A., Vanhaelen, Q., Oprea, T.I., Will artificial intelligence for drug discovery impact clinical pharmacology? *Clin. Pharmacol. Ther.*, 107, 4, 780–5, 2020 Apr.
47. Senior, A.W., Evans, R., Jumper, J., Kirkpatrick, J., Sifre, L., Green, T., Qin, C., Žídek, A., AW, N., Bridgland, A., Penedones, H., Improved protein structure prediction using potentials from deep learning. *Nature*, 577, 7792, 706–10, 2020 Jan 30.
48. Zhu, H., Big data and artificial intelligence modeling for drug discovery. *Annu. Rev. Pharmacol. Toxicol.*, 60, 573–89, 2020 Jan 6.
49. Mayr, A., Klambauer, G., Unterthiner, T., Hochreiter, S., DeepTox: toxicity prediction using deep learning. *Front. Environ. Sci.*, 3, 80, 2016 Feb 2.
50. Steiner, S., Wolf, J., Glatzel, S., Andreou, A., Granda, J.M., Keenan, G., Hinkley, T., Aragon-Camarasa, G., Kitson, P.J., Angelone, D., Cronin, L., Organic synthesis in a modular robotic system driven by a chemical programming language. *Science*, 363, 6423, eaav2211, 2019 Jan 11.
51. Ghasemi, F., Mehridehnavi, A., Fassihi, A., Pérez-Sánchez, H., Deep neural network in QSAR studies using deep belief network. *Appl. Soft Comput.*, 62, 251–8, 2018 Jan 1.
52. Bhuvaneshwari, B., Balusamy, B., Dhanaraj, R.K., Ravi, V., Artificial intelligence enabled Luong Attention and Hosmer Lemeshow Regression Window-based attack detection in 6G. *Int. J. Commun. Syst.*, 36, 15, e5571, 2023.

53. Wang, C. and Zhang, Y., Improving scoring-docking-screening powers of protein–ligand scoring functions using random forest. *J. Comput. Chem.*, 38, 3, 169–77, 2017 Jan 30.
54. Feinberg, E.N., Sur, D., Wu, Z., Husic, B.E., Mai, H., Li, Y., Sun, S., Yang, J., Ramsundar, B., Pande, V.S., Potential net for molecular property prediction. *ACS Cent. Sci.*, 4, 11, 1520–30, 2018 Nov.
55. Jin, W., Barzilay, R., Jaakkola, T., Junction tree variationalautoencoder for molecular graph generation, in: *International Conference on Machine Learning*, PMLR, 2018 Jul 32323–2332.
56. Wójcikowski, M., Zielenkiewicz, P., Siedlecki, P., Open Drug Discovery Toolkit (ODDT): a new open-source player in the drug discovery field. *J. Cheminf.*, 7, 1, 1–6, 2015 Dec.
57. Smith, J.S., Roitberg, A.E., Isayev, O., Transforming computational drug discovery with machine learning and AI. *ACS Med. Chem. Lett.*, 9, 11, 1065–9, 2018 Oct 8.
58. Brown, N., Ertl, P., Lewis, R., Luksch, T., Reker, D., Schneider, N., Artificial intelligence in chemistry and drug design. *J. Comput.-Aided Mol. Des.*, 34, 709–15, 2020 Jul.
59. Zhang, L., Tan, J., Han, D., Zhu, H., From machine learning to deep learning: progress in machine intelligence for rational drug discovery. *Drug Discov. Today*, 22, 11, 1680–5, 2017 Nov 1.
60. Lipinski, C.F., Maltarollo, V.G., Oliveira, P.R., Da Silva, A.B., Honorio, K.M., Advances and perspectives in applying deep learning for drug design and discovery. *Front. Rob. AI*, 6, 108, 2019.
61. Dwivedi, M., Tiwari, R.G., Ujjwal, N., Deep Learning Methods for Early Detection of Monkeypox Skin Lesion, in: *2022 8th International Conference on Signal Processing and Communication (ICSC)*, IEEE, pp. 343–348, 2022.
62. Tiwari, R.G., Misra, A., N.U., Image Embedding and Classification using Pre-Trained Deep Learning Architectures, in: *2022 8th International Conference on Signal Processing and Communication (ICSC)*, IEEE, pp. 125–130, 2022.

8

Heart CAP: Heart Disease Classification: Autoencoders and Principal Components

Kerenalli Sudarshana[1]*, Vamsidhar Y.[2] and SanthoshKumar D. K.[3]

[1]*Department of AI and DS, GITAM School of Technology, Bengaluru, India*
[2]*Department of CSE, GITAM School of Technology, Bengaluru, India*
[3]*Department of CSE, SJEC, Mangalore, India*

Abstract

Medical diagnostics is an ever-evolving domain. In recent times, heart diseases have spread rapidly in younger and older people. Thus, an urgent demand is to identify and classify heart illnesses accurately. Traditional invasive methods are available for detecting heart-related diseases. However, they are costly. Thus, in this investigation, we aim to diagnose heart diseases using modern data-driven and machine-learning techniques. Specifically, this work compares traditional and novel feature engineering techniques for heart disease classification. The first step in this study is to prepare the dataset carefully. Data preparation involves dealing with missing and categorical values. In the data preparation, we used feature scaling to ensure uniformity among features. Then, the model is developed and trained using the training data and tested using the testing dataset. A well-designed encoder and decoder-based Undercomplete Autoencoder (UAE) architecture is built for feature engineering. The Principal Component Analysis (PCA) technique is used for traditional feature engineering. The logistic regression model is trained using the data that has been AE-encoded or PCA-transformed. We have taken ten features for the heart disease classification task in both cases. The accuracy, precision, recall, F1-score, and receiver operating characteristic - area under the curve (ROC AUC) measures are considered to evaluate the performance of our model. The results demonstrate that the model identifies heart diseases effectively. The UAE outperforms PCA on the Cleveland Heart Disease Dataset. While PCA features are effective, the features of AE can help identify potential cases of heart disease with greater efficacy. The important features of the classification decisions

**Corresponding author*: skerenal@gitam.edu

R. Sathiyaraj, Rajesh Kumar Dhanaraj, K. Arun Kumar, Rutvij H. Jhaveri and A. Mohamed Abbas (eds.) Predictive Methods in Next-Generation Computing: An Approach Toward Sustainability, (149–174)

according to each method were also described in the study. Thus, this contribution will pave the way for more accurate medical diagnosis.

Keywords: Autoencoders, classification, heart diseases, data analysis, interpretation, machine learning

8.1 Introduction

The hunt for sustainable and intelligent solutions has become necessary in the dynamically evolving medical and healthcare domains. The rapidly changing field of next-generation computing is leading this hunt. The core of this effort is to create predictive tools to address societal concerns. Identifying and predicting cardiovascular and related abnormalities is one such challenge. The early detection of such disease symptoms plays a significant role, including improved treatment and delayed disease progression. Such measures would not only enhance the patient's quality of life but also save on healthcare expenses. In turn, it saves the national economy a significant amount of money [1].

Invasive and non-invasive procedures are the two primary methodologies in heart disease prediction. Each of these procedures comes with inherent rewards and downsides [2]. Invasive techniques offer better precision. Such methods include intravascular ultrasonography and angiography. However, invasive techniques come at the cost of significant resource allocation and potential risks to the patient's body [3]. On the other hand, non-invasive methods are deemed to be safer and painless. However, they exhibit limitations in sensitivity and discernibility [4]. This chapter applies artificial intelligence methods for early and effective heart disease diagnosis and detection. We explicitly investigate the transformative potential of artificial intelligence in predicting heart diseases [5]. These techniques include feature selection, risk assessment, early diagnosis, predictive modeling, real-time monitoring, therapy optimization, and data integration [41]. This can be achieved by discriminating dataset sample patterns, trends, and relationships.

A vital aspect of this study lies in data preparation and dimensionality reduction. It highlights the importance of data quality, feature engineering, and managing data formats. We introduce the Undercomplete Autoencoder (UAE) and Principal Component Analysis (PCA) models for feature extraction and reduction. We are specifically focusing on the ability of UAE and PCA to predict heart diseases. Then, the subsequent comparison addresses the effectiveness of heart disease classification [6].

The substantial contributions of this chapter include:

1. Build the artificial intelligence models for feature engineering.
2. Evaluate their efficiency to identify nonlinear correlations in the data.
3. Assessment of the model's adaptability to previously unseen data.
4. Exploration of interpretative latent characteristics enhances understanding of the critical factors contributing to the disease classification.

The structure of the remaining segments is as follows: An overview of related works is presented in Section 8.2. Section 8.3 outlines the detection and evaluation methodology employed in this study. Section 8.4 details the experimentation setting, results, and comprehensive analysis. Section 8.5 concludes the chapter and plans a course for forthcoming research endeavors.

8.2 Related Study

The relevant research described in the table below is the foundation for examining dimensionality reduction methodologies, notably the Autoencoder (AE) and Principal Component Analysis (PCA) models. Our aim is to enhance the prediction accuracy of heart disease classification. Table 8.1 delves into the thoroughness of the approach, experimentation settings, outcomes, and analysis, expanding on the insights garnered from these related works [7–40].

Table 8.1 Comparison of existing literature.

Study and model	Data source	Key findings and accuracy
Ambekar and Phalnikar [7]	UCI Repository	CNN-UDRP model achieved ~65% accuracy for heart disease risk classification. Data cleaning and imputation were performed.
Ramprakash *et al.* [8]	Cleveland (UCI Repository)	χ2-DNN model achieved a heart disease classification accuracy of 94%.

(Continued)

Table 8.1 Comparison of existing literature. (*Continued*)

Study and model	Data source	Key findings and accuracy
Maini *et al.* [9]	Cleveland (UCI Repository)	In the earlier stages, they explored a cloud-based data mining approach for heart disease risk detection.
Mohan *et al.* [10]	Cleveland (UCI Repository)	They built a hybrid model, HRFLM, and outperformed other models with an 88.4% accuracy.
Shah *et al.* [11]	Cleveland (UCI Repository)	They showed that the k-nearest neighbors classifier achieved an accuracy of 90% for heart disease prediction. That was the highest one.
Garg *et al.* [12]	Kaggle dataset	They built a Random Forest classifier and achieved 82% accuracy for heart disease classification.
Yadav *et al.* [13]	Cleveland (UCI Repository)	They Optimized DNN using Talos. This technique outperformed the other traditional models in accuracy.
Latha and Jeeva. [14]	Cleveland (UCI Repository)	Their ensemble technique significantly improved the heart disease prediction accuracy.
Singh *et al.* [15]	Cleveland (UCI Repository)	They built a special kind of prediction technique called MPSVM-DT. This method achieved 91% accuracy in binary class classification and 73% in multi-class classification problems.
Sowmiya and Sumitra [16]	Cleveland (UCI Repository)	Their Hybrid KNN showed efficiency and effectiveness for heart disease prediction.
Alotaibi *et al.* [17]	Cleveland (UCI Repository)	They used RapidMiner with different machine learning methods, including SVM, DT, and LR, which yielded higher accuracy.

(*Continued*)

Table 8.1 Comparison of existing literature. (*Continued*)

Study and model	Data source	Key findings and accuracy
Nikookar and Naderi [18]	SPECT heart disease dataset	Their Hybrid ensemble classifiers outperformed basic ensembles.
Tama *et al.* [19]	Various datasets	The authors proposed a two-tier ensemble approach that achieved high accuracy compared to existing models.
Li *et al.* [20]	Cleveland (UCI Repository)	The authors developed a novel technique, FCMIM-SVM, for feature selection. The method exhibited better accuracy with feature selection techniques.
Sarmah [21]	Cleveland (UCI Repository)	They showed that a deep learning-based DLMNN model that uses IoT sensors can improve heart disease prediction and authentication.
Chauhan *et al.* [22]	Cleveland (UCI Repository)	Authors have proposed an ANN model. This model outperformed other models with 85% accuracy for heart disease prediction.
Pan *et al.* [23]	N/A	Enhanced CNN architecture achieved an accuracy of 97%.
Fitriyani *et al.* [24]	Starlog, UCI datasets	The authors developed a hybrid model, HDPM. This model achieved 95% (Statlog) and 98% (Cleveland) accuracy for early heart failure detection.
Tate and Rao [25]	N/A	Proposed wearable-based system for early cardiac arrest prediction using vital data.
Prabhu *et al.* [26]	Medical dataset	CNN-MDRP outperformed CNN-UDRP in risk prediction for diseases.

(*Continued*)

Table 8.1 Comparison of existing literature. (*Continued*)

Study and model	Data source	Key findings and accuracy
Shankar *et al.* [27]	Structured and unstructured data	CNN model showed improvement over other algorithms in heart disease prediction.
Singh and Kumar [28]	Cleveland (UCI Repository)	KNN achieved 87% accuracy for early heart disease prediction.
Amin *et al.* [29]	Fitbit wearable data	The ML algorithms were used. They have achieved up to 82% accuracy in predicting heart disease.
Chen *et al.* [26]	Hospital data	The fusion of numerical and textual data achieved 90% sensitivity and 93% specificity.
Cohen *et al.* [30]	Quebec hospitals data	The authors developed a Multivariate logistic regression model. This model generates a risk score for each patient. The model achieved a higher performance.
Chang *et al.* [31]	Patient vital signs data	Their ML algorithms predicted vital signs with accurate results.
Youssef Ali Amer *et al.* [32]	Wearable vital signs data	An ensemble based on KNN, LS, and SVM improved early warning score prediction for vital signs.
Stehlik *et al.* [33]	Data from wearable sensors	The authors developed a remote monitoring model with wearable sensors. This model achieved high sensitivity and specificity.
Jia *et al.* [34]	Framingham dataset	Cox proportional hazards regression estimated risk probability for heart diseases.
Yang *et al.* [35]	National high-risk program dataset	Multivariate regression achieved improved accuracy.

(*Continued*)

Table 8.1 Comparison of existing literature. (*Continued*)

Study and model	Data source	Key findings and accuracy
Made *et al.* [36]	Sample data of men and women	SCORE model estimated a 10-year risk for coronary heart disease.
Budholiya *et al.* [37]	N/A	Optimized extreme Boost algorithm for heart disease identification.
Ali *et al.* [38]	Sensor and EMR data	Ensemble deep learning with feature fusion for improved heart disease prediction.
Cherian *et al.* [39]	Cleveland (UCI Repository)	Lion and particle swarm optimization and weighted optimal neural networks achieved improved accuracy.
Rani *et al.* [40]	Cleveland (UCI Repository)	A hybrid model with a feature selection technique.

While the existing literature has several comprehensive studies on various models and methodologies for predicting heart illness, our contribution intends to fill a significant gap. The most frequent strategies have primarily focused on using multiple machine learning algorithms and datasets to achieve high accuracy rates in cardiac disease prediction [44]. However, the assessment and comparison of dimensionality reduction approaches must be included, particularly for Autoencoder (AE) and Principal Component Analysis (PCA) models. We are motivated by the awareness that dimensionality reduction is critical for increasing the efficacy and comprehensibility of machine learning models. However, its use in heart disease prediction has yet to receive much attention in the literature. By introducing the AE and PCA models and analyzing their usefulness in identifying coronary artery disease, we want to increase our understanding of the factors influencing heart disease categorization.

8.3 Model Architecture

The model architecture, shown in Figure 8.1, for heart disease classification begins with preprocessing the dataset, resolving missing values, and translating categorical variables into a numeric representation using one-hot encoding. The dataset is divided into training and testing sets to support practical model training and assessment. Feature scaling is used to achieve homogeneity across the features in both groups. The algorithm is described in Table 8.2. The basis of the architecture is the creation and training of an autoencoder. It comprises an encoder and decoder block with a 10-dimensional bottleneck layer. The Autoencoder employs the Adam optimizer during training to minimize the mean squared error loss. The regularization approaches used are early halting and learning rate reduction. This is done to improve performance and prevent overfitting. The scaled training set is further subjected to Principal Component Analysis (PCA) to find the top ten principal components that capture significant dataset volatility.

A logistic regression classifier is built after the feature extraction step. The classifier predicts the target label using the encoded representation from the Autoencoder and the PCA-transformed data. Afterward, the logistic regression model is trained using the training data. The classifier is now well-trained to distinguish. The next step is to evaluate the trained

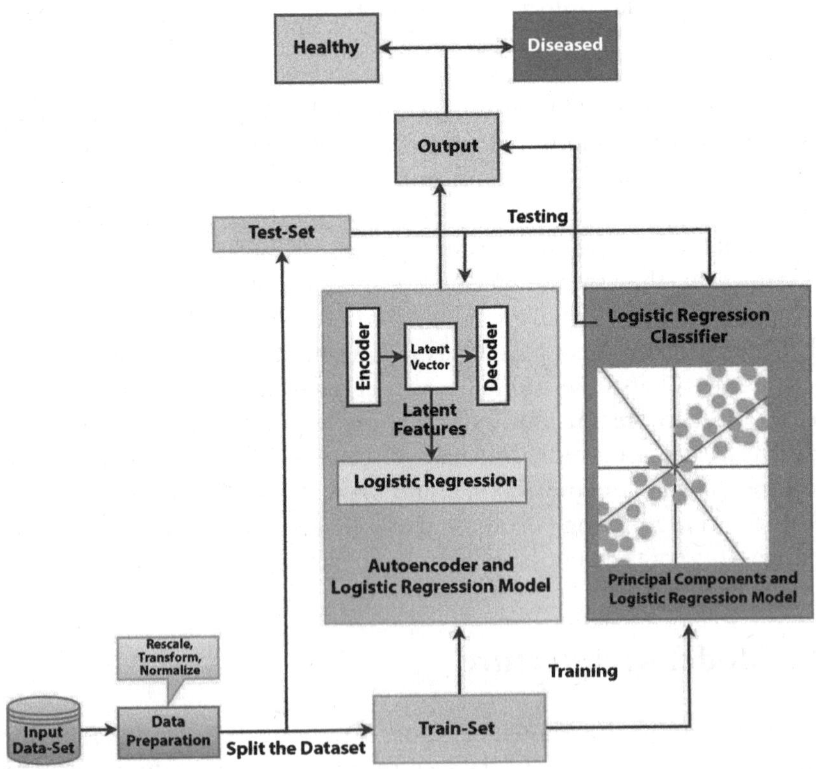

Figure 8.1 The architecture of the proposed model.

Table 8.2 Steps in the proposed HeartCAP model.

Algorithm: Heart Disease Classification
Input: Heart disease dataset D **Output: Trained logistic regression classifier and evaluation metrics.**
Preprocess dataset D to handle missing values and convert categorical variables to numeric using one-hot encoding. Split the dataset into a training set and a testing set. Apply feature scaling to train and test sets using Standard Scaler. Design an Autoencoder with a 10-dimensional encoding layer comprising an encoder E(x) and a decoder D(z). Train Autoencoder uses Adam optimizer to minimize MSE loss Apply early stopping and learning rate reduction during Autoencoder training. Apply PCA to scaled training set D_train, extracting the top 10 principal components capturing a significant portion of dataset variance. Design a logistic regression classifier to predict target label y' using encoded representation z (Autoencoder) or PCA-transformed data as input features. Train a logistic regression classifier using the training set to obtain the trained classifier model. Test trained logistic regression classifier on the testing set. Evaluate performance using precision, recall, F1-score, and ROC AUC classification metrics.

logistic regression classifier. We use the dedicated test set and evaluate its performance. The measures used are accuracy, recall, F1-score, and ROC AUC. In this work, we have integrated the Autoencoder and PCA methods. They extract the meaningful features for the classification task. The classification model effectively classifies heart diseases. It also ensures a robust, accurate predictions.

8.3.1 Cleveland Heart Disease Dataset

The Cleveland Heart Disease (CHD) dataset is an important dataset used for heart disease analysis. This CHD dataset is comprehensive and has many variables. It also has well-defined target labels. Thus, we can say that the CHD dataset is an excellent option for developing and testing prediction models in cardiovascular health [42]. We obtained the dataset from the University of California, Irvine (UCI) Machine Learning Repository. The dataset has detailed clinical and demographic information of the 303 individuals. Each sample consists of 14 features, including continuous and

Table 8.3 Cleveland dataset selected features [48].

S. n.	Attribute	Description of attribute
1	Age	Patient age in years
2	Gender	Female (0); male (1)
3	Chest Pain Type	Categorized as 1, 2, 3, or 4
4	Resting Blood Pressure	Measured in mm Hg
5	Serum Cholesterol	Blood cholesterol level (measured in mg/dl)
6	Fasting Blood Sugar	If FBS > 120 mg/dl, then True (1); False (0)
7	Resting ECG Results	Categorized as 0, 1, or 2
8	Max Heart Rate	The highest heartbeat measured
9	Exercise-Induced Angina	If yes, then 1; otherwise, 0.
10	ST Depression	ST depression levels due to exercise.
11	ST Segment Slope	Categorized as 1, 2, or 3
12	Vessels Fluoroscopy	Number of significant vessels highlighted
13	Thalassemia	Categorized as 3, 6, or 7
14	Heart Disease Presence	0 indicating absence, 1 indicating presence

categorical variables. Table 8.3, outlined below, shows the critical aspects of the dataset. It includes clinical data such as serum cholesterol levels, resting blood pressure, fasting blood sugar, and exercise-induced angina. Demographic data include age and gender. It also includes electrocardiogram (ECG) and maximal heart rate measurements achieved during exercise. The dataset also contains details on thalassemia and artery fluoroscopy. The target labels indicate the presence (1) or absence (0) of heart disease. The dataset is well-suited for training our learning models based on the available features.

8.3.2 Data Preparation

Data preparation is a crucial step in the analytical pipeline, involving the refinement and transformation of raw datasets to ensure suitability for subsequent analysis and modeling [43]. The heart disease dataset undergoes the following processes to facilitate adequate data preparation:

i. **Handling Missing Values**: The initial challenge is addressing missing values denoted by "?" in the raw dataset. A meticulous approach is taken, as these values can pose complications during analysis and modeling. The panda's libraries replace () method, which returns missing values with "NaN." Subsequently, the dropna() method eliminates rows containing NaN values, ensuring a cleaner dataset for further processing.

ii. **Converting Categorical Variables**: Categorical variables, such as "cp" (chest pain type), resting electrocardiographic scores, "slope," and "thal," exist in the dataset. These variables must be translated into a numeric format for machine learning models. The get_dummies() method is applied to one-hot encoding to generate the binary columns for categorical variables.

iii. **Target Variable Transformation:** The original target variable represents the presence or absence of cardiac disease with values greater than zero (1, 2, 3, or 4). The where () method aligns these labels with the binary classification requirements. This transformation generates a new binary target variable [1,0]. The value 1 indicates the presence of cardiac disease, while 0 signifies its absence. This binary format ensures compatibility with binary classification models.

After data preparation, the dataset is ready to split into training and testing sets. This facilitates the training and evaluation of machine learning models. The preprocessed dataset consists of numerical features. This makes it compatible with the Autoencoder and PCA models used to detect heart disease.

8.3.3 Feature Scaling

Feature scaling is essential in ensuring that every feature contributes equally. The machine learning models are then trained and tested using the scaled feature matrices. We used the Standard Scaler to perform feature scaling in diagnosing heart disease. After subtracting the mean, the scaling process standardizes each feature by mapping the sample to the unit variance. In the training data, the original feature value is x. The μ represents the mean, and σ represents the standard deviation of the data. The scaling formula is defined as in Equation (8.1).

$$\acute{x} = \sigma\left(\frac{x-\mu}{\sigma}\right) \tag{8.1}$$

8.3.4 Dimensionality Reduction Techniques

A critical stage in detecting heart disease is dimensionality reduction. An ideal dimensionality reduction step reduces the number of features without sacrificing dataset information. The benefits of this reduction are increased processing speed, better model performance, and better data visualization. We use both PCA-based and autoencoder-based dimensionality reduction techniques in our experimental settings.

8.3.4.1 Principal Component Analysis (PCA)

Principal component analysis, or PCA, is a mathematical approach to feature set reduction. The most crucial variances in the data are identified by a series of orthogonal lines called principal components. Eigenvectors that match the most significant eigenvalues are used to calculate these critical components [45]. The number of components in our arrangement is 10, and PCA is applied to the training data. PCA converts the data into a new feature space where each data point is represented as a linear combination of the principal components. The most significant fluctuations in the data samples are captured by the first principal components, then the next highest by the second principal components, and so on.

The dataset has m observations and n features, and the data is represented as a matrix X with size m×n, where each row corresponds to an observation and each column corresponds to a feature. The goal is to find a new set of orthogonal axes, i.e., principal components along which the data has the maximum variance.

Initially, the data is homogenized by deducting the arithmetic mean and dividing this difference by the standard deviation for every feature. Let $\underline{x_j}$ be the mean of the jth feature, and sj be its standard deviation. The standardized value zij for the ith observation and j[th] feature is given by:

$$z_{ij} = \frac{x_{ij} - \overline{x}_j}{s_j}$$

Next, compute the covariance matrix for the standardized data, C. The co-variance between the jth and k[th] features is given by:

$$cov\left(X_j, X_k\right) = \frac{1}{m-1} \sum_{i=1}^{m} \left(z_{ij} \cdot z_{ik}\right)$$

Compute the eigenvalue (λ) and the eigenvectors (V) of the covariance matrix C. The λ signifies the amount of variance captured by each principal component, and the corresponding eigenvectors represent the direction of these components. The top k eigenvectors that match the top k most significant eigenvalues. These are then chosen by sorting the eigenvalues in downward order. The matrix V_k is made up of these k eigenvectors. The standardized data Z is then projected into the newly created subspace the selected eigenvectors define [46]. Y is a m×k matrix representing the data in reduced-dimensional space. By choosing a subset of the critical elements, we can minimize dimensionality while retaining the majority of the variability in the data.

$$Y = Z \cdot V_k$$

8.3.4.2 *Autoencoder Architecture*

The Autoencoder network can learn compressed representations of input data in an unsupervised manner [47]. In our configuration, a 10-dimensional autoencoder architecture is implemented. Similar to the original data, the input layer of the autoencoder accepts the same number of features. The input data undergoes a sequence of fully connected hidden layers, ultimately reducing its dimensionality to 10 neurons at the bottleneck layer (encoding layer). The difference between the input data and the reconstruction of its output layer is referred to as the reconstruction error. The autoencoder is trained to minimize this error. Throughout the training phase, the network learns to capture the most significant elements describing the material while discarding less critical information. Consequently, the data is represented in a lower-dimensional manner, with each data point represented by a 10-dimensional vector in the encoding layer.

Let X be the input data represented as an n×m matrix and d be the desired encoding dimension. The encoder function defines the encoding phase of the Autoencoder:

$$\text{Encoder}(\mathbf{X}) = \sigma(\mathbf{X} \cdot \mathbf{W}_1 + \mathbf{b}_1)$$

Where W1 is the weight matrix of the first hidden layer, b1 is the bias vector of the first hidden layer, and σ represents the activation function ReLU.

The decoder function defines the decoding phase of the Autoencoder:

$$\text{Dencoder}(\mathbf{H}) = \sigma(\mathbf{H} \cdot \mathbf{W}_2 + \mathbf{b}_2)$$

Where H is the encoded data, W2 is the weight matrix, and b2 is the bias vector of the output layer. During the training phase of the Autoencoder, the reconstruction error between the Input data and the output data is minimized. The weights and biases of the Autoencoder model are updated during training. The optimization algorithm, Adam, updates it. The mean squared error loss function is used as a reconstruction loss. After training, the autoencoder hidden layer outputs serve as the input for the logistic regression classifier. This vector is a reduced representation of latent features.

8.4 Results

In this section, we provide and discuss the results in detail. The results are obtained by applying the PCA and Autoencoder models to the dataset. The results include classification performance metrics and Receiver Operating Characteristics (ROC) values. Each measure provides a comprehensive performance measure for the model's efficacy, interpretability, and discriminatory power. We present impactful insights and capabilities of both models. This is carried out through a rigorous examination of observed results.

8.4.1 Classification Performance

Consistent evaluation measures—such as Accuracy, Precision, Recall, and F1 scores—indicate a well-balanced performance by any classification model. In the given dataset, the test set has 60 examples. There are 36 Healthy and 24 Diseased patient records. The UAE-based model classifies the test samples into binary classes (0 and 1). The results, shown in Figure 8.2, are as follows: the model correctly classifies 34 out of 36 healthy and 21 out of 24 diseased records. The precision, recall, and F1 score measures are around 0.92 for healthy class example records. This result indicates a stronger ability to identify the instance of the Healthy class. The UAE performs admirably in the Disease Presence class (1) example records. The F1 score of the Diseased class is around 0.88. It also resulted in higher

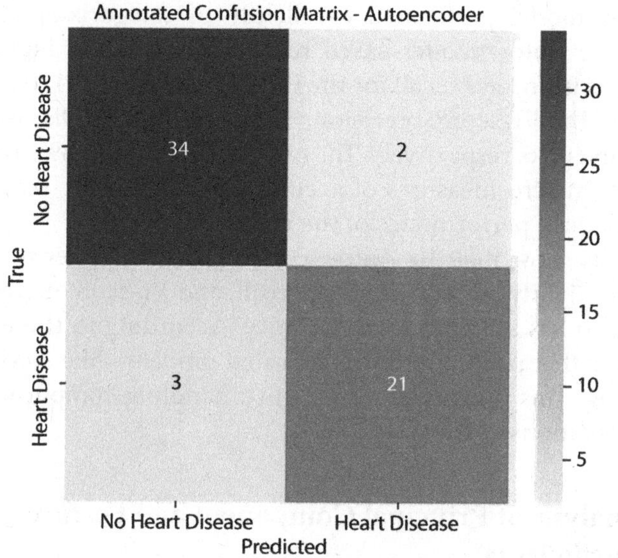

Figure 8.2 Confusion matrix for the Autoencoder based model.

recall and precision. According to the results, the classifier model with an autoencoded feature set has an overall accuracy of 90%. Thus, the results demonstrate that the features are effective for prediction. The precision, recall, and F1-score macro and weighted averages also support the balanced performance of the model in both cases.

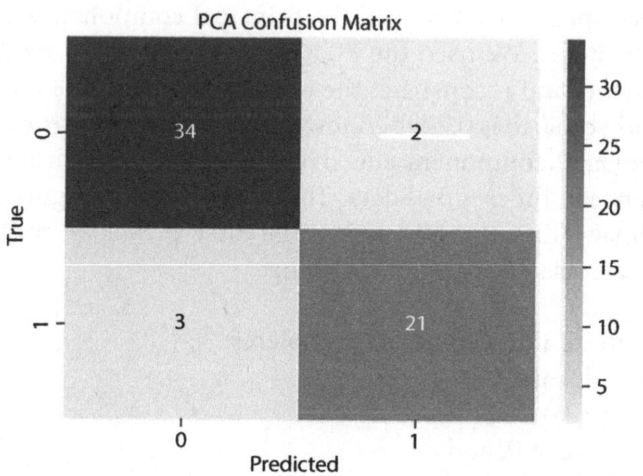

Figure 8.3 Confusion matrix for the PCA based model.

The PCA model performed excellently in categorizing the records, similar to the Auto-encoder-based results, as shown in Figure 8.3. The F1-score, precision, and recall for the Healthy class are 0.91, 0.89, and 0.90, respectively. The F1-score, precision, and recall for the Diseased class are 0.84, 0.88, and 0.86, respectively. The overall accuracy is 88%. The weighted averages and macro measures of accuracy, recall, and F1-score also confirm the balanced performance of the model.

The results show that the Autoencoder performs better than the PCA model, with slightly better precision, recall, and F1-score metrics for both classes. It also has a higher total accuracy. According to these results, we can conclude that using more sophisticated models—like autoencoders—is convincing. This is especially true when handling complicated patterns and representations in the data.

8.4.2 Analysis of Principal Component and Feature Coefficients

The coefficients of the original features within the first principle components are derived through PCA analysis. These coefficients are presented in this section. Each of these coefficients denotes the percentage of variance. The first principal components capture this variance from the original dataset attributes. The positive coefficients imply a correlating influence on the principal component, while negative coefficients indicate a negative contribution of that attribute to the results. We used the reconstruction error as a measure for this task. The reconstruction error is a statistic that assesses correspondence between the principal components and the original data attributes. We used the PCA model to learn the reduced principal components and reconstruct the original samples. The reconstruction error for this scenario is 0.2294. A lower reconstruction error suggests that the first principal component effectively captures a significant percentage of the variance in the original data. These are shown in Figure 8.4.

The primary drivers influencing the first principal component are parameters associated with the following:

- Exercise-induced cardiac problems:
  - oldpeak,
  - cp_3.0,
  - slope_1.0, and
  - thal_6.0,

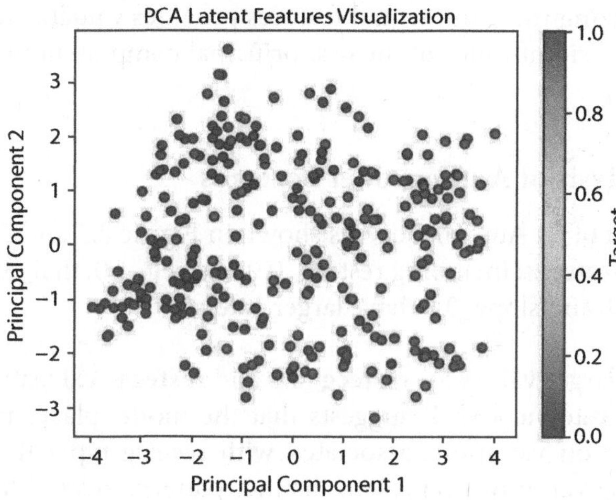

Figure 8.4 PCA latent feature space.

- Specific diagnostic test findings:
  - exang,
  - ca,
  - age,
  - restecg_1.0,
  - trestbps,
  - sex,
  - slope_2.0,
  - restecg_0.0,
  - chol, and
  - fbs.

Conversely, the following features negatively impact the first principal component:

- Parameters linked to particular forms of chest pain:
  - cp_4.0,
  - cp_2.0, and
  - cp_1.0

- Cardiac parameters such as:
  - thalach,
  - slope_3.0, and
  - restecg_2.0.

Characterizing these influential features provides valuable insights into the nature and significance of the first principal component in the context of the dataset.

8.4.3 Analysis of Autoencoder Features

In the context of an Autoencoder, as shown in Figure 8.5 and Figure 8.6, it appears that features, including restecg_0.0, restecg_1.0, thal_3.0, thal_6.0, exang, cp_2.0, and slope_3.0, have larger values.

- The larger values for **restecg_0.0** and **restecg_1.0** features in the Autoencoder. It suggests that the model places importance on variations associated with restecg types 0 and 1. These variations represent distinct patterns related to resting electrocardiographic (ECG) results. The Autoencoder emphasizes capturing such patterns in its compressed representation.
- Larger values for **thal_3.0** and **thal_6.0** indicate a focus on the variations associated with these specific types of thalassemia. The Autoencoder emphasizes the importance of capturing these distinctions. They related to different types of thalassemia in its data representation.
- Autoencoder attributes significance to variations associated with exercise-induced angina. It is evident from the next larger value for **exang parameter.** The Autoencoder considers exercise-induced angina a crucial factor in representing and reconstructing the input data.
- The Autoencoder emphasizes capturing the typical features of this type of chest pain. A higher value for cp_2.0 in the Autoencoder emphasizes variations associated with chest pain type 2 in its learned representation.
- Large value for the slope_3.0 suggests that the Autoencoder focuses on variations associated with a down-sloping ST segment during exercise.

In the context of an Autoencoder, smaller values for features like ca, thalach, oldpeak, chol, fbs, trestbps, and sex imply that these features have a relatively lesser impact or influence on the learned representation.

- A smaller value for **ca** suggests that the Autoencoder assigns less importance to variations in the number of significant

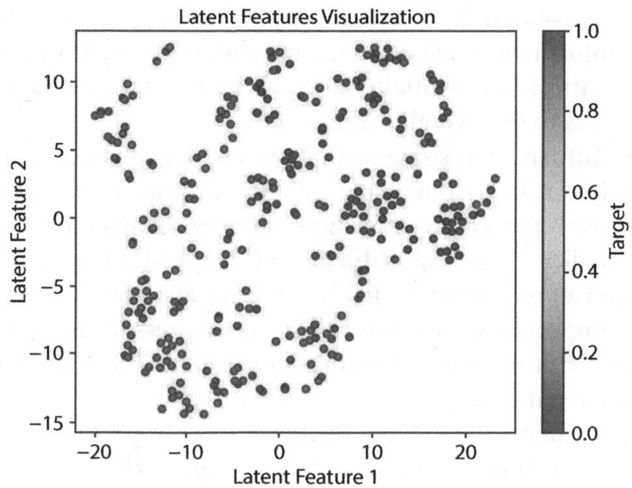

Figure 8.5 Autoencoder latent feature space.

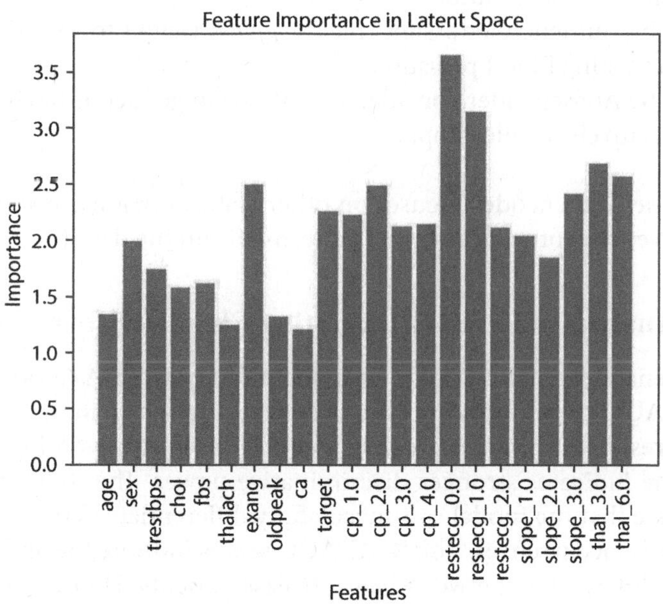

Figure 8.6 Feature importance in latent space for the Autoencoder.

vessels colored by fluoroscopy. The Autoencoder considers the information related to the number of colored containers less critical. It potentially indicates that this feature contributes less to the overall variability.

- The Autoencoder suggests that the smaller values of thalach-maximum heart rate achieved- has a minor impact on the learned representation for heart disease classification task.
- A smaller value for **oldpeak** (ST Depression Induced by Exercise) is recommended by the Autoencoder. It attributes less importance to variations in ST depression induced by exercise. It indicates that this feature contributes less to the learned patterns.
- The Autoencoder assigns relatively less weight to variations in serum cholesterol levels. It also suggests that serum cholesterol has a smaller impact on the learned representation.
- The Autoencoder considers variations in fasting blood sugar levels as having a lesser impact. It implies a comparatively smaller contribution.
- The Autoencoder assigns relatively less weight to variations in resting blood pressure.
- The Autoencoder considers variations in gender as having a relatively smaller impact.

Thus, the Autoencoder focuses on other features that it considers more informative for capturing essential patterns within the data.

8.4.4 Analysis of Receiver Operating Characteristics

The Autoencoder and Principal Component Analysis (PCA) models obtain the ROC AUC values for heart disease detection, as given in the Figure 8.7. Their corresponding values are 0.96 and 0.94, respectively. A higher ROC AUC value indicates stronger discriminative power. The ROC AUC values indicate that the model can successfully differentiate between positive and negative occurrences. The ROC-AUC scores indicate the ability of the model to differentiate between heart disease patients. Higher ROC-AUC highlights the superior predictive capacity of the model. Our experiment found that the UAE model's ROC-AUC score is 0.96, and the PCA-based model is 0.94. Therefore, the Autoencoder model demonstrates an extraordinary classification performance against the PCA model. We also observe that the UAE and PCA exhibit robust discriminatory skills. Even though

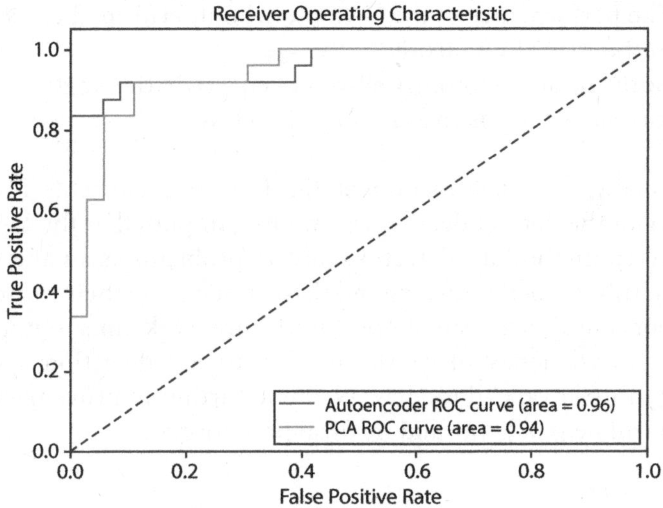

Figure 8.7 Receiver operating characteristics: UAE vs. PCA.

the ROC-AUC score of the PCA is slightly lower than the Autoencoder, it is still significant. This signifies that both the PCA and UAE feature set models could effectively differentiate between positive and negative examples.

8.5 Conclusion

The practical exploration and assessment of cardiac disease detection models are essential in the current societal context. These models provide valuable insights into standard feature engineering methods. This study emphasizes how well-suited sophisticated models handle intricate patterns and representations common in the medical field.

In this study, we have investigated two critical approaches for feature engineering: the Principal Component Analysis (PCA) and the Undercomplete Autoencoder (UAE). This study uses the prediction performance metrics such as accuracy, precision, recall, and F1-score metrics for model evaluation. Through the experiment results, we have observed that:

1. Identification and classification of cardiac disorders by the UAE and PCA models achieved an impressive 90% accuracy.
2. The Autoencoder demonstrated a promising 0.96 AUC-ROC predictive ability, while PCA achieved 0.94.

3. The performance of the UAE model outperformed the PCA in the AUC-ROC score.
4. Both models showed well-balanced predictive metric performance for positive and negative classes.

Additionally, our examination of the feature coefficients reveals the complexity of the dataset details. This finding implies that the UAE might be a preferred method for detecting cardiac problems as an alternative to PCA. With this, we better understand these models and their consequences for real-world healthcare situations. Our future work aims to improve the accuracy and efficiency of cardiovascular disease detection systems by designing more advanced models. We hope further improvements in this discipline will help patients and medical practitioners.

References

1. Cardiovascular Diseases (CVDs), June 11, 2021, https://www.who.int/news- room/fact-sheets/detail/cardiovascular-diseases-(cvds).
2. Muhammad, Y., Tahir, M., Hayat, M., To Chong, K., Early and accurate detection and diagnosis of heart disease using an intelligent computational model. *Sci. Rep.*, 10, 1, 19747, 2020.
3. Loffroy, R., Falvo, N., Galland, C., Fréchier, L., Ledan, F., Midulla, M., Chevallier, O., Intravascular ultrasound in the endovascular treatment of patients with peripheral arterial disease: current role and future perspectives. *Front. Cardiovasc. Med.*, 7, 551861, 2020.
4. Samuels, B.A., Shah, S.M., Widmer, R.J., Kobayashi, Y., Miner, S.ES., Taqueti, V.R., Jeremias, A., *et al.*, Comprehensive Management of ANOCA, Part 1—Definition, Patient Population, and Diagnosis: JACC State-of-the-Art Review. *J. Am. Coll. Cardiol.*, 82, 12, 1245–1263, 2023.
5. Chang, V., Bhavani, V.R., Xu, A.Q., Hossain, M.A., An artificial intelligence model for heart disease detection using machine learning algorithms. *Healthcare Anal.*, 2, 100016, 2022.
6. Bhatt, C.M., Patel, P., Ghetia, T., Mazzeo, P.L., Effective heart disease prediction using machine learning techniques. *Algorithms*, 16, 2, 88, 2023.
7. Ambekar, S. and Phalnikar, R., Disease risk prediction by using convolutional neural network, in: *2018 Fourth international conference on computing communication control and automation (ICCUBEA)*, IEEE, pp. 1–5, 2018.
8. Ramprakash, P., Sarumathi, R., Mowriya, R., Nithyavishnupriya, S., Heart disease prediction using deep neural network, in: *2020 International Conference on Inventive Computation Technologies (ICICT)*, IEEE, pp. 666–670, 2020.

9. Maini, E., Venkateswarlu, B., Gupta, A., Applying machine learning algorithms to develop a universal cardiovascular disease prediction system, in: *International Conference on Intelligent Data Communication Technologies and Internet of Things (ICICI) 2018*, Springer International Publishing, pp. 627–632, 2019.
10. Mohan, S., Thirumalai, C., Srivastava, G., Effective heart disease prediction using hybrid machine learning techniques. *IEEE Access*, 7, 81542–81554, 2019.
11. Shah, D., Patel, S., Bharti, S.K., Heart disease prediction using machine learning techniques. *SN Comput. Sci.*, 1, 1–6, 2020.
12. Garg, A., Sharma, B., Khan, R., Heart disease prediction using machine learning techniques, in: *IOP Conference Series: Materials Science and Engineering*, vol. 1022, p. 012046, IOP Publishing, 2021.
13. Yadav, K.K., Sharma, A., Badholia, A., Heart disease prediction using machine learning techniques. *Inf. Technol. Industry*, 9, 1, 207–214, 2021.
14. Latha, C.B.C. and Carolin Jeeva, S., Improving the accuracy of heart disease risk prediction based on ensemble classification techniques. *Inf. Med. Unlocked*, 16, 100203, 2019.
15. Singh, H., Navaneeth, N.V., Nath Pillai, G., Multisurface proximal SVM based decision trees for heart disease classification, in: *TENCON 2019-2019 IEEE Region 10 Conference (TENCON)*, IEEE, pp. 13–18, 2019.
16. Sowmiya, C. and Sumitra, P., RETRACTED ARTICLE: A hybrid approach for mortality prediction for heart patients using ACO-HKNN. *J. Ambient Intell. Hum. Comput.*, 12, 5, 5405–5412, 2021.
17. Alotaibi, F.S., Implementation of machine learning model to predict heart failure disease. *Int. J. Adv. Comput. Sci. Appl.*, 10, 6, 156–157, 2019.
18. Nikookar, E. and Naderi, E., Hybrid ensemble framework for heart disease detection and prediction. *Int. J. Adv. Comput. Sci. Appl.*, 9, 5, 2018.
19. Tama, B.A., Im, S., Lee, S., Improving an intelligent detection system for coronary heart disease using a two-tier classifier ensemble. *BioMed. Res. Int.*, 2020, 2020.
20. Li, J.P., Ul Haq, A., Ud Din, S., Khan, J., Khan, A., Saboor, A., Heart disease identification method using machine learning classification in e-healthcare. *IEEE Access*, 8, 107562–107582, 2020.
21. Sarmah, S.S., An efficient IoT-based patient monitoring and heart disease prediction system using deep learning modified neural network. *IEEE Access*, 8, 135784–135797, 2020.
22. Chauhan, U., Kumar, V., Chauhan, V., Tiwary, S., Kumar, A., Cardiac arrest prediction using machine learning algorithms, in: *2019 2nd international conference on intelligent computing, instrumentation and control technologies (ICICICT)*, vol. 1, pp. 886–890, IEEE, 2019.

23. Pan, Y., Fu, M., Cheng, B., Tao, X., Guo, J., Enhanced deep learning assisted convolutional neural network for heart disease prediction on the internet of medical things platform. *IEEE Access*, 8, 189503–189512, 2020.
24. Fitriyani, N.L., Syafrudin, M., Alfian, G., Rhee, J., HDPM: an effective heart disease prediction model for a clinical decision support system. *IEEE Access*, 8, 133034–133050, 2020.
25. Tate, A.R. and Rao, G., Activity trackers, wearables, noninvasive technologies for early detection, and management of cardiometabolic risks. *Int. J. Biomed.*, 10, 189–197, 2020.
26. Chen, Y., Zhang, L., Qin, X., Yi, B., Preoperative risk prediction of heart failure with numerical and textual attributes, 2020.
27. Shankar, VV., Kumar, V., Devagade, U., Karanth, V., Rohitaksha, K., Heart disease prediction using CNN algorithm. *SN Comput. Sci.*, 1, 3, 170, 2020.
28. Singh, A. and Kumar, R., Heart disease prediction using machine learning algorithms, in: *2020 international conference on electrical and electronics engineering (ICE3)*, IEEE, pp. 452–457, 2020.
29. Ramachandran, H.K., Rangarajan, A.K., Dhanaraj, R.K., Smart Hand-Hygiene Compliance and Temperature Monitoring System to Tackle COVID-19-like Pathogens in Healthcare Institutions, in: *Technological Advancement in Internet of Medical Things and Blockchain for Personalized Healthcare*, pp. 161–186, CRC Press, 2024. https://www.taylorfrancis.com/chapters/edit/10.1201/9781003405450-10/smart-hand-hygiene-compliance-temperature-monitoring-system-tackle-covid-19-like-pathogens-healthcare-institutions-hari-krishnan-ramachandran-aravind-krishnaswamy-rangarajan-rajesh-kumar-dhanaraj.
30. Cohen, S., Liu, A., Wang, F., Guo, L., Brophy, J.M., Abrahamowicz, M., Therrien, J., *et al.*, Risk prediction models for heart failure admissions in adults with congenital heart disease. *Int. J. Cardiol*, 322, 149–157, 2021.
31. Chang, D., Chang, D., Pourhomayoun, M., Risk prediction of critical vital signs for ICU patients using recurrent neural network, in: *2019 International Conference on Computational Science and Computational Intelligence (CSCI)*, IEEE, pp. 1003–1006, 2019.
32. Ali Amer, Y., Ahmed, F.W., Vranken, J., de Korte-de Boer, D., Smit-Fun, V., Duflot, P., Beaupain, M.-H., *et al.*, Vital signs prediction and early warning score calculation based on continuous monitoring of hospitalised patients using wearable technology. *Sensors*, 20, 22, 6593, 2020.
33. Stehlik, J., Schmalfuss, C., Bozkurt, B., Nativi-Nicolau, J., Wohlfahrt, P., Wegerich, S., Rose, K., *et al.*, Continuous wearable monitoring analytics predict heart failure hospitalization: the LINK-HF multicenter study. *Circulation Heart Fail.*, 13, 3, e006513, 2020.
34. Malviya, R., Sundram, S., Kumar Dhanaraj, R., Kadry, S. (Eds.), *Digital Transformation in Healthcare 5.0*, De Gruyter, 2024. https://www.degruyter.com/document/doi/10.1515/9783111327853/html.

35. Yang, L., Wu, H., Jin, X., Zheng, P., Hu, S., Xu, X., Yu, W., Yan, J., Study of cardiovascular disease prediction model based on random forest in eastern China. *Sci. Rep.*, 10, 1, 5245, 2020.
36. Made, F., Engelbert, A., Nonterah, N.T., Ntlebi, V., Naicker, N., Ten-year risk of fatal cardiovascular disease and its association with metabolic risk factors among waste pickers in South Africa. *BMC Cardiovasc. Disord.*, 21, 1, 1–8, 2021.
37. Kumar, P., Bhati, B.S., Dhanaraj, R.K., Iwendi, C., Balusamy, B., Bhati, N.S., Rai, P., Feature subset selection using heuristic and metaheuristic approaches for diabetes prediction on a binary encoded dataset, in: *International Journal of Modeling, Simulation, and Scientific Computing*, World Scientific Pub Co Pte Ltd, 2024. https://worldscientific.com/doi/abs/10.1142/S1793962324500314.
38. Ali, F., Alghamdi, W., Almagrabi, A.O., Alghushairy, O., Banjar, A., Khalid, M., Deep-AGP: Prediction of angiogenic protein by integrating two-dimensional convolutional neural network with discrete cosine transform. *Int. J. Biol. Macromol.*, 243, 125296, 2023 Jul 15. doi: 10.1016/j.ijbiomac.2023.125296. Epub 2023 Jun 8. PMID: 37301349.
39. Cherian, R.P., Thomas, N., Venkitachalam, S., Weight optimized neural network for heart disease prediction using hybrid lion plus particle swarm algorithm. *J. Biomed. Inf.*, 110, 103543, 2020.
40. Rani, P., Kumar, R., Sid Ahmed, N.MO., Jain, A., A decision support system for heart disease prediction based upon machine learning. *J. Reliab. Intell. Environ.*, 7, 3, 263–275, 2021.
41. Geetha, R., Jegatheesan, A., Dhanaraj, R.K., *et al.*, CVS-FLN: a novel IoT-IDS model based on metaheuristic feature selection and neural network classification model. *Multimed. Tools Appl.*, 83, 86557–86591, 2024. https://doi.org/10.1007/s11042-024-19617-7
42. Borboni, A., Vardhana Reddy, K.V., Elamvazuthi, I., AL-Quraishi, M.S., Natarajan, E., Azhar Ali, S.S., The Expanding Role of Artificial Intelligence in Collaborative Robots for Industrial Applications: A Systematic Review of Recent Works. *Mach.*, 11, 1, 111, 2023.
43. Cynthia, E.P., Mohamad Samuri, S.B., Shir Li, W., Ismanto, E., Afriyanti, L., Imam Arifandy, M., Improved Machine Learning Algorithm for Heart Disease Prediction Based on Hyperparameter Tuning, in: *2023 IEEE International Conference on Artificial Intelligence in Engineering and Technology (IICAIET)*, IEEE, pp. 176–181, 2023.
44. Shah, A., Ahirrao, S., Pandya, S., Kotecha, K., Rathod, S., Smart cardiac framework for an early detection of cardiac arrest condition and risk. *Front. Public Health*, 9, 762303, 2021.
45. Devare, V.S., Heart Disease Prediction Using Binary Classification, 2023.
46. Alshammari, H.H. and Alzahrani, A., Employing a hybrid lion-firefly algorithm for recognition and classification of olive leaf disease in Saudi Arabia. *Alex. Eng. J.*, 84, 215–226, 2023.

47. Kramer, M.A., Nonlinear principal component analysis using autoassociative neural networks. *AIChE J.*, 37, 2, 233–243, 1991.
48. Deivendran, G., Vishal Balaji, S., Paramasivan, B., Vimal, S., Coronary Illness Prediction Using the AdaBoost Algorithm, in: *Sensor Data Analysis and Management: The Role of Deep Learning*, 161–172, 2021.

9

Application of Intelligent Computational Techniques in the Development of Smart Cities

K. Kalaivani[1]*, S. Arun[1], K. Ulagapriya[1], A. Saritha[1], B. Shanthini[2] and R. Rani Hemamalini[3]

[1]*Department of Computer Science and Engineering, Vels Institute of Science, Technology and Advanced Studies, Pallavaram, Chennai, Tamil Nadu, India*
[2]*Department of CSE, St. Peter's Institute of Higher Education and Research, AVADI, Chennai, Tamil Nadu, India*
[3]*Department of EEE, St. Peter's Institute of Higher Education and Research, AVADI, Chennai, Tamil Nadu, India*

Abstract

In other words, a smart city uses Information and Communication Technology (ICT) to better use and more efficiently consume limited resources like space, mobility, and energy. Existing research has been conducted on recent developments on Internet of Things (IoT)-based smart city applications; however, there is a need to deliver an innovative idea, such as IoT-embedded vision for smart cities focused on various systems such as noise and air pollution monitoring, web monitoring, and fire detection system design along with the implementation aspects towards smart waste bins, etc., which have not been addressed precisely in previous works. This thesis aims to design a system for Air and Noise Imprint Monitoring/Control, Speed Monitoring/Web Monitoring, Temperature/Weather Monitoring for IoT, as well Fire Detection System, to be implemented soon after the start-up of this entire project for Smart Waste Bin Management and geographical information system (GIS)-based smart city innovation with high-level digitized software that is convenient enough and fast in providing effective actions using IoT. Under the proposed system, each time we collect readings of a given parameter, it is moved into the risk area. The status of the factors has been detected by them, in real-time, and an

**Corresponding author*: kalai.se@vistas.ac.in

R. Sathiyaraj, Rajesh Kumar Dhanaraj, K. Arun Kumar, Rutvij H. Jhaveri and A. Mohamed Abbas (eds.) Predictive Methods in Next-Generation Computing: An Approach Toward Sustainability, (175–192)

analysis is conducted on the data collected from various sensors. The suggested work has been verified using the real-time case study.

***Keywords*:** IoT-integrated smart city, air and noise impairments monitoring/ control system, speed and web monitoring system, temperature

9.1 Introduction

Among the many possible authentication methods for smart cities, biometric authentication offers the highest level of security. Biometric authentication systems come in a variety of forms. A thorough evaluation of available biometrics will be conducted in this study, with the goal of selecting the most accurate and secure option based on criteria such as the likelihood of fraud. Reducing theft and protecting the city from fraudulent users are the primary goals of biometric authentication. This thesis's authentication system makes use of a novel edge detection method called the fuzzy interference system.

9.1.1 Organization of the Chapter

The chapter is structured as follows. Section 9.2 provides an analysis of the performance of several biometric methods with respect to their uniqueness, permanence, fraud potential, and performance. A comprehensive outline of the Iris Recognition system is provided in Section 9.3. The iris recognition system's overall algorithm is described in Section 9.4. The block diagram of the Iris recognition system is described in depth in Section 9.5. Section 9.6 provides a study of the iris recognition system's performance. Section 9.7 wraps up the project.

9.2 Motivation and Justification

Password, multi-factor, certificate, biometric, and token-based authentication are the five primary categories of authentication methods. Due to its inconvenient nature and the ease with which an attacker might hack it, password authentication is not suitable for many environments. All three of these authentication methods—certification-based, multi-factor, and token-based—are labor-intensive, resource-intensive, and vulnerable to fraud. The use of biometric authentication addresses the aforementioned disadvantages, despite the availability of several biometric authentication technologies.

Due to its one-of-a-kind pattern, lightning-fast matching, and resilience to fraud, iris identification stands head and shoulders above the competition. Therefore, the iris authentication mechanism is used in this study.

9.3 Iris Recognition System

Image processing involves making adjustments to or removing unwanted information from a picture. The introduction of digital cameras and their seamless compatibility with other hardware devices, including computers, greatly simplified digital picture processing. The first step in processing images is identifying and then separating relevant areas within the picture. Algorithms such as cluster-based, threshold-based, and statistics-based approaches are used for segmentation in various ways.

Iris recognition systems rely on mathematical patterns in iris images to provide biometric identification of humans. One or both of the human eye's irises are considered for the purpose of iris recognition. The unique pattern seen in each person's iris is the basis for iris recognition technology. These distinct patterns remain visible from a given distance and remain stable throughout life.

The cornea is a highly permeable membrane that shields the iris, an internal organ, from harm. Fingerprints become more difficult to distinguish after a certain amount of time has passed, which is the major distinction between iris scans and fingerprints.

There are many different applications for iris recognition algorithms, including automatic border crossing systems that do not need a passport, educational institutions, airports, smart cities, email verification, multimedia workstations, theft detection, and many more. The key benefits of this iris identification system are its stability, protection of the organs, and rapid matching speed, as well as its high resistance to false matches.

The practice of comparing data sets with those belonging to specific individuals is known as human identification. The act of acknowledging or affirming one's identity as a certain individual is known as identification. Recognizing one another's efforts helps build trust and discourages dishonesty. Biometric identification encompasses a wide range of distinguishing physical and behavioral traits, including but not limited to fingerprints, iris scans, retina scans, facial features, hand geometry, voice, and signatures, among many others. Autonomous, precise, and rapid person recognition is the holy grail of biometric systems. Finding the false acceptance ratio of fraudulent users and the false rejection percentage of legitimate owners of biometrics is one way to test the performance and accuracy of a biometric system.

Table 9.1 Comparison of different biometrics.

Biometrics	Universal	Uniqueness	Permanence	Performance	Potential to fraud
Face	High	Low	Medium	Low	Low
Fingerprint	Medium	High	High	High	Low
Iris	High	High	High	High	Low
Signature	Low	Low	Low	Low	High
Voice	Medium	Low	Low	Low	High
DNA	High	High	High	High	Low

The accuracy level provided by iris biometrics is superior to that of other biometric approaches. The human eye's iris, a delicate circular diaphragm that sits between the cornea and lens, has a distinct epigenetic pattern that stays constant from birth to old age. Every human iris is distinct, and even identical twins can't help but look different. Research has shown that people also have different iris patterns on their left and right eyes. The reliability, accuracy, and longevity of different biometric methods may vary widely. Table 9.1 shows the comparability of these features.

From the comparison table, it is clear that iris and DNA have a high degree of universal, uniqueness, permanence, and performance. Since DNA is difficult to collect, iris is used in this work.

9.4 Algorithm for Iris Recognition System

Step 1: File Upload
The use of a digital camera allows for the collection of input images. This project makes use of the CASIA V4 database, which consists of approximately 54,000 iris samples.
Step 2: Standardize
Align and crop the iris images to a consistent size and orientation, ensuring uniformity across all samples.
Step 3: Resize
Resize the picture to alter the pixel intensity value by raising the contrast. The camera clip pictures can be gathered from a variety of distances, angles, and proximities. To save computation and time, the input picture is scaled to a 255 by 255 matrix.

Step 4: Equalize the Histogram
Histogram equalization is used after picture scaling to further improve contrast. This step is used to adjust the intensity value of the chosen photos. This is used to adjust the grayscale image's contrast. Using the notation l to describe the provided picture, we can see that there are 256 distinct values for the image's pixel intensity, which range from 0 to L-1. The next step is to use the mr matrix to represent the picture in a matrix format.
Step 5: Apply Masking
Fuzzy interference logic is used for the purpose of masking. It is able to identify almost every edge in a given input picture. A 2×2 window mask, dragged over the whole input picture, may be used to identify the input image's edges. Initially, the input is fuzzified in the Fuzzy Interference System (FIS) by establishing two trapezoidal membership functions, referred to as Black and White. All of the pixels in the input picture are made to fit into a fuzzy black-and-white set by comparing these two membership functions.
Step 6: Evaluation Based on Rules
The output is obtained using a rule-based assessment after fuzzification. The rule-based approach of fuzzy interference systems labels a sharp change from white to black pixels as an edge. To get the edge, the input picture was subjected to ten criteria. X1, X2, X3, and X4 are the four input pixels used by the Fuzzy Interference logic, which generates a single output variable. The OR (max) operation is used to aggregate these fuzzy results.
Step 7: Feature Extraction
Features for texture extraction and false detection are obtained. Verify that the supplied picture matches the original. With feature extraction, the original picture data is preserved while being converted into a numerical value that can be simply processed. The input picture is used to extract texture and characteristics for fraud detection. These characteristics may change depending on the pixel value of the supplied picture.
Step 8: Assessment
This step involves checking the retrieved features from the input picture against the features stored in the database. Analyzing the retrieved value by comparing it to previously recorded data is called evaluation.
Step 9: Classification
The characteristics of the input images are checked against those previously retrieved and stored in the database. The

individual will be categorized as either approved or unauthorized depending on whether both characteristics match. A dialog box indicates this classification. A Support Vector Machine (SVM) Classifier is used to classify images.

Classification using a support vector machine (SVM) classifier begins with the feature extraction phase, which involves extracting and storing a variety of characteristics from training data. The testing step involves matching the derived features with the features already recorded in the database. If the two characteristics are the same, then the individual is approved; otherwise, they are not.

9.5 Block Diagram of Iris Recognition System

One kind of biometric authentication that people utilize to be identified is iris recognition. Iris biometrics offers a high level of accuracy in contrast to other biometric techniques like fingerprint, face, voice, etc. While facial recognition and fingerprints are among the most commonly used biometric techniques, recent research has shown that fingerprint recognition systems have several limitations. Injuries to the finger, the cumulative effects of years of manual work, etc., can render fingerprint recognition ineffective. There are a lot of problems with biometric identification methods; therefore, we are switching to iris biometric identification, which is more secure. Iris biometric identification makes use of digital cameras to acquire pictures of a person's iris. The unique mathematical pattern seen in each human iris determines the unique iris picture. Iris patterns are one-of-a-kind and never change. Thanks to the eyelids, the iris is a well-protected organ. The two-part process of iris identification and authentication is the focus of the proposed effort.

The training process is the first step of an iris recognition system. While in training, the biometric system will be taught using a set of pre-existing data points. The second step of developing an iris recognition system is testing. The input picture will be compared to the biometric system's existing database during the testing phase. The user's iris will be identified if the two sets of data are identical; otherwise, a dialog box will be shown to inform the user that their iris was not recognized. Both steps include acquiring, preprocessing, and segmenting iris pictures from the CASIA Iris V4 database. Features are taken from the pictures that have been segmented.

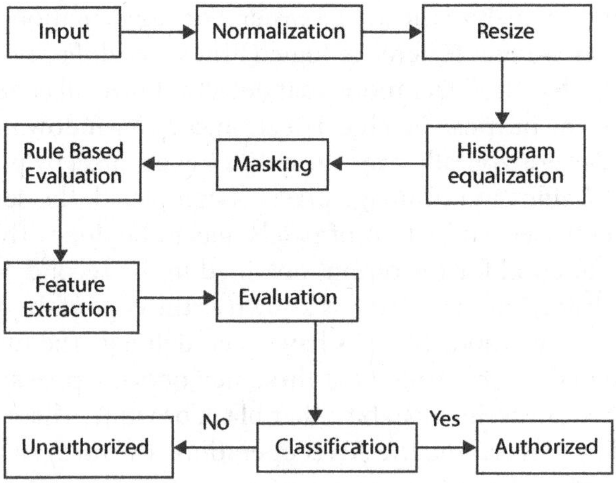

Figure 9.1 Block diagram of iris biometric security system.

The testing process concludes with an authorized match of the test image's retrieved features. If the two images match, then the test picture can be considered authorized. Otherwise, it cannot. Figure 9.1 shows the input image and the block diagram that shows the process of smart city growth and recognition.

Images used as input are sourced from the CASIA Iris V4 database. Any color, grayscale, or black-and-white picture may be used as input. The next step is to preprocess the picture to improve or enhance the image data by removing any undesirable noise or distortion. Image properties, such as contrast, are improved during preprocessing in preparation for further processing. Here, an RGB picture is transformed into a grayscale one; once converted, the image may be processed for further processing. Once the picture has been grayscaled, histogram equalization is used to tweak the density of the image to boost contrast.

To simplify the processing of the photograph, it will be downsized to 255×255.

Let the processed image be represented as f, and mc is a matrix representation of that image, denoted as mr.

9.5.1 Edge Detection

Edge detection is the process of detecting edges present in an image. It is used for the segmentation of an image. The main purpose of segmentation is to divide the image into a more meaningful form. The purpose of image segmentation is to analyze the image easier. For segmentation, a new technique known as fuzzy interference logic (FIL) is used. Fuzzy interference logic is an edge detection technique that detects almost all edges present in the image. For the purpose of edge detection, a 2×2 window mask is used. This mask slides horizontally over the entire image, pixel by pixel.

Once the fuzzification of image pixels is completed, the second phase, which is a rule-based evaluation of pixels, has to be done. The triangular membership function for the output obtained in the second phase, which is obtained by applying a rule base, is known as the edge of the given image. In the rule-based method, 10 rules have been defined. The fuzzy interference rule is based on the weights of three neighboring pixels, namely X1, X2, X3, and X4. The weight can be either black or white. These weights can be combined by performing the AND operation. The fuzzy outputs will be combined by using the OR (max) operator.

9.5.2 Variance

Variance can be defined as the measurement of the spread of pixels in an image. It is used to measure how much the pixels vary from the mean or average value in the data set.

The standard deviation (SD) is typically denoted by the Greek letter sigma (σ). The lower the value of standard deviation, the closer the pixels are to the mean value. A higher standard deviation in an image signifies greater variation in pixel intensity values, indicating increased contrast or diversity in brightness levels across the image. The contrast or intensity variation in an image is measured by

$$\mathrm{C} = \mathrm{x}\, \Sigma_{\mathrm{y}}\, \Sigma(x - y)2I(x, y)$$

Where, I(x,y) represents the pixel intensity at coordinates (x,y).

9.5.3 Support Vector Machine

In the SVM classifier, "svm-train" is used for the purpose of training data, and "svm-classify" is used for the purpose of classifying the data. To better understand the SVM classifier, refer to the following figure, where the x-axis represents positive data samples for training, and "o" denotes the negative data samples for training. A decision boundary is a hyperplane, also known as a separating hyperplane, as shown in Figure 9.3, with the points labeled as A, B, and C. Figures 9.2–9.9 exhibits the hyperplane, margin and the performance evaluation of biometric system.

X1	X2
X3	X4

Figure 9.2 Input pixels for the fuzzy interference logic (FIL).

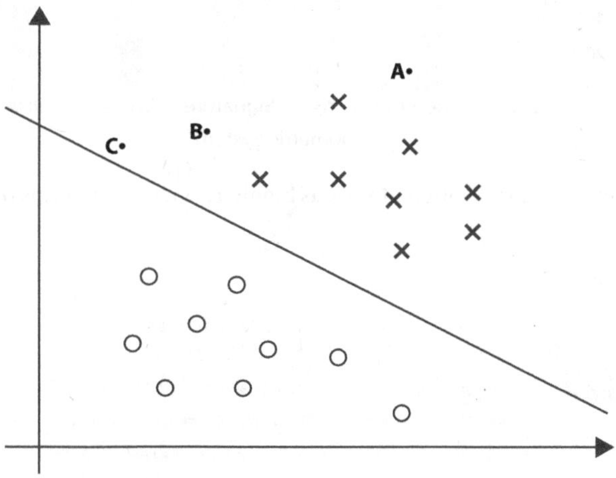

Figure 9.3 Hyperplane separation.

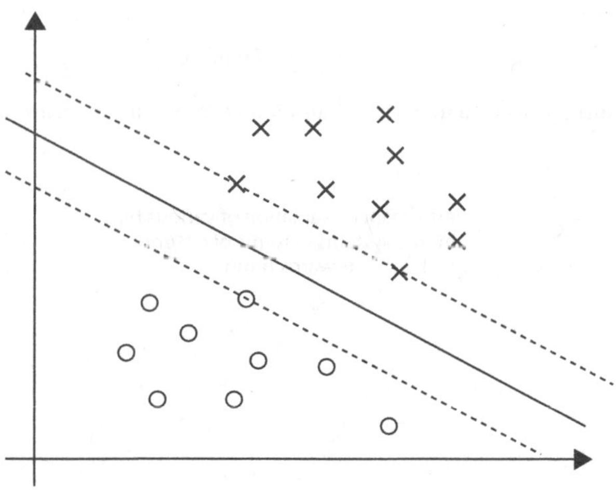

Figure 9.4 Maximum margin separation.

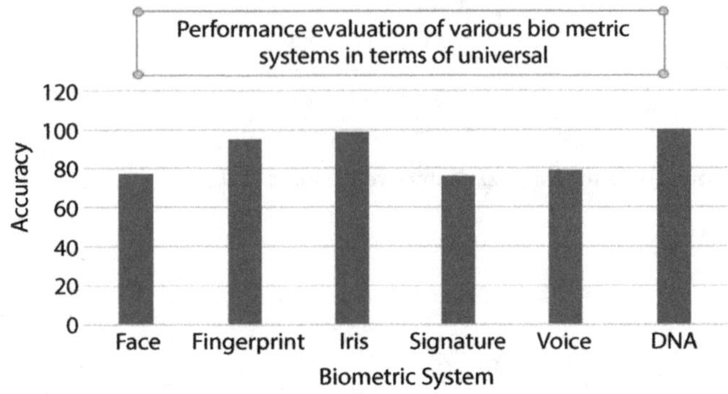

Figure 9.5 Performance evaluation of various biometric systems in terms of uniqueness.

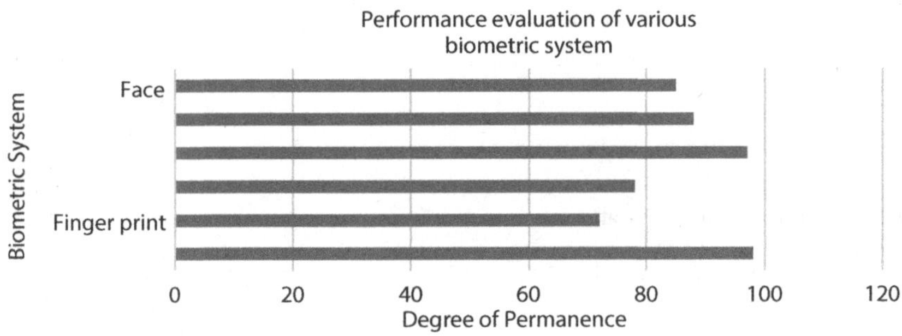

Figure 9.6 Performance evaluation of various biometric systems in terms of permanence.

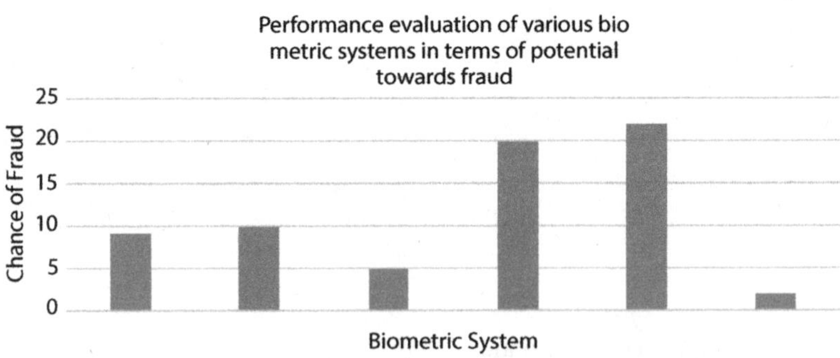

Figure 9.7 Performance evaluation of various biometric systems in terms of potential for fraud.

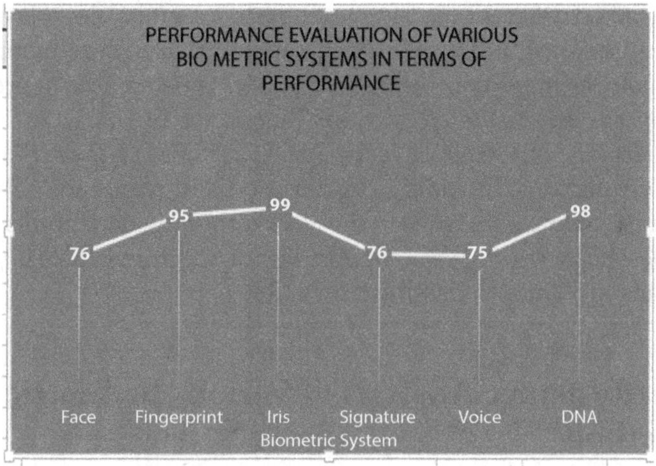

Figure 9.8 Performance evaluation of various biometric systems in terms of performance.

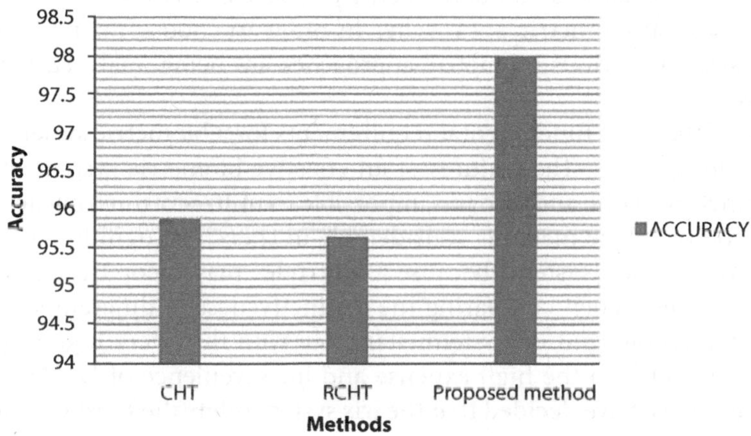

Figure 9.9 Classification of iris recognition system based on the method used.

Consider the figure below, in which the maximum margin separating the hyperplane is shown by the solid line.

Image data is classified using a support vector machine classifier. To identify a certain person, we use a support vector machine classifier. Human recognition relies on matching incoming data with pre-existing data stored in the dataset and then categorizing the results. It is possible to identify the individual if the two sets of data are identical. Moreover, SVM classifiers are capable of carrying out several classifications. The SVM classifier provides a very high level of accuracy and can generate multiple classifier outputs based on different decision boundaries or multi-class classification strategies. Instead of basing its design on empirical risk reduction, SVM takes a structural approach. The SVM classifier is better able to prevent the overfitting issue due to the architecture mentioned before.

The hyperplane of a support vector machine (SVM) allows it to perform a variety of functions, including classification and regression. The hyperplane with the greatest distance to the closest training data points will provide the best separation. With support vector machines (SVMs), a larger margin leads to a smaller classification error.

9.6 Performance Analysis of Various Biometric Method

Any system may be made more secure using biometric authentication. Research in the area of biometric systems is becoming popular, in addition to password locks and standard security systems. It is recommended to analyze several biometric approaches in order to choose the best recognition system. Various biometric approaches are being analyzed for this purpose.

One of the most fundamental requirements for a biometric system is its level of uniqueness. The features of an effective biometric system should be distinct from one another and impossible to utilize by third parties. The likelihood of a false match is considerable in speech recognition and signature recognition systems because an intruder may theoretically exploit these qualities. When comparing the distinctiveness of different systems, DNA and iris recognition systems stand out with their very high levels of uniqueness. Due to the high expense and inconvenience of DNA system installation, we have decided that the iris system offers the most distinctive benefits.

Similarly, the performance of a biometric system is classified based on the permanence feature. By analyzing the permanence value of different biometric systems, it is found that the DNA recognition system provides a high degree of permanence. Although the permanence of the DNA recognition system is high, due to the practical difficulties in the implementation process, we are going for the iris biometric system, which is easier to gather. The permanence feature of a biometric system denotes the stability of the biometric, such as face, voice, signature, fingerprint, etc., that remains unchanged despite external factors.

The permanence feature denotes the unchangeable characteristics of a biometric that remain the same throughout a lifetime. By analyzing various methods, it is found that certain biometric methods provide a low degree of permanence and, hence, cannot be used for security purposes. For accurate identification, the permanence of the system should be high. Since the implementation of the iris recognition system is easy and has a high degree of permanence, it can be used for security purposes in smart cities.

Potential for fraud describes the ability of the system to withstand or fail to recognize fraudulent users attempting to enter a smart city. While considering voice and signature recognition systems, the potential for fraud is very high. For example, in the case of a voice recognition system, the chances of fraud are high as one can imitate the voice of another person. Hence, it is not safe to use these recognition systems. As the potential for fraud is low in the iris recognition system, it is considered a better system for protection from intruders attempting to enter a smart city.

Because the effectiveness of biometric methods relies on the permanence and uniqueness of their features—as well as their resistance to fraud—biometric analysis demonstrates that DNA recognition systems are very effective, since their features are stable and do not change over the course of a person's lifetime. The DNA aspects remain the same, and the system performs to a great degree; however, implementing it is a pain. It is still challenging to identify individuals using the same methods, even if we build a system that relies on DNA collcction. It is hard to acquire DNA samples on a consistent basis due to the recognition system's authorization features. We are moving on to a more advanced biometric identification system, the iris recognition system, due to the aforementioned disadvantages.

Iris recognition technology is simple to set up and maintain, thanks to its analysis of many biometric traits. Due to its good performance, it is used for the purpose of authentication of the person.

For a good recognition system, it is important to choose the best method for authentication. In the proposed method Fuzzy Interference Logic System (FIS) was implemented. While going through previous research, it was found that the Circular Hough Transform, Right Circular Hough Transform, and many other methods have been implemented. In those cases, the rate of false rejection as well as false acceptance is high compared to the proposed method. The accuracy of a biometric system can be determined by calculating the false acceptance and false rejection ratios. The proposed method shows a high degree of accuracy.

9.6.1 Performance Evaluation

The performance of the system can be calculated in terms of accuracy. Accuracy is defined as the ratio of the summation of the number of false acceptances and false rejections to the total number of identifications attempted. Let us discuss the False Acceptance Ratio (FAR) and False Rejection Ratio (FRR) in a biometric system in detail.

9.6.1.1 *False Acceptance Ratio (FAR)*

The ratio of the number of false acceptances to the number of samples evaluated is called the False Acceptance Ratio. The term "false acceptance" describes the percentage of biometric samples that the system accepted as valid notwithstanding their falsity. The FAR ratio needs to fall below 0.10 to be considered an effective biometric system. An FAR may be expressed as:

$$FAR = FA / TA \tag{9.1}$$

where,
FAR = False Acceptance Ratio
FA = No. of False Acceptance
TA = Total no. of attempt

9.6.1.2 *False Rejection Ratio (FRR)*

The ratio of the number of samples examined to the number of erroneous rejections is called the False Rejection Ratio. The False Rejection Ratio measures the frequency with which an authorized user was not successfully verified or identified by the system. In a biometric system, variations in texture or dirt might cause a false rejection. For instance, a little cut or dirt on the finger might be the cause of a high false rejection percentage in a fingerprint system. Similarly, if the camera lens is malfunctioning, the iris recognition mechanism will reject the user's iris. An FRR may be expressed as:

$$FRR = FR/TA \tag{9.2}$$

where,
FRR = False Rejection Ratio

FR = No. of False Rejection
TA = Total no. of attempt

9.6.2 Result and Discussion

This work's security system was built using the best of various biometric systems after analyzing them. The CASIA V4 database is used to acquire iris pictures. After the iris pictures are normalized, a novel edge detection approach called Fuzzy Interference Logic is used to discover the edges. When compared to other methods like Canny, Hough, and Circular Hough Transform, this method offers the highest degree of edge identification. Following this, features are retrieved and saved in the database for future categorization. Images with recognized edges are used to extract texture and fraud detection characteristics. SVM is used for classification, ensuring that only approved individuals are granted access to the smart city based on the classification results.

9.7 Summary

This chapter examines and discusses a variety of biometric authentication mechanisms. Iris biometric authentication stands out as the most cost-effective and top-tier biometric authentication solution available today. Every human iris is distinct and remains the same size and shape throughout their lives. While there are a lot of different authentication techniques in use, the false rejection percentage is still significant. To provide more precise user verification, our suggested approach extracts additional information from the picture. This technology can be utilized for indoor security to prevent city invasions and can also enhance safety and access control in smart hospitals, schools, and urban environments.

Bibliography

1. Gomede, E., Gaffo, F.H., Briganó, G.U., De Barros, R.M., Mendes, L.D.S., Application of computational intelligence to improve education in smart cities. *Sensors, 18*, 1, 267, 2018.
2. Iqbal, R., Doctor, F., More, B., Mahmud, S., Yousuf, U., Big data analytics: Computational intelligence techniques and application areas. *Technol. Forecast. Soc. Change, 153*, 119259, 2020.

3. Tong, Z., Ye, F., Yan, M., Liu, H., Basodi, S., A survey on algorithms for intelligent computing and smart city applications. *Big Data Min. Anal.*, *4*, 3, 155–172, 2021.
4. Ali, M.A. and Dhanaraj, R.K., IoMT and blockchain oriented smart healthcare monitoring system. *AIP Conf. Proc.*, 2919, 1, 110001, 2024. https://doi.org/10.1063/5.0184364
5. Corchado, J.M., Pinto-Santos, F., Aghmou, O., Trabelsi, S., Intelligent development of smart cities: Deepint. net case studies, in: *Sustainable Smart Cities and Territories*. Lecture notes in networks and systems, pp. 211–225, Springer International Publishing, 2022. https://doi.org/10.1007/978-3-030-78901-5_19
6. Muhammad, A.N., Aseere, A.M., Chiroma, H., Shah, H., Gital, A.Y., Hashem, I.A.T., Deep learning application in smart cities: recent development, taxonomy, challenges and research prospects. *Neural Comput. Appl.*, *33*, 2973–3009, 2021.
7. Ullah, Z., Al-Turjman, F., Mostarda, L., Gagliardi, R., Applications of artificial intelligence and machine learning in smart cities. *Comput. Commun.*, *154*, 313–329, 2020.
8. Agarwal, P.K., Gurjar, J., Agarwal, A.K., Birla, R., Application of artificial intelligence for development of intelligent transport system in smart cities. *J. Traffic Transp. Eng.*, *1*, 1, 20–30, 2015.
9. Balasubramaniam, S., Kadry, S., Dhanaraj, R.K., *et al.*, Res-Unet based blood vessel segmentation and cardio vascular disease prediction using chronological chef-based optimization algorithm based deep residual network from retinal fundus images. *Multimed. Tools Appl.*, 83, 87929–87958, 2024.
10. Jha, A.K., Ghimire, A., Thapa, S., Jha, A.M., Raj, R., A review of AI for urban planning: Towards building sustainable smart cities, in: *2021 6th International Conference on Inventive Computation Technologies (ICICT)*, IEEE, pp. 937–944, 2021, January.
11. Giordano, A., Spezzano, G., Vinci, A., Smart agents and fog computing for smart city applications, in: *Smart Cities: First International Conference, Smart-CT 2016, Málaga, Spain, June 15-17, 2016, Proceedings 1*, Springer International Publishing, pp. 137–146, 2016.
12. Nayak, J., Vakula, K., Dinesh, P., Naik, B., Mohapatra, S., Swarnkar, T., Mishra, M., Intelligent computing in IoT-enabled smart cities: a systematic review. *Green Technology for Smart City and Society: Proceedings of GTSCS 2020*, pp. 1–21, 2021.
13. Bibri, S.E., Data-driven smart sustainable cities of the future: Urban computing and intelligence for strategic, short-term, and joined-up planning. *Comput. Urban Sci.*, *1*, 1, 8, 2021.

14. Balasubramaniam, S., Arishma, M., Satheesh Kumar, K., Dhanaraj, R.K., A Comprehensive Exploration of Artificial Intelligence Methods for COVID-19 Diagnosis, in: *EAI Endorsed Transactions on Pervasive Health and Technology*, vol. 10, European Alliance for Innovation n.o., 2024.
15. Rath, A., Patnaik, S., Panda, G., Comprehensive review of computational intelligence based smart city community. *J. Intell. Fuzzy Syst.*, *41*, 1, 975–991, 2021.
16. Sehito, N., Shouyi, Y., Alshahrani, H.M., Alamgeer, M., Dutta, A.K., Alsubai, S., Nkenyereye, L., Dhanaraj, R.K., Optimizing User Association, Power Control and Beamforming for 6G Multi-IRS Multi-UAV NOMA Communications in Smart Cities, in: *IEEE Transactions on Consumer Electronics*, Institute of Electrical and Electronics Engineers, IEEE, pp. 1–1, 2024.
17. Sánchez-Corcuera, R., Nuñez-Marcos, A., Sesma-Solance, J., Bilbao-Jayo, A., Mulero, R., Zulaika, U., Almeida, A., Smart cities survey: Technologies, application domains and challenges for the cities of the future. *Int. J. Distrib. Sens. Netw.*, *15*, 6, 1550147719853984, 2019.
18. Alavi, A.H., Jiao, P., Buttlar, W.G., Lajnef, N., Internet of Things-enabled smart cities: State-of-the-art and future trends. *Measurement*, *129*, 589–606, 2018.
19. Krishnamoorthi, S., Dhanaraj, R.K., Hafizul Islam, S., CCM-PRNG: Pseudo-random bit generator based on cross-over chaotic map and its application in image encryption. *Multimed. Tools Appl.*, 83, 80823–80846, 2024.
20. Chen, Q., Wang, W., Wu, F., De, S., Wang, R., Zhang, B., Huang, X., A survey on an emerging area: Deep learning for smart city data. *IEEE Trans. Emerging Top. Comput. Intell.*, *3*, 5, 392–410, 2019.

10

Security and Privacy Issues in Data Processing with Predictive Models

T. Sethukarasi[1]*, A. Thilagavathy[1], Balasubramanian M.[2], R. Rajitha Jasmine[1], Shilpa Murali[3] and Anusha S. L.[4]

[1]R.M.K. Engineering College, Kavaraipettai, India
[2]S.A. Engineering College
[3]LBS Institute Technology for Women Poojappura, Thiruvananthapuram, India
[4]Accenture Services Pvt, Ltd.

Abstract
With the advent of big data and machine learning, the increased capacity to process personal information with predictive models threatens issues regarding privacy and security more so now than ever before. Now, replace every noun in those sentences with any number of other sectors that are likely to become thrashed by unprecedented versions of predictive algorithms, loaded up on record levels of private information. However, the availability of these systems raises obvious questions of bias in an algorithmic configuration, unauthorized access prevention, and data security.

Data security is a significant issue with data processing using predictive models. This involves ensuring that the security of confidential data and sensitive information is protected so it does not become vulnerable to cyber attacks, e-gaming hacking, or password cracking. Implementing strong encryption methods, access control systems, and secure storage protocols can help reduce the severity of these security threats.

Also, the use of Personally Identifiable Information (PII) introduces major privacy issues in predictive modeling. Privacy is a right that belongs to the individual, and there are strong data protection laws such as GDPR (General Data Protection Regulation) or CCPA (California Consumer Privacy Act), which dictate how predictive models should be personally identifiable. By using privacy-preserving algorithms, anonymization approaches, and differential privacy strategies, we can protect the privacy of people while still gaining valuable insights from data.

**Corresponding author*: hod.cse@rmkec.ac.in

R. Sathiyaraj, Rajesh Kumar Dhanaraj, K. Arun Kumar, Rutvij H. Jhaveri and A. Mohamed Abbas (eds.) Predictive Methods in Next-Generation Computing: An Approach Toward Sustainability, (193–206)

Even more seriously, the issue of bias and prejudice in our prediction models risks worsening existing societal injustices and gaps. Biased training sets, algorithm design decisions, or even societal inclinations can be blamed for data bias. To ensure that predictive modeling is fair, it is important to take a careful look at the data collection (recording), model creation (generating), and evaluation measures.

More open and accountable prediction algorithms are, in part, a response to the general use of ever-more pervasive predictive analytics. When a prediction model is live, everyone involved needs an understanding of what goes into the models to make decisions and get out. Model interpretability tools, explainable AI methodology, and auditability metrics can likely help improve intrusion detection system for unstructured data (IDSUD) transparency in a way that allows stakeholders to evaluate the accuracy of both prediction models (i.e., whether they leverage single sources) as well as their equity over protected variables.

In summary, predictive models offer the potential for improved decision-making and innovation but also raise privacy and security challenges. These two big problems have to be part-solved *via* robust security measures, better privacy-enhancing technology mitigating bias, and transparency programs. While enterprises can benefit from big data analytics, the processing of the data with predictive models must be kept secure and private to protect individual rights and societal values.

Keywords: Predictive models, data processing, security, privacy, confidentiality, encryption

10.1 Introduction

According to Liu *et al.* (2015) [1], the intelligent self-configuring nodes that make up the Internet of Things are linked in a worldwide dynamic network. The traditional Internet enables a large number of limited devices and people to establish connections. The Internet of Things (IoT) provides a robust and efficient intelligent computer network that spans many devices, all of which operate independently of humans (Abidi *et al.* 2017). The IoT offers several practical uses for constant monitoring in numerous domains, including healthcare [2].

More and more industries are finding uses for the IoT because of its user-friendly and powerful characteristics. Now that IoT-cloud-based devices are commonplace, the Internet of Things has advanced significantly in the area of handling massive amounts of data. The healthcare system is one area where the IoT-Cloud [3] is finding new uses. Multiple trials are conducted to ensure the security of patient data. The IoT and cloud computing continue to face two major challenges: data security and computing overhead. A further difficult aspect of health systems is illness prediction utilizing patient data acquired *via* IoT sensors [4].

10.2 Literature Survey

Using the naïve premise that all characteristics are independently separate, the Naive Bayes classifiers build on the Bayes Theorem. For each given class Cv and feature vector F = (F1, F2... Fn), the following holds according to Bayes' Theorem [5–10].

To use cipher data to perform computations like addition or multiplication is the definition of full homomorphic encryption (FHE). The two most common methods for performing homomorphic encryptions are the additive and multiplicative types.

10.3 System Model

With the suggested architecture [11–15], we want to secure the Internet of Things (IoT) health cloud system while also making predictions about it. Pictured in Figure 10.1 is the System Model for the HERDE-MSNB architecture that has been suggested. Two distinct frameworks, the

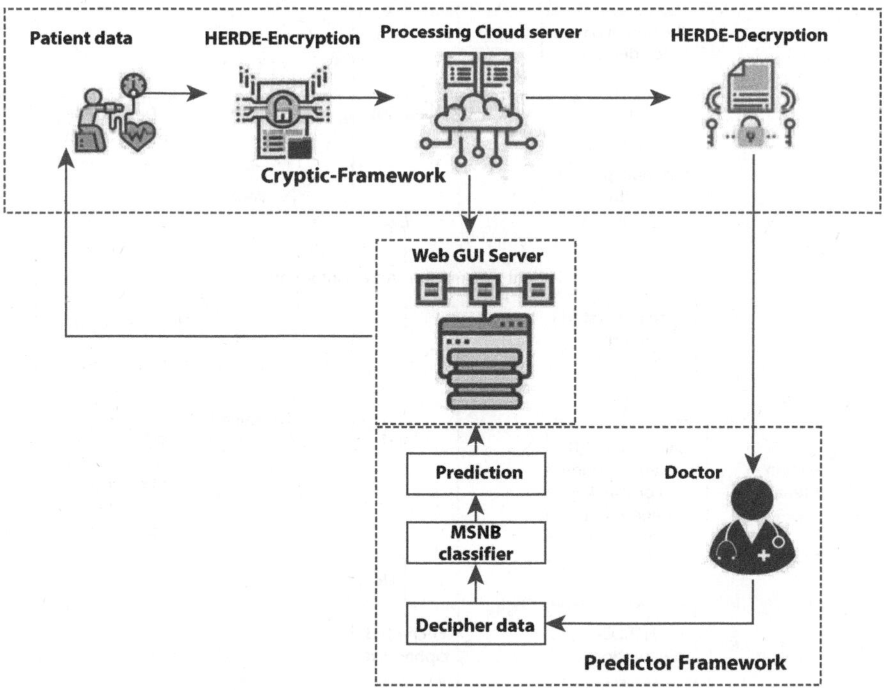

Figure 10.1 System model for proposed HERDE-MSNB architecture.

cryptic and predictive frameworks, make up the suggested system. By using Homomorphic Encryption with Random Diagonal Elliptical curve cryptography (HERDE), the cryptic architecture guards against unwanted access to patient data. There are four distinct steps to the cryptic structure, including patient data collection *via* IoT, data encryption by HERDE, data storage in the cloud, and data decryption *via* HERDE.

The second model is a predictor framework that uses the Multinomial Smoothing Naive Bayes (MSNB) model to forecast the patient's illness. The deciphered patient data is sent into the MSNB model within the prediction framework. The patient's disease is predicted using the MSNB classifier. Through the use of a web-based graphical user interface (GUI) [16–20], the predictor framework and the cryptic framework are linked. Doctors, clouds, and the Internet of Things can all communicate with one another over the web GUI.

10.3.1 Cryptic Framework

A cryptic framework and a prediction framework are the two main components of the suggested design. You can see the security model in Figure 10.2.

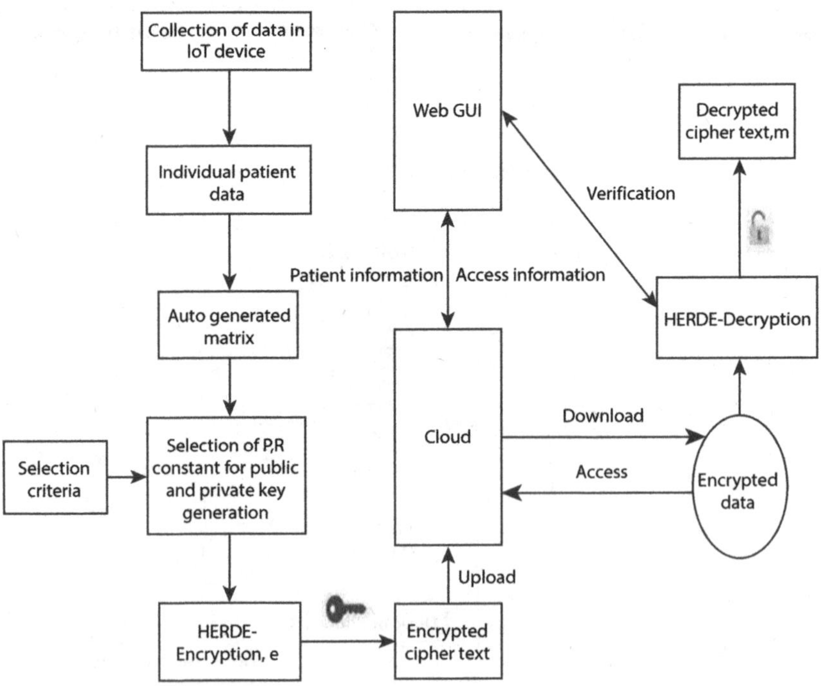

Figure 10.2 Cryptic framework.

A combination of Homomorphic Encryption (HE) and random diagonal elliptical curve cryptography forms the basis of the suggested security paradigm. Cloud data storage encrypts the information retrieved from IoT devices using the HERDE algorithm. A decryption key allows the doctor to access encrypted data stored in the cloud. Keys are created using an auto-generated matrix according to selection criteria in this suggested approach. Only some patient data can be decrypted so the doctor may access it. That is why every patient's key generation is different.

10.3.2 Prediction Framework

The MSNB prediction model uses patient data to provide illness predictions in this suggested framework [21–29]. Figure 10.3 displays the suggested MSNB prediction model. The patient's illness was predicted using the MSNB prediction model. Before feeding it into the MSNB model, the doctor decrypts the patient's data stored on a cloud server. The decrypted patient data is split into two sections: training data, which comprises 70% of the total, and test data, which accounts for 30%. By classifying characteristics, the MSNB prediction model is able to foretell the patient's illness. With both sets of data, we put the MSNB prediction model through its paces. The efficacy of the prediction model is evaluated using several performance measures.

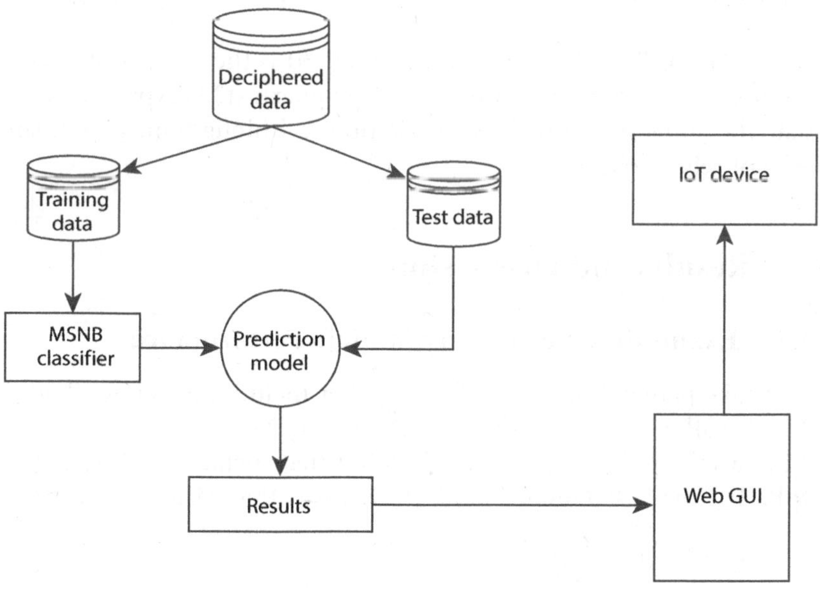

Figure 10.3 Prediction framework.

10.4 System Algorithm

A 4x4 matrix (RDm) is generated using random integers during the cryptographic framework setup process, which the administrator executes using the security parameter SD.

A random number and the location of the generator are the two parameters that the Keygen algorithm takes as input. The secret key (Sk) is a random number chosen from RDm by the IoT admin (IA) during patient registration in the proposed system. A secret key (Sk) and a generator point G are used to calculate the public key (Pk).

Indexing the keyword is done on plain text and a list of keywords (Ki) is retrieved during the index (e) procedure.

HEEN (ri, Pk, Ep, G, e, Ki): The elliptical curve points (Ep) are converted from the plaintext e using the map() function. With the help of G, Ep, and Pk, the IA generates an additional random number (r) from RDm, which is then used to encrypt the plaintext (CT1, CT2). Along with the cipher text, the keywords Ki are encrypted using the public key and combined as (CT1, CT2, KE1).

This method calculates the value of CT using the Sk and the cipher text $\mathbf{O}T1i$. It takes into account CT1i, CT2i, Sk, ri, and KE1. To get the Ep, decoding is done using both the CT and $\mathbf{O}T2i$. It is possible to decode the acquired e to its plaintext form. The suggested cryptic approach also encrypts the inquiry words in addition to the cipher text, which gives the keywords.

Check ($\mathbf{O}T$, $\mathbf{O}T2i$): The input to this method is the CT, and it uses the cipher text (cyphertext21, cyphertext22, cyphertext23~cyphertext2t) to validate the authentication. This verification technique stands apart since it does not rely on the Sk.

10.5 Results and Discussion

10.5.1 Examining the Security Model's Performance

Using a fake patient dataset (.CSV File) that includes P_Name, P_id, P_DoB, P_Email, P_GendeExamining the Security Model's Performance.

Using a fake patient dataset (.CSV File) that includes P_Name, P_id, P_DoB, P_Email, P_Gender, and P_Disease, the performance of the proposed HERDE is assessed in this section. I used Java to build the HERDE algorithm. This study takes into account the VPKE-HE and VMKDO16 existing mechanisms.

10.5.2 Duration of Key Generation

Current mechanisms, such as VPKE-HE and VMKD16, are compared to the suggested HERDE-MSNB framework's key generation time. Table 10.1 displays the results of comparing the times it takes to generate keys. Table 10.2 shows the query processing time comparison.

Table 10.1 Key generation time comparison.

Number of data owners	HERDE-MSNB (Seconds)	VPKE-HE (Seconds)	VMK DO16 (Seconds)
1000	6	8	18
It	10	13	38
3000	15	20	51
4000	21	30	70
5000	25	35	90

Table 10.2 Query processing time comparison.

Number of queries	HERDE-MSNB (Seconds)	VPKE-HE (Seconds)	VMK DO16 (Seconds)
150	4	5	16
300	6	8	17
450	10	14	18
600	13	18	15
750	16	22	19

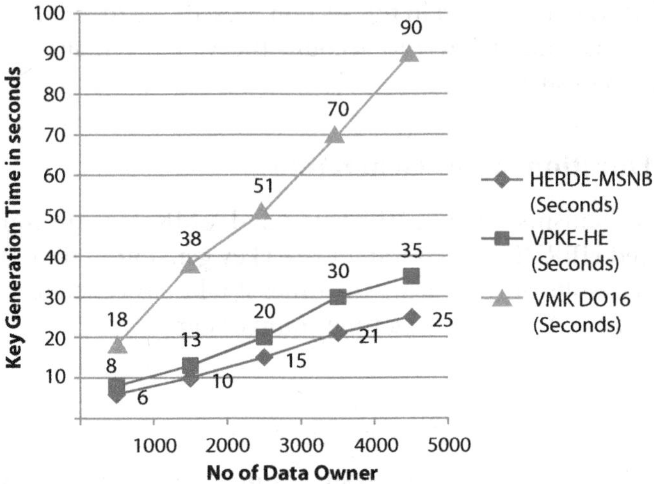

Figure 10.4 Comparison of key generation time.

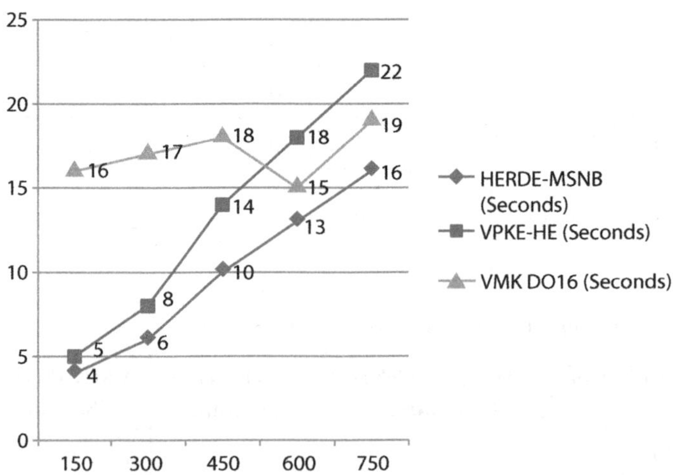

Figure 10.5 Comparison of query processing time.

10.5.3 Performance Analysis of Prediction Model

Accuracy, Sensitivity, Specificity, and the F-measure are some of the metrics that may be used to assess the suggested MSNB prediction model's performance. You may compare the suggested MSNB prediction model to other classification models like KNN, RF, and MLP. Using data stored in the UCI repository, the MSNB prediction model is suggested. Weka is a useful tool for evaluating the suggested MSNB prediction model's performance.

10.5.3.1 *Description of the Dataset*

The UCI repository dataset is used in the proposed innovative HERDE-MSNB architecture to forecast two interconnected serious diseases.

Eight characteristics are used in the proposed framework to predict the occurrence of heart disease:

- The seven characteristics that are used to forecast the occurrence of diabetes are:
- Age
- Measurement of Body Mass Index
- Sugar in the Blood
- Pressure during the end of diastole
- Diabetic Blood Sugar

10.5.4 Performance Metrics

10.5.4.1 *Sensitivity*

Sensitivity gives the fraction of correctly predicted positive observation out of overall positive observation. The sensitivity is calculated as follows:

$$\text{Sensitivity} = TP / TP+FN$$

10.5.4.2 *Specificity*

Specificity gives the fraction of correctly predicted negative observations out of overall predicted negative observations. The specificity is calculated as follows:

$$\text{Specificity} = TN / TN + FP$$

10.5.4.3 *F-Measure*

F-measures combine both recall (sensitivity or true positive rate) and precision into single measures. Table 10.3 shows the comparison of heart disease prediction. The F-measures are computed as follows:

$$\text{F-Measure} = (2 * \text{Precision} * \text{Recall}) / (\text{Precision} + \text{Recall})$$

Table 10.3 Comparison of heart disease prediction.

Algorithm	Heart disease prediction (Percentage)			
	Accuracy	Sensitivity	Specificity	F-measure
KNN	74.81	78.47	70.63	76.87
RF	81.48	82.47	80.17	810.55
MLP	82.22	84.46	79.51	810.89
MSNB	92.59	910.33	91.67	910.33

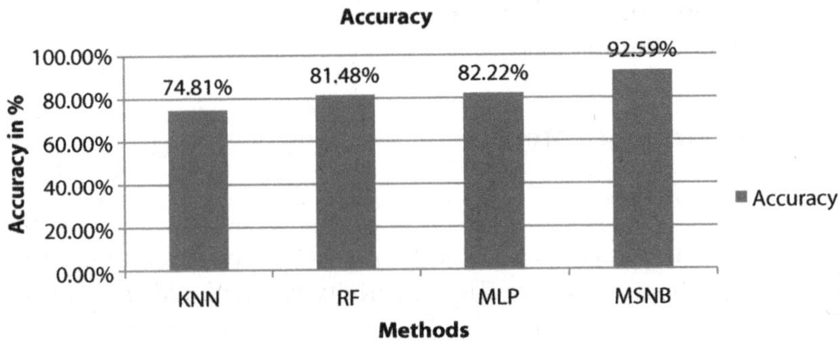

Figure 10.6 Heart disease prediction performance in terms of accuracy.

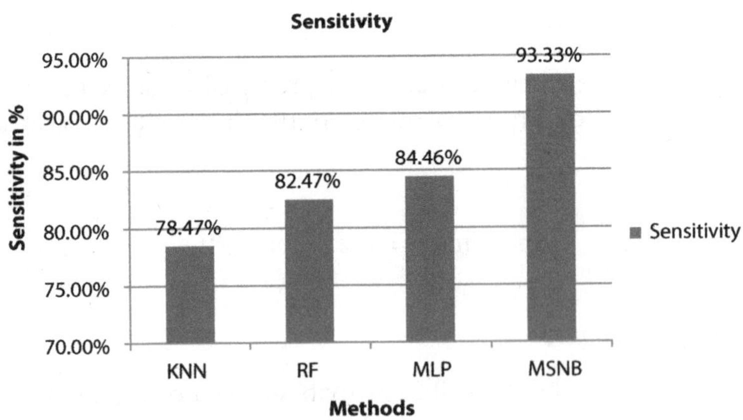

Figure 10.7 Heart disease prediction performance in terms of sensitivity.

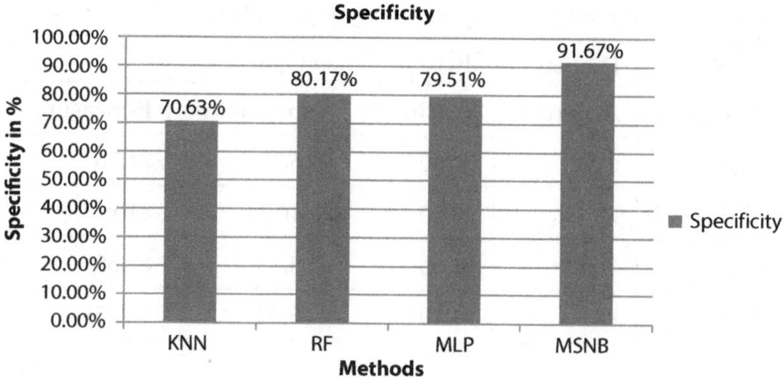

Figure 10.8 Heart disease prediction performance in terms of specificity.

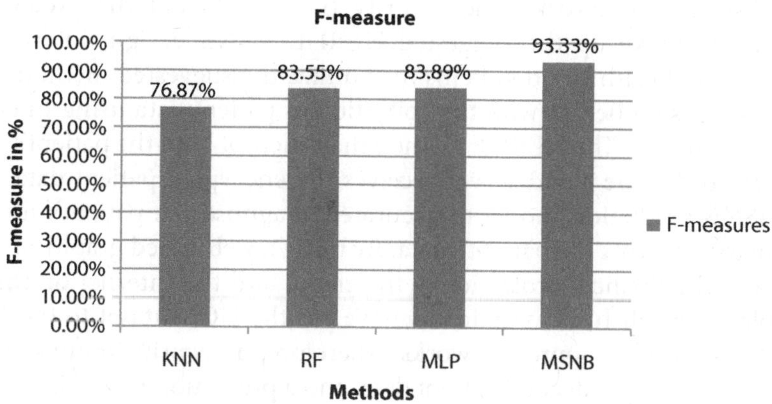

Figure 10.9 Heart disease prediction performances in terms of F-measure.

10.5.4.4 Diabetes Prediction

The comparison of the diabetes prediction of the proposed MSNB model and existing models is shown in Table 10.4. The accuracy of diabetes prediction using K-Nearest Neighbors (KNN), random forest (RF), multilayer perceptron (MLP), and Multi-Stage Naïve Bayes (MSNB) are 61.40%, 75.59%, 76.82%, and 88.93% respectively.

Table 10.4 Comparison of diabetes disease prediction.

	Diabetes prediction (Percentage)			
Algorithm	**Accuracy**	**Sensitivity**	**Specificity**	**F-measure**
KNN	61.40	72.00	46.25	71.76
RF	75.59	98.00	310.21	810.33
MLP	76.82	81.00	58.33	82.59
MSNB	88.93	910.94	68.00	910.58

10.6 Summary of Contributions

Two distinct frameworks, the security framework and the prediction framework, make up the suggested HERDE-MSNB design. Internet of Things (IoT) health cloud systems may utilize the suggested method. The suggested design begins with the collection of patient data using Internet of Things devices. The HERDE method may encrypt both the patient's data and keywords. The cloud server receives the encrypted patient data. For the MSNB prediction model to accurately diagnose the patient's illness, the doctor decrypts the patient's data. By using a web-based graphical user interface, the medical professional, the cloud, and the Internet of Things are able to establish communication. We use the UCI dataset to test how well the suggested approach works. Therefore, a security framework is used to encrypt and decode patient data, and a prediction model is used to forecast the patient's ailment. The suggested HERDE encryption technique has a polynomial time complexity of O(nk), according to the research. The decryption method has a time complexity of $O(\sqrt{T})$. Search queries have an O(m) time complexity. Based on the results of the performance investigation, the suggested security model outperforms the current approach in terms of query processing time and key generation cost. The suggested MSNB prediction model successfully anticipates cardiovascular disease with an accuracy of 92.59% and diabetes with an accuracy of 88.93%.

References

1. Dwork, C., Differential privacy, in: *Automata, languages and programming*, pp. 1–12, Springer, Berlin, Germany, 2006.

2. Ohm, P., Broken promises of privacy: Responding to the surprising failure of anonymization. *UCLA Law Rev.*, 57, 6, 1701–1777, 2010.
3. Narayanan, A. and Shmatikov, V., Robust de-anonymization of large sparse datasets, in: *Security and Privacy*, vol. 2008, no. SP 2008, pp. 111–125, IEEE, 2008.
4. Barocas, S. and Selbst, A.D., Big data's disparate impact. *Calif. Law Rev.*, 104, 3, 671–732, 2016.
5. Friedman, B. and Nissenbaum, H., Bias in computer systems. *ACM Trans. Inf. Syst. (TOIS)*, 14, 3, 330–347, 1996.
6. Zliobaite, I., On the relation between accuracy and fairness in binary classification, in: *Data mining (ICDM), 2015 IEEE international conference on*, IEEE, pp. 919–924, 2015.
7. Kamiran, F. and Calders, T., Classifying without discriminating, in: *Computer, Control and Communication, 2009. IC4 2009. International Conference on*, IEEE, pp. 1–6, 2009.
8. Diakopoulos, N., *Algorithmic accountability: A primer*, Tow Center for Digital Journalism, New York, USA, 2016.
9. Mittelstadt, B.D., Allo, P., Taddeo, M., Wachter, S., Floridi, L., The ethics of algorithms: Mapping the debate. *Big Data Soc.*, 3, 2, 2053951716679679, 2016.
10. Datta, A., Tschantz, M.C., Datta, A., Automated experiments on ad privacy settings. *Proc. Privacy Enhancing Technol.*, 2015, 1, 92–112, Springer, Berlin, Germany, 2015.
11. Greenwald, G., *No place to hide: Edward Snowden, the NSA, and the U.S. surveillance state*, Macmillan, New York, USA, 2013.
12. Angwin, J., Larson, J., Mattu, S., Kirchner, L., *Machine bias: There's software used across the country to predict future criminals. And it's biased against blacks*, ProPublica, New York, USA, 2016.
13. Sweeney, L., k-anonymity: A model for protecting privacy. *Int. J. Uncertainty Fuzziness Knowledge Based Syst.*, 10, 05, 557–570, 2002.
14. Abadi, M., *et al.*, Deep learning with differential privacy, in: *Proceedings of the 2016 ACM SIGSAC conference on computer and communications security*, pp. 308–318, 2016.
15. Poongodi, C., Lalitha, K., Dhanaraj, R.K., The Role of Blockchains for Medical Electronics Security, in: *Essential Enterprise Blockchain Concepts and Applications*, pp. 231–262, Auerbach Publications, Boca Raton, Florida, USA, 2021.
16. Acquisti, A. and Gross, R., Imagined communities: Awareness, information sharing, and privacy on the Facebook, in: *Privacy Enhancing Technologies*, pp. 36–58, Springer, Berlin, Heidelberg, Germany, 2006.
17. Solove, D.J., 'I've got nothing to hide' and other misunderstandings of privacy. *San Diego Law Rev.*, 44, 745, 2010.
18. Singh, A., Dhanaraj, R.K., Sharma, A.K., Balusamy, B., Sharma, G., Agrawal, S., Q-Learning Based Network Access Policy Management for Zero Trust

Security in IIoT, in: *2023 International Conference on Electrical, Electronics, Communication and Computers (ELEXCOM). 2023 International Conference on Electrical, Electronics, Communication and Computers (ELEXCOM)*, IEEE, 2023.

19. Singh, A., Dhanaraj, R.K., Hsu, C.-H., Sharma, A.K., Kumar, P., Deep Reinforcement Learning Aided Device Profiling for Anomaly Detection in IIoT Over Zero Trust Security Network, in: *2023 IEEE Asia-Pacific Conference on Computer Science and Data Engineering (CSDE). 2023 IEEE Asia-Pacific Conference on Computer Science and Data Engineering (CSDE)*, IEEE, 2023.
20. Edwards, L. and Veale, M., Slave to the algorithm? Why a 'right to an explanation' is probably not the remedy you are looking for. *Duke Law Technol. Rev.*, 16, 18, 2017.
21. Zarsky, T.Z., The trouble with algorithmic decisions: An analytic road map to examine efficiency and fairness in automated and opaque decision making. *Sci. Technol. Hum. Values*, 41, 1, 118–132, 2016.
22. Pasquale, F., *The black box society: The secret algorithms that control money and information*, Harvard University Press, Cambridge, Massachusetts, USA, 2015.
23. Diakopoulos, N., Accountability in algorithmic decision making. *Commun. ACM*, 59, 2, 56–62, 2016.
24. Singh, A., Dhanaraj, R.K., Ali, A., Balaji, P., Alharbi, M., Transfer Fuzzy Learning enabled Streebog Cryptographic Substitution Permutation based zero trust security in IIOT, in: *Alexandria Engineering Journal*, vol. 81, pp. 449–459, Elsevier BV, 2023.
25. Hardt, M., Price, E., Srebro, N., Equality of opportunity in supervised learning, in: *Advances in neural information processing systems*, pp. 3315–3323, 2016.
26. Kroll, J.A., Huey, J., Barocas, S., Felten, E.W., Reidenberg, J.R., Robinson, D.G., Felton, E.W., Accountable algorithms. *Univ. Pennsylvania Law Rev.*, 165, 3, 633–705, 2017.
27. Mitchell, M., *et al.*, Model cards for model reporting, in: *Proceedings of the conference on fairness, accountability, and transparency*, pp. 220–229, 2019.
28. Rudin, C., Stop explaining black box machine learning models for high stakes decisions and use interpretable models instead. *Nat. Mach. Intell.*, 1, 5, 206–215, 2019.
29. Lipton, Z.C., The mythos of model interpretability, 2016, arXiv preprint arXiv:1606.03490.

11

SmartMed: A Blockchain-Based Intelligent System for Managing Patient Data

Swapnil Pawar[1], Yogesh Jadhav[2] and Ashish Patel[3]*

[1]Computer Department, K J Somaiya College of Engineering, Mumbai, India
[2]Atlas SkillTech University, UGDX School of Technology, Mumbai, India
[3]Department of Computer Engineering, SVM Institute of Technology, Bharuch, India

Abstract

The management of medical records poses a significant global challenge in the commercial domain. The healthcare industry needs digitization so badly because its information management systems are so old that they are usually decades behind those of other sectors. The goal of the healthcare industry is to run without paper. More and more healthcare facilities are scanning paper medical data and entering the information into electronic health records (EHRs). They need to be more open and work better with other systems. Numerous individuals seek healthcare services from different providers due to the rapid evolution of the healthcare system. Blockchain technology fixes these problems and allows large amounts of health data to be shared safely and securely. So, the patient will have complete control over and access to their medical data. In this article, we have proposed 'SmartMed,' an intelligent and secure healthcare management system using blockchain architecture. People can choose who they want to share their medical information with as part of the proposal. They could also control the privacy and access to their health data. We have compared our proposed system using performance metrics for delay and resource utilization. The results show improvements over traditional approaches.

Keywords: Electronic health record (EHR), blockchain, healthcare, security, access control, patient

**Corresponding author*: ashish.patel@svmit.ac.in; ORCID: 0000-0002-8307-9425

R. Sathiyaraj, Rajesh Kumar Dhanaraj, K. Arun Kumar, Rutvij H. Jhaveri and A. Mohamed Abbas (eds.) Predictive Methods in Next-Generation Computing: An Approach Toward Sustainability, (207–232)

11.1 Introduction

The sharing of essential medical data with stakeholders while upholding data integrity and safeguarding patient privacy is one of the biggest issues the healthcare sector is now facing. The absence of Electronic Health Record (EHR) standards and secure data-sharing mechanisms poses a significant risk to human lives. The effectiveness of a particular course of therapy may be compromised if electronic medical records are left blank or overlooked at a crucial point in care [1, 34]. EHRs should be secure in today's world, and patients should actively participate in deciding who can access their data. It makes perfect sense to use blockchain given how sensitive and vulnerable personal health data is to the problems listed above. Our initiative, SmartMed, stores Electronic Health Records on the blockchain to make patient records more accessible while promoting interoperability and data quality. These EHRs would be updated, secured, and available for use by anybody with access rights on a distributed ledger of a blockchain [2, 3].

The medical data database in any healthcare system is the most significant intelligence resource. Building a successful and cohesive healthcare system requires sharing this data, which is usually scattered across multiple platforms. If a patient visits several doctors in different medical networks for different symptoms, it would be beneficial for each doctor to have access to the patient's complete medical history [4, 5]. Under these given circumstances, a doctor might be able to access the data kept by other institutions if there is no reciprocal sharing agreement for personal health information. A central location for data storage (such as a cloud-based solution) could also be a single target for a security breach [6, 7].

Recent reports indicate that healthcare data continues to be a target, for cyber attacks. Patients may face distress, social stigma, and financial risks as a result of breaches. The sharing of protected health information (PHI) [10] among healthcare facilities poses challenges due to the interoperability requirements. Consequently, a healthcare provider may not always have access to patient data even with proper authorization. Ideally, patients should have ownership of their records and be empowered to manage and share their information securely without compromising privacy [11, 12].

The concept behind technology is to provide a decentralized way of managing digital assets and data without relying on intermediaries or centralized authorities. The main proposal outlined in the document is SmartMed, a blockchain-powered platform designed to give patients control over their health records (EHRs) in real time, ensuring accuracy and security, without barriers. Additionally, the report discusses the importance of implementing an EHR-centered system and how blockchain technology could address the limitations of existing EHR systems.

The SmartMed solution is a platform that aims to create patient-focused Electronic Health Records (EHRs) through blockchain technology. This method is designed for both patients and medical professionals. Patients can easily access, upload, and control access to their EHRs for different healthcare providers. Medical professionals can view and submit EHRs for patients as well. Every action involving the medical records will be securely recorded and protected, ensuring transparency and accountability.

In addition, the SmartMed platform will provide patients with a comprehensive inventory of those with access to their medical records. Section 11.2 discusses the current state of blockchain research and identifies research gaps. Section 11.3 proposes 'SmartMed' as a platform for the secure exchange of medical data. Section 11.4 describes the model implementation. Section 11.5 discusses result analysis using hybrid model. Section 11.6 contain performance evaluation. In section 11.7 concludes the work and provide some essential perspectives.

11.1.1 The Need for the Digitization of Medical Records

Four reasons to digitize medical records:

- Access and Storage: The process of identifying a suitable location for storing patient charts, distinguishing between active and inactive patients, addressing issues related to misfiled data, and the physical retrieval and removal of charts for utilization are all difficult tasks. These charts can be readily accessed, always stored accurately, and you won't need to find space to store them once they have been scanned and placed into an EMR (Electronic Medical Records) system [8, 9, 13].
- Implementation: The implementation of an EMR system represents an expenditure. It will be expensive to initiate, and some practices cannot afford to make the changeover. However, every investment will yield returns until you have earned (or saved) more than the initial investment. With an EMR in place, you will need fewer employees to handle your records, less space to store them (meaning you can rent a smaller office), and less security to safeguard them. Paper

documents, particularly medical records, contain highly sensitive information that poses a substantial legal risk and must be protected. This may need the installation of surveillance cameras or even guards [14].

- Security: Electronic documents and the systems they are stored on facilitate increased office efficiency and productivity. Due to the fact that there is typically only one copy of paper documents, the loss of a document is irreparable. On the other hand, electronic papers are sorted with predefined automation, reducing the likelihood of human error, and they can be backed up on various systems and encrypted. With several copies saved and backed up, you can be assured that your files will be safe even during natural catastrophes or unexpected power outages. With cloud hosting, files are encrypted and stored on remote servers; only a unique login may decode them. This security helps keep out unwanted users and can trace who signed in with a specific ID and what they did. To maintain the authenticity of papers, you can also lock them to prevent future modifications or copying. Simply said, it is the finest possible security for your records [15, 16].
- Accuracy and Readability: Everyone has heard the jokes about how difficult it is to read a doctor's handwriting, which can range from misreading a few letters to being unable to understand an entire scrawl. This uncertainty affects all other medical personnel who need to check that information later, not simply the patient trying to fill a prescription. Individuals who attempt to understand the contents of an electronic medical record can do so with a sense of confidence when the text is presented in a readable typeface [17, 18].

11.1.2 What is Blockchain?

The emerging technology known as blockchain operates on a distributed ledger that only allows appends. The fact that new entries may only ever be added by appending them to the end of the series of chronological blocks that comprise the ledger is the source of the ledger's name. The features of blockchain technology are, ironically, (i) consensual; (ii) decentralized; and (iii) unchangeable. Blockchain is a collection of hosts with a time-stamped transaction history. Every new block is linked to the one that came before it. When paired with cryptographic hashes, this time-stamped chain of blocks provides a theoretically unchangeable record of every transaction made within a network, starting from the genesis block and ending with the most recent block. Unlike a traditional relational database where data may be deleted or modified, a blockchain does not have administrator permissions that permit the deletion or modification of the recorded data. A group of nodes that are completely independent of one another and comprise a blockchain are connected by a peer-to-peer network. Every node will host a blockchain in the same decentralized fashion. However, for a system like this to work, there needs to be a way for the nodes to come to an agreement on adding the next legitimate block to the chain. Consensus methods are procedures that make sure that, prior to a transaction being added to the blockchain, all nodes—the computers that manage the blockchain and sometimes process transactions—are in sync with one another and agree on its validity. For a blockchain to function correctly, specific consensus procedures must be in place. Some of the executed strategies for reaching such a distributed consensus are Proof of Work, Proof of Stake, Proof of Capacity, Proof of Human Work, Proof of Activity, and Proof of Elapsed Time [19].

In addition to decentralization, consensus, and immutability, a blockchain network possesses two more significant properties: provenance and finality. Finality refers to the existence of a single shared ledger that provides a definitive location for determining asset ownership or transaction completion. Provenance, on the other hand, enables network participants to track the origin of an asset and its ownership history. Smart contracts, serving as agreements or a set of regulations governing a commercial transaction, can also be employed with a blockchain. There are two forms of blockchain: permissioned and permissionless.

Individuals have the liberty to participate in a network on a permissionless (public) blockchain. Prior verification of the participating entities who possess mutual familiarity within the network is required for a permissioned (private) blockchain. The choice between the two types is mainly determined by an application's capacity to standardize trust. Bitcoin and Ethereum are examples of permissionless blockchains, where parties can transact without the need to authenticate each other's identities. Electronic Health Records (EHRs), for example, are an ideal scenario where permissioned blockchain can be effectively utilized [20, 29].

11.1.3 How to Use Blockchain to Digitize Medical Records

The application of cryptography on the blockchain ensures the encryption and security of each data block, made feasible by the utilization of blockchain technology. Public-key cryptography is employed to encode a block, and the data contained within can be deciphered using a private key or password. Blockchain technology in healthcare enables businesses to access patients' data using blockchain medical records, eliminating the need for several healthcare providers to maintain separate versions of the data. This is achieved by utilizing cryptographic keys. Blockchain medical records would be inaccessible without the key that is attached to them. Moreover, due to the interconnectedness of each block in the chain through chronological order, it is unattainable to obtain control over an individual piece of data. This feature also prohibits any modifications to the data blocks on the blockchain. Cryptocurrency enables transactions to be conducted on the blockchain. Transactions in the healthcare business may encompass interactions between consultants, physicians, diagnostic imaging, test results, medication prescriptions, or surgical interventions. The blockchain stores the complete medical history of the patient; therefore, any new data must undergo a validation process before it can be appended to the chain. Blockchain medical records, which ensure data privacy while allowing universal accessibility, would greatly benefit healthcare professionals and patients. Due to the provisions of the Health Insurance Portability and Accountability Act of 1996 (HIPAA), healthcare providers are allowed to impose fees for providing copies of medical data. As a result, the current process for patients to obtain their information is arduous, costly, time-consuming, and sometimes burdensome for the patient. Blockchain technology in healthcare enables patients to instantly access their data without the need to file formal requests. Despite being a nascent technology in the healthcare sector, recent trials utilizing blockchain for medical data have yielded highly promising outcomes [21, 22].

11.2 Literature Survey

Historically, blockchain technology was invented to prevent financial data forging. Due to its ability to maintain data security and its decentralized nature, it is a good contender for secure healthcare systems. Blockchain technology enables patient management systems to ensure data integrity, transparency, and efficient sharing. However, there are a few challenges, such as the legal procedures, the system's complexity, and the parties' willingness to share the information with others. The work presented here provides an effective solution to deal with the problems stated earlier and offers an improved solution for the healthcare system.

11.2.1 State-of-the-Art

Smith and Johnson [23] examine the advantages and complications involved in using blockchain technology to manage Electronic Patient Records (EPRs) in the healthcare domain. They mainly focused on the fundamental blockchain concepts, like decentralization and transparency. These features provide benefits like privacy, transparency, and sharing. The authors also discussed the problems of blockchain, such as network bandwidth, scalability of the system, cost involved, and legal issues. The article by Agbo *et al.* [24] explores the limitations and complexity of integrating blockchain technology in healthcare. The article offers a detailed study of the state-of-the-art of blockchain in the healthcare sector.

The article [25] provides a good discussion on the legal challenges of blockchain in healthcare because the government highly regulates this sector. Because of this, it is tough to develop applications that comply with the standards. The article [6] explores the above issues and provides a good discussion on the involvement of various stakeholders in blockchain applications. The authors of the article [26] offered detailed future directions of blockchain technology in the healthcare sector. They discussed personalized medicine, the sharing of records, and new healthcare models with the involvement of the stakeholders.

Blockchain can be used to manage clinical trials in the healthcare industry. Blockchain technology provides a reliable and easily verifiable means of tracking the progress of clinical trials and assuring the accuracy of data reporting [27]. The authors [11] observed an increasing trend in the healthcare industry where electronic health records (EHRs) are being adopted more frequently as healthcare providers aim to convert patient records to digital format and provide functionality. These efforts have been successful. However, existing electronic health record systems are prone to security breaches and data manipulation, threatening patient confidentiality and medical record integrity. The solution offered by [5] is that an electronic health records (EHR) system will provide a secure and transparent use of available blockchain attributes technology, such as immutability and decentralization. The system uses a permissioned blockchain, which ensures that only authorized healthcare providers and users can access and exchange patient data. The system also uses smart contracts to create functional and quality healthcare systems.

The article [28] explores the potential benefits of using blockchain technology in the healthcare industry, especially in the context of the COVID-19 pandemic. Blockchain technology is believed to provide a secure and decentralized way of storing and exchanging patient data, which can be particularly useful in times of crisis, such as the COVID-19 pandemic. This technology facilitates the reliable exchange of medical records, test findings, and other vital information, enabling healthcare providers to make informed decisions about patient care while saving money. This is followed by an experimental approach to other widely used blockchain platforms such as Bitcoin, Ethereum, Hyperledger, and Corda. These platforms are evaluated according to criteria such as conceptual approaches, scalability, and programming language support. The authors explore intersections and provide a variety of healthcare systems for each platform, highlighting the advantages and disadvantages in each context. The article [30] discusses limitations to implementing blockchain technology in the healthcare industry, such as scalability, regulation, and a framework. This proposal employs a blockchain ecosystem by presenting the rules for operating this ecosystem efficiently.

Kumar *et al.* [31] discussed the practical use of blockchain technology and the Interplanetary File System (IPFS), which strengthens the security of the patient's medical records. They also presented a detailed study on the advantages and disadvantages of blockchain and IPFS. Furthermore, the article offered a hybrid solution that combines the above two technologies. Madin *et al.* [32] discussed the healthcare systems' challenges, such as patient data privacy, access control mechanisms, and acceptance of blockchain-based applications.

Johari *et al.* [33] presented BLOSOM (Blockchain for Security Of Medical records), which enhanced the security of patient's medical records. The article discussed how blockchain technology can increase the security and transparency of medical records management. To avoid illegal searches of conversations, coordinate the exchange of health services, improve patient management, and distribute EMRs for electronic records.

An electronic medical record system using open-source blockchain technology called "Hyperledger" has been prototyped. This system assures confidentiality, security, and availability of medical records. [35] proposed a system that uses advanced blockchain and network technologies to explore distributed electromedical information. To ensure the authenticity and integrity of the data, a hash calculation is performed on the electronic medical information, and the resulting value is stored on the blockchain. The electronic medical information is encrypted and secured by adopting a method on a distributed storage known as an interplanetary file system.

Subsequently, the encrypted keyword index data of electronic medical records was stored on the Ethereum blockchain. Instead of relying on a central third party, they used smart contracts implemented on the Ethereum blockchain to perform keyword searches. In addition, attribute-based encryption methods are used that guarantee that only those attributes that follow the access rules are decrypted electronic medical data.

11.2.2 Research Gap

- The first challenge in blockchain technology in healthcare is exploring how blockchain is best used in managing medical data. Researchers must examine how blockchain technology can store and manage patient medical records, focusing on privacy and confidentiality.
- Another challenge is using blockchain technology to improve supply chain management. To manage medical records integrity and transparency, one must address the legal issues of the governing bodies.
- Another critical issue with blockchain technology is its impact on healthcare data transfer. The use of different health information techniques may restrict the ability of healthcare providers to deal with patient information.
- Blockchain uses a decentralized approach to maintain records. Incorporating its use in medical research can improve information sharing and cooperation between researchers.

11.3 SmartMed: Proposed System

The proposed SmartMed blockchain solution presents a more secure and trustworthy approach for the transparent exchange of patient data. The benefits of the proposed system are:

- Security and Privacy: Blockchain provides a solution for healthcare providers to exchange patient information. Patients can check with whom the information is shared, and healthcare providers receive accurate and truthful information.
- Reducing Human Mistakes: Blockchain technology can reduce medical errors by providing all healthcare providers

with universal patient data access. By sharing the information effectively, prescribing errors, false diagnoses, and other issues can be reduced.

- Data Management: Blockchain technology offers a better way to manage the tasks of managing patient data. Blockchain technology provides more efficient and cost-effective healthcare solutions.
- Research: Blockchain technology can be used to collect and store data in a secure and highly transparent manner for clinical trials and research projects. This facilitates rapid advances in medical research and can improve healthcare.
- Patient Empowerment: Patients can exercise greater freedom in using their health information and have the right to designate individuals who have been granted access. This will lead to a healthcare system that prioritizes patients' needs and preferences, enabling them to actively participate in their healthcare.

The SmartMed System shown in Figure 11.1 aims to showcase its functionality from the perspective of two different user groups: patients and healthcare providers, especially physicians. Upon registration, individuals have the option of choosing a patient or physician role. Upon successful registration, keys are allocated to individual users. When an individual registers as a patient, they are given two RSA keys, including a public and

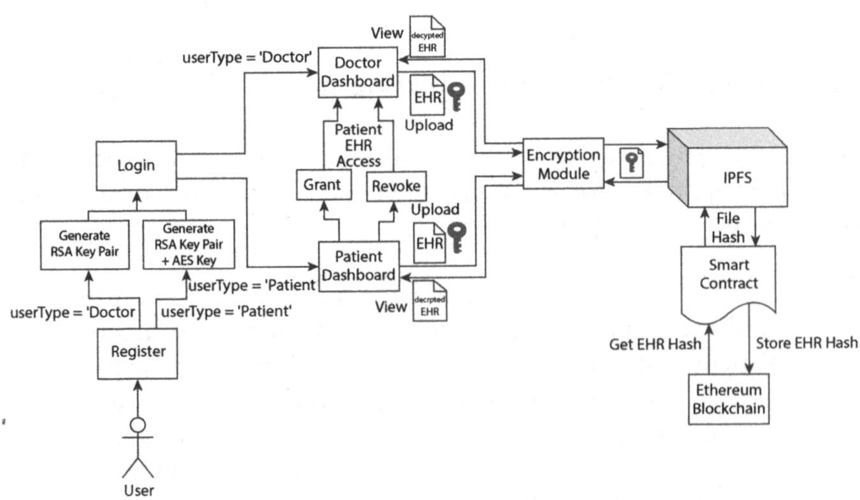

Figure 11.1 SmartMed: Proposed model for patient and health care provider.

a private key, as well as an advanced encryption standard (AES) private key. However, when the user registers as a doctor, they are given only two Rivest, Shamir, Adleman (RSA) keys. After completing the registration process, a user can gain access to the system by using their authentic credentials. Once logged in, users will be directed to the relevant dashboard based on their user type: patient or physician.

11.4 SmartMed: Model Implementation

To follow the agile methodology, the implementation of the system has been divided into different modules that were delivered iteratively and incrementally. The sections mentioned below explain the process followed for the implementation of each of these modules in a detailed manner.

11.4.1 Software Requirements

- ReactJS: ReactJS is a framework for building user interfaces in JavaScript.
- Solidity: Solidity is a language to develop smart contracts.
- Truffle: Built on top of Ethereum, Truffle lets you build and test smart contracts and then put them into use on the Ethereum network. It has tools and other resources that can be used to test and launch DApps on Ethereum.
- Ganache: Ganache is a developer tool enabling users to replicate blockchain environments on their local machines and do smart contract testing. A decentralized blockchain system operates within a single computer's memory and is created for software development and testing. It replicates the characteristics of an actual Ethereum network, including many accounts that are provided with test Ether.
- MetaMask: MetaMask is a browser extension that can conduct Ethereum transactions on standard websites. It serves as the connection between the local blockchain and the front end of the application.
- IPFS: IPFS is a decentralized protocol where every node preserves a set of hashed files. The system is decentralized and independent of a central authority. It stores and references files using hashes, giving users increased control over their data.

11.4.2 User Registration

The registration module offers a detailed explanation of the registration procedure for two different categories: the patient and the doctor. During the registration process, the user initially provides essential information such as their first name, last name, email address, and password. Next, the user must decide whether they would like to register as a patient or as a doctor. After making a choice, the user is then presented with conditional fields. If the user chooses to register as a patient, the user is prompted to enter his/her age and blood group. If the user chooses to register as a doctor, he/she is asked for his/her qualification, the field in which he/she has specialized, and his/her license number as per the Indian Medical Register. Once the user clicks on the register button, the validity of all the fields is checked. If all the fields are valid, an HTTP POST request is sent to the server along with the form details.

After receiving the request, the form data is verified on the server side. Once the data is determined to be legitimate, we proceed to construct a distinct salt for the user. Subsequently, we employ the SHA512 cryptographic hash method to hash the user's salt and password. To facilitate the implementation of asymmetric encryption for the patient-specific secret key, an RSA key pair (consisting of public and private keys) is generated for the user. Ultimately, the database stores all the user details, including the produced hash, salt, and RSA key pair. Currently, we verify the user's classification. If the user has enrolled as a patient, we create a distinct cryptographic key for the user, which may be utilized to encrypt and decrypt records that are specific to the user. The confidential key is securely maintained on the blockchain in an encrypted format. The patient can access the system at any time to upload or examine their medical records, as well as to provide a doctor access to their records. The subsequent sections provide a comprehensive explanation of the procedure for retrieving the key from the blockchain.

11.4.3 Login

After successful registration, the user can log in by entering the email and password used at registration. These fields are also subject to validation. Next, to verify the user's identity, we extract the password provided by the user from the request and the salt from the user's database entry. Then, we perform a hashing algorithm on the provided password and salt, and compare the resulting hash to the user's hash stored in the database. If the user's hash matches the created hash, then the password is deemed correct, resulting in a successful user login and redirection to the user's dashboard.

11.4.4 Upload Records

This module focuses on the primary aspect of the project, which is the uploading of medical records and their storage on the blockchain. Due to the limited capacity of a blockchain to store data, particularly complex data like entire medical records, the process of storing such records on the blockchain becomes laborious. Therefore, we utilize an external data storage system known as IPFS to store the medical records. IPFS stores data and produces a distinct hash for each piece of data that can be put on the blockchain. An inherent issue with utilizing IPFS is that anyone in possession of the hash of the record file can effortlessly access it via IPFS. To address this problem, we employ an extra level of protection that encrypts the medical records prior to putting them on IPFS. Section 11.2 provides a comprehensive explanation of the method of encrypting records. To preserve the medical history of a certain patient, we store an array of their medical records in the blockchain. Each patient has a unique array that may be retrieved using their unique ID. According to the proposed system concept, both patients and clinicians have the ability to upload files. Once the user's medical record is uploaded, the record is initially sent to the encryption module where it is encrypted. The encrypted record is subsequently placed on IPFS, which generates a hash. The hash, together with additional information such as the file name, the name of the patient or doctor who uploads the record, and the current timestamp, is appended to the array representing the patient's medical history. To upload a new record, the patient can navigate to the 'Upload New Record' tab located on their dashboard. In the 'View Patients' tab, doctors can access a comprehensive list of all registered patients and determine if each patient has granted them permission to view their medical records or if access is restricted. When a doctor desires to upload a fresh record for a certain patient, they can select the 'View' link next to the patient's name, which will bring them to a page showcasing the complete medical history of that patient. Subsequently, the doctor can navigate to the 'Upload New Record' section, where they can proceed to upload the record. The hash value of this record is appended to the medical history of the specific patient.

11.4.5 View Records

This module explains the process of viewing the previously uploaded records. The medical records uploaded by the patient or the doctor (for a particular patient) can be viewed by both the patient as well as the doctors to whom the patient has granted access.

To view the records, the patient can go to the 'View Records' tab on his/her dashboard. The entire medical history consisting of all the records uploaded for the patient can be seen there, along with other details like file name, the name of the user who uploaded the file, and the time and date when the record was uploaded. To access a specific record, the patient can click on the "view" link next to the record. This action will open a new tab where the record can be seen. On the 'View Patients' tab, doctors can access a complete list of all registered patients and see if any patient has given permission to view their medical records or if access is restricted. If a doctor wants to access the records of a particular patient, the 'View' hyperlink next to the patient's name can be selected. This process redirects them to a page that shows that patient's entire medical history. To access a specific record, the doctor can simply click on the "view" link next to the record. This action will open a new tab where the record can be viewed.

11.4.6 Grant/Revoke Permissions

This section describes how a patient can authorize or obtain permission from a physician to view their medical record. The 'Permissions' tab on the patient's dashboard displays a complete list of all registered physicians. First, physicians are not allowed to examine patient records. To grant permission to see a doctor, a patient can simply click on the 'Grant' button next to the doctor's name. Following this simple procedure, the physician is authorized to access and search the patient's medical history and upload additional records specific to that patient. If he/she were to revoke the authorization from the physician, the patient can simply click the 'Revoke' button. If the patient does this, the physician will lose access to the patient's records and will not be able to send any more records to the patient.

11.4.7 Encryption of Medical Records

Encryption is essential to ensure data security and privacy in blockchain technology. Encryption provides data privacy and protects confidentiality, but its use and use must be scrutinized. In order for encryption to remain effective in the blockchain ecosystem, it is important to implement proper key schemes, carefully select algorithms, and conduct frequent security audits.

11.4.8 Need for Encryption

The proposed system allows patients and healthcare professionals to upload health records and access them for retrieval and viewing at a later time.

Moreover, patients have the ability to assign access privileges and authorize specific healthcare practitioners to access their medical records or contribute new information [28]. As stated in Section 11.1, we utilize an external data storage system known as IPFS. However, there is a clear and easily exploitable vulnerability in the security system. Given the hash of a file, anyone can retrieve it from IPFS. Therefore, IPFS is not ideal for storing sensitive files such as medical records in their original form. Without taking any action on these data, sharing these sensitive files is not suitable for IPFS. Fortunately, we have encryption readily available to us, which complements IPFS effectively in order to safeguard files prior to uploading them onto IPFS.

11.4.9 Symmetric vs. Asymmetric Encryption

Symmetric or secret key encryption relies on the use of a mutually known secret key held by both the sender and the recipient of an encrypted communication. This key can be a genuine word, a numerical value, or a random string of letters. It is constantly applied to the content of communication to modify it in a manner that renders it illegible to both casual and more attentive observers. Asymmetric or public key encryption is based on a pair of interconnected keys. One is private—a confidential code that is only known to the intended receiver. An additional, publicly available key can be freely provided to anyone whom the individual desires to receive encrypted messages from. Encrypted documents and data may only be decrypted by utilizing the corresponding private key and employing the identical encryption technique employed by the sender. While asymmetric key lengths, such as 1024 and 2048 bits, are typically longer than symmetric key lengths, such as 128 and 256 bits, it does not automatically mean that a file encrypted with a 2048-bit RSA key (an asymmetric key) is more difficult to decrypt than a file encrypted with a 256-bit AES key (a symmetric key). Therefore, we will evaluate asymmetric and symmetric encryptions based on two specific characteristics:

i. Computational demands
ii. Distribution convenience

Generally, symmetric key encryption is faster than asymmetric key encryption since it requires fewer CPU cycles. Nevertheless, symmetric keys possess a significant drawback when employed for the purpose of securing file transfers. Since the encryption and decryption processes require the usage of the same key, it is necessary to establish a method for delivering the key to the recipient if they do not already possess it. The challenge of distributing encryption keys is particularly evident in a file transfer setting when there may be a significant number of users spread across a wide geographic region. Certain users, the majority of whom you may have never encountered, could potentially be situated at a considerable distance from your current location. It is exceedingly difficult to securely distribute a symmetric key to each of these users. Asymmetric key encryption is not affected by this issue. As long as the private key remains undisclosed, it would be impossible for anyone to decipher the encrypted file. Therefore, we can effortlessly disseminate the relevant public key without any concerns regarding the transmission method [36, 37].

11.5 Result Analysis Using Hybrid Model

Given the distinct advantages of both symmetric and asymmetric key encryptions, we choose to include both methods in our system. To create a patient-centric model, we employ a distinct key for each patient, which is utilized to symmetrically encrypt the patient's medical records. Subsequently, we employ asymmetric encryption to cipher this distinct symmetric key and securely store the encrypted symmetric key on the blockchain. The decision to choose AES-256 as the symmetric key encryption method was based on its resistance to known realistic attacks and its superior speed compared to TripleDES, its closest competitor, which is six times slower. We employ the RSA method for asymmetric key encryption due to its robustness, as it necessitates the factorization of prime integers, a task that is challenging to do. Upon successful registration, the keys for these algorithms are generated. The technique is thoroughly explained in the Registration Module of the previous section.

We now split down the encryption process into various scenarios, outlining each one in detail. These are some key terms that will be used in the explanation before we begin:

- secretKey: A 256-bit patient-specific key is generated when a patient registers, which is used for both encrypting and decrypting the patient's medical records using AES encryption.
- public key: RSA public key that is specific to the user and is generated during the registration process.
- private key: RSA private key that is unique to each user and is generated during the registration process.

11.5.1 Scenario 1: Patient Uploads a Record

- In order to initiate the process of encryption, we first extract the RSA-encrypted AES secretKey from the blockchain.
- Next, we decrypt this RSA-encrypted AES secretKey using the patient's RSA private key to get the actual AES secret key.
- We then use this decrypted secretKey to encrypt the medical record uploaded by the patient.
- Then, we add this encrypted file buffer to IPFS, which in turn returns a hash that can be used to access the encrypted file stored on IPFS.
- Finally, we add this file hash to the patient's medical history array stored on the blockchain along with other details like file name, uploader's name, and the current timestamp.

11.5.2 Scenario 2: Patient Views the Uploaded Record

- Since we use symmetric encryption to encrypt the uploaded medical records, to access and decrypt the record, we will need the same AES secretKey used for encryption.
- First, we extract the RSA-encrypted AES secretKey from the blockchain.
- Next, we decrypt this RSA encrypted AES secretKey using the patient's RSA private key to get the actual AES secret key.
- Then, we extract the file hash of the required file from the medical history array stored on the blockchain.
- Using this file hash, we can get the encrypted file from IPFS.
- Finally, we use the decrypted AES secret key to decrypt this encrypted file and the patient is then able to view the record.

11.5.3 Scenario 3: Patient Grants Access to His/Her Records to a Doctor

- For a doctor to access a patient's records, we need to securely share the AES secretKey used for encryption of the patient's record with that particular doctor.
- To achieve this, we first extract the RSA-encrypted AES secretKey from the blockchain.
- Then, we decrypt this RSA-encrypted AES secretKey using the patient's RSA private key to get the actual AES secret key.
- Next is the process of re-encryption of this AES secret key.

- For this, we re-encrypt the AES secret key with that particular doctor's RSA public key.
- This re-encrypted AES secret key can only be decrypted using the doctor's RSA private key, thus ensuring secure sharing of the AES secret key. A malicious party cannot decrypt the file because they lack the doctor's private key.
- Next, we add this re-encrypted AES secret key to that doctor's access control list.
- Finally, we add this doctor to the patient's access control list.

11.5.4 Scenario 4: Patient Revokes Access to His/Her Records from a Doctor

- This is a relatively simple step. We remove the re-encrypted AES secret key from the doctor's access control list.
- Finally, we remove the doctor from the patient's access control list.

11.5.5 Scenario 5: Doctor Views the Patient Record

- We extract the re-encrypted AES secret key from the doctor's access control list.
- Next, we decrypt this re-encrypted AES secret key using the doctor's RSA private key to get the actual AES secret key.
- Then, we extract the file hash of the required file from the medical history array stored on the blockchain.
- Using this file hash, we can get the encrypted file from IPFS.
- Finally, we use the decrypted AES secret key to decrypt this encrypted file and the doctor is then able to view the record.

11.5.6 Scenario 6: Doctor Uploads a Record for the Patient

- We extract the re-encrypted AES secret key from the doctor's access control list.
- Next, we decrypt this re-encrypted AES secret key using the doctor's RSA private key to get the actual AES secret key.
- We then use this decrypted secret key to encrypt the medical record uploaded by the doctor.
- Then, we add this encrypted file buffer to IPFS, which in turn returns a hash that can be used to access the encrypted file stored on IPFS.

- Finally, we add this file hash to the patient's medical history array stored on the blockchain along with other details like file name, uploader's name, and the current timestamp.
- Since the AES secret key used for encryption remains the same, this record uploaded by the doctor can be easily decrypted and viewed by the patient.

11.6 SmartMed: Performance Evaluation

Experiments were carried out to measure the efficacy of SmartMed, and the findings were evaluated using the approved criteria mentioned below. Latency or delay refers to the amount of time it takes for data to travel from one point to another in a network or system. Latency refers to the duration required for a transaction's impact to propagate across the network. The duration encompassing the period between the moment of submission and the moment when the outcome becomes accessible within the blockchain system is considered part of the total time. Resource utilization refers to the measurement of the amount of CPU and memory usage of a proposed blockchain system within a specific time period. To assess the performance of our system, we examined a cohort of patients consisting of 50, 100, 150, 200, and 250 individuals.

11.6.1 Latency/Delay

The performance metric delay is calculated for SmartMed with patient groups mentioned in the following table. The SmartMed system takes 1.1 seconds for 50 patients; 1.17 seconds for 100 patients, 1.45 seconds for 150 patients, 1.73 seconds for 200 patients, and 2.01 seconds for 250 patients as shown in Table 11.1. Figure 11.2 shows the graph of delay for SmartMed compared to the existing non-blockchain traditional system.

Table 11.1 Comparison between SmartMed and non-blockchain based traditional system.

No. of patients	50	100	150	200	250
SmartMed	1.1	1.17	1.45	1.73	2.01
Traditional System	1.25	1.41	1.56	1.87	2.11

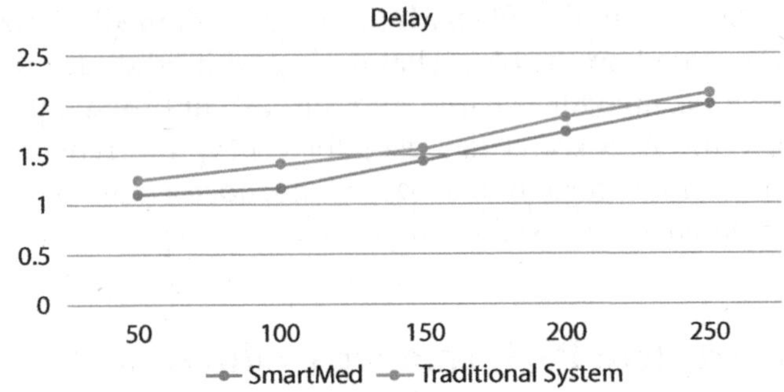

Figure 11.2 Transaction delay of the SmartMed compared to the existing non-blockchain traditional system.

11.6.2 Resource Utilization

For resource utilization, CPU and memory utilization are considered. There are five categories of patient groups considered, i.e., 50, 100, 150, 200, and 250. Firstly, the resource utilization of the SmartMed system is measured, as shown in Table 11.2. For 50 patients with a file size of 100 MB, CPU utilization is reported as 60%; for 100 patients with a record of size 150 MB, CPU utilization was 74%. For 150 patients with a file size of 200 MB, CPU utilization is reported as 85%. For 200 patients with a file size of 250 MB, CPU utilization is reported as 91%. For 250 patients with a file size of 300 MB, CPU utilization is reported as 97%. Figure 11.3 shows the graph of CPU and memory utilization for the proposed SmartMed blockchain model.

The resource utilization for the traditional system without blockchain for the same patient groups is mentioned in Table 11.3. For the 50 patients with a file size of 100 MB, CPU utilization is reported as 65%; for 100 patients with a record size of 150 MB, CPU utilization was 78%. For 150

Table 11.2 Resource utilization for SmartMed based on different groups of patients.

No. of patients	50	100	150	200	250
CPU Utilization (%)	60	74	85	91	97
Memory Utilization (MB)	100	150	200	250	300

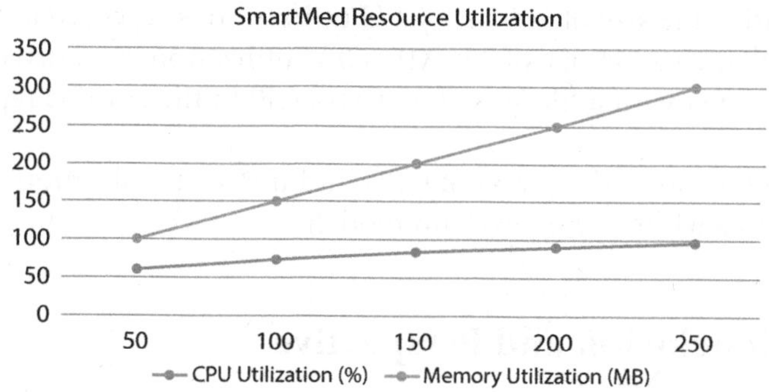

Figure 11.3 Resource utilization for SmartMed based on different patient groups.

Table 11.3 Resource utilization for the traditional system based on different groups of patients.

No. of patients	50	100	150	200	250
CPU Utilization (%)	65	78	86	93	98
Memory Utilization (MB)	100	150	200	250	300

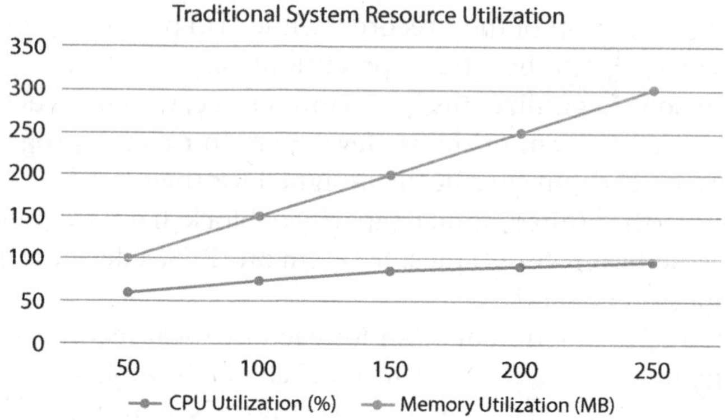

Figure 11.4 Resource utilization for the traditional system based on different patient groups.

patients with a file size of 200 MB, CPU utilization is reported as 86%. For 200 patients with a file size of 250 MB, CPU utilization is reported as 93%. For 250 patients with a file size of 300 MB, CPU utilization is reported as 98%.

Figure 11.4 shows the graph of CPU and memory utilization for traditional systems without a blockchain model.

11.7 Conclusion and Perspective

The implementation of blockchain technology has the potential to revolutionize the storage and distribution of electronic health records for patients. It achieves this by securely sharing medical data within the healthcare business and safeguarding it through a decentralized peer-to-peer network. The irreversibility of blockchain stems from the fact that any attempt to alter a block that has already been added to the chain will need the recalculation of the modified block as well as all subsequent blocks. This leads to the necessity of a significant amount of computer power, rendering the attack virtually difficult. Furthermore, due to the data being stored in several replicas across various nodes, there is no centralized architecture that an attacker may target. Due to these advantages, blockchain is an excellent method for overseeing healthcare data. The SmartMed system described in this article is outlined below.

- SmartMed is a blockchain-based medical data management system that ensures security and enables patients to maintain ownership of their records, while also providing convenient access for healthcare practitioners.
- Our solution utilizes the Ethereum service, which is a decentralized platform enabling developers to execute programs on a blockchain specifically designed for their needs.
- Due to the limited storage capacity of blockchain, we encrypt the medical records and store them on IPFS, a decentralized data storage service.
- IPFS returns a unique hash for each medical record stored, which is securely stored in blockchain through the smart contracts thus achieving our objective of secure storage.
- For access control, we have used the ACL (Access Control List) approach where we maintain a list of all the approved doctors in the patient ACL and the re-encrypted keys for patients in the doctor ACL.

- We guarantee that patients have full ownership of their medical records, with the right to grant or cancel access to clinicians at their discretion. This ensures effective access control.

By utilizing blockchain technology to develop a patient-centric EHR system, we may alter the healthcare hierarchy by giving control of medical records to the patient. This transfer of authority may result in an overall shift toward patient-centered care; the blockchain movement for patients is only getting started. SmartMed's objectives were deliberately limited to what was deemed achievable within the allocated time frame and budget. Therefore, numerous enhancements can be made to this original model. Despite this, the established system is believed to represent a tiny model that might be replicated on a much bigger scale. The following suggestions are presented as possibilities for future research expansion:

- The blockchain's provision of shared, authenticated, and secure access to information can facilitate doctors and insurers in optimizing the insurance claims processing procedure. Smart contracts have the capability to be configured with the health plan information of the payer. When a doctor intends to prescribe a treatment, they only authorize the smart contract to access the required patient records. The payer's intelligent contract subsequently compares the aforementioned records with the insurer's health plan data, renders a decision, and promptly communicates the outcome to the doctor. This can lead to precise, instantaneous decisions that save resources and eliminate service interruptions.
- One can explore the utilization of blockchain and the Internet of Things (IoT) in healthcare to enhance network scalability and accommodate low-end devices.
- Smart contracts have the potential to facilitate agreements among patients, drug manufacturers, and pharmacies in the pharmaceutical sector, hence reducing the necessity for pharmacy benefit managers.
- It is possible to design mobile EHR applications to improve health care and empower patients with data management capabilities. Access to permanent health records via a smartphone, for instance, can give a game-changing chance for patient engagement.

Blockchain is a widely accepted contemporary domain that can strengthen and turn EHR systems into a patient-centric approach. Recent improvements in the use of blockchain in healthcare show that the number of people using it will grow. To significantly improve the role of blockchain technology, organizations need to develop practical use cases and encourage ecosystem collaboration.

References

1. Peterson, K., Deeduvanu, R., Kanjamala, P., Boles, K., Blockchain in healthcare: opportunities, challenges, and recommendations. *J. Healthcare Inf. Manage. JHIM*, 32, 2, 39, 2018.
2. Zhao, J., Zhang, X., Zhang, X., Chen, X., Chen, Y., Liu, X., Blockchain-based personal health records: A systematic review. *J. Med. Syst.*, 43, 8, 174, 2019.
3. Shahin, M., Bayati, M., Shishavan, B.H., Blockchain technology and health care: A review. *Health Inf. Manage. J.*, 48, 2, 62–68, 2019.
4. Abu-Elezz, I., Hassan, A., Nazeemudeen, A., Househ, M., AbdAlrazaq, A., The benefits and threats of blockchain technology in healthcare: A scoping review. *Int. J. Med. Inf.*, 142, 104246, 2020.
5. Tanwar, S., Parekh, K., Evans, R., Blockchain-based electronic healthcare record system for healthcare 4.0 applications. *J. Inf. Secur. Appl.*, 50, 102407, 2020.
6. Farouk, A., Alahmadi, A., Ghose, S., Mashatan, A., Blockchain platform for industrial healthcare: Vision and future opportunities. *Comput. Commun.*, 154, 223– 235, 2020.
7. Hussien, H.M., Yasin, S.M., Udzir, N., II, Izuan, M., Ninggal, H., Salman, S., Blockchain technology in the healthcare industry: Trends and opportunities. *J. Ind. Inf. Integr.*, 22, 100217, 2021.
8. Azaria, A., Ekblaw, A., Vieira, T., Lippman, A., Medrec: Using blockchain for medical data access and permission management. *2016 2nd International Conference on Open and Big Data (OBD)*, pp. 25–30, 2016.
9. Yue, X., Wang, H., Jin, D., Li, M., Jiang, W., Blockchain-based data storage and sharing for medical records in the era of electronic health records. *Int. J. Med. Inf.*, 114, 94–102, 2018.
10. Khatoon, A., A blockchain-based smart contract system for healthcare management. *Electronics*, 9, 1, 94, 2020.
11. Shahnaz, A., Qamar, U., Khalid, A., Using blockchain for electronic health records. *IEEE Access*, 7, 147782–147795, 2019.
12. Yaqoob, I., Salah, K., Jayaraman, R., Al-Hammadi, Y., Blockchain for healthcare data management: opportunities, challenges, and future recommendations. *Neural Comput. Appl.*, 34, 11475–11490, 2022.

13. Attaran, M., Blockchain technology in healthcare: Challenges and opportunities. *Int. J. Healthcare Manage.*, 15, 1, 70–83, 2022.
14. Ratta, P., Kaur, A., Sharma, S., Shabaz, M., Dhiman, G., Application of blockchain and internet of things in healthcare and medical sector: applications, challenges, and future perspectives. *J. Food Qual.*, 2021, 1–20, 2021.
15. Haleem, A., Javaid, M., Singh, R.P., Suman, R., Rab, S., Blockchain technology applications in healthcare: An overview. *Int. J. Intell. Netw.*, 2, 130–139, 2021.
16. Merlo, V., Pio, G., Giusto, F., Bilancia, M., On the exploitation of the blockchain technology in the healthcare sector: A systematic review. *Expert Syst. Appl.*, 213, 118897, 2022.
17. Schinckus, C., A nuanced perspective on blockchain technology and healthcare. *Technol. Soc.*, 71, 102082, 2022.
18. Ramzan, S., Aqdus, A., Ravi, V., Koundal, D., Amin, R., Al Ghamdi, M.A., Healthcare applications using blockchain technology: Motivations and challenges. *IEEE Trans. Eng. Manage.*, 70, 8, 2874–2890, Aug. 2023, doi: 10.1109/TEM.2022.3189734 2022.
19. Erol, I., Oztel, A., Searcy, C., Medeni, T., Selecting the most suitable Blockchain platform: A case study on the healthcare industry using a novel rough mcdm framework. *Technol. Forecast. Soc. Change*, 186, 122132, 2023.
20. Aloini, D., Benevento, E., Stefanini, A., Zerbino, P., Transforming healthcare ecosystems through blockchain: Opportunities and capabilities for business process innovation. *Technovation*, 119, 102557, 2023.
21. Azbeg, K., Ouchetto, O., Andaloussi, S.J., Blockmedcare: A healthcare system based on iot, blockchain and ipfs for data management security. *Egypt. Inf. J.*, 23, 2, 329–343, 2022.
22. Pratima, S., Namasudra, S., Gonzalez Crespo, R., Parra-Fuente, J., Trivedi, M.C., Ehdhe: Enhancing security of healthcare documents in iot-enabled digital healthcare ecosystems using blockchain. *Inf. Sci.*, 629, 703–718, 2023.
23. Sathyamoorthy, M., Vanitha, C.N., Dhanaraj, R.K., Balusamy, B., Introduction to Cyborgization Systems, in: *Studies in Computational Intelligence*, pp. 1–15, Springer Nature Singapore, Singapore, 2023.
24. Agbo, C.C., Mahmoud, Q.H., Eklund, J.M., Blockchain technology in healthcare: a systematic review, in: *Healthcare*, vol. 7, no. 2, p. 56, MDPI, Basel, Switzerland, 2019.
25. Qahtan, S., Sharif, K.Y., Zaidan, A.A., Alsattar, H.A., Albahri, O.S., Zaidan, B.B., Zulzalil, H., Osman, M.H., Alamoodi, A.H., Mohammed, R.T., vol. 18, pp. 6415–6423, IEEE Transactions on Industrial Informatics, 2022.
26. Chelladurai, U. and Pandian, S., A novel blockchain based electronic health record automation system for healthcare. *J. Ambient Intell. Hum. Comput.*, 13, 693–703, 2022.
27. Ali Siyal, A., Zahid Junejo, A., Zawish, M., Ahmed, K., Khalil, A., Soursou, G., Applications of blockchain technology in medicine and healthcare: Challenges and future perspectives. *Cryptography*, 3, 1, 3, 2019.

28. Fusco, A., Dicuonzo, G., Dell'Atti, V., Tatullo, M., Blockchain in health- care: Insights on covid-19. *Int. J. Environ. Res. Public Health*, 17, 19, 7167, 2020.
29. Krishnasamy, L., Dhanaraj, R.K., Balusamy, B., Sabharwal, M., Chinnasamy, P. (Eds.), Healthcare 4.0: Health Informatics and Precision Data Management (1st ed.), Chapman and Hall/CR, 2022. https://doi.org/10.1201/9781003217435.
30. Kassab, M., DeFranco, J., Malas, T., Laplante, P., Destefanis, G., V.V.G.N., Exploring research in blockchain for healthcare and a roadmap for the future. *IEEE Trans. Emerging Top. Comput.*, 9, 4, 1835–1852, 2019.
31. Kumar, S., Bharti, A.K., Amin, R., Decentralized secure storage of medical records using blockchain and ipfs: A comparative analysis with future directions. *Secur. Privacy*, 4, 5, e162, 2021.
32. Dhanaraj, R.K., Paramasivam, A., Vijayalakshmi, S., Emmanuel, C., Pallavi, P., Metkewar, P.S., Ashwin, M., Design and Implementation of an IoT Based Smart Digestive Health Monitoring Device for Identification of Digestive Conditions. *Eng. Proc.*, 58, 1, 33, https://doi.org/10.3390/ecsa-10-16253 2023.
33. Johari, R., Kumar, V., Gupta, K., Vidyarthi, D.P., Blosom: Blockchain technology for security of medical records. *ICT Express*, 8, 1, 56–60, 2022.
34. Usman, M. and Qamar, U., Secure electronic medical records storage and sharing using blockchain technology. *Procedia Comput. Sci.*, 174, 321–327, 2020.
35. Sun, J., Ren, L., Wang, S., Yao, X., A blockchain-based framework for electronic medical records sharing with fine-grained access control. *PLoS One*, 15, 10, e0239946, 2020.
36. Kumar, P., Kumar, R., Gupta, G.P., Tripathi, R., Jolfaei, A., Najmul Islam, A.K.M., A blockchain-orchestrated deep learning approach for secure data transmission in iot-enabled healthcare system. *J. Parallel Distrib. Comput.*, 172, 69–83, 2023.
37. Chen, H.S., Jarrell, J.T., Carpenter, K.A., Cohen, D.S., Huang, X., Blockchain in healthcare: a patient-centered model. *Biomed. J. Sci. Tech. Res.*, 20, 3, 15017, 2019.

12

Trinity: A Blockchain-Based Stablecoin Lending Protocol Using Decentralized Credit Default Swaps

Shyam Mohan J. S.[1*], Akshit Vig[2], Parameswaran T.[3], Kota Harsha Surya Abhishek[4] and Sathiyaraj R.[5]

[1]*Dept. of CSE, GITAM University, Bengaluru, Karnataka, India*
[2]*Co-Founder and CEO, Autonomint Technologies Pvt. Ltd (Awaiting for Approval), Hyderabad, India*
[3]*Department of CSE, School of Engineering and Technology, CMR University, Bengaluru, Karnataka, India*
[4]*Co-Founder and CEO, Autonomint, Hyderabad, India*
[5]*Manipal Institute of Technology, MAHE Bengaluru Campus, Karnataka, India*

Abstract
The need for stablecoins, or stable internet money, is now rapidly being accepted across the world by institutions and governments alike. These stablecoins are issued on-chain on a global ledger and pegged to a relevant transactional currency like USD or EURO. The features of instantaneous settlement, high velocity, high programmability, low volatility (unlike other cryptocurrencies), and 24/7 availability are the most sought-after qualities for every user and business. There are multiple stablecoin designs but the most scalable are the cash-backed or custodial stablecoins. However, these cash-backed stablecoins have inherent risks in terms of censorship by governments through banking rails and high collateral silos of short-term government securities, which can wreak havoc in case of high stablecoin redemptions by users or businesses due to sudden flash crashes in cryptocurrency space. A purely decentralized stablecoin that can easily scale like these custodial stablecoins and is programmable to support a wide variety of use cases is the need of the hour. This research chapter presents a novel decentralized stablecoin design stabilized by derivatives and programmable like money market

**Corresponding author*: jsshyammohan@gmail.com

R. Sathiyaraj, Rajesh Kumar Dhanaraj, K. Arun Kumar, Rutvij H. Jhaveri and A. Mohamed Abbas (eds.) Predictive Methods in Next-Generation Computing: An Approach Toward Sustainability, (233–270)

funds to instill yield-bearing characteristics in stablecoins. The issues solved are capital inefficiency, de-pegging risks, high crypto collateral, native token collateral requirements, heavy reliance on arbitrageurs to maintain a stablecoin peg, lack of long-term value cohesion, and ineffective liquidation management. The stablecoin design can offer up to 100% capital efficiency in spite of being backed by crypto collaterals. It is done through backing by decentralized Credit Default Swaps (dCDS) and collateral options or derivatives. The design ensures high scalability, high programmability to support various use cases, and in-built derivative-based volatility hedging to handle the issue of liquidations due to crypto flash crashes.

Keywords: Decentralized, crypto, credit default swaps, stablecoin, loan-to-value ratio, privacy

12.1 Introduction

Trust serves as the cornerstone of all global human interactions, established through strong backing. Currency acts as a medium of exchange due to the robust support it receives from governments. Trust operates at two levels: trust in currency and trust in counterparties, fueling economic activities. During the Free Banking Era, private currency issuance was allowed, albeit with the requirement of government bond backing. Although state bonds carried some risk, banknotes issued against them maintained their par value [1]. This ensured highly trusted backing, resulting in capital efficiency. Banks could offer loans backed by illiquid assets like property or intangible assets such as education. Similarly, corporations issued corporate bonds against their book assets, benefitting from reasonable interest rates based on credit ratings. However, the decline in the value of transactional currencies has led to reduced capital efficiency across asset classes [2]. To counter this, a store of value that is relatively stable yet volatile is needed. Stability relies on both psychological value measurements and the understanding of purchasing power. Stablecoins not only capture the deterioration of transactional currency value but also introduce volatility as a hedge against such losses [3]. The proposed protocol aims to create a highly capital-efficient stablecoin with solid backing from counterparties to maintain trust in the system. Unique mechanisms have been devised to limit risk for parties seeking above-average returns on their investments.

Trinity is the world's first stablecoin and lending platform offering a Loan-to-Value ratio of 100%. We are also the first protocol utilizing a combination of decentralized derivative instruments like Credit Default swaps (dCDS) and "Collateral options" to manage the risks and provide adequate incentives for every stakeholder through collateral volatility. It has three core components: stablecoins, Credit Default Swaps, and options. It also has a lending protocol where the stablecoin is minted and sent to users who deposit some crypto assets as collateral. Trinity ensures that it can provide a 100% Loan-to-Value ratio so that clients can borrow stablecoins against the entire value of their collateral. To manage the downside risk of collateral deposited, we have devised a unique mechanism to keep the collateral value neutral to price variations. This is enabled by taking a short position on the underlying collateral against the long side of trade handled by the protocol on behalf of our Credit Default swap holders. These dCDS owners deposit the stablecoins in our dCDS contract, and their funds are utilized to take a long position on the underlying collateral borrowers' deposit. These dCDS owners are compensated with a combination of upfront fees and ongoing periodic fees for taking the long side of the position and providing downside protection to collateral assets for borrowers. The borrowers pay these fees to dCDS holders in exchange for downside protection of their collateral and a call option on the underlying collateral asset at some out-of-the-money strike price. The call option allows them to capture the upside of their collateral, automatically making the dCDS owners option sellers as they are also paid some fixed fees for taking the long side of the trade at some out-of-the-money strike price. The protocol ultimately ensures high capital efficiency of the deposited assets and brings a stablecoin that caters to both retail and institutional returns and risk tolerance capacity needs.

12.1.1 Background and Related Work

Some of the most popular stablecoins in the market are USDT (Tether) and USDC (Circle), both of which are centralized and backed by Proof of Reserves. Many crypto companies pay their employees' salaries in USDT and USDC, which is also the preferred option among employees. As the value of the USDT is fully backed by fiat currencies, the peg always remains stable, and you will always be redeemed $1 for 1 stablecoin. Other stablecoins are over-collateralized stablecoins like Maker Dai, which has a native blockchain cryptocurrency like Ethereum (ETH) or other established project tokens as collateral. These stablecoins are minted at the Loan-to-Value ratio of 60% or below. These have gained the most adoption due to their over-collateralized nature, which makes the protocol less susceptible to default, and the stablecoin does not lose its peg widely. Interest rate mechanisms are put in place to manage the demand and supply of stablecoins in the market, which in turn helps manage the peg of the stablecoin to $1 [4]. Stablecoins are backed by on-chain algorithms with an algorithmic rule that manage the supply and demand of stablecoins and the assets backing them. They can be burned and minted algorithmically to ensure a 1:1 peg [5]. Then there are partially collateralized and partially algorithmic stablecoins like FRAX [6]. Their collateral consists of established blockchain projects like ETH and protocol tokens in a ratio that varies based on the supply and demand of stablecoins, affecting the stablecoin price. If the stablecoin price is above the peg, then there is a higher demand for the stablecoin, which can be utilized by the protocol to increase the percentage of their protocol token as backing for the stablecoin minted. This leads to broader adoption of their receipt and an increase in the price of the token. This increases the project's market capitalization of the project and broader success and strength of the protocol. Some stablecoins are minted in return for supplying native blockchain assets like ETH or established project tokens. These projects have these deposited assets in their balance sheet, which are volatile. Any change in the value of these assets is compensated by the minting of protocol tokens, which are sold or bought as per the decrease or increase in asset value at a particular discount. There has been de-pegging in all four scenarios mentioned above, with major bank runs in algorithmic stablecoins and partially collateralized stablecoins. For example, the Terra Luna crash was based on an algorithmic stablecoin design with the protocol's own asset being used as collateral to back their stablecoin [7]. Another big crash occurred with Iron Finance stablecoin, which was a partially collateralized and algorithmic stablecoin [8]. Over-collateralized stablecoins have faced de-pegging during periods of high collateral volatility, affecting the auction of collateral assets at a discounted price. Even centralized stablecoins like USDC backed by Proof of Reserves had a de-pegging of more than 10% due to their budgets being affected in banks that went bankrupt due to bank runs. Sometimes, the funds are utilized in government bonds or other assets [9], which decrease in value, leading to a fall in reserves [10]. After analyzing various stablecoins, some observations have been made as given below based on core user tendencies toward minting and borrowing stablecoins.

1. Users aim to maximize their yield opportunities in the dynamic DeFi space while holding onto their volatile assets. To achieve this, they leverage their capital by borrowing stablecoins, allowing them to explore various opportunities in the market, including platforms and yield farms.
2. Stablecoins as a currency are widely accepted across all new and established platforms. New platforms prefer stablecoins because they do not want their platform to be affected by

some external risk factors or overall DeFi volatility [11]. Established platforms prefer stablecoins to diversify their TVL (Total Value Locked) to stable assets, which will grant backing to their governance tokens or utility tokens. Stablecoin backing is similar to cash equivalent backing, which commands the highest trust among the user base [12].

3. Users want to take advantage of the peg off balance, especially when the stablecoin value is above the peg. This way, they can borrow stablecoins at 1 USD from the protocol and sell them at the market price of > 1 USD to generate a net profit [13].

When designing the protocol, measures were implemented to avoid minting stablecoins by exchanging volatile cryptocurrencies as assets. Instead, the protocol securely stores the underlying assets (such as ETH or Solana (SOL)) upon which the DeFi protocol is built. This approach offers users a risk-free opportunity while allowing them to retain their volatile cryptocurrencies and maintain a long position on the base layer assets.

Blockchain technology is becoming more and more popular on a global basis. Numerous sectors and use cases are being uncovered that could profit from the use of blockchain as the investigation from professionals and academics intensifies. One of the most prominent and potential use cases in this area is frequently mentioned as being peer-to-peer finance *via* initial coin offerings. In this study, the principles of initial digital currency offerings are explained, their distinctions from traditional fundraising are emphasized, and their possible effects on crowdfunding are investigated [14]. Decentralized finance (DeFi) is still an intricate trend that needs more in-depth study, even if it has the ability to mimic and even surpass current financial systems. In addition to discussing the current state of knowledge on the subject of decentralized finance, this paper proposes a consolidated definition of decentralized finance [15], to accomplish this while modifying the suggested blockchain research approach [16]. The purpose of this study is to stimulate additional research to reduce the present dangers associated with decentralized finance, with the ultimate goal of improving the financial ecosystem. Value Token Transfer Protocol, a decentralized financial protocol, is presented in this article. It allows value or tokens to be exchanged for fiat money in fiat wallets, bank accounts, and blockchain networks that are involved [17]. For tokens or digital currency, the protocol permits both intra- and inter-chain transfers. Unquestionably, one of the most cutting-edge financial services innovations of the preceding generation is blockchain. The present state of financial applications and services provided by blockchain technology has been reviewed along with the effects, ramifications, and rules surrounding the integration of blockchain technology in the banking sector. Together with offering a vision for the upcoming generation of monetary services based on this cutting-edge technology, it also addresses the adaption model for the use of blockchain in the global economy [18].

Proprietary authorized blockchains are being utilized in increasing quantities to ease cross-organizational procedures in numerous industries, especially in managing supply chains. Through a comprehensive performance investigation of Hyperledger Fabric, this paper seeks to address this problem. The Distributed Ledger Performance Scan is improved upon, and the report provides a comprehensive compilation of several performance metrics [19]. The hyperledger fabric system can be configured and implemented more effectively by researchers and practitioners by using several different performance aspects that have been determined and clarified as guidance. The article discusses facts on the development of blockchain technology, as well as the background of the various cryptographic primitives—public key cryptography, digital signatures, and cryptocurrency—and consensus methods. The focus of this study is on the blockchain's mechanisms for consensus [20]. It focuses on consensus techniques, specifically proof of work and furthermore.

12.2 Motivation and Problem Statement

Blockchain technology can be used in a distributed manner to address the aforementioned issues because of its inviolability, privacy, decentralization, transparency, concealment, transactional information, and automation capabilities. To highlight potential future prospects and recommendations, findings deficiencies, and constraints are stated [21]. The results of this study can be used as a roadmap to help the new distributed generation rapidly embrace blockchain technology. The review's research findings offer a broader understanding of blockchain's adaptability and usefulness in the distributed production industry, specifically with regard to peer-to-peer energy trading, decentralized grid operations, and energy optimization. Blockchain is a technology for decentralized digital ledgers that has completely changed trade, industry, and business by eliminating the requirement for a centralized authority for storage and management. Because blockchain technology is immutable and decentralized, it offers a rapid, transparent, pseudo-anonymous solution that has completely altered identification, trust, ownership, and financial systems. This essay offers a thorough analysis of blockchain technology, emphasizing its underlying theories, historical context, and unexpected surge in popularity. Several blockchain consensus algorithms are also covered in the study [22]. Subsequently, the study centers on the diverse application domains and conceivable applications of blockchain technology, along with the associated obstacles and concerns. The study also offers a few unusual applications for blockchain technology.

Existing collateralized lending protocols and algorithmic stablecoins have the following issues:

1. These protocols have a low capital efficiency: DeFi lenders require collateral over the value of the loan so that if the value of the borrowed asset drops or the value of the collateral drops, the lender still has a cushion in the form of excess collateral. This helps in saving the protocol from insolvency but it also limits the amount of capital to be borrowed.
2. Protocols need to constantly monitor the market to set an efficient liquidation discount: Some protocols like Maker and dYdX use an auction mechanism where liquidators bid with increasing amounts of the protocol currency/borrowed asset to liquidate under-collateralized accounts. These bidders will be able to get the collateral at a discount named an LD (Liquidation Discount) and then sell the collateral back in the open market at the market price, thus pocketing the profit. However, there is slippage in decentralized exchanges like Uniswap, which varies with the liquidation size. This slippage might lower or eliminate the arbitrage while selling the collateral. Thus, these protocols need to constantly monitor the market and re-evaluate their liquidation discount (LD) to both ensure overpaying of collateral when the market rate is lower as well as ensure not underpaying when the market rate is higher, which will lead to no one bidding for liquidation leading to insolvency risks.
3. Algorithmic stablecoins backed by another stablecoin: These stablecoins are backed by a stablecoin asset, which doesn't fulfill the need of users to stay long in their current crypto asset and capture the yields through price appreciation. Motivated by the above challenges, we tried to develop a new protocol design, specifically addressing the below issues:

1. There is a need to create a stablecoin that is highly capital efficient with solid backing by the counterparties to ensure trust in the system is maintained.
2. Current stablecoin protocols need to design better incentives and user-friendly mechanisms for their borrowers. Currently, Borrowers have to monitor their collateralization ratios to avoid the risk of getting liquidated. This limits the borrowing capacity to a lower Loan-to-Value ratio so that the borrowers have some leeway to manage liquidation risk, which decreases the capital efficiency of the protocol. Although there are projects out there that through some subscription fees provide services of maintaining the collateral ratios, it introduces another overhead on top of the borrowing fees.
3. The current stablecoin does not provide downside protection for borrower collateral. So, during bearish times, there is a higher risk of collateral liquidation, leading to less utilization of these projects and less minting of stablecoins, which can have a ripple effect on the strength or crypto economics of these projects.
4. Current stablecoin projects still need to build a capital-efficient way to manage liquidations as the incentive structures are not attractive enough for liquidators. The best way now is to create a readily available pool of stablecoins utilized to manage liquidations at a particular discount. However, this mechanism is reliant on using liquidations to reward stablecoin pool users, making it highly pro-cyclical.

Real data may be recorded at several supply chain nodes using blockchain technology, which can also facilitate rapid data sharing and complete product lifetime traceability. This study undertakes a systematic literature evaluation based on the Web of Science database, concentrating on the research issue of the implementation of blockchain-based technology in managing the supply chain [23]. They ultimately obtained 591 target studies by putting up explicit search and selection requirements based on four research topics. Additionally, a thorough analysis of the target literature's distribution by entity, country/region, publication, and research field was also carried out. Two revolutionary technologies that have come out of the fourth industrialization and significantly changed the industry are bitcoin and intelligent machines. The existing corpus of research on the subject of artificial intelligence as well as blockchain technology integration is accessible, but a thorough grasp of the viability and efficiency of this integration in a corporate setting is lacking. To close this current knowledge gap, the main goal of this research project is to thoroughly examine and define the different uses and benefits of artificial intelligence (AI) and blockchain integration in a range of commercial application domains [24].

12.3 Methodology

We present a stablecoin solution that serves as a reliable store of value, targeting individual users, businesses, DAOs (decentralized autonomous organizations), and financial institutions seeking to stay engaged in the growing digital asset ecosystem while capitalizing on diverse opportunities in global markets. Our lending protocol allows leveraging crypto collateral while offering downside protection for the deposited assets. This opens up new possibilities for borrowers who can secure a loan against their crypto collateral and invest the funds in their businesses without the risk of liquidation. Our objective is to deliver optimal capital efficiency to all participants. The project encompasses three key components, outlined as follows:

1. Stablecoins - They are minted upon locking collateral like ETH. The LTV (Loan-to-Value) ratio will be 100%.
2. Decentralized dCDS (Credit Default swaps) - Depositors can enter into dCDS with the protocol and get regular funding payments apart from the interest rates they earn by depositing their stablecoins on the protocol. Participants can earn more than 100% APY over and above the meager interest rates they receive from depositing their assets. The dCDS owners will also act as option sellers and will be getting fixed option premiums in return for their assets being readily available in case of default by the borrower. The dCDS will effectively be getting compensated with option premiums from multiple borrowers in return for offering downside protection and taking the long side of the trade on collateral price.
3. Collateral options - The collateral options are the source of fees for dCDS owners. The idea behind collateral options is to give an option to the borrower for creating lossless strategies. In traditional finance, people buy options to hedge their

downside and create a limited loss strategy. Using the same method, the upside is maintained as the collateral options are a form of call options that allow the borrower to earn all the upside above a particular strike price. Borrowers will be able to buy a call option and downside protection while taking a loan against Ethereum or any other collateral through our borrowing contract. Upon paying an upfront option price, the borrower can hedge the downside risk.

These three will work together to maintain the peg of stablecoin and manage collaterals and defaults. The protocol will have two types of user bases with different risk tendencies and opinions about the market.

1. The first type of users will be borrowers who want to mint stablecoins and stay long in the volatile crypto asset that they hold. These users also want to maximize their deposited capital's efficiency. To achieve this, they can mint and borrow the stablecoins against their deposited capital at the maximum LTV ratio of 100%.
2. The second type of users will be dCDS owners. A dCDS position allows one to swap the credit/default risk in exchange for some periodic fixed fees. In its aim to provide a 100% LTV ratio to borrowers, the protocol faces the credit/default risk when there is a fall in deposited capital (collateral) value. This protocol will protect itself against these credit risks with the help of dCDS owners. The protocol will swap the credit risk from itself to the dCDS owners. These users will deposit the stablecoins in dCDS contracts. The stablecoins deposited will act as a counterpart and their capital will be utilized to counter the credit risk generated by falling collateral value. These dCDS owners' capital will be locked, and in return, they will be compensated with a combination of upfront fees and periodic fees, which will help them achieve returns near 100% annual percentage yield (APY).

12.3.1 Option Fees Exchanged Among the Participants

The collateral option fees are shared from borrowers to dCDS owners and achieved through an options derivative. The protocol will also have a 'delta neutral contract' where borrowers' capital and dCDS capital will take short and long positions, respectively. This will help achieve downside protection on the borrower's capital and help the protocol to capture an upside of the borrower's capital and utilize that upside to provide excessive returns to dCDS owners and borrowers. For the initial few years, the protocol parameters will be handled by our core team to ensure stablecoin peg is maintained with appropriate incentives created. We will automate most of the parameters over the course of this stabilization period to achieve an equilibrium state where the protocol runs smoothly.

12.4 Discussions

Figure 12.1 shows the functional model of the proposed work.

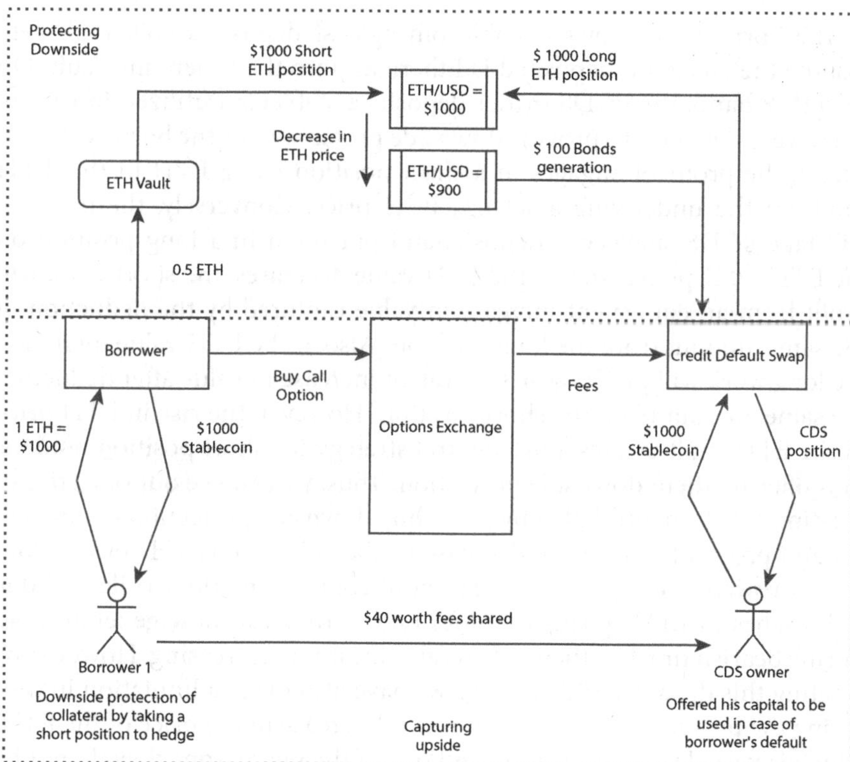

Figure 12.1 Functional mechanism of project trinity.

12.4.1 Stakeholders in Protocol

1. Borrowers – Borrow stablecoins by depositing acceptable volatile assets (Ethereum) as collateral.
2. Credit Default Swap Owners – Deposits stablecoins, which are utilized by the system to provide downside protection for the ETH deposited by borrowers.

12.4.2 Tokens in Protocol

1. Stablecoin
2. Option
3. Protocol Token/Reserve currency (generated to manage risk and act as a savings account)

The borrower borrows a stablecoin against deposited collateral. Let's assume the collateral deposited is Ethereum into the Ethereum Vault. On the other hand, the dCDS owner deposits a stablecoin utilized in case of borrower's defaults. To provide downside protection for the borrower's collateral, the protocol engages in a short position using ETH in the 'ETH vault' on the underlying asset i.e., ETH price. Conversely, the protocol will take dCDS stablecoin deposits and put them in a long position on the ETH/USD price. Now, if the ETH value decreases, the short work will profit from an equivalent increase in value captured by the deduction of the same amount from the long position. Also, if the ETH value increases, the long work will profit by an equivalent increase in value after deducting the same amount from the short position. However, the rise in ETH price in the ETH vault creates a net-neutral strategy for short position holders, thus offering them downside protection. Thus, we achieve our objective of creating a delta-neutral plan by providing downside protection to borrowers and protocol during the decrease in the collateral (ETH) price. Now, the borrowers don't have to worry about confiscating their collateral due to breaches in LTV (Loan-to-Value) ratios. They can now generate yield during bearish times as their collateral value is not decreasing. However, by creating this delta-neutral strategy, we have also made a limitation in capturing the upside of the collateral, i.e., an increase in the price of the ETH, which is very dear to borrowers and one of the big reasons they do not let go of their collateral. The deposits of stablecoin are locked for some duration. Also, the dCDS owners will be getting option fees from borrowers in return for offering their stablecoin deposits to offer downside protection. Minting of protocol tokens is done when the collateral value is 90% of the borrowed amount and when the collateral value has touched 80% of the borrowed amount. In the initial stages of the protocol, we will be offering downside protection based on the volatility of Ethereum.

We plan to offer 20% downside protection for collateral at the start. There is an alternative mechanism for providing protection of dCDS deposits by generating a bond or hedge token, which will be given to dCDS once they unlock their deposit after fulfillment of contract unlock conditions. This bond or hedge token will have a maturity of 6–12 months. Its value will depend on the total amount pending for maturity at different time durations. This token can be with other participants.

12.4.3 Components of the Protocol

Borrowing of Stablecoins

A borrower deposits ETH as collateral, and the protocol mints the equivalent value of stablecoin in a 100% Loan-to-Value ratio as shown in Figure 12.2.

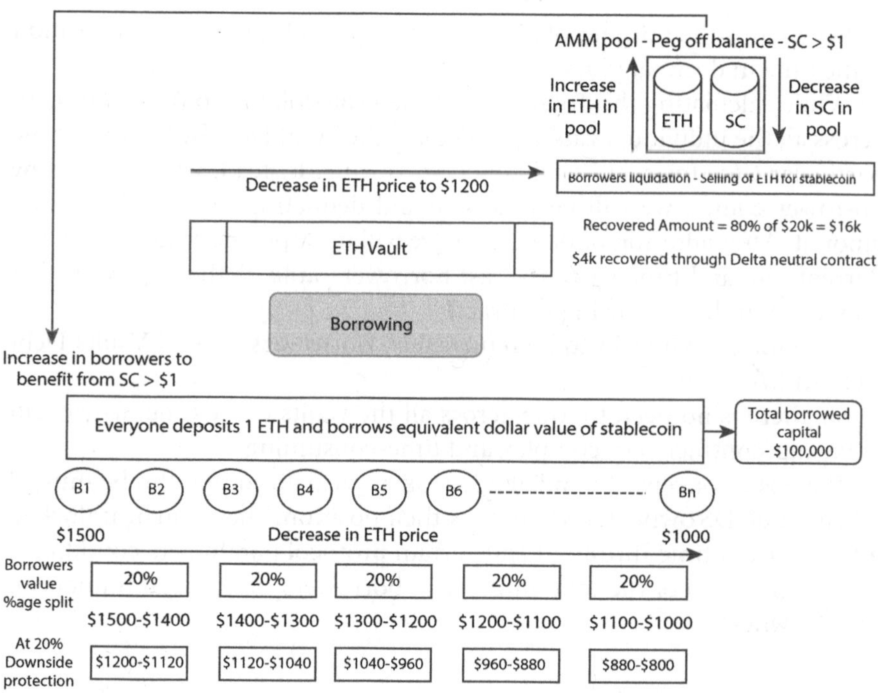

Figure 12.2 Borrowing module.

1. Track the price of ETH at the time of borrowing to store the USD worth of collateral deposited by the borrower. Every borrower will have their dollar worth collateral amount stored in the smart contract parameters when borrowing.
2. The protocol immediately deposits ETH into the ETH vault and takes a short position on the delta-neutral contract.
3. The protocol mints stablecoins equivalent to the USD worth of ETH collateral deposited.

Total Debt for a Particular Vault = Amount borrowed + Borrowing Fees

At t = 0, APR = 12% (where APR is the Annual Percentage Rate of borrowing written in decimals)

Total Debt Calculation

If ETH Price = $1000
Collateral Deposited = 1 ETH = $1000
Stablecoin Borrowed, B = $1000
Total Debt at time t = B*(1+APR/n)^nt

Where n is the number of compounding periods per unit of time and t is the time in decimal years.

While calculating the Total Debt of the Protocol, we don't need to loop across all the individual vaults to calculate the Total Debt by looking at the particular time for every vault since borrowing. Instead, whenever a new borrower comes, we will keep adding and deducting the total borrowed amount. After addition or deduction, we will multiply the amount with the current rate and time since the last borrower came or the last event that happened in the borrowing contract.

Therefore, Total Debt to be returned by borrowers = Total Vaults Debt * (1+APR/n) ^ nt

So, there is no need to loop across all the vaults every time, which can make our contract very complex and time-consuming.

There is a concept of bonds/hedge tokens visualized that can be minted when the dCDS owner tries to unlock their position. These can be unlocked after a certain time threshold and certain protocol parameters conditions, such as the ratio of the total number of borrowers to the total number of dCDS owners.

Credit Default Swap Entry by Holders

1. Each dCDS holder will deposit the Trinity stablecoins after buying them from a market into the dCDS contract in multiples of $500.
2. The contract will save each dCDS holder's position.
3. The pooling of the total amount and taking a long position on a delta-neutral contract will be done.
4. An option seller will utilize the pooled amount in an options contract on behalf of dCDS holders. This way, the dCDS holders will get the option fees from borrowers.
5. The decision to unlock dCDS holder stablecoins is based on tracking a combination of fixed term and protocol parameters.
6. The ratio of dCDS holders to borrowers must be ≥ 0.2.
7. The above ratio should be greater than 2 to unlock the dCDS positions.

Delta-Neutral Contract (Downside Protection for Borrowers)

A delta-neutral contract involves taking two opposite positions on the price of ETH/USD:

1. One is the short position taken by the borrowers on ETH/USD, and the other is the long position taken by the dCDS holder on ETH/USD.
2. Assuming a 10% decrease in the price of ETH, the dCDS holder's short position will cause a corresponding 10% increase in USD value to be added for each ETH held in the ETH vault. This additional amount will be subtracted from the dCDS holder's long position.
3. These are synthetic positions, and no cash settlement is happening on every change in price after every periodic interval.
4. Cash settlement only happens if a dCDS holder wants to withdraw their amount after a 1-month lock-in period is over. At that moment, we will calculate the final balance of the total pooled amount. If the amount is positive than the amount pooled, then a fraction of the amount will be deducted and given to the dCDS holder.

Calculation of Balances of a Long Position and Short Position

1. Short Position (Borrowers)
   a. Calculate the quantity of ETH deposited in the ETH vault.
   b. Track the price of ETH in periodic intervals (1 min).
   c. If the price of the ETH in the current periodic interval is higher/lower than the previous periodic interval, then the total balance of the short position will be deducted by the below formula:

X = (Total number of ETH in ETH Vault * ETH Price change (Between Periodic intervals)

Short Position Balance = Total Short Position Balance – (Total number of ETH in ETH Vault * ETH Price change (Between Periodic intervals)).

2. Long Position (dCDS Holder)
   a. Calculate the total amount of stablecoin deposited in the pool.
   b. As the price of collateral (ETH) changes, there is a change in the dCDS pool long position balance:

Total Long Position Balance = Long position balance in previous interval + X (Real)

Option's Contract

Earlier versions based on the ERC20 standard failed to adequately distinguish between principal and interest payments while also accommodating differing rolling maturities. In the past, holders encountered theta decay as all positions neared maturity simultaneously, leading to a prisoner's dilemma [25]. The duration is measured in seconds utilizing Unix timestamps, as permitted by Solidity shown in Figure 12.2.

1. The design of the option contract aims to offer borrowers a means of benefiting from a potential increase in the price of ETH. This is accomplished through the purchase of a call option at a specified strike price.
2. Furthermore, the option contract facilitates the transfer of option fees from option buyers (i.e., borrowers) to option sellers (i.e., dCDS holders), thereby allowing dCDS holders to earn a high yield APY on their deposited funds while

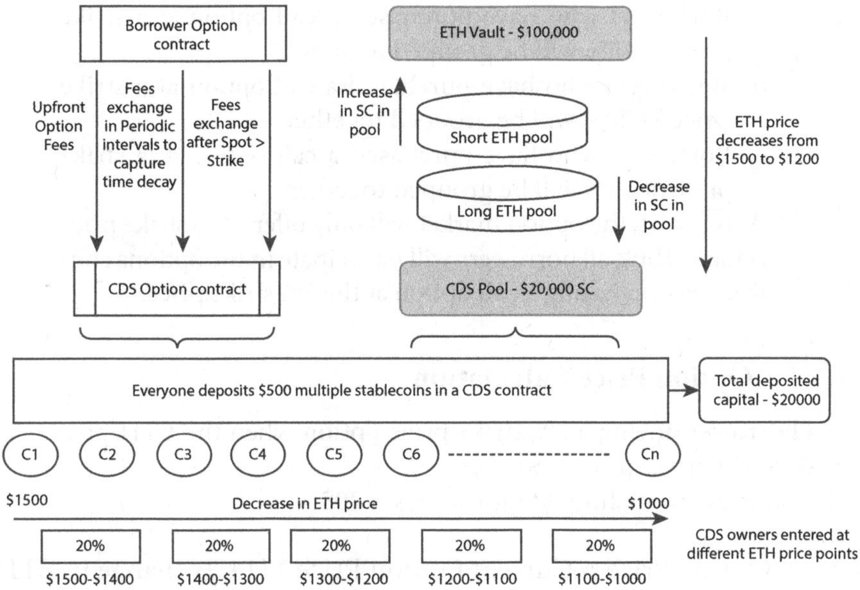

Figure 12.3 dCDS module.

maintaining a delta-neutral position for borrowers shown in Figure 12.3.

3. There are five variations of strike prices that borrowers can take: 5%, 10%, 15%, 20%, and 25%. It implies that borrowers can buy a call option on ETH price on the above percentage ranges for strike prices only.
4. The option price will decrease from a 5% strike price option to a 25% strike price option as per the risks.

There are three different approaches to designing an option fees exchange mechanism:

First Approach

1. There will be only five markets for option prices:
   a. Borrowers who have purchased a call option at a strike price of 5% will be grouped together.
   b. Borrowers who have purchased a call option at a strike price of 10% will be grouped together.

c. Borrowers who have purchased a call option at a strike price of 15% will be grouped together.
d. Borrowers who have purchased a call option at a strike price of 20% will be grouped together.
e. Borrowers who have purchased a call option at a strike price of 25% will be grouped together.

2. At the start, the option market will only offer a 5% strike price option. Thus, all borrowers will participate in the options contract by purchasing a call option at the 5% strike price.

12.4.4 Option Price Calculation

For a borrower buying a 5% strike price option when the ETH price is at \$1000, so the strike price is \$1050.

He/she pays some Initial Option Fees = 20\$

Option Price = Current Option Price * (1+ % change in ETH price from the contract start * 10) - (Time decay effect on Price)

Option price also changes if some borrower comes in between to sell their option at the current price. So, the seller will be given the increase in option price by deducting the same amount over the remaining borrowers who are still holding the option, implying they are bullish on the option price and thus acting as counterparty to the borrower looking to exit from his option contract.

Second Approach

1. Once an option buyer enters into an options contract, they will receive an non-fungible tokens (NFT) representing their position at the 5% strike price. They may then choose to list the NFT in a marketplace for sale at a specific price.
2. Potential buyers of the NFT may purchase it at the listed price and subsequently deposit it into our protocol, enabling them to receive any benefits resulting from the ETH price being above the strike price on the specified expiry date.

Third Approach

The option prices with no maturity dates and five strike price options

1. Borrowers who have purchased a call option at a 5% strike price will be grouped together.

2. Borrowers who have purchased a call option at a 10% strike price will be grouped together.
3. Borrowers who have purchased a call option at a 15% strike price will be grouped together.
4. Borrowers who have purchased a call option at a 20% strike price will be grouped together.
5. Borrowers who have purchased a call option at a 25% strike price will be grouped together.

Total Option fees = 40% Upfront Payment + Continuous stream of option payments for time decay in option price with no maturity dates

For Instance, ETH spot price = $1000

The borrower deposits 1 ETH as collateral to borrow a $1000 stablecoin.

The borrower takes a call option at a 5% strike price with no expiry of the maturity date. So, the strike price is $1050.

Total fees = Upfront Option Fees + Continuous stream of option payments to capture theta decay + Option Fees to maintain position (If Spot > Strike)

Total Fees = $10 + $20 (Continuous fees deduction from $20 in 1% percentage points corresponding to theta decay) + (%age Deduction of overall upside as long as the position is kept open)

12.4.5 Risk Management and Protocol Tokens/Reserve Currency

Our protocol is designed to provide borrowers with downside protection on their collateral while also enabling them to capture the upside potential of collateral. This is currently achieved through a combination of dCDS capital [26] and collateral options used as incentives.

It is crucial for our protocol to have the necessary flexibility to manage risk and incentivize participants appropriately. This will be achieved through the use of protocol tokens/reserve currency, which will only be minted and burned based on the actions of participants. We recognize the importance of the time value of money in providing yields to parties, whose assets are utilized by a counterparty to manage project operations, drawing upon traditional finance principles. In our protocol, we also utilize the assets of dCDS owners to manage the downside risk of collateral. As compensation, they receive upfront fees and a continuous flow of fees for time decay in options. The Protocol Tokens will serve as a risk management tool for both the protocol and dCDS owners.

12.4.5.1 Use of Protocol Tokens/Reserve Currency in Risk Management

We will be utilizing the protocol tokens as a risk management tool for both the protocol and dCDS owners. The protocol has downside protection built in through its delta-neutral function, but it also needs flexibility to manage risk by reducing its reliance on collateral assets' volatility.

It provides incentives through protocol tokens to diversify the risk from collateral assets to protocol tokens. The protocol tokens' mint function will be activated when the borrower's collateral has fallen to 90%, and the number of protocol tokens minted will be twice the fall in collateral value. These tokens will be provided to the borrower upon returning the stablecoins borrowed. The provided tokens are double the value of the loss in collateral, so they act as an incentive for the borrower to earn an upfront yield. This higher yield compensates for the higher yields that the borrower could have earned by locking or staking their stablecoins on some protocol.

By diversifying the risks from collateral volatility to protocol tokens, the protocol has higher flexibility in managing risks. The protocol will mint tokens that will be distributed to dCDS owners after some term or time duration. This will act as the yield for locking the dCDS capital for longer durations with the protocol.

It can be observed in current decentralized lending platforms such as Compound Finance that stablecoins provide significantly higher supply APYs (20–40 times) compared to volatile assets like ETH. This yield is even more substantial for tokens with active yield farming programs [27].

By depositing Ethereum to borrow stablecoins, individuals can potentially earn higher yields by efficiently utilizing their stablecoins. Despite the deduction of borrowing fees, the yields offered on stablecoins are higher due to their non-volatile nature.

dCDS owners take on a significant amount of risk in exchange for large option fees. However, their participation is based solely on their view of the collateral assets' volatility. If the collateral asset's volatility is low, they will benefit from higher returns through option fees. Conversely, if the volatility is high, their returns are more likely to be negatively impacted. By diversifying the risk from collateral volatility to protocol tokens, we gain greater flexibility in managing risks within the protocol. The protocol will mint tokens that will be distributed to dCDS owners after a specific time duration, providing a yield for locking dCDS capital for longer periods with the protocol.

One potential issue with the protocol's 100% LTV is that users may attempt to game the system by borrowing stablecoins to buy ETH, and then using that ETH as collateral to take out another loan. However, since fees are deducted from the original stablecoin loan, the actual loan value is closer to 95%. This means that repeatedly opening borrowing positions in this way would not significantly impact the system, as the borrowed value is eventually returned. The only systemic risk would be if the collateral for all these borrowing positions were to fall in value, which could impact the dCDS pool.

12.4.5.2 Managing Liquidation in Protocol

Method 1

We have a set of borrowers Br = {b1, b2, b3, b4.............bn)

Where bi denotes the i-th borrowing position

It is a single collateral lending protocol with stablecoin borrowed in an LTV ratio of 100%

Assuming the collateral utilized is the ETH, we have all these borrowers coming at different points of time at different ETH prices and borrowing stablecoin loans at 100% LTV.

Thus, the ETH prices associated with this group of borrowers can be represented as:

$$Er = (E1, E2, E3,E4...............En)$$

Where Ei represents the ETH price for the i-th borrowing position.

The collateral amount will be a fraction or multiple of ETH value, with Ci denoting the collateral deposited by the i-th borrower.

The debt taken in stablecoin is equivalent to the price of the ETH at an LTV of 100% LTV.

As the borrower also needs to engage in an option contract along with the borrowing, the borrower needs to pay some option fees to provide downside protection to collateral and capture ETH upside if the price rises above a particular strike price. We will deduct these fees at the time the borrowing occurs from the Loan value taken by the borrower.

These option fees are a combination of upfront and fees for taking a perpetual position in the call option. After deducting the perpetual call option fees corresponding to the time decay of a particular borrowing position, some of them will be returned. If a borrowing position is closed early, the borrower will receive the fees back.

The prices will be calculated on the below factors:

1. The fees will have a $10 minimum cap.
2. The fees will be dependent on the strike price of the perpetual call option. Payments will be higher for a higher strike price option.
3. The upfront fees will be determined based on the percentage of downside protection provided to the collateral amount. Initially, the protocol will offer 20% downside protection.

$$\text{Upfront fees} = 10\% * 20\% * Ci*Ei$$

Perpetual Option Fees will be calculated based on the strike price.

1. We will group together borrowers who purchased a call option at a 5% strike price.

$$40\% * (\text{Strike Price of ETH} - Ei)$$

2. We will group together borrowers who purchased a call option at a 10% strike price.

$$30\% * (\text{Strike Price of ETH} - Ei)$$

3. We will group together borrowers who purchased a call option at a 15% strike price.

$$20\% * (\text{Strike Price of ETH} - Ei)$$

4. We will group together borrowers who purchased a call option at a 20% strike price.

$$10\% * (\text{Strike Price of ETH} - Ei)$$

5. We will group together borrowers who purchased a call option at a 25% strike price.

$$5\% * (\text{Strike Price of ETH} - Ei)$$

The perpetual option fees will have a time decay deduction of fees every day from the perpetual option fees.

$$\text{Time decay} = 0.1\$ + 10\% * (\text{ETH price change every day})$$

12.4.5.3 Liquidation Management

We manage liquidation by minting protocol tokens. However, we can still wait for liquidation to happen and then take action. We will proactively protect the protocol against any liquidation or strive to earn some yield until the liquidation happens (in two ways):

1. Earning yield from collateral deposited: We will split the collateral value into two parts. Half of the collateral will be deposited in some other protocol to earn yield, and half will be kept here to offer downside protection in our See-Saw function.
2. Minting of protocol tokens at various stages: This will be done when the collateral value is 90% of the borrowed amount and when the collateral value has touched 80% of the borrowed amount. When the collateral value touches 80% of the borrowed amount, we give them protocol tokens in return for stablecoins. We will apply a liquidation discount before giving protocol tokens. This mechanism will ensure that we do not have to take our collateral back from an external protocol, which might charge us some fees and lose out on the yield on the collateral deposited.

If Di is the debt in stablecoin taken by the borrower bi, then at 100% LTV:

$$Di = Ci * Ei$$

Rt denotes the value of collateral ETH at time t.
So, the health of the borrowing position:

$$Hi = (Ci * Rt) / Di = (Ci * Rt) / (Ci * Ei) = Rt / Ei$$

The health of the borrowing position will mainly vary from approximately 0 to 2. Considering that with the rise in the value of Hi, the borrower has increased incentive to close their position and take the increase in value. We will mint protocol tokens at different stages.

1. When Hi approaches 0.9, the protocol tokens will be minted based on the below formula:

$$\text{If the market price of protocol tokens} = Pm$$
$$\text{Protocol Tokens} = [(Ei - Rt) * 2] / Pm$$

2. When Hi approaches 0.8, we will mint the protocol tokens again. We will use a Hypothetical Liquidation discount (U) to determine the value of the protocol tokens minted for Liquidators.

$$\text{Protocol Tokens} = [0.1 * (Ei - Rt)] / Pm$$

Here, Hi of 0.9 and 0.8 are dependent on the ETH volatility and dCDS volumes/borrower volumes.

Example

Assuming the current market price of ETH, Rt = $1000:

The borrower, bi, puts 1 ETH as collateral. In return, the protocol mints $1000 Trinity SC.

So, here Ci is the collateral as a multiple of ETH = 1.

Also, Ci*Ei = 1*1000 = $1000.

The borrower also chooses the 5% strike price, i.e., $1050.

So, the option price for borrower = Upfront Option fees + Perpetual option fees:

$$= 0.1*0.2*Ci*Ei + 0.3*(\text{Strike Price} - Ei)$$

$$= 0.1*0.2*1000 + 0.4*(1050-1000)$$

$$= 20 + 20 = \$40$$

So, out of 1000 Trinity SC minted, we will take 40 SC as Option Fees, leaving the borrower with 960 SC.

We have different scenarios as follows:

1. ETH fell to $900 or 90%
   So, here Hi = 0.90
   Let's assume, Protocol tokens price, Pm = $2
   The protocol will mint Protocol tokens = [(Ei - Rt) * 2] / Pm

   = [(1000 - 900) * 2]/ 2

   = 100 Protocol tokens

In this case, if the borrower decides to return $1000 SC, they will receive their ETH back after 3 months, but they will immediately receive 100 Protocol tokens. Essentially, the borrower will only need to return $900 SC to receive the 100 Protocol tokens.

2. ETH fell to $800 or 80%
   Here, Hi = 0.8
   In this case, the borrower's collateral assets will become protocol assets, meaning the protocol will become the owner of the ETH. The liquidator will receive the earlier 100 Protocol tokens plus an additional 10% of Protocol tokens, and in exchange, will give 200 SC to Protocol for the Protocol tokens.
   So, the liquidator will get = [0.1 * (Ei - Rt)] / Pm

   = 100 + 0.1* (1000 - 800)/2

   = 100 + 10 = 110 Protocol tokens

Liquidator will get = 1.1 * [(Ei - Rt) / Pm]
It will be a direct call from the user (the depositor of that particular index cannot be a liquidator/user).

12.4.5.4 *Calculation of dCDS Holder Accrued Amount During Withdrawal/Close*

We should know the total amount to be returned to the dCDS depositor after a particular time period. The exchange of funds between the ETH pool and the dCDS pool will be calculated after every dCDS action or borrower action. As soon as a dCDS deposits funds into our platform, we will identify the below parameters:

1. Current ETH market price, Er
2. Amount of dCDS funds deposited/Total dCDS deposited funds till now (Cd/C)
3. Total number of ETH holdings in our ETH pool

We will then calculate the current value of dCDS funds in our protocol:

$$\text{Total dCDS Deposited Funds} = C$$

$$\text{dCDS deposited funds} = Cd$$

$$\text{dCDS current funds} = Cr1$$

So, Cr = Cd + (Cd/C)*(Er - Ei)*(Total Eth Holdings)

We will calculate the division of exchanged funds among the total dCDS depositors using the above formula. As soon as there is a new depositor or borrower or any sort of new event, the value of different figures in the formula will change. After the new event, the division percentage of exchanged funds will be changed accordingly.

Thus, Cr2 = Cd + (Cd/C)*(Er- Ei+1) * (Total ETH Holdings)

So, after every event, the reward percentage split changes, which requires us to calculate the rewards split between two deposit intervals among all the dCDS depositors until that moment. This exercise will be too computationally intensive for the smart contract considering there might be hundreds of thousands of dCDS depositors. Also, calculating the reward split before every new dCDS deposit would delay the transaction completion time and considerably affect the user experience. Table 12.1 shows the dCDS depositors calculation and Table 12.2 shows the dCDS depositors values obtained - daywise.

Table 12.1 dCDS depositors calculation.

Day	Total ETH	Initial ETH capital	ETH price	Initial dCDS amount	dCDS pool	dCDS depositors	Total	Net value of dCDS pool
1	51	50000	1000	10000		1000	11000	11000
2	52		1010		510	1000	12000	12510
3	53		1020		1030	1000	13000	14030
4	54		1030		1560	1000	14000	15560
5	55		1040		2100	1000	15000	17100
6	56		1030		1550	1000	16000	17550
7	57		1020		990	1000	17000	17990
8	58		1010		420	1000	18000	18420
9	59		1000		-160	1000	19000	18840
10	60		950		-3110	1000	20000	16890

Table 12.2 dCDS depositors values obtained—day-wise.

	Day 2	Day 3	Day 4	Day 5	Day 6	Day 7	Day 8	Day 9	Day 10
dCDS 1	1046.4	1043.3							
dCDS 2		1043.3							
dCDS 3			1040.8						
dCDS 4				1038.6					
dCDS 5					963.3				
dCDS 6						965.0			
dCDS 7							966.5		
dCDS 8								967.8	
dCDS 9									844.7

To manage the above situation, we will maintain a record of reward split for only one standardized deposit amount. For a start, we have considered that deposit amount to be $1000. So, before every new dCDS deposit transaction, we will calculate the proportionate reward for $1000 worth of deposits and update the total amount after every transaction. By recalculating the division percentage of exchanged funds, we will be able to determine the final amount to be returned to the dCDS when they try to close their position. The total amount for a particular dCDS will be a fraction or multiple of the current total amount of the standard $1000 deposit figure. This allows us to identify the value accrued to a dCDS position during the time of withdrawal, which is one of the critical values to calculate in the operation of our See-Saw contract.

12.4.6 Utilization of Protocol Tokens as Reserve Currency

As we intend to offer 20% downside protection on collateral deposited by borrowers, we will potentially deal with a situation where users won't return the loan amount until and unless their collateral is near 80% of the value deposited while opening a borrowing position. This is a probable situation because users will try to take the maximum benefit of the downside protection offered. Most of the time, the collateral volatility varies between 20,% so dCDS capital will be protected most of the time. If and when the borrower comes to return the stablecoins, then the returned amount will be the current collateral value. Thus, the borrower doesn't need to return the whole borrowed amount. Instead, giving a lesser amount equivalent to the present value of collateral ensures that stablecoins confiscated from dCDS capital remain with the protocol and never really leave the system. A minting protocol will simultaneously generate tokens, which will be returned to the borrower. The process involves maintaining a pool of stablecoins and protocol tokens. Half of the returned stablecoin amount will be burned, while the other half will be deposited into the pool. This pool will serve as collateral for the protocol tokens minted from it.

To create a strong mechanism, we can analyze the daily volatility of collateral price and construct a normal distribution graph. By doing so, we can identify the limits within which the volatility typically fluctuates, distinguishing outlier events that fall outside these limits. Assuming that ETH volatility usually varies around 20%, we can offer ETH downside protection

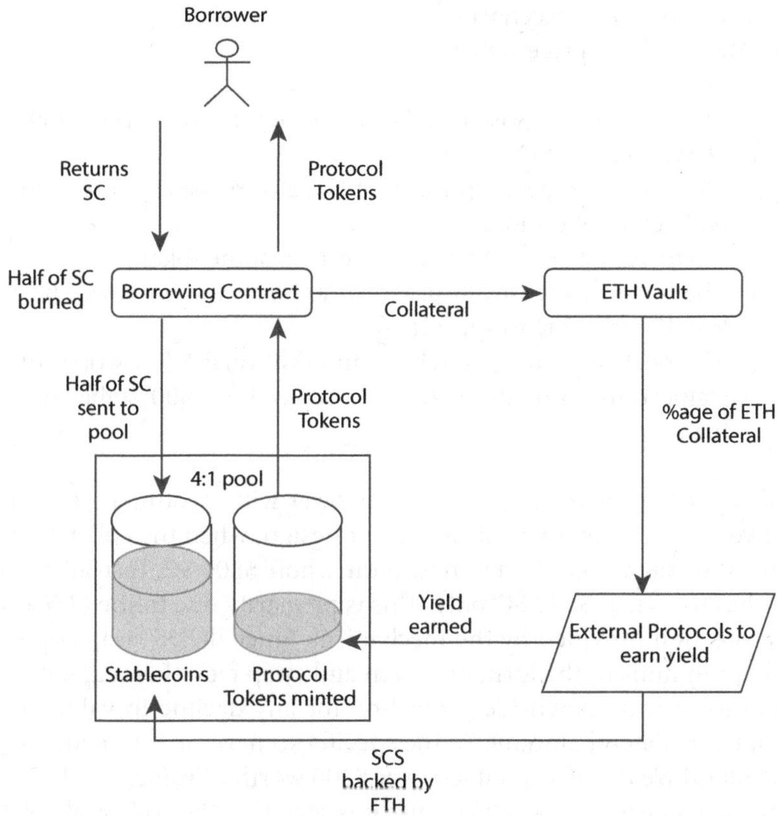

Figure 12.4 Protocol tokens as a reserve currency.

beyond the 20% fall in ETH price. Our robust mechanism ensures that we will only seize dCDS capital when the collateral value drops below 20% of its initial deposit value. As a result, our Credit Default Swaps module effectively transfers credit risk beyond an 80% decline in collateral value from dCDS depositors to borrowers and the protocol shown in Figure 12.4.

An Alternate Design for the Protocol

Here, we will offer the Loan-to-Value (LTV) ratio of 80% with the protection offered for 80% of the collateral amount in return for option fees the borrowers are paying. Liquidation will not occur unless the collateral value falls below 80%.

If we take the below scenario:
Collateral = ETH price = $1000

1. The borrower deposits 1 ETH as collateral and borrows 80% of SC, i.e., 800 SC.
2. The borrower pays option fees to get downside protection and get a call option.
3. Borrower takes 800 SCs and invests in some token.
4. The token decreases in price by 50 %, so the borrower has lost 400 SCs due to speculation.
5. The borrower must purchase an additional $400 worth of stablecoins from the market to repay the $800 stablecoin loan.

So, as per the above scenario, the borrower will encounter a bigger loss in the volatile market. Instead, as per our design, when the collateral value falls to 60%, there is no need to return the whole $800 SC. Instead, the borrower has to return $600 SC only. This is primarily due to the 80% downside protection provided by the mechanism. Since dCDS swap depositors receive premiums in the form of option and swap fees, their capital will be utilized to provide downside protection for any decline in value beyond 80% of the collateral amount. In the specific scenario mentioned, the protocol will utilize dCDS capital to cover $200 worth of value.

This mechanism will work because it is seen that the collateral volatility usually varies between 20% over a 3-month time span. Therefore, dCDS capital will be protected most of the time and will be able to earn enough fixed fee revenues through collateral options and downside protection fees which are paid periodically.

12.5 Conclusion

The issuer issues the Trinity stablecoin to borrowers while enabling full protection of their collateral amount through a combination of Credit Default swaps and taking a delta-neutral position on the price of the collateral at the time of borrowing. The protocol allows a Loan-to-Value ratio of 100% for borrowers and a high yield return for users with a Credit Default swap position. The protocol also utilizes derivatives like options to facilitate fee exchange among different users and capture the upside of the collateral amount. The main innovation of this protocol is the utilization of Credit Default swaps and options derivatives, which work together to deliver high capital efficiency for borrowers and lenders. Another unique innovation is the diversification of risky positions through transferring risk from short-term holders to longer-term positions and proactive management of positions near liquidation territory. This stablecoin will serve an immediate need of retail and institutional participants with respect to risk and return tradeoff. The protocol also brings to the market new financial products like Credit Default swap and options, which, instead of being an independent product in themselves, facilitate high capital efficiency and peg of stablecoin, thus capturing an established demand and needs of the market.

Appendix

We are adding a financial model where we tested our model. We have built the model for ten borrowers and 10 dCDS depositors which comes at different timestamps at different ETH prices (Table 12.3). Our model has the potential to be extrapolated to thousands of borrowers and dCDS depositors. We have also incorporated calculations for changes in the P/L of the dCDS pool with the fluctuation of the ETH price (Table 12.4). Additionally, we have determined the split of P/L among all dCDS depositors during each new event, such as opening a new dCDS position, a new borrower entering, a borrower closing their position, or any contract calls by external users. This core model of our See-Saw function is where assets move between the ETH Vault and dCDS pool with changes in ETH prices.

Table 12.5 shows the ETH price changes over a couple of days. We observed the change in ETH price over a four-month period from 26/07/2022 to 27/11/2022 and calculated the daily and annual ETH volatility.

Table 12.6 applies a random number generator function for dCDS deposit amounts over 100 days by tracking ETH prices over the same period. We then calculate the LTV ratios and sum them up to the values that breach the LTV ratio beyond a standard industry-wide figure of 60% LTV. We can determine the total amount required from the dCDS pool and dCDS depositors by using this method.

Table 12.3 Borrowers and 10 dCDS depositors at different ETH prices.

Day	Total ETH	Initial ETH capital	ETH price	Initial dCDS amount	P/L of dCDS pool	dCDS depositors	dCDS depositor %age of ETH price
1	51	50000	1000	10000		1000	1
2	52		1010		510	1000	0.9900990099
3	53		1020		1030	1000	0.9803921569
4	54		1030		1560	1000	0.9708737864
5	55		1040		2100	1000	0.9615384615
6	56		1030		1550	1000	0.9708737864
7	57		1020		990	1000	0.9803921569
8	58		1010		420	1000	0.9900990099
9	59		1000		-160	1000	1
10	60		950		-3110	1000	1.052631579
							9.896899947

Table 12.4 Total/Net ETH Vault and Total/Net dCDS Pool with Pool ratios.

Initial dCDS amount	Total dCDS pool	Net value of dCDS pool	P/L of ETH pool	ETH pool at market price	ETH pool with P/L	Net ETH pool value	Ratio	Inverse of ratio
10000	11000	11000		51000	51000	51000	0.216	4.636
	12000	12510	-510	52520	52010	52010	0.238	4.198
	13000	14030	-1030	54060	53030	53030	0.260	3.853
	14000	15560	-1560	55620	54060	54060	0.280	3.575
	15000	17100	-2100	57200	55100	55100	0.299	3.345
	16000	17550	-1550	57680	56130	56130	0.304	3.287
	17000	17990	-990	58140	57150	57150	0.309	3.232
	18000	18420	-420	58580	58160	58160	0.314	3.180
	19000	18840	160	59000	59160	59160	0.319	3.132
	20000	16890	3110	57000	60110	60110	0.296	3.375

Table 12.5 Annual volatility.

Eth price	**Date**	**Daily returns**	**Daily volatility**	**Annual volatility**
1215.480165	11/27/22 0:00			
1216.120944	11/26/22 0:00	0.001	3.35%	32.02%
1190.840868	11/25/22 0:00	-0.021		
1199.777785	11/24/22 0:00	0.007		
1163.074472	11/23/22 0:00	-0.031		
1110.720153	11/22/22 0:00	-0.046		
1122.223882	11/21/22 0:00	0.010		
1193.216625	11/20/22 0:00	0.061		
1210.534792	11/19/22 0:00	0.014		
1214.575382	11/18/22 0:00	0.003		
1205.69334	11/17/22 0:00	-0.007		
1230.465701	11/16/22 0:00	0.020		
1259.073674	11/15/22 0:00	0.023		
1230.783049	11/14/22 0:00	-0.023		

Table 12.6 Calculation of dCDS amount.

SI. no.	Collateral deposited	Stablecoin borrowed at 60% LTV	Collateral value after week	LTV ratio after 1 week	Breach of LTV	Difference	Total amount required from dCDS pool
1	345	207	318.53	0.65	15.88	138	20818
2	236	141.6	231.56	0.61	2.67	94.4	
3	156	93.6	158.58	0.59	-1.55	62.4	
4	803	481.8	812.90	0.59	-5.94	321.2	
5	258	154.8	267.45	0.58	-5.67	103.2	
6	224	134.4	248.15	0.54	-14.49	89.6	
7	851	510.6	954.78	0.53	-62.27	340.4	
8	371	222.6	382.68	0.58	-7.01	148.4	
9	912	547.2	935.88	0.58	-14.33	364.8	
10	287	172.2	298.99	0.58	-7.19	114.8	

(Continued)

Table 12.6 Calculation of dCDS amount. *(Continued)*

Sl. no.	Collateral deposited	Stablecoin borrowed at 60% LTV	Collateral value after week	LTV ratio after 1 week	Breach of LTV	Difference	Total amount required from dCDS pool
11	911	546.6	958.09	0.57	-28.25	364.4	
12	441	264.6	441.18	0.60	-0.11	176.4	
13	723	433.8	705.52	0.61	10.49	289.2	
14	890	534	1055.66	0.51	-99.39	356	

References

1. The Free-Banking Era: A Lesson for Today?, in: *Economic Insights, Third Quarter 2016*, Federal Reserve Bank of Philadelphia Research Department, 9–14, 2016.
2. https://country.eiu.com/article.aspx?articleid=1532551136&Country=United+States&topic=Economy&sub_1.
3. Volatility and the Allegory of the Prisoner's Dilemma – False Peace, Moral Hazard, and Shadow Convexity, 2015.
4. https://docs.makerdao.com/.
5. Clements, R., Built to Fail: The Inherent Fragility of Algorithmic Stablecoins (October 28, 2021). *11 Wake For. L. Rev.*, 131, 131–145, October 2021, Available at SSRN: https://ssrn.com/abstract=3952045 or http://dx.doi.org/10.2139/ssrn.3952045.
6. https://hackernoon.com/tokenomics-of-different-stablecoins-ttg33ut.
7. Briola, A., Vidal-Tomás, D., Wang, Y., Aste, T., Anatomy of a Stablecoin's failure: The Terra-Luna case. *Financ. Res. Lett.*, 103358.
8. Saengchote, K., A DeFi Bank Run: Iron Finance, IRON Stablecoin, and the Fall of TITAN, July 16, 2021, Available at SSRN: https://ssrn.com/abstract=3888089 or http://dx.doi.org/10.2139/ssrn.3888089.
9. Kandasamy, M., Shanmugam, R., Adesara, H., Patel, V., Dhanaraj, R.K., The impact of ubiquitous computing on heterogeneous next generation networks, in: *Ubiquitous and Transparent Security*, pp. 236–264, CRC Press, United States, 2024.
10. Kumar, A.S., Dhanaraj, R.K., Maleh, Y., Arockiam, D., *Ubiquitous and Transparent Security*, CRC Press, United States, 2024.
11. Jarno, K. and Kołodziejczyk, H., Does the Design of Stablecoins Impact Their Volatility? *J. Risk Financ. Manage.*, 14, 2, 42, Jan. 2021, doi: 10.3390/jrfm14020042.
12. Darlin, M., *et al.*, Debt-Financed Collateral and Stability Risks in the DeFi Ecosystem, 7 Jun 2022, arXiv:2204.11107v2 [q-fin.TR].
13. Lyons, R.K. and Viswanath-Natraj, G., What keeps stablecoins stable? *J. Int. Money Financ.*, 131, 102777, 2023, ISSN 0261-5606.
14. Arnold, L., Brennecke, M., Camus, P., Fridgen, G., Guggenberger, T., Radszuwill, S., Urbach, N., Blockchain and initial coin offerings: Blockchain's implications for crowdfunding. *Bus. Transform. Through Blockchain*, I, 233–272, 2019.
15. Kour, K., Madavarapu, J.B., Gupta, D., Dhanaraj, R.K., Saini, S., Design of Sensor Based Walnut Cracking Device and By-Product Classification *via* K-Means, in: *2023 6th International Conference on Contemporary Computing and Informatics (IC3I). 2023 6th International Conference on Contemporary Computing and Informatics (IC3I)*, IEEE, 2023.

16. Risius, M. and Spohrer, K., A blockchain research framework: What we (don't) know, where we go from here, and how we will get there. *Bus. Inf. Syst. Eng.*, *59*, 385–409, 2017.
17. Bahga, A. and Madisetti, V.K., A Value Token Transfer Protocol (VTTP) for Decentralized Finance. *J. Software Eng. Appl.*, *13*, 11, 303, 2020.
18. Miah, A., Rahouti, M., Jagatheesaperumal, S.K., Ayyash, M., Xiong, K., Fernandez, F., Lekena, M., Blockchain in Financial Services: Current Status, Adoption Challenges, and Future Vision. *Int. J. Innov. Technol. Manage.*, *20*, 08, 2330004, 2023.
19. Guggenberger, T., Sedlmeir, J., Fridgen, G., Luckow, A., An in-depth investigation of the performance characteristics of Hyperledger Fabric. *Comput. Ind. Eng.*, *173*, 108716, 2022.
20. Vyas, K. and Deshmukh, A., A Survey Paper on Blockchain Technology and Consensus Algorithms, in: *2023 11th International Conference on Emerging Trends in Engineering & Technology-Signal and Information Processing (ICETET-SIP)*, pp. 1–6, IEEE, USA, 2023, April.
21. Yap, K.Y., Chin, H.H., Klemeš, J.J., Blockchain technology for distributed generation: A review of current development, challenges and future prospect. *Renew. Sustain. Energy Rev.*, *175*, 113170, 2023.
22. Tripathi, G., Ahad, M.A., Casalino, G., A comprehensive review of blockchain technology: Underlying principles and historical background with future challenges. *Decis. Anal. J.*, 100344, 2023.
23. Liu, R., Ran, W., Liu, S., Blockchain Technology Applied to Supply Chain Management: A Systems' Analysis. *Mobile Inf. Syst.*, *2023*, 1–23, 2023.
24. Xuan, T.R. and Ness, S., Integration of Blockchain and AI: Exploring Application in the Digital Business. *J. Eng. Res. Rep.*, *25*, 8, 20–39, 2023.
25. Bech, M.L., Intraday Liquidity Management: A Tale of Games Banks Play, FRBNY Economic Policy Review, September 2008.
26. Hassan, M., Ngow, T., Yu, J.S., *et al.*, Determinants of credit default swaps spreads in European and Asian markets. *J. Deriv. Hedge Funds*, 19, 295–310, 2013, https://doi.org/10.1057/jdhf.2014.1.
27. Rajasekar, V., Premalatha, J., Dhanaraj, R.K., Security analytics, in: *System Assurances*, pp. 333–354, Elsevier, USA, 2022.

13

Renewable Energy Integration in Data Centers: Strategies and Challenges

Esha Dhamija[1], Kamali Singla[1], Deepali Gupta[1], Vidhu Kiran[2] and Sapna Juneja[3]*

[1]Chitkara University Institute of Engineering and Technology, Chitkara University, Punjab, India
[2]CDLSIET, Panniwala Mota, Sirsa, Haryana, India
[3]KIET Group of Institutions, Ghaziabad, India

Abstract

Data centers are major energy consumers, but there are growing environmental motivations and cost incentives to transition their power supply from fossil fuels to renewable sources. Integrating renewables like solar and wind energy introduces unpredictability and variability that pose new challenges for maintaining the 24×7 uptime and quality of service demanded by cloud applications and internet services. This paper provides a comprehensive review of strategies and technologies to increase renewable penetration in data center facilities. We analyze the impact of supply intermittency on power distribution, cooling, server operation, and network infrastructure within modern data centers. Techniques to mitigate these effects are surveyed, including intelligent workload scheduling, real-time performance modulation, fast server suspension/resume, advanced battery systems, geo-distributed failover computing, and integrated photovoltaic panels. The effectiveness of renewables integration approaches and the feasibility of a full transition to sustainable power are assessed across data center scales. We highlight open research problems related to reliable and economical 100% renewable data center implementation. The discussion focuses on both today's grid-supported facilities and forward-looking fully off-grid designs. Our analysis aims to inform and accelerate advances toward carbon-neutral internet infrastructure.

**Corresponding author*: sapnajuneja1983@gmail.com

R. Sathiyaraj, Rajesh Kumar Dhanaraj, K. Arun Kumar, Rutvij H. Jhaveri and A. Mohamed Abbas (eds.) Predictive Methods in Next-Generation Computing: An Approach Toward Sustainability, (271–288)

Keywords: Renewable energy integration, data centers, sustainability, power supply transition, solar energy, wind energy, supply intermittency

13.1 Introduction

Society's surging digital dependence has raised public concerns over the environmental impacts of power-hungry server farms behind our online services. Data centers now rival major industrial sectors in electricity consumption, using an estimated 200 TWh per year—over 1% of worldwide demand [1]. This concentration of computation enables efficiency through conservation techniques, yet absolute consumption continues increasing with growth trends in cloud computing, artificial intelligence, internet video, etc. [2]. Industry leaders like Google, Facebook, and Microsoft have responded by aiming to fully offset fossil fuel usage *via* renewable energy purchases, carbon credits, and biodiversity campaigns [3]. Getting rid of carbon-based grids is difficult.

Data centers need stable power for load balancing, backup generators, battery reservoirs, and infrastructure redundancy [4]. Renewable generation's unpredictability makes matching supply with this power-critical workload problematic. Server design depends on power budgets, and abrupt shortfalls can cause computational errors and central processing unit (CPU) and disk degradation [5]. Despite being sized for full load, cooling systems respond slowly to sudden generating spikes that risk excessive temperatures. Quality of service contracts can be violated by adaptive rate-limiting network delay. Voltage fluctuations can shorten component lifespans. Data centers provide advantages over sensitive manufacturing and equipment for green power integration. Time flexibility smooths power variance through demand shifts. Performance margins allow computation intensity to be actively matched to supply [6].

Service replication permits failovers to distant locations under local disruption. Recent work also demonstrates the feasibility of fully sustainable data center design driven only by on-site solar, wind, batteries, and novel direct current (DC) architectures [7].

This article surveys established and proposed techniques for integrating renewable power into data center operations with minimal performance or availability impact. The challenges introduced by supply variability and intermittency are analyzed, including harmful effects across cooling, power distribution, server operation, and networking equipment. Promising solutions are reviewed, such as intelligent workload scheduling, adaptive performance modulation, geographic workload shifting, integrated

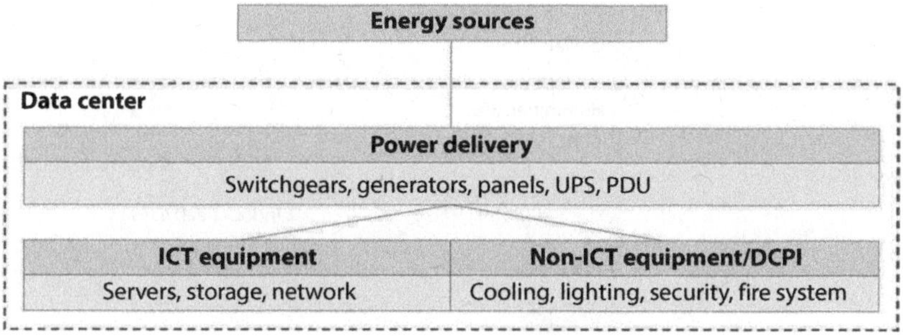

Figure 13.1 Energy use in a data center.

photovoltaics (PV), advanced batteries, and holistic facility eco-design [8]. Comparisons quantify potential renewable penetration achievable *via* different approaches. We assess the feasibility of a fully sustainable green data center across ownership scales—from hyper-scale operator campuses down through colocation multi-tenant sites. Multiple motivations are considered, including corporate social responsibility, reduced electricity costs, regulatory compliance, and demonstration of technical leadership [9, 10]. Figure. 13.1 guides energy use in a data center.

The remainder of this paper is organized as follows. Section 13.2 introduces sources of renewable power generation viable for integration at data center sites. Section 13.3 details the infrastructure subsystems impacted within traditional data centers by supply variability. Section 13.4 surveys techniques and architectures to mitigate these effects for increased renewable penetration, load balancing, and isolation. Section 13.5 reviews research toward fully sustainable net-zero energy data centers with 100% on-site renewable supply and storage. Section 13.6 concludes with a summary of key findings and open challenges in enabling carbon-neutral cloud services powered only by clean energy sources.

13.2 Renewable Generation Technologies

Transitioning data centers from fossil fuel reliance first requires viable renewable energy sources available at proportions capable of powering these computationally intense workloads. Figure 13.2 shows the evidence of power flows in a typical data centre. While green power can be obtained through utility contracts, on-site generation offers the greatest control over integration with the computational load. We briefly review primary technologies—solar, wind, and geothermal—discussing practical limits on capacity versus demand at various data center scales [11–28].

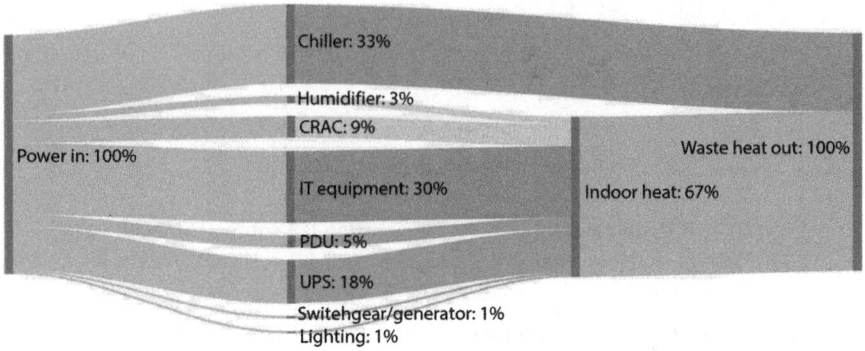

Figure 13.2 Power flows in a typical data center.

13.2.1 Photovoltaic Solar

Photovoltaics (PV) convert sunlight directly into electrical current *via* the photoelectric effect in panels mounted outside or on rooftops. Output scales easily through array expansion, with advanced sunlight tracking to increase yield. Today's monocrystalline silicon cells approach 26% efficiency in commercial products [11], double the levels of the early 2000s levels. Thin-film materials promise further cost and efficiency gains.

Feasibility studies consistently identify solar PV as the most universal renewable option for data centers, thanks to technological maturity, implementation simplicity, scalability, and energy density. Meteorological variability does pose availability challenges versus load profiles. Output shifts diurnally, following irradiation patterns that peak midday—only partially matching IT electricity demand that spikes each evening [12]. Short-term solar intermittency also arises from cloud transients that can drop production by 50% over tens of seconds before recovering [14]. Still, intelligent demand response and energy storage techniques (detailed in Sections 13.4 and 13.5) demonstrate high potential to mitigate these solar power fluctuations.

Small- and mid-scale data centers (<5 MW) already implemented rooftop solar successfully [22]. Large cloud service operators like Microsoft [13] and Apple [20] are also increasingly turning to distributed solar installations at multi-hundred-megawatt centralized facilities to offset daytime usage, with some reaching 70–80% annual solar penetration [29]. More ambitious proposals call for situating future data centers within solar farms for direct access to GigaWattt (GW)-scale PV generation [24]. With current technology, on-site solar PV is demonstrably capable of powering data centers at any scale.

13.2.2 Wind Power

Wind generation leverages airflow kinetic energy to spin turbines, producing AC current output up to multi-megawatt capacity. Wind farms commonly satisfy data center electricity needs in northern European countries, thanks to both high wind levels and clean power grid mandates [16]. For example, Google data centers in Finland and Sweden source over 40% of their total energy from regional wind farms [15].

But unlike solar's distributed advantage, air motion constraints require large, raised horizontal-axis turbines, which are poorly suited to urban data center locations [18]. Smaller vertical-axis turbines adapt better but generate less power. Intermittency also exceeds solar, with multiple-day lulls whenever wind patterns shift. So while exemplary cases demonstrate great promise for wind balancing regional energy grids [17], on-site wind remains impractical to power major data centers directly compared to more consistent solar resources [19, 35].

13.2.3 Geothermal Heat

Iceland's naturally cold climate and year-round subterranean heat uniquely situated the island for leadership in green data hosting. Renewable electricity stemming from geothermal and hydroelectric generation exceeds 70% of total generation [20]. Facilities located over volcanic zones tap into natural hot springs *via* heat exchangers, enabling 95% of building heating in Reykjavík, for instance [31]. These conditions allow data centers to reduce cooling demands through direct heat dissipation rather than electricity-driven refrigeration [10]. Microsoft, Verne Global, and others now operate major server clusters partially cooled through geothermal heat transfer [33].

Unfortunately, such ideal natural synergies remain geographically constrained. Most data center sites lack accessible geothermal resources beyond Earth's average underground temperature unsuitable for heat rejection. While desirable for specialized locales like Iceland, on-site geothermal does not provide generally viable renewable generation for global-scale computing infrastructure, especially considering risks like unexpected well field depletion [32]. Global distribution and redundancy requirements further discount dependence on isolated regions with distinctive renewable advantages such as Iceland or Scandinavia.

Based on scalability, ubiquity, and reliability factors, photonic solar power emerges as the most universally deployable renewable generation asset for integration with data centers of any size. We, therefore, focus our subsequent analysis primarily on strategies for maximizing solar penetration and mitigating its availability fluctuations. However, many techniques can also be generalized to other renewables including wind or hydroelectric energy obtained through utility contracts rather than generated on-site.

13.3 Impacts of Supply Variability

Renewable integration into traditional data center architecture reveals cascading ramifications across subsystems provisioned for stable power feed. Effects propagate from the utility interconnection impacting power distribution, cooling, IT equipment, and network infrastructure in ways that degrade efficiency, quality, or availability. Figure 13.3(a) annual electricity use world wide for ICT; (b) annual electricity share world wide for ICT; (c) annual electricity use worldwide for data centers; (d) annual electricity share world wide

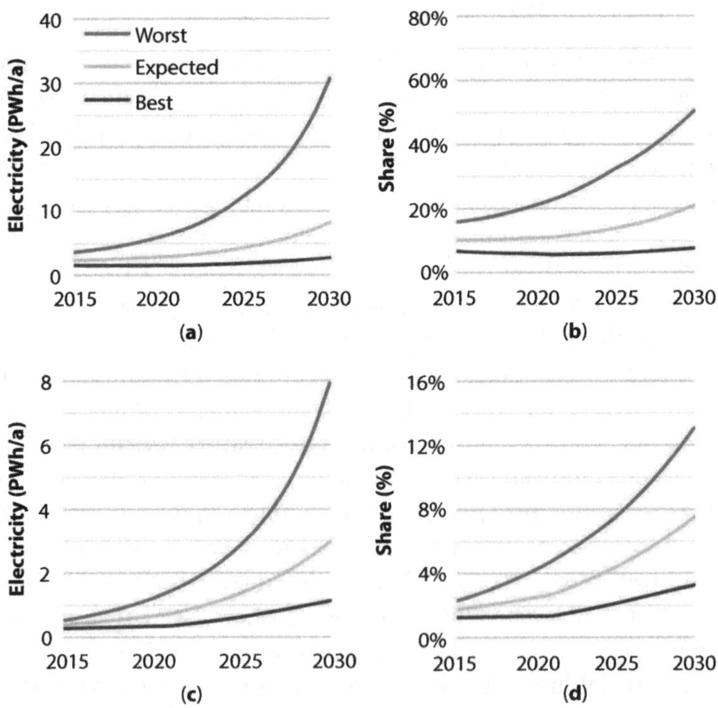

Figure 13.3 (a) Annual electricity use worldwide for ICT; (b) annual electricity share worldwide for ICT; (c) annual electricity use worldwide for data centers; (d) annual electricity share worldwide for data centers.

for data centers. These interactions must be holistically addressed to avoid fault conditions. We survey primary failure modes when layering variable generation atop standard data center designs.

13.3.1 Power Distribution

Data centers conforming to Tier 3 or 4 resiliency specifications incorporate redundant utility paths, centralized uninterruptable power supply (UPS) banks, extensive distribution wiring, and on-site diesel generators to maintain seamless operation through external power failures [34–37]. These systems rely on stability in the upstream supply for efficiency and longevity. However, injecting variable renewable generation adds harmful new dynamics. For example, reverse current flows may arise when momentary solar surges overfeed available data center demand, threatening standard UPS topologies optimized for unidirectional operation. Sudden renewable drop-offs could force unexpected transitions onto UPS buffer and backup power with less transient tolerance. Power distribution transformers also operate most efficiently when continuously loaded near their rating [34]. Rapid fluctuations cause thermal strain and lifetime detriments [35], necessitating overprovisioning. Smart solid-state transformers offer an alternative, leveraging integrated data monitoring and algorithms to actively regulate voltage, provide buffering, and synchronize with the smart grid [36]. These advances enable stability despite variable supply but add costs currently tenable only for new construction. Retrofitting renewable power into existing data centers therefore poses greater infrastructure challenges.

Oversizing PV capacity exacerbates several issues by maximizing variance as cloud transients fully cut off production. Table 13.1 summarizes the key effects of supply fluctuations across the power delivery path.

Table 13.1 Impacts of variable renewable generation on data center power infrastructure.

Component	Issue	Effect
Utility Feed	Reverse Power Flow	Safety Risk
Transformers	Thermal Cycling	Lifetime Reduction
UPS	Shock Transfers	Reliability Risk
Generators	Start/Stop Cycling	Wear Increase
Batteries	Charge Variance	Degraded Capacity

13.3.2 Cooling Systems

Data center cooling apparatus removes heat generated by compute servers to maintain safe operating temperatures for IT equipment. Typically, an order of magnitude more energy is spent powering computer room air conditioners (CRACs) and fluid chillers than actually running the servers. Careful thermal optimization and waste heat recycling thus provide major efficiency opportunities. However, proportioning cooling capacity for peak computation again relies on a stable electric supply to fans and pumps. Unexpected irradiance loss undermines assumptions during control system design [30].

Sudden solar plant output drops slow CRAC fans, reduce coolant flow rates, and cut chiller compressor power. Server inlet temperatures then spike rapidly [11], triggering hardware throttling or shutdown if they exceed safe operating thresholds [22]. Thermal inertia causes a lag before the air conditioning system can catch up when input power recovers. These scenarios may violate service level agreements and cause computational mistakes. Supply changes make efficiency increases like economizer cooling using "free" exterior air temperature differentials, harder to execute [32]. Air-side economizers often have regulated louvres and dampers. These economizers fail to close when server hall temperatures rise abruptly due to a decline in renewable energy. This negates any efficiency improvements from consuming more electricity for mechanical chilling. Using renewable energy sources to cool data centers requires adaptive set points, active thermal buffers, and predictive control rather than steady-state rules [14].

13.3.3 IT Equipment

Unlike the unpredictability of renewable sources, computing hardware expects a steady electricity flow within stricter limits. All common server power supplies meet the criteria if the input is a pure sine wave from 60 Hz with controlled voltage regulation. Modern CPUs adjust clock speed to increase throughput within thermal restrictions. These built-in power balancing devices can absorb supply changes, but they cannot avoid failures induced by electrical noise or interruptions that surpass 10–20% thresholds.

Hard disk drive (HDDs) are more sensitive to quality issues than other storage systems. A little voltage drop disrupts their dense magnetic bit encoding. I/O errors can shut down the redundant arrays of independant disk (RAID) volume, threatening data integrity. Inadequate equipment coordination increases the risks: a partially darkened server hall may use

Table 13.2 Server hardware impacts from renewable supply intermittency.

Component	Issue	Effect
CPU	Thermal Emergency	Throttling
Dynamic Random Access Memory (DRAM)	Write Disruption	Memory Fault
Storage	Magnetic Flux Loss	Disk Errors
Power Supply	Brownout	System Reboot

full mechanical cooling, exposing the blades to freezing inlet temperatures and moisture far outside their operational range. Integrated control solutions are needed to gracefully scale compute and cooling speeds while maintaining harmony. Table 13.2 lists frequent hardware issues caused by solar fluctuation that threaten workload processing and data integrity.

The lack of commercially available variable power input computer gear hinders the development of green data centers. Hot-swappable blade servers with uninterruptable power supply (UPS) buffering [10], next-generation nor-and flash memory (NAND) flash storage with intrinsic radiation hardness [12], and non-volatile CPUs that keep state during supply failures [11] are under development. Broad usage of specialist equipment like this is still needed to realize the potential of integrated renewable energy sources at a facility scale.

13.4 Network Architecture

Fault-tolerant servers and uninterrupted networking resources are needed to maintain cloud application performance and quality. Modern data centers do this by distributing traffic across redundant top-of-rack switches that link thousands of workstations at over 50 gigabits per second [13]. Splitting delay-sensitive workloads between geographically distant centers reduces latency and interruption hazards [14]. These systems may now be threatened by renewable supply volatility.

Data centers need adaptive demand response to stay within safe thermal ranges owing to local fluctuation. Due to workload reduction or transfer, this reaction dynamically modifies traffic patterns [15]. These transient spikes strain the network's architecture, which was built for seamless access. Video streaming and other bandwidth-intensive businesses are worst hurt.

Consolidating workloads emphasizes the need for well-planned shared topologies that can handle peak demand. To reestablish equilibrium, containers or virtual machines may need to be rescheduled or moved quickly to optimize resource consumption across fault zones. Disruptions can occur when runtime migrations transfer terabytes of state [0], overwhelming the network fabric and possibly surpassing capacity. Without intentional orchestration, cascade effects might generate systemic quality issues or regional outages [46].

Due to electrical and optical network infrastructure scalability issues, renewable energy adoption is currently low. This is done before considering variability-related availability or quality loss. Improving next-generation hardware to gracefully adjust to changing demand and supply enables new research and innovation options.

13.4.1 Renewable Energy Integration Methods

Transdisciplinary technologies may solve the problems preventing seamless green data center building. To preserve stability, intelligent control systems redistribute flexible workloads between sites, ease the transition from grid to local generation, smooth supply intermittency, and dynamically right-size computation based on availability. We provide a comprehensive overview of the latest methodologies and open research areas in green power compatibility to achieve cost-effectiveness and sustainability.

13.4.2 Task Time Management

Technologies for provisioning offer a fundamental software approach for batching computing tasks and co-optimizing demand and dynamic supply. These limitations take the availability and flexibility of renewable resources into account.

We can suspend low-priority model convergence threads during supply outages with these jobs. By employing efficiency and accuracy factors in video and image processing pipelines, adaptive approximation can reduce computing workload during generating deficits. Performance modulation gradually slows processing speeds to match capacity to prevent a complete shutdown.

Methodical "green scheduling" based on automated process flexibility analysis can help data centers handle renewable power interruptions cost-effectively [10]. Predictive coordination will be limited by model precision under complex service relationships. Online learning can mitigate the unpredictability of large-scale infrastructure [1].

Table 13.3 Software approaches for co-optimizing workload and variable power supply.

Method	Strategy	Tactics
Forecasting	Predict generation/demand transients	Weather data, seasonality modeling
Flexibility Analysis	Quantify the malleability of computational graphs	Parallelism, approximation knobs
Performance Modulation	Continuously tune server utilization to supply	CPU scaling, adaptive networks
Time Shifting	Exploit deadline flexibility	Deferrable maintenance, backups
Location Shifting	Distribute load geographically	Follow the renewables
Real-time Control	Reactive adaptation rules	Fast VM migration, brownout

Table 13.3 summarizes common intelligent workload scheduling techniques to increase renewable utilization.

13.4.3 Integrated Architectures

Data center designers historically separated power supply, cooling infrastructure, and IT equipment into independent, siloed subsystems, which may lead energy losses in data center diagram, shows in Figure 13.4. However, the synergistic facility-computational approach necessary for high renewable integration requires seeing the whole as more than the sum of its parts. Emergent integrated architectures instead coordinate these domains *via* unified sensing, control planes, and holistic system awareness [2].

Joint optimization delivers substantial efficiency gains even in the absence of renewables [3] but promises a much greater impact by surviving their volatility. For example, fine-grained telemetry tracking production, consumption, and temperatures at time scales below one minute allows rapid automated compensation for abrupt irradiance drops [14]. Detecting an upstream solar plant fault promptly suspends adiabatic cooling to prevent thermal runaway while gracefully scaling down servers [25].

Integrating functionality tightens feedback loops both digitally and physically. Low-level sharing of thermal buffers and fluid loops cuts waste

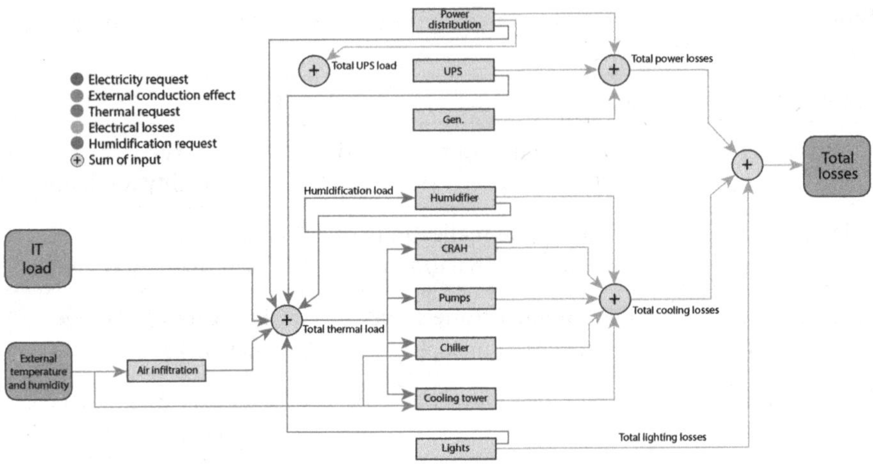

Figure 13.4 Diagram of energy losses in a data center.

and reaction lag [26]. Unified power infrastructure enables bi-directional conversion, storage shifting, and fast switching among grid, solar, and battery sources to present a stable supply to servers [27].

Platform architectures facilitate agility thanks to software-defined hardware resources, pooled connectivity through flexible network fabrics, and real-time visibility exposing optimization opportunities. Component life shortening and fault risks drop substantially once generation volatility stays hidden behind smart integrated facilities rather than directly exposing servers. Workload analysis additionally guides renewable capacity planning based on flexibility dimensions at various time scales [20].

Getting integration right requires cross-domain expertise and iterative design thinking. Reference architectures and open-source infrastructure blueprints lower barriers for third parties through common starting points like Project Natick's submersed data center modules [12] and Romonet's EcoDC templates [22]. Validation at smaller scales also helps de-risk innovations [23]. Overall, seamless facility integration stands out as essential for unlocking the full potential of renewable energy in sustainable data centers moving forward.

13.5 Proposed Smart and Sustainable Framework

Building upon the strategies and techniques discussed in the previous sections, we propose a smart and sustainable framework for energy optimization in data centers. This architecture influences the functionalities of artificial intelligence, Internet of Thing (IoT), and machine learning technologies to enable an efficacious feasible energy integration system [38–45].

13.5.1 Geo-Distributed Load Balancing

For large-scale data center operators with multiple facilities in different locations, the framework can utilize load-balancing techniques that are specifically designed for distributed environments. Through a thorough examination of renewable energy availability and demand patterns in various geographic regions, the framework can efficiently allocate workloads to facilities with greater access to renewable energy. This intelligent distribution optimizes energy usage and effectively decreases the overall carbon footprint. The advanced framework combines cutting-edge technologies such as AI, ML, and IoT to support efficient energy management, accurate predictive analysis, and intelligent decision-making. This paves the way for smooth and sustainable data center operations that rely on renewable energy sources [47, 48, 59].

13.6 Conclusions

This paper surveyed established techniques and emerging innovations for integrating renewable power sources like solar photovoltaics into data center facilities. Unique efficiency, stability, and reliability challenges posed by supply variability were shown to cut across physical infrastructure sub systems and computational workloads. We discussed software scheduling policies, hardware advances, and integrated architectural approaches to mitigate these effects [49].

Analysis reveals high feasibility today for smaller distributed data centers to operate predominantly on renewable supply by combining smart workload analysis, behind-the-meter batteries, and aggressive efficiency gains [50–53]. However, cost and technology limitations still prevent the industry's largest mega-scale cloud server farms from running anywhere close to fully carbon-free until further hardware improvements emerge [54].

Nonetheless, continuous expansion of renewable electricity options along with modular data center design and algorithmic flexibility improvements appear likely in the coming years to facilitate more companies adopting 100% sustainable power. Paradigm shifts loom as next-generation platforms embrace variable supply as a native condition rather than an outlier case. Through holistic innovation integrating power, cooling, and software, green data infrastructure will shed its reputation as an improbable vision to become the normal mode of powering our digital world [55–58].

References

1. Dhillon, G., Council Post: From the Age of Computing to The Age of Data: Are You Ready?, Available online: https://www.forbes.com/sites/forbestechcouncil/2019/03/27/from-the-age-of-computing-to-the-age-of-data-are-you-ready/ (accessed on 1 March 2021).
2. Allen, R., Siukonen, P., Cattermull, N., Brown, M., Eaves, S., *Devouring Data: 5G, Edge Computing & the Future of Data Centres*, Kingston Technology Europe, Sunbury-on-Thames, UK, 2020, [Google Scholar].
3. Donno, M.D., Tange, K., Dragoni, N., Foundations and Evolution of Modern Computing Paradigms: Cloud, IoT, Edge, and Fog. *IEEE Access*, 7, 150936–150948, 2019, [Google Scholar] [CrossRef].
4. World Bank. Europe and Central Asia Economic Update, May 2018, in: *Cryptocurrencies and Blockchain*, World Bank, Washington, DC, USA, 2018, [Google Scholar].
5. Eaves, S., The Demand on Data Centers in the Time of Coronavirus, 2021, https://www.kingston.com/italy/us/solutions/servers-data-centers/coronavirus-demands-on-data-centers (accessed on 1 January 2021, Available online.
6. Nicholson, J., How is Coronavirus Impacting the News? Our Analysis of Global Traffic and Coverage Data—Chartbeat Blog, 2020, Available online: https://blog.chartbeat.com/2020/03/25/coronavirus-data-news-traffic-impact-analysis/ (accessed on 1 January 2021).
7. Cisco, Cisco Annual Internet Report (2018–2023), 2020, Available online: https://www.cisco.com/c/en/us/solutions/collateral/executive-perspectives/annual-internet-report/white-paper-c11-741490.pdf (accessed on 1 February 2021).
8. Liu, Y., Peng, M., Shou, G., Chen, Y., Chen, S., Toward Edge Intelligence: Multiaccess Edge Computing for 5G and Internet of Things. *IEEE Internet Things J.*, 7, 6722–6747, 2020, [Google Scholar] [CrossRef].
9. Chih-Lin, I., Han, S., Bian, S., Energy-efficient 5G for a greener future. *Nat. Electron.*, 3, 182–184, 2020, [Google Scholar].
10. Panwar, N., Sharma, S., Singh, A.K., A survey on 5G: The next generation of mobile communication. *Phys. Commun.*, 18, 64–84, 2016, [Google Scholar] [CrossRef][Green Version].
11. Ashford, K., What Is Cryptocurrency?, 2020, Available online: https://www.forbes.com/advisor/investing/what-is-cryptocurrency/ (accessed on 1 February 2021).
12. Lansky, J., Possible State Approaches to Cryptocurrencies. *J. Syst. Integr.*, 9, 19–31, 2018, [Google Scholar] [CrossRef].
13. Li, J., Li, N., Peng, J., Cui, H., Wu, Z., Energy consumption of cryptocurrency mining: A study of electricity consumption in mining cryptocurrencies. *Energy*, 168, 160–168, 2019, [Google Scholar] [CrossRef].

14. Krause, M.J. and Tolaymat, T., Quantification of energy and carbon costs for mining cryptocurrencies. *Nat. Sustain.*, 1, 711–718, 2018, [Google Scholar] [CrossRef].
15. Mora, C., Rollins, R.L., Taladay, K., Kantar, M.B., Chock, M.K., Shimada, M., Franklin, E.C., Bitcoin emissions alone could push global warming above 2 °C. *Nat. Clim. Chang.*, 8, 931–933, 2018, [Google Scholar] [CrossRef].
16. Dittmar, L. and Praktiknjo, A., Could Bitcoin emissions push global warming above 2 °C? Nat. *Clim. Chang.*, 9, 656–657, 2019, [Google Scholar] [CrossRef].
17. Sedlmeir, J., Buhl, H.U., Fridgen, G., Keller, R., The Energy Consumption of Blockchain Technology: Beyond Myth. *Bus. Inf. Syst. Eng.*, 62, 599–608, 2020, [Google Scholar] [CrossRef].
18. Fairley, P., The Ridiculous Amount of Energy It Takes to Run Bitcoin—IEEE Spectrum, 2017, Available online: https://spectrum.ieee.org/energy/policy/the-ridiculous-amount-of-energy-it-takes-to-run-bitcoin (accessed on 1 February 2021).
19. IEEE Blockchain Initiative, 2021, Available online: https://blockchain.ieee.org/about (accessed on 1 April 2021).
20. Laroiya, C., Saxena, D., Komalavalli, C., Applications of Blockchain Technology, in: *Handbook of Research on Blockchain Technology*,.S. Krishnan, V.E. Balas, E.G. Julie, Y.H. Robinson, S. Balaji, R. Kumar, (Eds.), pp. 213–243, Academic Press, Cambridge, MA, USA, 2020, Chapter 9, [Google Scholar].
21. Frauenthaler, P., Sigwart, M., Spanring, C., Sober, M., Schulte, S., ETH Relay: A Cost-efficient Relay for Ethereum-based Blockchains, in: *Proceedings of the in 2020 IEEE International Conference on Blockchain (Blockchain)*, pp. 204–213, 2–6 November 2020, [Google Scholar].
22. Howson, P., Tackling climate change with blockchain. *Nat. Clim. Chang.*, 9, 644–645, 2019, [Google Scholar] [CrossRef].
23. Andoni, M., Robu, V., Flynn, D., Abram, S., Geach, D., Jenkins, D., McCallum, P., Peacock, A., Blockchain technology in the energy sector: A systematic review of challenges and opportunities. *Renew. Sustain. Energy Rev.*, 100, 143–174, 2019, [Google Scholar] [CrossRef].
24. Gunasekeran, D.V., Tseng, R.M.W.W., Tham, Y.-C., Wong, T.Y., Applications of digital health for public health responses to COVID-19: A systematic scoping review of artificial intelligence, telehealth and related technologies. *NPJ Digit. Med.*, 4, 40, 2021, [Google Scholar] [CrossRef].
25. Gao, L., Wu, C., Yoshinaga, T., Chen, X., Ji, Y., Multi-channel Blockchain Scheme for Internet of Vehicles. *IEEE Open J. Comput. Soc.*, 2, 192–203, 2021, [Google Scholar] [CrossRef].
26. Ghosh, E. and Das, B.A., Study on the Issue of Blockchain's Energy Consumption, in: *Proceedings of the International Ethical Hacking Conference 2019*, pp. 63–75, 2020, [Google Scholar].

27. Microsoft. Update #2 on Microsoft Cloud Services Continuity. 2020. Available online: https://azure.microsoft.com/en-us/blog/update-2-on-microsoft-cloud-services-continuity/ (accessed on 1 March 2021).
28. Facebook. Keeping Our Services Stable and Reliable During the COVID-19 Outbreak—About Facebook. 2020. Available online: https://about.fb.com/news/2020/03/keeping-our-apps-stable-during-covid-19/ (accessed on 1 March 2021).
29. Yuan, E.S. A Message to our Users. 2020, Available online: https://blog.zoom.us/a-message-to-our-users/ (accessed on 1 March 2021).
30. Morgan, J.P., Media Consumption in the Age of COVID-19, 2020, https://www.jpmorgan.com/insights/research/media-consumption (accessed on 1 March 2021, Available online.
31. Klebnikov, S., 5 Big Numbers That Show Amazon's Explosive Growth during the Coronavirus Pandemic, 2021, https://www.forbes.com/sites/sergeiklebnikov/2020/07/23/5-big-numbers-that-show-amazons-explosive-growth-during-the-coronavirus-pandemic/ (accessed on 1 March 2021, Available online.
32. Ong, D., Moors, T., Sivaraman, V., Complete life-cycle assessment of the energy/CO2 costs of videoconferencing vs face-to-face meetings, in: *Proceedings of the 2012 IEEE Online Conference on Green Communications (GreenCom)*, pp. 50–55, 25–28 September 2012, [Google Scholar].
33. Ong, D., Moors, T., Sivaraman, V., Comparison of the energy, carbon and time costs of videoconferencing and in-person meetings. *Comput. Commun.*, 50, 86–94, 2014, [Google Scholar] [CrossRef].
34. Jones, N., How to stop data centres from gobbling up the world's electricity. *Nat. Cell Biol.*, 561, 163–166, 2018, [Google Scholar] [CrossRef].
35. *Blockchain-Based Systems for the Modern Energy Grid*, 285–310, Elsevier, Academic Press, 2023, https://doi.org/10.1016/c2020-0-04640-2.
36. Andrae, A.S.G. and Edler, T., On Global Electricity Usage of Communication Technology: Trends to 2030. *Challenges*, 6, 117–157, 2015, [Google Scholar] [CrossRef][Green Version].
37. World's Top. Data Centers, 2014, Available online: http://worldstopdatacenters.com (accessed on 1 February 2021).
38. Cambridge Centre for Alternative Finance, Cambridge Bitcoin Electricity Consumption Index (CBECI), 2021, Available online: https://cbeci.org/ (accessed on 1 February 2021).
39. Shehabi, A., Smith, S., Sartor, D., Brown, R., Herrlin, M., Koomey, J., Masanet, E., Horner, N., Azevedo, I., Lintner, W., United States Data Center Energy Usage Report, 2016, Available online: https://www.osti.gov/servlets/purl/1372902 (accessed on 1 January 2021).
40. Nadjahi, C., Louahlia, H., Lemasson, S.A., review of thermal management and innovative cooling strategies for data center. *Sustain. Comput. Inform. Syst.*, 19, 14–28, 2018, [Google Scholar] [CrossRef].

41. Levy, M. and Raviv, D., An Overview of Data Center Metrics and a Novel Approach for a New Family of Metrics. *Adv. Sci. Technol. Eng. Syst. J.*, 3, 238–251, 2018, [Google Scholar] [CrossRef][Green Version].
42. Rasmussen, N., *Electrical Efficiency Measurement for Data Centers—White Paper 154—Revision 2*, Schneider Electric's Data Center Science Center, Rueil-Malmaison, France, 2011, [Google Scholar].
43. Directorate General for Communications Networks Content and Technology. Shaping Europe's Digital Future, 2020, vailable online: http://op.europa.eu/it/publication-detail/-/publication/33b6e417-53c8-11ea-aece-01aa75ed71a1 (accessed on 1 February 2021).
44. Analytics Vidhya, Available online: https://www.analyticsvidhya.com/blog/ (accessed on 1 May 2021).
45. Chawla, V., Yotta Infrastructure Inaugurates India's Largest Data Center Facility, 2020, Available online: https://analyticsindiamag.com/yotta-infrastructure-inaugurates-indias-largest-data-center-facility/ (accessed on 1 May 2021).
46. Sharma, B. and Hooda, S., AI-Based Prediction Models for Network Security Attacks: A Comparative Study, 1–4, Available at SSRN 4638515, 2023.
47. Hooda, S., Lamba, V., Kaur, A., AI and soft computing techniques for securing cloud and edge computing: a systematic review, in: *2021 5th International Conference on Information Systems and Computer Networks (ISCON)*, pp. 1–5, IEEE, 2021, October.
48. Singh, S.P., *et al.*, Dual adaption based evolutionary algorithm for optimized the smart healthcare communication service of the Internet of Things in smart city. *Phys. Commun.*, 55, 1018935, 2022.
49. Singamaneni, K.K., *et al.*, An efficient hybrid QHCP-ABE model to improve cloud data integrity and confidentiality. *Electronics*, 11.21, 3510, 2022.
50. Monga, C., *et al.*, Sustainable network by enhancing attribute-based selection mechanism using Lagrange interpolation. *Sustainability*, 14.10, 6082, 2022.
51. Kautish, S., *et al.*, Enhanced cloud storage encryption standard for security in distributed environments. *Electronics*, 12.3, 714, 2023.
52. Singh, N., *et al.*, Load balancing and service discovery using Docker Swarm for microservice based big data applications. *J. Cloud Comput.*, 12.1, 4, 2023.
53. Singh, P., *et al.*, A fog-cluster based load-balancing technique. *Sustainability*, 14.13, 7961, 2022.
54. Gupta, N., *et al.*, Enhanced virtualization-based dynamic bin-packing optimized energy management solution for heterogeneous clouds. *Math. Probl. Eng.*, 2022, 1–115, 2022.
55. Zhang, Y., *et al.*, Edge intelligence in the cognitive Internet of Things: Improving sensitivity and interactivity. *IEEE Netw.*, 33.3, 58–64, 2019.
56. Hao, Y., *et al.*, Smart-Edge-CoCaCo: AI-enabled smart edge with joint computation, caching, and communication in heterogeneous IoT. *IEEE Netw.*, 33.2, 58–64, 2019.

57. Abualkishik, A.Z., Alwan, A.A., Gulzar, Y., Disaster recovery in cloud computing systems: An overview. *Int. J. Adv. Comput. Sci. Appl.*, 11.9, 1–9, 2020.
58. Radi, M., Alwan, A.A., Gulzar, Y., Genetic-based virtual machines consolidation strategy with efficient energy consumption in cloud environment. *IEEE Access*, 11, 48022–48032, 2023.
59. Vijayalakshmi, S., Balusamy, S.,.B., Dhanaraj, R.K. (Eds.), AI-Powered IoT in the Energy Industry, in: *Power Systems*, Springer International Publishing, 2023.

14

Optimizing Energy Efficiency in Computing Systems: An In-Depth Exploration: Analytics for Sustainable Global Resources

Esha Dhamija[1], Kamali Singla[1], Deepali Gupta[1], Sapna Juneja[2]* and Yonis Gulzar[3]

[1]*Chitkara University Institute of Engineering and Technology, Chitkara University, Punjab, India*
[2]*Department of CSE(AI), KIET Group of Institutions, Ghaziabad, India*
[3]*Department of Management Information Systems, College of Business Administration, King Faisal University, Al-Ahsa, Saudi Arabia*

Abstract

Energy efficiency has become a critical issue in computing systems design and operation due to economic, environmental, and practical constraints. This paper provides an in-depth exploration of techniques and strategies for optimizing energy efficiency across all layers of computing systems, from circuits and architectures to systems and data centers. We review common sources of energy inefficiency and present both hardware and software approaches to address them, including dynamic voltage and frequency scaling, heterogeneous architectures, resource virtualization and workload consolidation, and adaptive resource provisioning. Design trade-offs between performance and energy efficiency are analyzed. The effectiveness of different optimization methods is compared across target systems ranging from mobile devices to high-performance computing platforms. We also examine innovations in sustainable computing through the joint management of computation, cooling, and power delivery subsystems. The discussion focuses on established techniques as well as emerging technologies and their potential impact. We conclude with a set of open challenges and directions for future research.

**Corresponding author*: sapnajuneja1983@gmail.com

R. Sathiyaraj, Rajesh Kumar Dhanaraj, K. Arun Kumar, Rutvij H. Jhaveri and A. Mohamed Abbas (eds.) Predictive Methods in Next-Generation Computing: An Approach Toward Sustainability, (289–308)

***Keywords*:** Energy efficiency, computing systems, optimization techniques, dynamic voltage and frequency scaling, heterogeneous architectures, resource virtualization, workload consolidation, adaptive resource provisioning

14.1 Introduction

Rising energy costs and impending constraints on CO2 emissions have made energy efficiency a top concern across the computing industry. At the same time, practical limits on battery life, packaging, power delivery, and cooling have made energy optimization essential for continued performance gains. As a result, power and energy management have become as important as traditional metrics like speed and cost in the design of modern computing systems.

The need for energy-efficient computing touches all segments of IT, from tiny sensors and mobile devices to massive data centers. For battery-powered mobile platforms, energy efficiency directly impacts usability by determining active lifetime. In larger systems, increased energy use drives up costs, wastes resources, and aggravates global warming. Even if energy remains cheap and abundant, the heat dissipation limits of air cooling ultimately cap the performance that can be delivered at a sensible cost. The importance of eco-aware computing will only grow over time. Multiprocessing computing is shown in Figure 14.1.

Fortunately, widespread awareness of the energy crisis in computing has sparked an explosion of research into system designs that offer improved performance per watt. Techniques have emerged to optimize energy efficiency at every level of the computing stack, from low-level hardware like circuits, processors, and memory, up through networks, virtualization platforms, operating systems, middleware, and applications [1–8].

This paper surveys the established and emerging methods for optimizing energy efficiency across this spectrum of layers and technologies. We explore the sources of energy inefficiency in computing systems and identify technical approaches to curbing waste. Architectural innovations that prioritize energy efficiency over absolute performance are reviewed. We compare strengths and limitations among competing strategies. Trends covered range from chip manufacturing processes and dynamic power management schemes, through compiler optimizations and energy-aware scheduling algorithms, up to data center construction guidelines and models for smart power grids. Improving data center energy efficiency is shown in Figure 14.2.

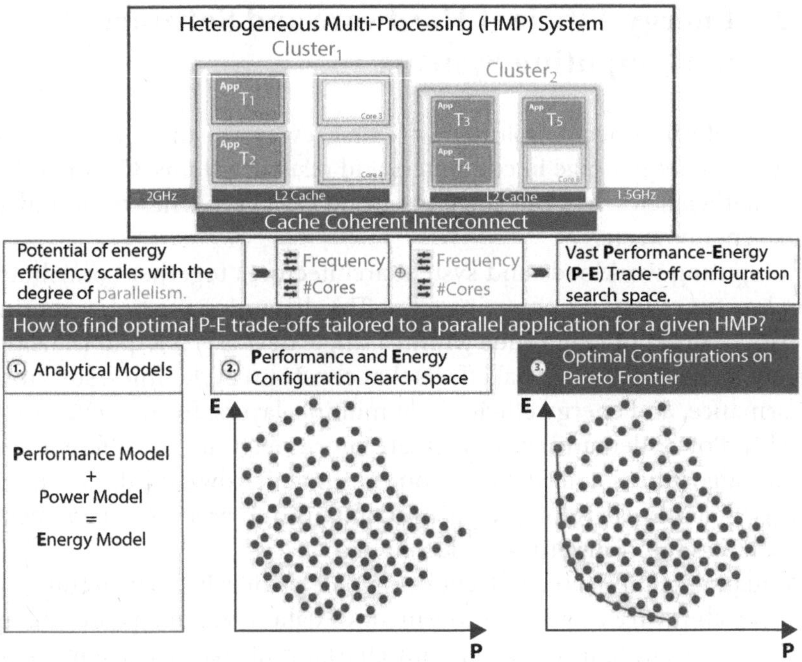

Figure 14.1 Multiprocessing computing.

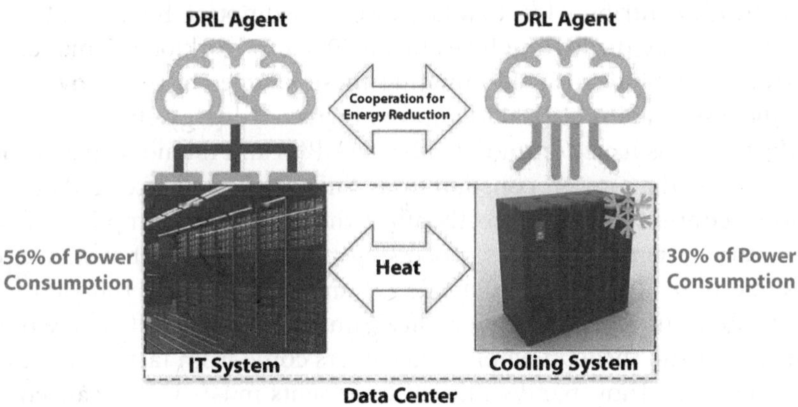

Figure 14.2 Improving data center energy efficiency.

14.2 Energy-Efficient Hardware and Software in Computing Systems

Before exploring specific solutions, we first review the unique sources and patterns of energy usage in computers and related systems. Characterizing these inefficiencies sets the stage for technical approaches to bound and reduce energy waste.

Computing workloads and system architectures together contribute to complex, time-varying power profiles. The dynamic range now routinely exceeds an order of magnitude within a single device [1]. Rapid transitions trigger electrical and thermal effects that constrain cycle times, sustainable performance, and energy efficiency at multiple layers, from circuits to systems [2]. Power demands also fluctuate enormously across different applications, algorithms, and data sets on the same hardware [3]. Optimizing energy efficiency, therefore, requires adaptivity and precision from mechanisms across the computing stack.

Fundamental limits on efficiency originate primarily from circuits, logic gates, on-chip wires, and the movement of data. Dynamic power dissipation due to transistor switching and charging of load capacitances now exceeds static leakage effects for most fabrication processes [4]. Yet, recent trends toward dark silicon suggest leakage currents could constrain future chips if not adequately addressed [5]. Higher levels of the system hierarchy typically contribute less to total power consumption but still introduce significant waste through policies mismatched to workload demands and hardware capabilities [6]. Eliminating these sources of overprovisioning and idleness remains critical to improving overall energy efficiency.

Most systems have common loads like CPUs and memory that account for most of the power consumption. Still, dedicated accelerators and network connectivity also greatly affect the energy consumption of contemporary systems. Graphics processing units (GPUs), for instance, can consume over 50 watts even at idle [7] and run between 100–300 watts to provide peak computing capability. Similar threats to efficiency trends from circuits up through whole data centers come from fast-growing data movement [8]. Thus, bandwidth enhancements must aim at least equally for energy efficiency with capacity increases. We investigate technologies and methods especially targeted at increasing these several aspects of energy proportionality and precision at every level of computer systems in the sections that follow. Energy-efficient computing's basis is better hardware designs ranging from the circuit level up through system architecture. We review developments in processors, memory, interconnects, and accelerators directly affecting system-level energy use and performance-per-watt trends in this part.

14.3 Smart Solutions to Optimize Energy Efficiency in Computing Systems

14.3.1 Low-Power Processors

The energy efficiency of computation depends much on the strategies of processor architecture [9]. Designs that lower cost per instruction without compromising performance increase computational energy economy. Common techniques include incorporating domain-customized accelerators such as graphics engines or crypto processors, and using superscalar and very long instruction word (VLIW) architectures to utilize instruction-level parallelism (ILP) [10–16].

By lowering static leakage currents at lower voltages, nano- Complementary Metal-Oxide-Semiconductor (nano-CMOS) manufacturing processes also help [17, 18]. More recent process nodes, however, also cause parametric fluctuation and necessitate adaptive components such as Razor flip-flops with *in situ* error detection [19]. Beyond energy, cost criteria such as EDAP (energy-delay-area product) catch these difficult trade-offs to direct low-power design [20].

Future extreme-scale systems will require disruptive architectures, devices, and materials to maintain scaling trends without hitting power and thermal limits [21, 22]. Prospects like optical and chemical switching, carbon nanotube interconnects, and customized nanophotonic networks promise continued efficiency gains only through coordinated innovation across the hardware and software stack [23–25].

14.3.2 Low-Power Memory

Large pool sizes, frequent access, and high fanout make main memory a critical determinant of system energy efficiency [26]. Access optimizations like intelligent prefetching and caching help reduce off-chip traffic, while voltage scaling, sub-banking, and low-power sense amplifiers cut energy per access [27, 28]. Increasing parallelism allows for lower speeds to save significant dynamic power with little loss in bandwidth [29].

New memory technologies also show potential but lack capacity and scalability. For example, spin-transfer torque RAM (STT-RAM) eliminates the refresh costs of DRAM while matching performance at lower voltage [30]. STT-RAM caches configured as L1/L2 buffers save considerable energy [31], but remain too expensive for main memory [32]. Similar scalability concerns hamper competing resistive RAM technologies like phase-change memory (PCM) and memristors despite favorable density and leakage [33]. System-level modeling that co-optimizes the scheduling of processors, caches, main memory banks, and virtual memory pages may help transitional technologies reach broader viability [34].

14.3.3 On-Chip Interconnects

As feature sizes continue to shrink per Moore's law, energy efficiency of movement both on and off-chip increasingly impacts systems from embedded system on chips (SoCs) to server CPUs [35]. Bus, crossbar, and network-on-chip (NoC) architectures all address communication bottlenecks with different trade-offs. Grid-based NoCs provide the best scalability and performance through massive parallel switches [36], but machine learning now enables adaptive topologies for much greater energy efficiency [37]. Wireless options using integrated antennas promise even lower NoC power costs, nudging toward the 1–10 fJ/bit dream [38]. Stacking memory and logic into 3D systems shortens interconnect lengths at the cost of thermal hotspots [39]. Holistic analysis from circuits through layout and packaging is required to determine optimal organizations balancing bandwidth, power, and cost [40].

14.3.4 Hardware Accelerators

While customizable processors and memory systems handle a wide range of workloads efficiently, customized hardware accelerators maximize energy efficiency for specific tasks in high-performance or embedded computing contexts [41]. Hardwired logic avoids instruction fetch and decode costs while eliminating unnecessary generality [42]. Accelerators also simplify parallelism essential for efficiency. For example, GPUs leverage small repeated units to enable throughput an order of magnitude higher than complex superscalar CPUs on graphics and machine learning [43]. Recent research further co-optimizes data movement with computation using novel interconnects like wireless networks-on-chip [44]. Table 14.1 summarizes several standard offload workloads and associated accelerator architectures.

The 77% annual growth rate for accelerators now outpaces Moore's law as algorithms expose massive parallelism. However, heterogeneity also adds complexity across the software/hardware stack and challenges traditional CPU-centric analysis. Tools like Intel's Heterogeneous Architecture

Table 14.1 Common hardware accelerator targets and typical organizations.

Workload	Accelerator architecture
Media processing	Stream processors with dedicated functional units for coding/decoding
Graphics rendering	Many simple shader cores with matrix math units, texture samplers, and raster output
Learning & AI	Vector processors, matrix multiply units, nearest neighbor caches
Search, mining	Hash generators, tree traversal engines
Compression	Custom codecs, encryption blocks

Research Platform (HARP) tackle these issues *via* unified system modeling, optimization, and simulation. The Autotuning Compiler Environment (ACE) takes a higher-level approach by generating code for custom accelerators from domain libraries. Optimally partitioning workloads between accelerators and general processors remains an open challenge.

Beyond hardware advances, software also impacts system-level energy efficiency across areas from operating systems and compilers to algorithms and applications. In this section, we survey established and emerging techniques at these various levels.

14.3.5 Operating Systems

The operating system coordinates all processes, resources, devices, and policies on a computing platform. Energy aware resource management and scheduling, therefore, provide powerful system-level mechanisms for improving efficiency. The growing diversity of low power states in modern systems offers both opportunity and complexity [20]. Effective dynamic power management (DPM) requires accurate modeling of idle intervals to predict breakeven times for state transitions [1]. Linux, Windows, and all major mobile OSs now incorporate such predictive policies [2], dynamically adapting timeouts based on observed patterns [3]. The exponential range of power/latency trade-offs requires multi-tiered idle states, necessitating research on cost metrics and control theory for optimal state selection [4].

Similar opportunities exist for dynamic voltage and frequency scaling (DVFS), which can modulate processing capacity to precisely match

Table 14.2 Standard operating system power management methods.

Method	Description	Mechanisms
Dynamic Power Management	Transition devices/ components to lower power states during idle periods	CPU sleep states, bus power down, disk spin-down
Dynamic Volt/ Freq Scaling	Modulate performance to match workload throughput needs	Processor voltage/ frequency setting
Power-aware Scheduling	Batch tasks to maximize idle intervals *via* packing and ordering optimizations	OS task queue manipulation
Energy Accounting	Provide visibility into system and application-level power usage	Software monitors: Joulemeter, PowerTOP

workload needs. Linux on-demand governors pioneered autonomous DVFS, while advanced configuration and power interface (ACPI) standardizes voltage/frequency control interfaces [5]. Multicore systems add complexity through shared resources and temperature effects impacting reliability and signaling [21]. Current research addresses these issues *via* distributed agents [25], formal control policies [22], machine learning [23], and utility optimization to unlock additional efficiency gains. Table 14.2 summarizes common power management techniques exploited at the operating system (OS) level.

Future systems may require more disruptive OS advances to address the dark silicon era's shift toward specialized heterogeneous architectures [1]. Proposals include spatial task scheduling among discrete power domains [2] and voltage stacking to compensate for lowering voltage device means device (Vdd) [3]. Co-optimization of scheduling, voltage allocation, and task placement could then maximize efficiency for a fixed thermal design power budget [4].

14.3.6 Compilers and Runtimes

Compiler analysis provides extensive opportunities to improve energy efficiency by transparently optimizing software downstream from the programmer [5]. Typical approaches include minimizing costly operations like memory accesses, eliminating redundancy, maximizing parallelism, and adapting precision to workload [6]. For example, feedback-directed optimization adjusts function layout to reduce instruction cache misses [31], approximate computing shortens costly calculations with tolerable precision loss [30], and strict alias analysis enables effective auto-vectorization on SIMD units [32].

Compiler-based software tuning relies heavily on accurate architectural models. However, the proliferation of heterogeneous multi-accelerator SoCs challenges traditional assumptions [40], requiring novel intermediate representations like the Heterogeneous Abstract Syntax Tree (HAST) [1]. The Virtual Machine Interface (VMI) instead offers a platform to abstract such architectural differences and automatically explore optimizations with evolutionary algorithms [2]. Other recent techniques apply deep learning to circumvent the need for explicit modeling [3]. Ultimately, runtime adaptation will prove essential to respond to phase changes. DynamoRIO supports online hotspot optimization by patching frequently executed code [4], while Green allows annotated functions to substitute approximations dynamically [5].

Languages and frameworks also provide leverage, enabling compact, expressive code without sacrificing performance. For example, algorithmic skeletons abstract complex parallel patterns for easy reuse [6] while distributed frameworks like MapReduce transparently scale out across clusters [7]. Recent domain-specific languages like Halide (image processing) and Liszt (mesh algorithms) raise abstraction further, permitting explicit schedule and storage optimization during just-in-time compilation [8].

14.3.7 Algorithms and Applications

Ultimately, the choice of algorithms and adherence to efficiency principles determine the total application and system-level energy usage [30]. Standard methods include right-sizing computation and data types, minimizing expensive I/O, leveraging efficient libraries, and simplifying control flow [21]. For example, scanning satellite images can reduce memory traffic by over 90% by skipping touch tests for interior pixels [2]. Broad surveys highlight hundreds of additional application-level optimizations [23]. Dynamically tuning input data size also provides a simple lever for adapting efficiency to meet real-time constraints during execution [14]. More examples appear in Table 14.3.

Emerging algorithms built on approximation [25], compression [26], and probability [7] promise to raise efficiency further by trading marginal

Table 14.3 Typical application-level energy optimizations.

Technique	**Description**	**Impact on energy efficiency**
Code Optimization	Writing efficient code to reduce computational complexity.	Lowers CPU usage and power consumption.
DVFS	Adjusting voltage and frequency based on workload.	Reduces power during low-intensity tasks.
Resource Scheduling	Allocating resources based on energy profiles.	Optimizes resource use, lowering energy.
Memory Management	Optimizing memory access patterns.	Decreases power usage from memory operations.
Task Consolidation	Grouping tasks to minimize state transitions.	Reduces energy spikes and improves efficiency.
Algorithm Optimization	Using energy-efficient algorithms.	Reduces computational energy needs.
Energy-Aware Design	Designing software with modular, energy-efficient code.	Integrates energy-saving from the start.

loss of quality for substantial gains in speed or storage. Applications already successfully employ such techniques in domains like analytics [8], visualization [32], and recognition [30]. Quantifying trade-off curves helps users balance accuracy and efficiency [1]. Integrating these approximate computing methods into common libraries could greatly simplify adoption [2].

14.3.8 Energy-Efficient Data Centers

The previous sections addressed technologies and policies for improving the energy efficiency of individual devices and systems. Yet modern computing depends equally on warehouse-scale data centers composed of thousands of servers, switches, and storage arrays interconnected by optical fiber [45]. Total data center electricity usage now rivals that of medium-sized nations [23], motivating extensive research on facility-level optimization [29].

Metering and profiling identify the largest savings opportunities. Studies consistently show that computing and communication are dominated by a small subset of servers, with utilization averaging 30% or less [40]. Simple spreadsheet models can then prioritize efficiency tactics based on return on investment [41]. For example, tuning supply air temperature allows a greater fraction of waste heat recapture. Higher operating temperatures also improve chiller efficiency with minor risk [45]. Workload shifting similarly exploits time-of-day electricity pricing differentials that often exceed 50% [46].

With detailed telemetry as a guide, common infrastructure optimizations deliver over 40% energy savings [46], significantly extending the benefits of optimized components. Virtualization, already widely adopted for server consolidation, additionally enables fine-grained rightsizing by shifting load in real-time. Container platforms like Docker extend such flexibility down to single processes while minimizing runtime overhead [49, 50]. Integrated rack architectures go further still, combining high-efficiency power supplies, optimized cooling paths, and lower loss DC distribution to raise facility capacity by over 35%.

Ultimately, the survival of computing systems requires total decoupling from fossil fuel energy use. Renewable sources, coupled with advanced batteries, offer a path to sustainable operation, though locational mismatches between sun, wind, and data centers necessitate a national smart

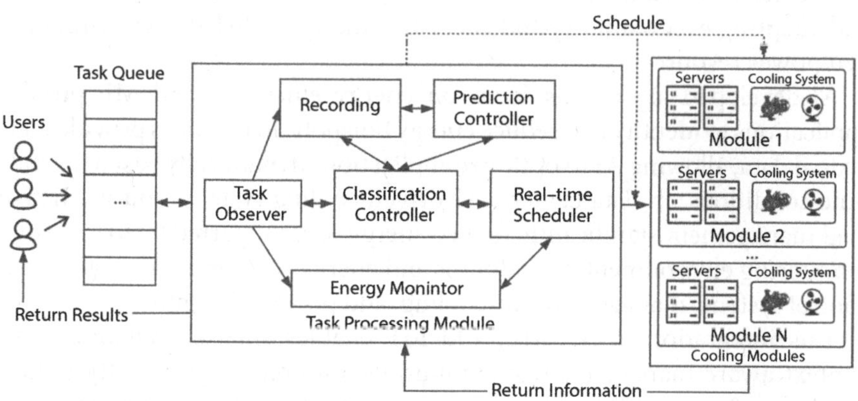

Figure 14.3 The structure of the data center.

grid. Holistic clean energy integration will require coordination among IT architects, policymakers, and utility companies to reshape infrastructure for the next century. Figure 14.3 shows the structure of data Centre [51–54].

14.4 Augmentations of Artificial Intelligence (AI)/Machine Learning (ML)/IoT in Optimizing Energy Efficiency in Computing Systems

Integrating AI, ML, and IoT technologies significantly enhances energy efficiency across computing systems. In low-power processors, AI predicts workload patterns to adjust performance dynamically, ensuring optimal power states [55]. IoT devices facilitate real-time monitoring and control of processor temperatures and loads. For low-power memory, ML optimizes access patterns to minimize energy consumption, while IoT-enabled modules communicate usage data for better data placement strategies [57].

On-chip interconnects benefit from AI-driven traffic management, avoiding congestion and reducing power use. IoT sensors provide real-time data, helping AI models optimize interconnect operations. Hardware accelerators, such as GPUs and FPGAs, use AI to offload intensive tasks and tune performance, while IoT integration at the edge enables efficient local processing, reducing the need for energy-intensive data transfers.

Operating systems use AI for energy-aware scheduling and resource management, optimizing CPU, memory, and I/O usage based on real-time analysis. IoT devices, managed centrally, benefit from coordinated task and power state optimization. AI-driven compilers and runtimes enhance code efficiency, reducing energy consumption by optimizing instructions and adapting execution in real time, particularly for IoT devices with limited power resources.

AI-developed algorithms focus on energy efficiency, and ML profiles applications to identify and reduce energy hotspots. IoT devices provide contextual data, allowing AI to optimize applications dynamically based on real-time conditions. In data centers, AI-driven cooling systems and predictive load management significantly reduce energy use, supported by IoT sensors monitoring environmental conditions and energy consumption. Automated control systems manage lighting, cooling, and power efficiently [47].

This integration of AI, ML, and IoT enables smarter, dynamic, and context-aware management of computing resources, significantly reducing the energy footprint and contributing to a sustainable, environmentally friendly computing infrastructure [48].

14.5 Sustainable Computing

The fast expansion of cloud computing and online services fuels ever more heated discussion on their environmental effect. On target to reach 8% by 2030, data centers today account for over 2% of US electricity use. Although this concentration of computation allows efficiency by means of conservation strategies described in Section 14.6, public awareness of absolute usage keeps driving the need for more obvious change. Industry leaders have responded with carbon credits, bio-diversity initiatives, and balancing legacy fossil impacts through renewable energy purchases. However, eliminating reliance on carbon-based grids is still difficult given availability, cost considerations, and dependability issues.

Habitat restoration under sustainable IT equipment power consumption. Such innovative ideas seek to translate data centers from symbols of waste into models of systems thinking. Proposed self-sufficient data centers have ground-water cooling loops, rainwater collecting and reuse, on-site renewable generation including solar panels and wind turbines, and strong energy storage capacity architecturally. By use of thermal energy storage and mixed reality workload simulation, careful modeling balances local climate with dynamic computational load. Even with changing supply, tight integration of power distribution, battery buffers, health monitoring, and intelligent scheduling guarantees quality of service. Software-defined wireless mesh networks, rather than rigid fiber, take the front stage in last-mile connection. Edge computing designs spread availability and capacity risks all around. Taken together, these developments move the sector towards practical off-grid operation [56].

More generally, whole life cycle studies expose areas of optimization across hardware manufacture, transportation, building, facility maintenance, and electronic waste issues. Reducing sustainability costs by means of redundant components, extending product lifetimes through repair and upgrades, and enhancing the recoverability of rare earth metals and plastics at end-of-life all greatly help to lower sustainability costs. Through buy-back programs, some companies even encourage the return and reuse of server equipment [46, 47].

Many challenges still stand before data-driven services can bring overall net positive environmental impact. Still, public pressure and the growing acceptance of domestic carbon fees help to propel more rapid development. Furthermore, enhancing knowledge of sustainability issues among practitioners and policy officials through cross-industry alliances. With continuous exponential efficiency increases across devices, data centers, algorithms, and business processes, computing can obviously outgrow its reputation as a dirty industry with suitable paths now readily available.

14.6 Conclusions

Growing energy prices and sustainability issues are changing information technology, so system designs that clearly aim for efficiency gain have an evident competitive advantage. From small embedded sensor nodes to large cloud server farms, this article examined technologies and approaches for maximizing energy efficiency across the spectrum of computing equipment. We investigated hardware methods, software rules, and facility-level practices designed to reduce inefficiencies and surveyed the causes of energy waste particular to computer workloads.

Established techniques already provide multiplicative gains covering the computer stack. To lower the cost per operation, circuits optimize voltage scaling, leakage currents, and physical layout. Heterogeneous multi-core CPUs fit workloads to effective engines. Runtimes check codes, adjusting parallelism and precision to fit limitations. Operating systems schedule forcefully over power states to balance performance and energy consumption. Compiler optimization of memory traffic, data types and eliminating redundant operations such as: Loop unrolling & vectorization, memory layout optimization and code elimination and redundancy removal. Applications pick algorithms that balance performance, accuracy, and quality of service. Data centers address cooling, service location for sustainable operation, and topologies. Over the past decade, these developments have raised efficiency by more than 1000x across all measurements, from FLOPS/watt to searches/Joule. However, open challenges still exist. Dynamic adaptation of provisioning, routing, scheduling, and approximation in runtime learning systems could release even more benefits. Clean-slate redesigns of sustainable computation and data infrastructure promise transformation rather than small improvement. Investigating alternative nano-devices, 3D integration, wireless communication, and free-air cooling will help keep efficiency constraints at both high and low levels under constant challenge. Most importantly, cross-layer feedback and control strategies must spread learning between layers to coordinate system-level progress. Over the next ten years, overcoming these obstacles will firmly establish energy-efficient computing as a pillar of technical and environmental advancement.

Acknowledgment

This work was supported by the Deanship of Scientific Research, Vice Presidency for Graduate Studies and Scientific Research, King Faisal University, Saudi Arabia, under Project GRANT6,025.

References

1. Pham, D., Aipperspach, T., Boerstler, D., Bolliger, M., Chaudhry, R., Cox, D., Harvey, P., Harvey, P., Hofstee, H., Johns, C., *et al.*, Overview of the architecture, circuit design, and physical implementation of a first-generation Cell processor. *IEEE J. Solid-State Circuits*, 41, 179–196, 2006, [Google Scholar] [CrossRef].
2. Corp, A. big.LITTLE Technology–ARM, Available online: https://www.arm.com/products/processors/technologies/biglittleprocessing.php (accessed on 6 April 2019).
3. Chitlur, N., Srinivasa, G., Hahn, S., Gupta, P.K., Reddy, D., Koufaty, D., Brett, P., Prabhakaran, A., Zhao, L., Ijih, N., *et al.*, QuickIA: Exploring heterogeneous architectures on real prototypes, in: *Proceedings of the IEEE International Symposium on High-Performance Comp Architecture*, pp. 1–8, New Orleans, LA, USA, 25–29 February 2012, [Google Scholar] [CrossRef].
4. Wang, G., Li, W., Hei, X., Energy-aware real-time scheduling on Heterogeneous Multi-Processor, in: *Proceedings of the 2015 49th Annual Conference on Information Sciences and Systems, CISS 2015*, pp. 1–7, Baltimore, MD, USA, 18–20 March 2015, [Google Scholar] [CrossRef].
5. Herbert, S. and Marculescu, D., Analysis of dynamic voltage/frequency scaling in chip-multiprocessors, in: *Proceedings of the 2007 International Symposium on Low Power Electronics and Design (ISLPED '07)*, pp. 38–43, Portland, OR, USA, 27–29 August 2007, [Google Scholar] [CrossRef].
6. Benini, L., Bogliolo, A., De Micheli, G.A., survey of design techniques for system-level dynamic power management. *IEEE Trans. Very Large Scale Integr. VLSI Syst.*, 8, 299–316, 2000, [Google Scholar] [CrossRef].
7. De Sensi, D., Torquati, M., Danelutto, M.A., Reconfiguration Algorithm for Power-Aware Parallel Applications. *ACM Trans. Archit. Code Optim.*, 13, 1–25, 2016, [Google Scholar] [CrossRef][Green Version].
8. Gupta, U., Patil, C.A., Bhat, G., Mishra, P., Ogras, U.Y., DyPO: Dynamic Pareto-Optimal Configuration Selection for Heterogeneous. *ACM Trans. Embed. Comput. Syst.*, 16, 1–20, 2017.

9. Morokoff, W.J. and Caflisch, R.E., Quasi-Random Sequences and Their Discrepancies. *SIAM J. Sci. Comput.*, 15, 1251–1279, 1994.
10. Saez, J.C., Pousa, A., Castro, F., Chaver, D., Prieto-Matias, M., Towards completely fair scheduling on asymmetric single-ISA multicore processors. *J. Parallel Distrib. Comput.*, 102, 115–131, 2017.
11. Sawalha, L., Wolff, S., Tull, M.P., Barnes, R.D., Phase-Guided Scheduling on Single-ISA Heterogeneous Multicore Processors, in: *Proceedings of the IEEE 2011 14th Euromicro Conference on Digital System Design*, pp. 736–745, Oulu, Finland, 31 August–2 September 2011.
12. Hill, M.D. and Marty, M.R., Amdahl's Law in the Multicore Era. *Computer*, 41, 33–38, 2008.
13. Endrei, M., Jin, C., Dinh, M.N., Abramson, D., Poxon, H., DeRose, L., de Supinski, B.R., Energy Efficiency Modeling of Parallel Applications, in: *Proceedings of the International Conference for High Performance Computing, Networking, Storage, and Analysis, Dallas, TX, USA, 11–16 November 2018*, pp. 212–224, IEEE Press, Piscataway, NJ, USA, 2018.
14. Singh, A.K., Shafique, M., Kumar, A., Henkel, J., Mapping on multi/many-core systems: Survey of current and emerging trends, in: *Proceedings of the 2013 50th ACM/EDAC/IEEE Design Automation Conference (DAC)*, pp. 1–10, Austin, TX, USA, 29 May–7 June 2013.
15. Manumachu, R.R., Lastovetsky, A., Bi-Objective Optimization of Data-Parallel Applications on Homogeneous Multicore Clusters for Performance and Energy. *IEEE Trans. Comput.*, 67, 160–177, 2018.
16. Tzilis, S., Trancoso, P., Sourdis, I., Energy-Efficient Runtime Management of Heterogeneous Multicores using Online Projection. *ACM Trans. Archit. Code Optim.*, 15, 1–26, 2019.
17. Loghin, D. and Teo, Y.M., The time and energy efficiency of modern multicore systems. *Parallel Comput.*, 86, 1–10, 2018.
18. Vasilakis, E., Sourdis, I., Papaefstathiou, V., Psathakis, A., Katevenis, M.G., Modeling energy-performance tradeoffs in ARM big.LITTLE architectures, in: *Proceedings of the 2017 27th International Symposium on Power and Timing Modeling, Optimization and Simulation, PATMOS 2017*, pp. 1–8, Thessaloniki, Greece, 25–27 September 2017.
19. De Sensi, D., Predicting Performance and Power Consumption of Parallel Applications, in: *Proceedings of the 24th Euromicro International Conference on Parallel, Distributed, and Network-Based Processing, PDP 2016*, pp. 200–207, Heraklion, Greece, 17–19 February 2016.
20. Aalsaud, A., Shafik, R., Rafiev, A., Xia, F., Yang, S., Yakovlev, A., Power–Aware Performance Adaptation of Concurrent Applications in Heterogeneous Many-Core Systems, in: *Proceedings of the 2016 International Symposium on Low Power Electronics and Design, San Francisco, CA, USA, 8–10 August 2016*, pp. 368–373. ACM: New York, NY, USA.
21. Gustafson, J.L., Reevaluating Amdahl's Law. *Commun. ACM*, 31, 532–533, 1988.

22. Amdahl, G.M., Validity of the single processor approach to achieving large scale computing capabilities, in: *Proceedings of the AFIPS 1967 Spring Joint Computer Conference*, pp. 483–485, Atlantic City, NJ, USA, 18–20 April 1967.
23. Woo, D.H. and Lee, H.H.S., Extending Amdahl's law for energy-efficient computing in the many-core era. *Computer*, 41, 24–31, 2008.
24. Donyanavard, B., Mück, T., Sarma, S., Dutt, N., SPARTA: Runtime task allocation for energy efficient heterogeneous manycores, in: *Proceedings of the 2016 International Conference on Hardware/Software Codesign and System Synthesis (CODES+ISSS)*, pp. 1–10, Pittsburgh, PA, USA, 1–7 October 2016.
25. Sarma, S., Muck, T., Bathen, L.A.D., Dutt, N., Nicolau, A., SmartBalance: A sensing-driven Linux load balancer for energy efficiency of heterogeneous MPSoCs, in: *Proceedings of the 2015 52nd ACM/EDAC/IEEE Design Automation Conference (DAC)*, pp. 1–6, San Francisco, CA, USA, 8–12 June 2015.
26. Kim, M., Kim, K., Geraci, J.R., Hong, S., Utilization-aware load balancing for the energy efficient operation of the big.LITTLE processor, in: *Proceedings of the Design, Automation & Test in Europe Conference & Exhibition (DATE) 24–28 March 2014*, Dresden, Germany, pp. 1–4.
27. Endrei, M., Jin, C., Dinh, M.N., Abramson, D., Poxon, H., DeRose, L., de Supinski, B.R.A., Bottleneck-Centric Tuning Policy for Optimizing Energy in Parallel Programs, in: *Proceedings of the Parallel Computing is Everywhere-International Conference on Parallel Computing, ParCo 2017*, pp. 265–276, Ologna, Italy, 12–15 September 2017.
28. Balaprakash, P., Tiwari, A., Wild, S.M., Multi objective optimization of HPC kernels for performance, power, and energy. *Lect. Notes Comput. Sci. (Incl. Subser. Lect. Notes Artif. Intell. Lect. Notes Bioinform.)*, 8551, 239–260, 2014.
29. Malathy, S., Vanitha, C.N., Dhanaraj, R.K., Kotteswari, C., Impact of Blockchain-IoE on economy, in: *Blockchain-Based Systems for the Modern Energy Grid*, pp. 135–156, Elsevier, 2023.
30. Bailey, P.E., Marathe, A., Lowenthal, D.K., Rountree, B., Schulz, M., Finding the Limits of Power-constrained Application Performance, in: *Proceedings of the International Conference for High Performance Computing, Networking, Storage and Analysis, Austin, TX, USA, 15 November 2015*, pp. 1–12, ACM: New York, NY, USA, 2015.
31. Coutinho, D.A.M., Georgiou, K., Eder, K.I., Nunez-Yanez, J., Xavier-de-Souza, S., Performance and Energy Efficiency Trade-Offs in Single-ISA Heterogeneous Multi-Processing for Parallel Applications, in: *Proceedings of the 2019 IFIP/IEEE 27th International Conference on Very Large Scale Integration (VLSI-SoC)*, pp. 232–233, Cuzco, Peru, 6–9 October 2019.
32. Koufaty, D., Reddy, D., Hahn, S., Bias scheduling in heterogeneous multi-core architectures, in: *Proceedings of the 5th European Conference on Computer Systems—EuroSys '10, Paris, France, 13–16 April 2010*, p. 125, ACM Press: New York, NY, USA, 2010.

33. Jin, C., de Supinski, B.R., Abramson, D., Poxon, H., DeRose, L., Dinh, M.N., Endrei, M., Jessup, E.R.A., survey on software methods to improve the energy efficiency of parallel computing. *Int. J. High Perform. Comput. Appl.*, 31, 517–549, 2017.
34. Barros, C., Silveira, L., Valderrama, C., Xavier-de Souza, S., Optimal processor dynamic-energy reduction for parallel workloads on heterogeneous multi-core architectures. *Microprocess. Microsys.*, 39, 418–425, 2015.
35. Morad, T., Weiser, U., Kolodny, A., Valero, M., Ayguade, E., Performance, Power Efficiency and Scalability of Asymmetric Cluster Chip Multiprocessors. *IEEE Comput. Archit. Lett.*, 5, 4, 2006.
36. Furtunato, A.F.A., Georgiou, K., Eder, K., de Souza, S.X., When parallel speedups hit the memory wall, arXiv 2019, arXiv:1905.01234.
37. Uppal, M., Metkewar, P.S., Kumar Dhanaraj, R., Kour, K., Gupta, D., Saini, S., ESSS: Energy Saver Smart Shoes for Energy Harvesting using Multi-Sensors Technique, in: *2023 International Conference on Advances in Computation, Communication and Information Technology (ICAICCIT)*, 2023.
38. Alonso, P., Dolz, M.F., Mayo, R., Quintana-Ortí, E.S., Modeling power and energy of the task-parallel Cholesky factorization on multicore processors. *Comput. Sci. R D*, 29, 105–112, 2014.
39. Kim, N.S., Austin, T., Blaauw, D., Mudge, T., Flautner, K., Hu, J.S., Irwin, M.J., Kandemir, M., Narayanan, V., Leakage Current: Moore's Law Meets Static Power. *Computer*, 36, 68–75, 2003.
40. Suleiman, D., Ibrahim, M., Hamarash, I., Dynamic voltage frequency scaling (DVFS) for microprocessors power and energy reduction, in: *Proceedings of the 4th International Conference on Sustainable Energy and Environmental Engineering (ICSEEE 2015)*, pp. 5–9, Shenzhen, China, 20–21 December 2005.
41. Venkatachalam, V. and Franz, M., Power reduction techniques for microprocessor systems. *ACM Comput. Surv.*, 37, 195–237, 2005.
42. Cardoso, J.M., Coutinho, J.G.F., Diniz, P.C., Chapter 2—High-performance embedded computing, in: *Embedded Computing for High Performance*, J.M. Cardoso, J.G.F. Coutinho, P.C. Diniz, (Eds.), pp. 17–56, Morgan Kaufmann, Boston, MA, USA, 2017.
43. Tang, A., Sethumadhavan, S., Stolfo, S., Tang, A., Stolfo, S., CLKSCREW: Exposing the Perils of Security- Oblivious Energy Management, in: *Proceedings of the 26th USENIX Security Symposium*, pp. 1057–1074, Vancouver, BC, Canada, 16–18 August 2017.
44. Usman, S., Khan, S.U., Khan, S., A comparative study of voltage/frequency scaling in NoC, in: *Proceedings of the IEEE International Conference on Electro-Information Technology EIT 2013*, pp. 1–5, Rapid City, SD, USA, 9–11 May 2013.
45. ODROID-XU3 - Hardkernel, Available online: https://www.hardkernel.com/shop/odroid-xu3/ (accessed on 12 April 2019).

46. Mittal, S., *et al.*, Light weight cryptography for cloud-based e-health records. *2022 7th International Conference on Communication and Electronics Systems (ICCES)*, IEEE, 2022.
47. Hooda, S., Lamba, V., Kaur, A., AI and soft computing techniques for securing cloud and edge computing: a systematic review. *2021 5th International Conference on Information Systems and Computer Networks (ISCON)*, IEEE, 2021.
48. Gupta, N., *et al.*, Enhanced virtualization-based dynamic bin-packing optimized energy management solution for heterogeneous clouds. *Math. Probl. Eng.*, 2022, 1–115, 2022.
49. R. Anand, (Ed.), *et al.*, *Integration of IoT with Cloud Computing for Smart Applications*, CRC Press, 2023.
50. Bali, M.S., *et al.*, An effective technique to schedule priority aware tasks to offload data on edge and cloud servers. *Meas.: Sens.*, 26, 1006705, 2023.
51. Kautish, S., Juneja, S., Mohiuddin, K., Karim, F.K., Elmannai, H., Ghorashi, S., Hamid, Y., Enhanced cloud storage encryption standard for security in distributed environments. *Electronics, 12*, 3, 714, 2023.
52. Singamaneni, K.K., *et al.*, An efficient hybrid QHCP-ABE model to improve cloud data integrity and confidentiality. *Electronics*, 11.21, 3510, 2022.
53. Singh, N., *et al.*, Load balancing and service discovery using Docker Swarm for microservice based big data applications. *J. Cloud Comput.*, 12.1, 4, 2023.
54. Singh, S.P., *et al.*, Dual adaption based evolutionary algorithm for optimized the smart healthcare communication service of the Internet of Things in smart city. *Phys. Commun.*, 55, 1018935, 2022.
55. Sathya, K. and Rajesh Kumar, D., Energy efficient clustering in sensor networks using Cluster Manager. *2012 International Conference on Computing, Communication and Applications*, IEEE, 2012.
56. Dhanaraj, R.K., *et al.*, Optimal clone attack detection model using an energy-efficient GSA based simulated annealing in wireless sensor networks. *Asian J. Res. Social Sci. Humanit.*, 6.11, 201–217, 2016.
57. S. Rajendran, M. Sabharwal, G. Ghinea, R.K., Dhanaraj, B. Balusamy, (Eds.), *IoT and Big Data Analytics for Smart Cities: A Global Perspective*, CRC Press, 2022.

About the Editors

Dr. R.Sathiyaraj
Associate Professor,
Manipal Institute of Technology,
MAHE Bengaluru Campus, Karnataka, India
rsr026@gmail.com
+91-8328249506

Dr. R.Sathiyaraj is currently working as an Associate Professor at Manipal Institute of Technology, Bangalore. He received the B.Tech. degree in Information Technology from Anna University Chennai, India in 2009 and M.Tech from Vel Tech University Chennai, India in 2012 and Ph.D. degree in Computer Science and Engineering from Anna University, Chennai, India, in 2020. He has contributed 2 Authored books and served as lead editor for 3 books on various technologies, 5 Patents and 20+ articles and papers in various refereed journals and international conferences and contributed chapters to the books. His research interests include Big Data Analytics, Machine Learning, and Intelligent Systems.

Dr. Rajesh Kumar Dhanaraj
Symbiosis International (Deemed University), India,
sangeraje@gmail.com
+91-9488668833

Rajesh Kumar Dhanaraj is a Professor in Symbiosis International (Deemed University), Pune, India. Prior to this assignment he was Professor, School of Computing Sciences & Engineering, Galgotias University, Greater Noida, India. He received the B.E. degree in Computer Science and Engineering from the Anna University Chennai, India in 2007 and the M.Tech from the Anna University Coimbatore, India in 2010 and Ph.D. degree in Computer Science from Anna University, Chennai, India, in 2017. He has contributed 45+ Authored and Edited books on various technologies, 21 Patents and 90+ articles and papers in various refereed journals and international conferences and contributed chapters to the books. His research interests include Machine Learning, Cyber-Physical Systems and Wireless Sensor Networks. He is a Senior Member of the Institute of Electrical and Electronics Engineers (IEEE), member of the Computer Science Teacher Association (CSTA); and International Association of Engineers (IAENG). He is serving as an Associate Editor and Guest Editor for reputed journals Elsevier Computers and Electrical Engineering, Human-centric Computing and Information Sciences, Emerald - International Journal of Pervasive Computing and Communications, Hindawi - Mobile Information Systems, etc. He is an Expert Advisory Panel Member of Texas Instruments Inc USA.

Dr. K. Arun Kumar
Department of CSE
GITAM School of Technology
GITAM University, NH 207
NagadenehalliDoddaballapur, taluk, Bengaluru, Karnataka 561203, India
akanagan@gitam.edu
+91-9515555519

K. Arun Kumar is currently working as an Assistant professor in the Department of Computer Science and Engineering at GITAM University, Bangalore. He received his Doctorate Degree from the Dept of CSE JNTUA University, his M. Tech Degree from the Dept of CSE, JNTUA University, and his B.E from Dept of IT, Anna University, Chennai. He has been serving as a reviewer for leading journals like Springer and Elsevier. His Research interests lies in the areas of Wireless Networks, Data Mining, Deep Learning, and Big Data. He had contributed 15+ articles published in various reputed journals.

Dr. Rutvij H. Jhaveri
Department of Computer Science and Engineering, School of Technology, Pandit Deendayal Energy University, India
E-mail: rutvij.jhaveri@gmail.com

Dr. Rutvij H. Jhaveri is working as an Associate Professor in the Department of Computer Science & Engineering, Pandit Deendayal Energy University (PDEU/PDPU), India. He completed his Postdoctoral Research from Delta-NTU Corporate Lab for Cyber-Physical Systems, Nanyang Technological University, Singapore in 2019. He completed his Ph.D. in Computer Engineering in 2016 and Master's degree in 2012.

Apart from numerous academic assignments, he shouldered the responsibility as Head of the Department (IT) for 5 years in S.V.M. Institute of Technology. In 2024, he received "Best Ph.D. Supvervisor" award, while in 2017, he received prestigious "Pedagogical Innovation Award" from Gujarat Technological University. He is among the top 2% of scientists around the world in 2024, 2023, 2022, and 2021, listed by Stanford University and Elsevier. He authored 200+ articles including over 25 in IEEE/ACM Transactions along with flagship IEEE/ACM conferences. Moreover, he has several national and international patents and, copyrights to his name. He is a senior member of IEEE (SMIEEE). He is a member of the prestigious IEEE IES Technical Committee on Building Automation, Control, and Management. He is an editorial board member in various journals of repute including IEEE Transactions on Industrial Informatics, Scientific Reports (Springer NATURE) and International Journal of Wireless Information Networks (Springer). He also serves as a reviewer in several international journals and as an advisory/TPC member in renowned international conferences.

Dr. A.Mohamed Abbas
Faculty-Information Technology Department,
University of Technology and Applied Sciences-Sur,
Sultanate of Oman, P.O. Box: 484,
Zip Code: 411, Sur.
abbasasfaq@gmail.com
+968 91707183

Mohamed Abbas is currently working in IT Department at University of Technology and Applied Sciences, Sultanate of Oman. He has published 23 research articles in reputed international journals and presented 16 papers in International Conferences. Dr Abbas has registered 4 patents and 1 patent was granted. He is working on 2 funded research projects and completed 2 funded research projects which was funded by The Research Council, Sultanate of Oman. Dr Abbas severed in many administrative managerial positions, acted as keynote speaker and session chair in international conferences and symposium.

Index

Also of Interest

Check out these related titles from Scrivener Publishing

Deep Learning and Its Applications Using Python, Edited by Niha Kamal Basha, Surbhi Bhatia Khan, Abhishek Kumar and Arwa Mashat, ISBN: 9781394166466. This practical book gives a detailed description of deep learning models and their implementation using Python programming relating to computer vision, natural language processing, and other applications.

Networked Sensing Systems, Edited by Rajesh Kumar Dhanaraj, Malathy Sathyamoorthy, Balasubramaniam S., and Seifedine Kadry, ISBN: 9781394310869. *Networked Sensing Systems* is essential for anyone seeking innovative and sustainable solutions across diverse sectors, as it explores the integration of cutting-edge IoT technologies and digital transformation aimed at enhancing resource efficiency and addressing climate change challenges.

Multimodal Data Fusion for Bioinformatics Artificial Intelligence, Edited by Umesh Kumar Lilhore, Abhishek Kumar, Narayan Vyas, Sarita Simaiya, and Vishal Dutt, ISBN:9781394269938. *Multimodal Data Fusion for Bioinformatics Artificial Intelligence* is a must-have for anyone interested in the intersection of AI and bioinformatics, as it not only delves into innovative data fusion methods and their applications in omics research but also addresses the ethical implications and future developments shaping the field today.

Data Structure and Algorithms Using C++: A Practical Implementation, By Sachi Nandan Mohanty and Pabitra Kumar Tripathy, ISBN: 9781119750543. The book is intended to assist university faculty members and students to realize the principles and acquire the practical skills of programming using the C++ programming language.

Artificial Intelligence-Based System Models in Healthcare, Edited by A. Jose Anand, K. Kalaiselvi and Jyotir Moy Chatterjee, ISBN: 9781394242498. Artificial Intelligence-Based System Models in Healthcare provides a comprehensive and insightful guide to the transformative applications of AI in the healthcare system.

EXPLAINABLE MACHINE LEARNING MODELS AND ARCHITECTURES: Real-Time System Implementation, Edited by Suman Lata Tripathi and Mufti Mahmud, ISBN: 9781394185849. This cutting-edge new volume covers the hardware architecture implementation, the software implementation approach, and the efficient hardware of machine learning applications.

Natural Language Processing for Software Engineering, Edited by Rajesh Kumar Chakrawarti, Ranjana Sikarwar, Sanjaya Kumar Sarangi, Samson Arun Raj Albert Raj, Shweta Gupta, Krishnan Sakthidasan Sankaran, and Romil Rawat, ISBN: 9781394272433. Discover how Natural Language Processing for Software Engineering can transform your understanding of agile development, equipping you with essential tools and insights to enhance software quality and responsiveness in todays rapidly changing technological landscape.

MACHINE LEARNING TECHNIQUES FOR VLSI CHIP DESIGN, Edited by Abhishek Kumar, Suman Lata Tripathi, and K. Srinivasa Rao, ISBN: 9781119910398. This cutting-edge new volume covers the hardware architecture implementation, the software implementation approach, and the efficient hardware of machine learning applications with FPGA or CMOS circuits, and many other aspects and applications of machine learning techniques for VLSI chip design.

Intelligent Green Technologies for Smart Cities, Edited by Suman Lata Tripathi, Souvik Ganguli, Abhishek Kumar, and Tengiz Magradze, ISBN: 9781119816065. Presenting the concepts and fundamentals of smart cities and developing "green" technologies, this volume, written and edited by a global team of experts, also goes into the practical applications that can be utilized across multiple disciplines and industries, for both the engineer and the student.

Hybrid Intelligent Optimization Approaches for Smart Energy: A Practical Approach, Edited by Senthilkumar Mohan, A. John, Sanjeevikumar Padmanaban, and Yasir Hamid, ISBN: 9781119821243. Written and edited by a group of experts in the field, this is a comprehensive and up-to-date description of current energy optimization techniques, such as artificial intelligence techniques, machine learning, deep learning, and IoT techniques and their future trends.

NANODEVICES FOR INTEGRATED CIRCUIT DESIGN, Edited by Suman Lata Tripathi, Abhishek Kumar, K. Srinivasa Rao, and Prasantha R. Mudimela, ISBN: 9781394185788. Written and edited by a team of experts in the field, this important new volume broadly covers the design of nano-devices and their integrated applications in digital and analog integrated circuits (IC) design.

DESIGN AND DEVELOPMENT OF EFFICIENT ENERGY SYSTEMS, edited by Suman Lata Tripathi, Dushyant Kumar Singh, Sanjeevikumar Padmanaban, and P. Raja, ISBN: 9781119761631. Covering the concepts and fundamentals of efficient energy systems, this volume, written and edited by a global team of experts, also goes into the practical applications that can be utilized across multiple industries, for both the engineer and the student.

Electrical and Electronic Devices, Circuits, and Materials: Technical Challenges and Solutions, Edited by Suman Lata Tripathi, Parvej Ahmad Alvi, and Umashankar Subramaniam, ISBN: 9781119750369. Covering every aspect of the design and improvement needed for solid-state electronic devices and circuit and their reliability issues, this new volume also includes overall system design for all kinds of analog and digital applications and developments in power systems.

MODELING AND OPTIMIZATION OF OPTICAL COMMUNICATION NETWORKS, Edited by Chandra Singh, Rathishchandra R Gatti, K.V.S.S.S.S. Sairam, and Ashish Singh, ISBN: 9781119839200. *Modeling and Optimization of Optical Communication Networks* is a comprehensive and authoritative book that delves into the optical networks, principles, technologies, and practical applications of optical networks, equipping readers with the knowledge needed to design, implement, and optimize optical networks for various applications, from telecommunications to scientific research. With its comprehensive coverage and up-to-date insights, this book serves as an essential reference in the field of optical networks.

WIRELESS COMMUNICATION SECURITY: Mobile and Network Security Protocols, Edited by Manju Khari, Manisha Bharti, and M. Niranjanamurthy, ISBN: 9781119777144. Presenting the concepts and advances of wireless communication security, this volume, written and edited by a global team of experts, also goes into the practical applications for the engineer, student, and other industry professionals.

ADVANCES IN DATA SCIENCE AND ANALYTICS, Edited by M. Niranjanamurthy, Hemant Kumar Gianey, and Amir H. Gandomi, ISBN: 9781119791881. Presenting the concepts and advances of data science and analytics, this volume, written and edited by a global team of experts, also goes into the practical applications that can be utilized across multiple disciplines and industries, for both the engineer and the student, focusing on machining learning, big data, business intelligence, and analytics.

ARTIFICIAL INTELLIGENCE AND DATA MINING IN SECURITY FRAMEWORKS, Edited by Neeraj Bhargava, Ritu Bhargava, Pramod Singh Rathore, and Rashmi Agrawal, ISBN: 9781119760405. Written and edited by a team of experts in the field, this outstanding new volume offers solutions to the problems of security, outlining the concepts behind allowing computers to learn from experience and understand the world in terms of a hierarchy of concepts.

MACHINE LEARNING AND DATA SCIENCE: Fundamentals and Applications, Edited by Prateek Agrawal, Charu Gupta, Anand Sharma, Vishu Madaan, and Nisheeth Joshi, ISBN: 9781119775614. Written and edited by a team of experts in the field, this collection of papers reflects the most up-to-date and comprehensive current state of machine learning and data science for industry, government, and academia.

MEDICAL IMAGING, Edited by H. S. Sanjay, and M. Niranjanamurthy, ISBN: 9781119785392. Written and edited by a team of experts in the field, this is the most comprehensive and up-to-date study of and reference for the practical applications of medical imaging for engineers, scientists, students, and medical professionals.

SECURITY ISSUES AND PRIVACY CONCERNS IN INDUSTRY 4.0 APPLICATIONS, Edited by Shibin David, R. S. Anand, V. Jeyakrishnan, and M. Niranjanamurthy, ISBN: 9781119775621. Written and edited by a team of international experts, this is the most comprehensive and up-to-date coverage of the security and privacy issues surrounding Industry 4.0 applications, a must-have for any library.

CYBER SECURITY AND DIGITAL FORENSICS: Challenges and Future Trends, Edited by Mangesh M. Ghonge, Sabyasachi Pramanik, Ramchandra Mangrulkar, and Dac-Nhuong Le, ISBN: 9781119795636. Written and edited by a team of world renowned experts in the field, this groundbreaking new volume covers key technical topics and gives readers a comprehensive understanding of the latest research findings in cyber security and digital forensics.

DEEP LEARNING APPROACHES TO CLOUD SECURITY, Edited by Pramod Singh Rathore, Vishal Dutt, Rashmi Agrawal, Satya Murthy Sasubilli, and Srinivasa Rao Swarna, ISBN: 9781119760528. Covering one of the most important subjects to our society today, this editorial team delves into solutions taken from evolving deep learning approaches, solutions allow computers to learn from experience and understand the world in terms of a hierarchy of concepts.

MACHINE LEARNING TECHNIQUES AND ANALYTICS FOR CLOUD SECURITY, Edited by Rajdeep Chakraborty, Anupam Ghosh and Jyotsna Kumar Mandal, ISBN: 9781119762256. This book covers new methods, surveys, case studies, and policy with almost all machine learning techniques and analytics for cloud security solutions.

SECURITY DESIGNS FOR THE CLOUD, IOT AND SOCIAL NETWORKING, Edited by Dac-Nhuong Le, Chintin Bhatt and Mani Madhukar, ISBN: 9781119592266. The book provides cutting-edge research that delivers insights into the tools, opportunities, novel strategies, techniques, and challenges for handling security issues in cloud computing, Internet of Things and social networking.

DESIGN AND ANALYSIS OF SECURITY PROTOCOLS FOR COMMUNICATION, Edited by Dinesh Goyal, S. Balamurugan, Sheng-Lung Peng and O.P. Verma, ISBN: 9781119555643. The book combines analysis and comparison of various security protocols such as HTTP, SMTP, RTP, RTCP, FTP, UDP for mobile or multimedia streaming security protocol.

SMART GRIDS FOR SMART CITIES VOLUME 2: Real-Time Applications in Smart Cities, Edited by O.V. Gnana Swathika, K. Karthikeyan, and Sanjeevikumar Padmanaban, ISBN: 9781394215874. Written and edited by a team of experts in the field, this second volume in a two-volume set focuses on an interdisciplinary perspective on the financial, environmental, and other benefits of smart grid technologies and solutions for smart cities.

SMART GRIDS AND INTERNET OF THINGS, Edited by Sanjeevikumar Padmanaban, Jens Bo Holm-Nielsen, Rajesh Kumar Dhanaraj, Malathy Sathyamoorthy, and Balamurugan Balusamy, ISBN: 9781119812449. Written and edited by a team of international professionals, this groundbreaking new volume covers the latest technologies in automation, tracking, energy distribution and consumption of Internet of Things (IoT) devices with smart grids.

Printed in the USA/Agawam, MA
June 30, 2026

907142.002